76 Years of Entertainment

Bournemouth Pavilion

A Celebration

HUGH ASHLEY

**Published and Sponsored by ROBERT WETTON,
HUGH ASHLEY and the
PAVILION ORGAN FUND
2006**

By the Same Author.....

Dorset Village Book *(with Harry Ashley)*
History of Bournemouth *(with Harry Ashley)*
Sixty Hymns to Remember
A New Forest Journey
Glossary of Church Terms
Dave the Rave (Lyrics for Musical)
Born to Save (Lyrics for Musical)
Caesar Must Go (Lyrics and Book for School Musical)

THANK YOU

Acknowledgements.....

To Technical Co-Ordinator Christian Knighton for his help and encouragement
To all the front of house staff
To the Receptionists who always made me feel welcome
To the Stage Crew of Simon Bagnall, Sean Tomkins, Kristen Greenep, Ryan Oliver and Graham Shearing, who gave me so much time
To Bob Wetton and John Knighton who checked through the proofs
To Manager Bob Bentley for his support
To Tim Trenchard for his advice on the Compton Organ
To Scott Harrison and Michaela Horsfield of the Bournemouth Daily Echo Archive and Library
To Neal Butterworth, Editor of the Bournemouth Daily Echo
To John Cresswell for his generosity in sharing his research
To Michael Lunn for his knowledge and enthusiasm
To Sally Shepard of Rotherham Archives
To Katherine Ashley for historical material
To Councillor Stephen Chappell for the Indenture
To Jon Primrose of Strand Archive for pictures of switchboard
To Iain Robinson, Origination Manager at Henry Ling Ltd for guidance with file production
And to Bournemouth Central Library, Grace Pullen, Hazel Chambers, Evelyn Dilks, Pat Dyson, and countless folk who gave me ideas and memories

Photographs.....

Front Cover by Christian Knighton, taken from the roof of the Metro Palace Court Hotel
Rear Cover by the author
I am grateful to the Pavilion Archives Bank for historical photographs, and to the following for original pictures from their own collections: Simon Bagnall, Sean Tomkins, Christian Knighton, and David Woodley. Other pictures were taken especially by the author
Bournemouth Daily Echo
Other photographs were provided by editorial contributors, and, where known, every attempt has been made to contact copyright owners. I apologise for any we have been unable to trace.

Printed by.....

Henry Ling Ltd., The Dorset Press, Dorchester, Dorset. DT1 1HD

Design by the Author.....

Set in CorelDraw. Main Text Font: Palatino Linotype

To my two grandsons,
Joseph and Harry,
in the hope the Pavilion
will stay with us for
them to enjoy

Introduction

HUGH ASHLEY

Welcome to a celebration of the Bournemouth Pavilion, an entertainments complex which took nearly a century in the making and which was, when opened, the finest of its kind in the land. Then, sadly, it seemed as if everybody lost interest, and nothing has ever been written in detail about this gem of architecture.

Most Bournemouth people don't hate it, nor do they love it, but they certainly ignore it - and yet, whenever there is the slightest suggestion that it might be pulled down, there is a rallying call to keep it alive. What the future holds is unknown, but this book looks back over 76 years of glorious entertainment and leisure.

The history is incomplete, because no formal records exist and no complete record of the shows and events has ever been kept. But, through the knowledge we have, through the nostalgic memories of people who've enjoyed the building, and through the thoughts of those who have worked and who do work here, emerges a picture of a warm and loving old lady who has tried desperately to please us over the years, against all odds, suffering many slings and arrows, but who has triumphed in providing the people of Bournemouth, and countless millions of visitors, with a home for drama, for melodrama, for farce, for comedy, for culture, for films, for information, for wrestling, for bands, for eating, for fun, for vaudeville, for variety, for musicals, for ballet, for opera, for dancing, for virtually every star of the stage and television - in fact, for everything in the way of entertainment and relaxation.

As you read, remember that the memory plays tricks with the truth, but the emotions are untouched. Enjoy this celebration of the wonderful

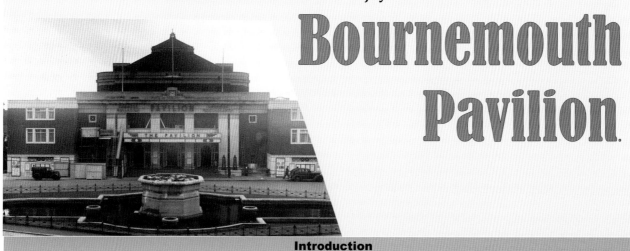

Bournemouth Pavilion.

PREFACE

Before a new Pavilion could be built, land was needed. The building has as its legal foundation an indenture dated "**the twelfth day of August One Thousand Eight Hundred and Seventy Three**". In this indenture, the land was provided for the people of Bournemouth, at a small cost.. The indenture runs to six sides of A3 paper, was entitled **APPROPRIATION OF LAND FOR PUBLIC GARDENS** and bears these remarks:

"Now this indenture witnesseth that the said trustees by virtue and in exercise of the powers in this behalf given them in and by the said recited Act of Parliament and with such sanction and approbation as aforesaid and with the consent of Sir George Eliott Meyrick Tapps Gervis as such Tenant for life........<u>A L L</u> those pieces and parcels of land containing together fifteen acres or thereabouts situate at Bournemouth and delineated on the plan drawn........for public Gardens for the use of the Inhabitants of Bournemouth and the vicinity <u>PROVIDED</u> always and it is hereby declared that the use and enjoyment of the said public Gardens shall be subject to such reasonable bye laws and regulations as shall from time to time be made.......<u>PROVIDED ALSO</u> it shall be lawful for the said commissioners to erect on some convenient part of the said pieces or parcels of land allotted as aforesaid a Building to be used as a Public Building........and also other erections for the use of persons enjoying the Pleasure Grounds (as Waiting Rooms Lavatories and the like) such Building and Erections to be approved by the said Sir George Eliott Meyrick Tapps Gervis........the yearly rents........<u>ONE HUNDRED AND TWENTY-THREE POUNDS THREE SHILLINGS</u>.......the yearly sum or rent of <u>ONE HUNDRED AND NINETY-TWO POUNDS FIFTEEN SHILLINGS</u> such rents to be paid in each year by equal quarterly payments on the usual quarter days."

So, the land was provided, but it was to be another fifty-six years before the building was completed. The story is in this book.

Contents:

Contents

Page 2:

One of several 'false' doorways in the front part of the building. This one is facing the Top west terrace outside the Costa Coffee Bar

To Be or Not?

Would There Ever Be a Bournemouth Pavilion?

To most people, the workings of local government are a complete mystery; year after year of discussion, dozens of decisions, a multitude of mind-changes, and plenty of seemingly broken promises. For the Bournemouth Pavilion to be built, there were **eighty-seven years of pre-planning**, beginning in 1842, when Sir George Gervis died. He was the owner of the estate on which the building now stands, and the land was inherited by his son, at that time a child, who became Sir George Elliot Meyrick Tapps-Gervis-Meyrick. The land was administered by trustees who suggested a future scheme of development which embraced the whole area **between Westover Road and the sea-front**.

Their proposal suggested a "**Pleasure Gardens Pagoda**" and this is seen as the first-ever move towards providing a public pavilion and entertainments centre for Bournemouth. Two designs came from the eminent Christchurch-born architect, **Benjamin Ferrey** (who had designed the first building for the Royal Bath Hotel); one was a rather pretentious large rectangular structure, drawn with three tiers and surmounted by a tall square tower, something more than an hotel, looking more like a pavilion - in some ways quite

similar to the current Pavilion.

What is interesting is that the site proposed for this building was on the site where the present Pavilion eventually came to be. So in one way, Ferrey was quite prophetic.

After much talking and argument, the **Pagoda idea was moth-balled** through lack of any real interest, and the money used for other public utility buildings. Later, the less imposing **Belle Vue**

Hotel (originally nothing more than a boarding-house) was built and this occupied this prestigious site for many years. In the picture below, notice the sand dunes which were replaced by the West Cliff promenade and cliff walk.

Visitors found it elegant and comfortable for a quiet mode of life - it even boasted a **billiard table**! There was no pressing need for any kind of public meeting place at that time, because the Belle Vue Hotel answered all the purposes for such gatherings in its **Assembly Rooms**. So versatile were they that touring entertainments were happy there, as were concerts, dances and official gatherings - including the Board of Commissioners which governed the town. At this time, Bournemouth was little more than a marine village with a **population of about 2,000 people**. But, versatility was an essential spice in Bournemouth's planning, and so, even though many years were to elapse before anything substantial was built, these Assembly Rooms formed the basis of thinking for the town's entertainment needs.

It's quite amusing to notice some other sites which were considered for the site of the Pavilion; what would the town be like today had it been built on Horseshoe Common in the middle of a complex of municipal buildings? And how about the Pavilion at the pier head? Both these, and others, were considered.

So, more than **thirty years on**, and still no pavilion, but in 1873 the then **Sir George Meyrick** gave the town a permanent lease of the Central Pleasure Gardens. In the discussions which led to this gift, the Improvement Commissioners were granted permission to build a **'rendezvous or pavilion on the plateau site'** of the Winter Gardens behind the Arcade and overlooking what we now call Pine Walk. In those days it was known as 'Invalids Walk'! This site forms part of the site on which some of the present Pavilion stands.

From this time on, **for fifty years**, the idea of building something to be proud of continually cropped up, but, in another example of how local government never runs smoothly, there were sharp conflicts of opinion as to what the finished building should contain and what design it should have. **Proposals and counter-proposals** were brandished about as weapons in the fight, and ideas were vetoed three times through protracted discussions.

That the town needed some place of entertainment is clear. To be fair, the idea was gaining momentum among the residents who were made well aware that **visitors in the 1870s and 1880s found the town incredibly dull**; at about that time, in the mid-nineteenth century, one Mr. Grantley Berkeley - a man, apparently, of racy style, described Bournemouth as *"the prettiest, most pretending, but generally stupidest"* place he was ever in. *"At Bournemouth, man has no amusement of any kind; and what is stranger still, when men and women meet at this watering place there is no association, no promenade as at other watering places, where the people walk; and not an opportunity sought in which to exchange an idea."* To him, the residents were too decorous and unsocial. *"Bournemouth seems to be made for social enjoyment, and to welcome the heart to genial sympathy, yet the visitors apparently shrink within themselves, remaining in their lodgings or hotels, or secreting themselves in the cover afforded by the neighbouring bushes. It is a very pretty place; it is also a very strange place."*

The intention to build was not in doubt, and before the turn of the century, **five architects submitted designs** to the Council for a competition to find the best building to cost £5,000. Nothing came of the competition and there was no further action at that time.

Quite co-incidentally - but importantly, a band of **itinerant Italian musician**s who played in various venues in the open air began to develop some prestige as the **Municipal Orchestra** and they were to have an overbearing influence on the future. Under **Dan Godfrey**, a man of great determination and vigour, the town realised that some permanent home was required for them as they established their high-class music. They were allowed the use of the **Winter Gardens**, an extremely large greenhouse - which had opened in 1877 - from 1893, but the building didn't become the property of the local Council until 1908.

Those who didn't see the need for anything else thought that the Winter Gardens would be a solution to the problem of where to house the orchestra. But not so; **the orchestra's reputation grew** alongside the popularity of the expanding town, and many people thought the prestigious orchestra **should have a worthy concert hall** - hence the revival of the pavilion scheme.

Mr. Merton Russell Cotes, who was a vociferous supporter of a new pavilion, made it very clear as early as 1901 that "**a seaside Pavilion is an absolute necessity**". This was backed by a report two years later from a Deputation assigned the task of investigating possibilities; they made a "**strong recommendation that a pavilion embracing a concert room, reading rooms, cafes (indoor and outdoor refreshments) and all other accommodation and advantages found in the very**

best of the kind we have seen in our travels", should be provided in Bournemouth.

After much concentrated debate and disagreement, with heavy defeats for those who wanted a new building, eventually, the **Belle Vue property was acquired** by the Council in 1908. Plans to build a pavilion at the cost £45,000 were drawn up and a loan sanctioned by the Local Government Board. All seemed in place and **the long-awaited entertainments centre seemed on course**. But not so! The final decision was held up for another twelve years because of a licensing difficulty with the Belle Vue Hotel.

In April 1911, one George William Bailey wrote a report in praise of the Pavilion development in which he listed five points:

1) The Pavilion is desirable and needed in the interests of Bournemouth and its future, and near the sea amid the beauty of the Pleasure Gardens.

2) The building should be central and readily accessible from all parts of the Borough.

3) It would improve and enhance the value of adjoining property.

4) It would bring an end to the idea that Bournemouth is not taking advantage of the beauties of the place to establish a pleasant central rendezvous, where visitors may meet and where the Municipal Orchestra can be suitably housed.

5) The issue is of paramount importance as affecting the future of Bournemouth long after those who have to deal with its affairs today have ceased to do so.

Following these comments, yet another scheme for a building costing £60,000 was approved in 1912, but deadlock prevailed and the **outbreak of the Great War** stopped any further negotiations. There would still 17 years without a Pavilion.

Once the War was over, **Alderman Charles Cartwright** proposed an entirely new scheme, now at the increased cost of £100,000. **A loan was sought** from the Ministry of Health, but the public enquiry incited such protests that the meeting, in 1922, had to be adjourned and reconvened in a Church Lecture Hall nearby. The enquiry estimated that the eventual cost would be nearer £170,000, but the **approval was given by the government** and so plans were put in place to advertise another competition for designs. The advert stated, *"The Mayor and Corporation*

of the County Borough of Bournemouth invite designs for the erection of a Concert Pavilion to seat approximately 2,000, with the necessary adjuncts." Entry to the competition cost £2.2s (two guineas), and all but one hundred competitors submitted designs, with architects from across the country - an indication of the prestige that the building would have. The top prize was £300, and the winners were **Messrs. G. Wyville Home and Shirley Knight of London** a virtually unknown team of architects - with **Messrs. James and Seward**, a local building company, who were given the contract to demolish the Belle Vue Hotel and build the new Pavilion. The **top prize sounds small** by today's standards, but would have been worth in the region of £6,000 today. This illustrates how important the project was, and how desperate the Borough Council was to receive top quality entrants.

County Borough of Bournemouth.

PROPOSED PAVILION AT BOURNEMOUTH.

COMPETITIONS.

COUNTY BOROUGH OF BOURNE-MOUTH.

The Mayor and Corporation of the County Borough of Bournemouth invite designs for the erection of a Concert Pavilion to seat approximately 2,000, with the necessary adjuncts, as set forth in conditions of competition, on a site in the Pleasure Grounds belonging to the Corporation.

Conditions of Competition, together with a plan of the site and sections, will be supplied by the Town Clerk after February 12th on receipt of a cheque for £2 2s. 0d., which will be returned to competitors submitting a *bona fide* design. The estimated cost of the building is £100,000.

Premiums of £300, £200 and £100 are offered for the designs placed first, second and third respectively.

The Assessor is Sir Edwin Cooper, F.R.I.B.A., whose decision is final.

CONDITIONS OF COMPETITION.

1. Architects are invited to submit drawings in competition for the proposed New Pavilion to be erected in the Westover Gardens and on the site of the Belle Vue Hotel, between the Westover Road and the Pier Approach.

2. The Main Entrance will be from the former, and the Lower Floor Entrance from the latter.

3. The site and the levels and sections of the ground are shown on the plan accompanying these particulars and coloured pink thereon.

4. It will be observed that a small Pumping Station and water tower on the ground may be in the way of the proposed building; in this case provision must be made for incorporating them in the building.

5. Designs are to be prepared in accordance with these Conditions, copies of which may be obtained of the Town Clerk on application, with a deposit of Two Guineas, which deposit will be returned on the receipt of a *bona fide* design or on return of the Conditions within a fortnight of their receipt.

The submitted designs represented an interesting study in the forward-looking architecture of the 1920s, and had the general public been allowed to select the winner - perhaps through interactive television on their red buttons! - the winning design would probably have been very different. As ever throughout history, it was the economics which played an important role - the Borough could not afford anything too lavish. The winner presented a design which was to become a **central feature of Bournemouth** for ever - well, at least until 2005, anyway! The style was considered as free, and able to create an **atmosphere of a building eminently suitable** for a town like Bournemouth. This picture of the proposed building can be seen in the east corridor of the Pavilion.

inscription: *"A Hall of Music, Theatre, Assembly Rooms, place of refreshment, and generally for the entertainment of the many thousands of visitors annually flocking to Bournemouth for health and recreation, as well as for the recreation of the inhabitants themselves."* And that's an ideal every much as relevant today as it was nearly eighty years ago. *(Casket details on Page 18)*

Seven to eight hundred people gathered for the ceremony in specially erected marquees while many others were unable to get in. This throng was entertained by the **Municipal Orchestra under Sir Dan Godfrey** - appropriate indeed, since it was largely for them that the building had been designed. Music played included some dances by Edward German and an overture by Arthur Sullivan, and

After a year of preparation, the **foundation stone** of the building was laid by **Alderman Charles Cartwright** at 3.00 p.m. on Wednesday, 23rd September, 1925, and a **copper casket filled with documents**, newspapers and books, along with money notes and coins was placed in a cavity. A document buried under a slab carried the following

other music by British composers. The ceremony took place at the northern end (Westover Road) of the site. The **Mayor, Alderman F.S. Mate**, said, *"We have today arrived at another epoch in the history of Bournemouth. Today we are met to lay the foundation stone of the Bournemouth Pavilion, a project on which contrary opinions have been held for nearly a century, but* as you see, 'the ayes have it'. I am privileged and proud to assist in the ceremony. I congratulate very heartily the chairman and members of the Pavilion Committee on having arrived at this stage in their progress, and I trust that at a distant date we shall see a Pavilion erected on the site on which we now stand, which shall be worthy of the County Borough."

Chairman of the Committee, **Alderman Charles Cartwright** spoke of the Winter Gardens as an *"old conservatory, unworthy of the town, and no fit home for an orchestra that had spread the fame of* **Bournemouth as a musical centre** *far and wide; the very traditions of the town which prided itself that when it did a thing it did it well, cried aloud for something better, for a worthier building more in accord with modern day requirements. Upon the ground on which we are now gathered will arise a dignified building, a stately home for municipal music, and other varied entertainments, extending I hope to grand opera, for which a suitable stage is being provided, whilst among its amenities will be the provision of accommodation* **in comfort and pleasure**, *to the large audience which we hope to attract during all the seasons of the year. Adjoining it yet forming part of the same building, will be large and commodious rooms for the entertainment in other ways of its patrons -* **reading, recreation and refreshment rooms** *in accordance with modern requirements."*

> *INSCRIPTION ON STONE*
> *The Foundation Stone,*
> *which can be seen just to the left of the main entrance of the foyer, is now partly obscured by a metal safety hand-rail.*
> *The Stone was 4 ft x 2 ft x 1 ft 9 inches and weighed about 18 cwts.*
> *It was made in Whitbed Portland Stone. The inscription reads:*

> **THIS STONE WAS LAID BY**
> **ALDERMAN CHARLES HENRY**
> **CARTWRIGHT, J.P.**
> **ON THE 23rd DAY OF SEPTEMBER,**
> **1925**
> **Architects: G. Wyville Home, A.R.I.B.A**
> **Shirley Knight, A.R.I.B.A.**
> **Builders: Jones and Seward, Bournemouth**
> **Alderman Frederick Skinner Mate, Mayor**
> **Herbert Ashling, Town Clerk**

To ensure that the stone was "well and truly laid", a special set of instruments was used; **an ivory-handled silver trowel** was provided by the architects, **the mallet** to tap the stone into place was made **from ebony**, and the **level was a hard-wood**

replica of the pine tree which surmounts the Bournemouth Borough Coat of Arms, standing on an ebony base. Some flowery Edwardian journalism sums up the day in lovely over-the-top style - from the *Bournemouth Daily Echo*: *Many a controversial storm had been weathered, and vicissitudes encountered until today they emerged into a quieter haven. And the sun came out to bless their labours, and that of those in the present council who had taken an active part in the furtherance of their ideals.*

Visit of the Prince of Wales in 1928

In 1928, the **Prince of Wales** made a civic visit to the town and was taken to the Bournemouth Pavilion in the middle of its construction. It couldn't have been known at the time, but this was the Prince who would become King and then abdicate in 1936. The tour of the town was what we would call today "whistle-stop", and **six minutes were put aside** for him to view the site, before he was whisked off to the Royal Bath Hotel. Large crowds clambered about at the Pier Approach and on Bath Road, many climbing to the roof of the Baths opposite, and when the Prince got inside the grounds of the Pavilion site, a loud rousing cheer broke out across the area from the workmen who were lining up on the scaffolding and roof of the building. The Prince retaliated by removing his hat and waving it in the air. **His Highness looked at the skeleton** of the construction and gained a good impression of its dimensions. He spent a few seconds in conversation with the site manager and enquired whether the workers were local and seemed pleased that the great majority were.

On this day, the Daily Echo described the building as follows: **"It is like a great skeleton, but the many departments are gradually taking shape. At the south end, by the Pier Approach, where the restaurant sections are situated, the roofing is** already considerably advanced, and it is hoped that soon it will be possible to start work on the roof of the concert hall. The building is rearing itself above the foliage and can be seen now from the Square as well as from the seafront." This picture is taken from the official programme for the Prince's visit, and it shows the larger part of the building to be well under way.

In April, 1928, the **first manager was appointed**, and a year later the **licence transferred** from the Belle Vue Hotel to the Pavilion. So ended those 87 years of controversy; at last, Bournemouth was to have a building to be proud of, to show off and to enjoy. Its planning had been tempestuous - would the future journey be **plain sailing**? Certainly it was the beginning of an **exciting voyage**.

The Pavilion

THE new Pavilion when completed, will in all probability, be the largest of its kind in the country, and will certainly be the biggest municipal enterprise ever undertaken for the entertainment and recreation of the public.

The design for the building was selected from nearly 100 schemes submitted by architects in open competition, and the work is now being successfully carried out by the appointed architects, Messrs. Home and Knight, A.A.R.I.B.A., of London.

In addition to providing a new home for the Municipal Orchestra, the Concert Hall has been designed to present operatic, theatrical and cinematographic performances. The accommodation in this hall will be approximately for 1,700 people.

Picture from Opening Programme 1929

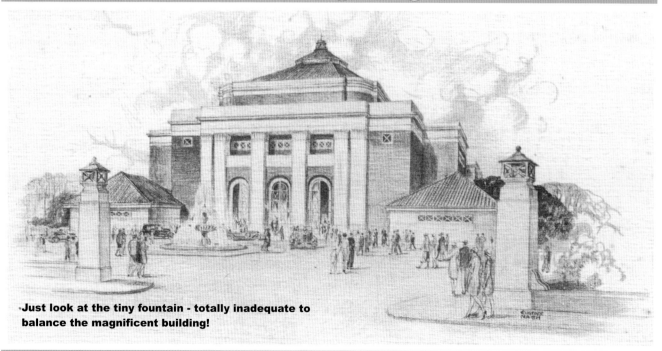

·Just look at the tiny fountain - totally inadequate to balance the magnificent building!

AT LAST!!
And Worth Waiting For

As we look back over the history of Bournemouth, many events have been of **tremendous importance** - in more recent history, in April 1969, many of us can recall the Sunday afternoon when the final trolley-bus drove to Pier Approach, marking the end of 'silent' travel in the town, when thousands of residents made their farewells from the streets.

When AFC Bournemouth were promoted to the old Division Two in 1987, they took an open-top bus ride through town and, again, thousands waved from the pavements below. In earlier years, the arrival of the railway and the development of the pier and seafront were of immense importance and pride; but the biggest ever occasion to date in 1929 was the opening of the **Bournemouth Pavilion**.

Years of **struggle and determination** had ended and the town could proudly boast an **entertainments centre second to none**. Many might argue that it is still the greatest event ever in the entire history of the town, but others might be a little sceptical! Those who had believed in the need for such a place were relieved that it had come to pass, and even those who thought the idea a complete waste of time and money must have felt a **warm sense of occasion** on that long-awaited day. Try to imagine the sense of excitement in the residents and envisage the smart clothing and smiling faces which they were wearing for this day. **Tuesday, March 19th, 1929** - the day of the **official royal opening**.

The picture shows the Mayor and the Duke of Gloucester, travelling around town to the Official Opening.

The *Bournemouth Daily Echo* wrote: "Rising phoenix-like from the ashes of the **Belle Vue Hotel**, the Pavilion replaces the original 'Assembly Room' which was the only place of resort for the elite settlers who founded the '**Marine village of Bourne**'." Under the front-page banner headline "BOURNEMOUTH'S SUNNY WELCOME TO THE KING'S SON", almost the entire front page was dedicated to the visit of **His Royal Highness the Duke of Gloucester** - the royal visit actually taking precedence and **overshadowing the actual Pavilion opening**. This was the first time that a member of the royal family had travelled by a train filled with "all types of passengers" to an official opening ceremony. The other passengers were "excursionists who were making a holiday trip to the seaside town. A **spotlight of brilliant sunshine** fastened on the Duke as he stepped down from the train." On this glorious day, the Duke was welcomed by the town with great enthusiasm. Crowds gathered at the railway station, along Holdenhurst Road, down Old Christchurch Road and at the War Memorial, and the Prince" - reports the *Daily Echo* - "acknowledged his welcome by **bowing and raising his hat** to the delighted crowd. If pleasure is indicated by expression, there was no happier person there than the Duke himself." All work had been suspended along the route so that workers could watch the procession, which was in a magnificent **Rolls Royce** loaned by Mr. A. E. Pearman of Branksome Park - in the neighbouring Borough of Poole!

Hundreds of **brightly-coloured flags** hung from the roofs of buildings near the railway station, and gold letters told the Duke that the town was pleased to see him. In the Square, **blue, yellow and green artificial flowers** swung gently from the breeze, and the lamp standards supported flags of fish-tail shape in **deep hues of red, yellow, orange and mauve**. The Town Hall was almost totally covered in Union Jacks, and **spring flowers adorned the route** of the procession. At the Pier Approach, a seventy-foot lamp standard in the centre of the roadway had been transformed into a decorative pillar from which radiated streamers and garlands. Westover Road itself was draped with a **blaze of colour** and the entrance to the Bournemouth Arcade had an enormous floral archway. All in all, it was **a truly memorable day** and wonderful sunshine highlighted all the colour.

The opening ceremony was formal yet bright, with a superbly set stage and a long queue of people directed to their allotted seats in the wide and **spacious concert hall**. In yet more florid language from the *Daily Echo*, we learn that "it **was impossible to suppress an agreeable murmur** at the very fine sight which was offered. A warm and genial glow was cast on all around by the handsome sunburst and sunray's lamps which lit up the **star-spangled ceiling and the richly-coloured walls**. The stage was handsomely draped with a rich gold curtain, with towering palms at either end of the platform. In the centre was a vase of red tulips, and secreted behind was a microphone for the broadcasting of the speeches."

Once the Duke and the official party had taken their seats, the formal speeches began with the Mayor, **Alderman Charles Cartwright**, who had pressed for the Pavilion scheme for many years, and whose work and dedication had seen the idea come to fruition. He said, "**We feel ourselves particularly fortunate that this opening ceremony should be undertaken by a member of our Royal House, and we look upon it as an excellent omen of prosperity and success for the important undertaking upon which we embarked with perhaps a little feeling of trepidation, and which is now about to be tried and proved upon its merits.**"

The Deputy Mayor, **Alderman H.J. Thwaites**, took up the relay baton of praise by speaking of how the building was designed. "In order to obtain the best design possible, we invited plans from architects in open competition naming as assessor a notable architect, **Sir Edwin Cooper**. Many excellent designs were sent in, but

Time Table

11.30	Arrival of H.R.H. at Central Station
11.45	At the War Memorial
	H.R.H. will place a wreath on the Memorial and inspect a Guard of ex-Service men
11.55	At the Pavilion Approach, Westover Road
	Inspection of Guard of Honour by H.R.H.
12 noon	Opening Ceremony at Pavilion
1.0	Luncheon
2.30 to 4.30	The first Concert, at which H.R.H. will attend
5.10	H.R.H. leaves Central Station for Waterloo

NOTE.—From 4 till 6 p.m. there will be a Thé Dansant in the Pavilion

ultimately, Sir Edwin Cooper decided that the plans sent in by **Messrs. Home and Knight** were, in his opinion, the best, having regard to all circumstances; and the building in which we now are in, is the result of that decision, and has been erected, I am glad, to say by local contractors **Messrs. Jones and Seward Ltd**. I venture to say that the building must be considered a magnificent and imposing structure, and it is, I believe, the finest building of its kind in this country." Then, he gave an endorsement which seems quite strange by today's standards.

"Incidentally, I may say that the construction has been approved by the Ministry of Health, and the scheme has been referred to by the Ministry in one of their annual reports as **unique of its kind among schemes promoted by English municipalities** and the results will be awaited with interest." It should be remembered that, at this time, Bournemouth was seen as **a place for invalids and for recuperation**, as well as for the general holiday-maker. The Deputy Mayor then drew attention to some of the problems that had been encountered over the years of planning and discussion. "There has been division of opinion on various matters in connection with the site, construction and use of the building. Now that the building is in existence and the project a fact, I am sure that putting aside all differences of opinion will be the earnest desire of every resident in the Borough that the Pavilion shall be of the greatest advantage to the visitors and residents and conduce to the **well-being, happiness and prosperity of the town** of Bournemouth." Worthy sentiments, not, probably, endorsed by everyone at the time - just one of those public pronouncements made at times of emotional heights and designed to quell any possible criticism.

The pomp and circumstance continued with the words of the Principal Guest, **H.R.H. The Duke of Gloucester**. "I am so glad to have this opportunity of visiting your town to open this fine building. As I have been here before, I don't have to remind you of the **high position held by your Borough among other towns** which take upon themselves the pleasing duty of acting as physicians to the sick, renewal of vigour to the convalescent,

and a playground to those in full health. I have made myself acquainted with many of the facts regarding the history of the construction of this building, and **I congratulate you on its completion. I hope you will in due course see the fulfilment of your desire, that it will make for the benefit and prosperity of the beautiful town which already affords so many amenities to those who are so favoured by residing here or are fortunate enough to be able to visit it.** It is evidently to serve two purposes: first, as a home for music for which you are so famous and of which you are so justly proud, and secondly, for the less artistic but still essential purpose of catering for the more material necessities of residents and visitors, for it is intended to provide for the mind and body."

And so to the moment everyone had been waiting for: "**I now have the utmost pleasure formally to declare** (notice that H.R.H. did not split his infinitive**!) this building open for the use of the public, and in doing so, I express the hope very sincerely that it may prove a great advantage to the inhabitants of Bournemouth and visitors.**"

The Deputy Mayor then rose again to say a few words about the facilities in the new building. "Mr. Mayor, let me assure you, sir, as chairman of the committee appointed to deal with the administration of this Pavilion, that we will see that the various functions and entertainments in this building will be carried out in a manner worthy of the best traditions of our beautiful town. **May I say to the residents present and to the whole of the inhabitants of this town that this building with its beautiful concert hall, its palatial ballroom, its restaurant, recreation and refreshments room, have been erected for you under the directions of your representatives.** You are all shareholders in this great concern, and I appeal to you, one and all, to take an interest in and whole-heartedly support this undertaking which is **one of the greatest municipal enterprises of this country.**"

After the speeches, some of which were broadcast 'live' by Bournemouth's own radio station, 6BM, the Mayor presented **a gold cigarette casket** to His Royal Highness to mark the memorable occasion. Then the Duke was escorted from the concert hall through a side door into the west passage - the one nearer the Pleasure Gardens - to be taken to the ballroom. He was supposedly delighted by the view from the rear windows right across the Pier Approach with the sea and the Purbecks in the distance. He tested the spring of the floor and was instantly attracted by the fine and distinctive mural paintings around the band alcove, the work of a **Miss Sydenham** from the **Bournemouth Art School**. The Duke and party then had lunch before he made apologies that he would be leaving before the opening concert was over, and left for **another engagement at Christchurch Priory**. Folk-law and hearsay has it that many Bournemouth people were greatly offended by the Duke's **apparent rudeness** in leaving the opening ceremony so abruptly, before its completion. For some, it has been said, the entire day had been marred. He did return, and it seems that the visit to Christchurch Priory was not without problems! The Vicar of Christchurch (Revd. Canon Gay) was in Winchester with the Bishop and not present when the Duke arrived! Also, police from Bournemouth and Ringwood had to reinforce their Christchurch colleagues, because they had not been told about the visit until 2 o'clock that afternoon.

Some Quirky Moments

As with any grand occasion, some amusing and quirky side-stories are worth recounting. **Lieutenant R. Kennedy** of the 5/7th Battalion Hampshire Regiment was to have carried the **King's Colour in the Guard of Honour** at the Pavilion entrance, but a few days before, he sprained his leg while playing rugby and had to be replaced by **Second-Lieutenant Randall-Jones**. Amidst other folk tales of the day is the allegation that at quarter to ten on the

morning of the royal visit, the Pier Road entrance was **still being steam-rollered**. Crowds were reported to be ten deep at the bottom of Richmond Hill, and a gaily decorated tricycle caused much levity as it was cycled through the Square ahead of the Duke's procession. The *Daily Echo* also reports that "several people in the Square were operating **miniature cinema cameras**." What a shame no one thought to video the occasion! At **J.J. Allen Ltd. Furniture Store** (they supplied the carpets and furniture for the new Pavilion), you could buy an oak bedroom suite, bedstead and bedding, consisting of a wardrobe, a dressing table, a tall chest, two chairs, a bedstead, a wire mattress, a hair mattress, a feather bolster and two feather pillows for £35.0.0. **Robertson's Thick Marmalade** was six and half old pence for a pound, and in **J. Kay's in Winton**, you could buy afternoon frocks at 6/11p - that's about 35p in today's money! And that's not all - your satisfaction was guaranteed!

Programme of Music   *March 19th, 2.30-4.30 p.m.*

THE MUNICIPAL ORCHESTRA
DIRECTOR   -   SIR DAN GODFREY

1. GRAND MARCH	.. " Land of Hope and Glory "	..	Elgar
2. OVERTURE ..	" Tannhauser "	..	.. Wagner
3. SERENATA (No. 2)	.. .. Solo Violins : BERTRAM LEWIS and JOSEPH GOVÆRE		.. Toselli
4. SELECTION ..	" Merrie England "	..	Edward German
5. CELLO SOLI ..	(a) Peasant Dance (b) Intermezzo (c) Gavotte W. H. SQUIRE	.. ..	Wolstenholme Saint Saens .. Popper
6. CARLSBAD DOLL'S DANCE ..	..	..	.. Pleier
7. MARIMBA XYLOPHONE SOLO..	" Gee Whizz " W. W. BENNETT		Byron Brooke
8. EXTRACTS FROM THE POPULAR MUSICAL PLAY	" Show Boat " (Including " Ole Man River ")		Kern

INTERVAL.

10. ORGAN SOLO	PHILIP DORE, F.R.C.O.	
11. ETHEL ALDERSON	Danseuse	
12. SYBIL VANE	The Welsh Prima Donna At the Piano, LEON DOMQUE	
13. Two CO-OPTIMISTS	STANLEY HOLLOWAY and WOLSELEY CHARLES	
14. WILL MORRIS ..	Nonsense on Wheels.	

It's interesting to place the ceremony historically in line with other events - on the same front page there was news of a Norwegian Royal wedding and a record-breaking attempt by two airmen to fly from France to Australia in twelve days! The *Bournemouth Daily Echo* cost 1d (one old penny). On the same day as the royal visit, it was reported that the County Court cases for the parish of Kinson would move from Wimborne to Bournemouth. Other 'rival' attractions in town that very afternoon included Al Jolson's "The Singing Fool" at the Westover Super Cinema (not the present building), and Percy Pearce and his London Dance Band were at the Westover Ballroom. The Regent Theatre (later Gaumont and now Odeon) opposite the Pavilion was not quite finished and opened later in the year.

Let's leave the last word about the opening ceremony to the official programme of the day, where was printed this policy statement: >

Eager to Serve!!

The Pavilion and its Policy

BOURNEMOUTH has long been noted for the high standard of its Entertainments and the Council in continuance of its oft declared policy of providing only the best, has built and equipped the Pavilion, which is not only the greatest Municipal Enterprise of its kind, but, as visitors will agree, one of the finest places of public resort in the country.

Recognising the trend of public taste, the intention is to provide entertainments grave and gay which will be acceptable both to the visitors Bournemouth is proud to welcome and eager to serve, and to her own citizens.

At Last - the Bournemouth Pavilion was Open

. . PAVILION BALLROOM . .

Maurice Smart and his Pavilion Dance Orchestra

AFTERNOON TEA DANCES

Each weekday from 3.30 to 5.30
Admission (including Afternoon Tea) 2/-. Saturdays 2/6.

EVENING DANCES

Each weekday from 7.45 to 11.45 p.m.
Admission : 4/-. Saturdays 5/-.
(See weekly Bills for Special Dances)

EVERY SUNDAY

THE RENDEZVOUS PLAYERS

MORNING CONCERT	AFTERNOON TEA
11 to 12.15	CONCERT
Admission Free	3.30 to 5.30
Light Refreshments Served	Admission (including Tea) 1/6

Visit the **LUCULLUS RESTAURANT** for
LUNCHEONS - DINNERS (From 6.15 p.m.)

Suttons, Printers. Boscombe

Pattern of Tea Dances in 1949

THE BOURNEMOUTH DAILY ECHO, SATURDAY, MARCH 16, 1929.   7

THE PAVILION
OPENS on TUESDAY NEXT
IT IS YOURS TO USE . . . USE IT!

IN THE ..
BALLROOM
To which there is
No Charge for Admission
YOU
will find

Herman Darewski's "PAVILIANS"
THE DANCE BAND WITH THE COMPELLING RHYTHM.

This room with its spacious dimensions, its splendid outlook over the Sea, and its wonderfully sprung DANCE AREA, will become the recognised meeting place, where, from 10 a.m. to 11 p.m. Morning Coffee, Afternoon Teas, and Light Refreshments of Every Kind will be served.

Here is THE LARGEST AND MOST UP-TO-DATE
SODA FOUNTAIN
. . IN THE DISTRICT .

THERE WILL BE AN OPENING
THÉ DANSANT
On TUESDAY (March 19th)
from 4 p.m. to 6 p.m., Tickets for which will be 2/6, including Tea.
On FUTURE AFTERNOONS THE CHARGE FOR DANCING will be 1/-

WEDNESDAY EVENING (March 20th)
8 to Midnight   DANCING, 2/6

THURSDAY & FRIDAY EVENINGS
MARCH 21st and 22nd
8 p.m. to 11 p.m.   DANCING, 1/6

SATURDAY EVENING (March 23rd)
DANCING, 2/6
It will be observed that the above prices are for Dancing Only. Refreshments being as per Menu.   Admission is FREE.

On SUNDAY AFTERNOON (Mar. 24th)
from 4 p.m. to 6 p.m.
A TEA CONCERT
will be given by a section of the Municipal Orchestra.
Tickets 1/6 inclusive.

IN THE ...
CONCERT HALL
(EACH EVENING at 8 p.m.)
YOU will find
THE MUNICIPAL ORCHESTRA
Director : SIR DAN GODFREY
in delightful new and magnificent surroundings. The Silver Rostrum, Gilt Chairs and Music Stands, with a Silver background, upon which coloured Limelights will give tone colour effects to a specially selected Programme, will enhance the enjoyment of the music of this famous Orchestra in a manner hitherto unrealised.

MR. PHILIP DORE
will play a short programme upon
THE ORGAN
after which
SYBIL VANE
(the Welsh Prima Donna)
will charm you in selections from her repertoire, accompanied by
LEON DOMQUE
to be followed by
ETHEL ALDERSON
(Danseuse)
in a delightful exposition of the TERPSICHOREAN ART.
THEN THE TWO CO-OPTIMISTS
STANLEY HOLLOWAY & WOLSELEY CHARLES
will amuse you with their inimitable humour, and
WILL MORRIS
will astound you with his NONSENSE ON WHEELS.
Prices: Ground Floor: 3/6, 2/4, 1/6 and 1/-; Balcony, 3/- and 2/-
EVERY SEAT MAY BE BOOKED IN ADVANCE

THE FIRST SYMPHONY CONCERT
when THE ORCHESTRA WILL BE AUGMENTED TO
50 PERFORMERS
will take place on
Thursday Next, March 21st, at 3 p.m.
Programme: Overture, "Cockaigne" (London Town), Elgar; A LONDON SYMPHONY (Vaughan Williams); Violin, Concerto in G Minor (Max Bruch).
Soloist, SONIA MOLDAWSKY.
Prices: Ground Floor: 3/6, 2/4, 1/6 and 1/-; Balcony, 3/- and 2/-
EVERY SEAT MAY BE BOOKED IN ADVANCE

Saturday Next, March 23rd, at 3 p.m.
Last Appearance in England this Season of
JOHN McCORMACK
Supported by LAURI KENNEDY (Violoncello).
Prices: Ground Floor: 10/6, 7/6, 5/9, 3/6; Balcony 8/6, 4/9.

Sunday, March 24th, at 8 p.m.
Special Engagement of
MURIEL BRUNSKILL
(The Celebrated Contralto).
supported by
THE MUNICIPAL ORCHESTRA
Prices: Ground Floor: 3/6, 2/4, 1/6 and 1/-; Balcony, 3/- and 2/-

DON'T LEAVE IT TO CHANCE
BOOK YOUR SEAT IN ADVANCE
IT COSTS NO MORE

IN THE ...
RESTAURANT
(which is fully licensed)
YOU
will find
The Lucullus Room
Set apart for
A LA CARTE SERVICE
OF
LUNCHEONS, DINNERS and THEATRE SUPPERS
This room is admirably equipped for Private Parties, Banquets, Wedding Receptions, etc.

In the MAIN RESTAURANT
Table d'Hote Luncheon (2/6)
will be served from 12—2.30 Daily.

A Selection of Short Menus
at various prices has been compiled with a view to saving Patrons trouble of choosing from the General Menu.

SILVER GRILL
High Teas and Fruit Teas
at various prices a speciality.

These rooms have been designed to give the public, visiting and residential alike, facilities for dining and refreshment in perfect surroundings, and the aim is to offer only the best with efficient service at a moderate price.

The various rooms are available for private functions, and the Manager will be happy to furnish details to those contemplating private dances, dinner parties, or, indeed, any function which demands for success the resources of a fully equipped establishment and the services of a highly skilled staff.

Why not Dine at the Pavilion?
You Will Find the Experience Interesting

COMING EVENTS
Week commencing March 25th— LESLIE FULLER'S PEDLERS in their "REVUE OF REVUES"
Good Friday (Mar. 29th) at 3 & 8—First Appearance out of London of PAUL ROBESON of "Show Boat" Fame
Easter Sunday (March 31st) at 8—HERMAN DAREWSKI (Himself) and HIS BAND

12

The Opening Ceremony Programme

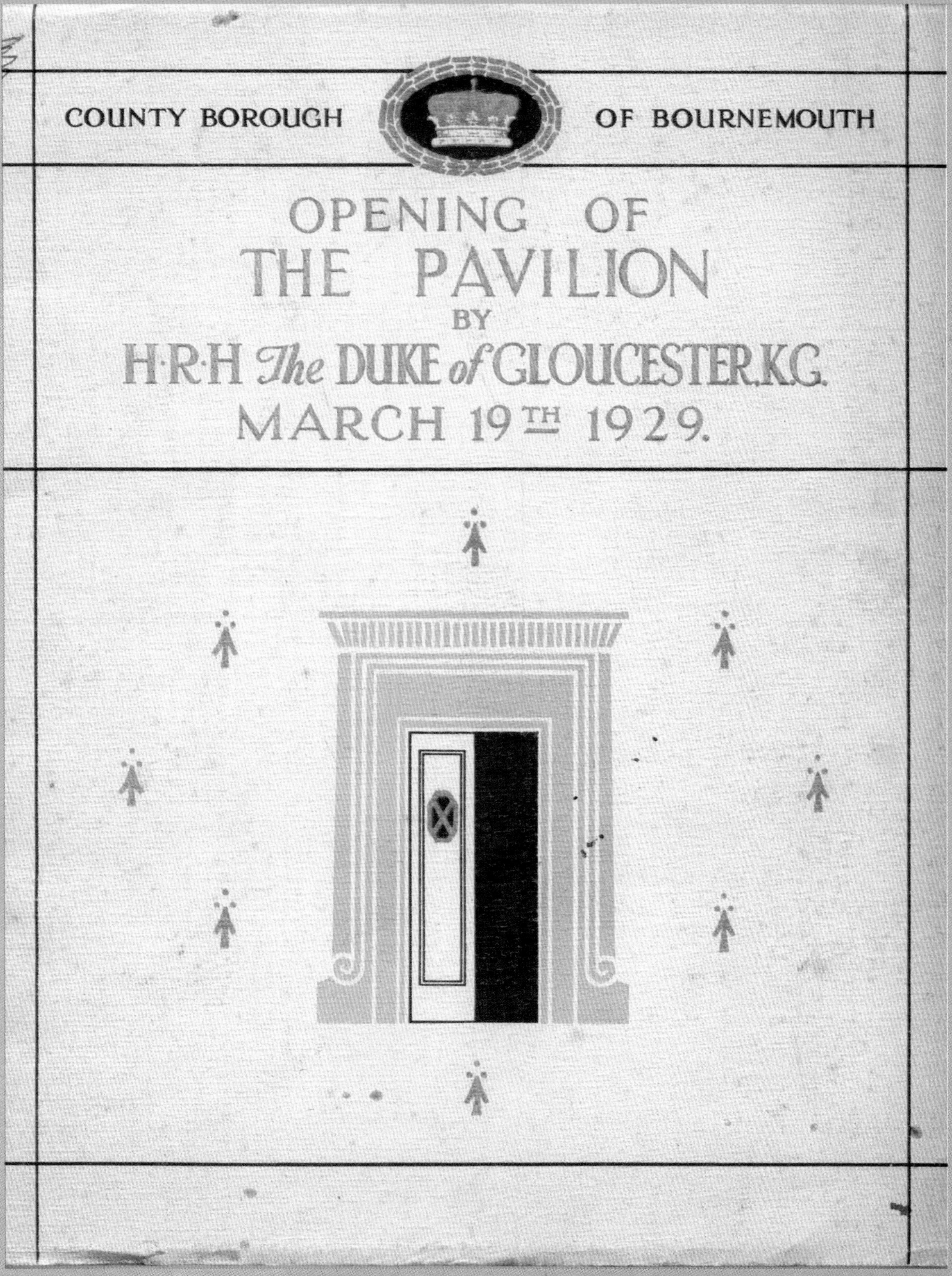
COUNTY BOROUGH OF BOURNEMOUTH
OPENING OF
THE PAVILION
BY
H·R·H The DUKE of GLOUCESTER.K.G.
MARCH 19TH 1929.

This rather sombre programme cover for a bright and auspicious occasion is a detail from the architects' drawing of the six entrance doorways to the auditorium. These still exist (though the glass sections are painted out) and are a clear reference to the 'Egyptian' influence on Art Deco at the time.

THE PRINCIPAL DINING ROOM

HESE rooms have been designed to give the public, visiting and residential alike, facilities for dining and refreshment in perfect surroundings, and the aim is to offer only the best with efficient service at a moderate price.

The various rooms are available for private functions and the Manager will be happy to furnish details and to suggest menus to those contemplating private dances, dinner parties or indeed any function which demands for success the resources of a fully equipped establishment and the services of a highly skilled staff.

14

Relaxing pastel shades in pure elegance

TEA LOUNGE AND DANCE HALL

*W*HEN amusement and relaxation from the cares and worries of the daily round are demanded, where better can they be found than in surroundings such as these?

A magnificent room, ultra modern in decoration, bright and stimulating in colour, yet glowing with the subtle atmosphere of refinement and hospitality, which modern conditions demand, the morning coffee, the afternoon tea, the evening's refreshment, may all be obtained here.

Those who dance will find ample opportunity of indulging in that pleasure to the strains of Herman Darewski's "Pavilians"—a modern dance combination of rare skill and ability who will provide not only the latest dance music but also the glorious old melodies whose charm never ceases.

The multi-coloured lighting will add further to the enjoyment of dancers and spectators alike, while the elaborate ventilating system ensures the comfort of patrons in all weathers.

4

Courtly, graceful and refined

THE CONCERT HALL

THE Concert Hall has been designed to furnish a worthy setting for every form of entertainment. No effort or expense has been spared to achieve the ideal Concert Hall. The provision of tip up chairs throughout the auditorium, the installation of a ventilating system which propels purified air through the building and extracts the vitiated air, the delightful colouring and the elaborate stage settings, combine to provide that physical and mental satisfaction which is essential for the full enjoyment of an entertainment.

The performances themselves will vary in nature but not in quality, from time to time, and in this direction the comprehensive stage and lighting equipment will enable the Management to present many attractions and novelties of charm and interest.

13

Warmth and nobility

Perfect symmetry of design - who could but be impressed?

CONTENTS OF THE CASKET LAID AT FOUNDATION STONE CEREMONY
On Wednesday, 23rd September, 1925

The lid of the copper casket had been hermetically
sealed by a soldering process, in the presence of
The Mayor, The Deputy Mayor, the Town Clerk
and the Deputy Town Clerk.

Inside was - and presumably still is:

1. A copy of **The Times** of Saturday, 19th September, 1925

2. A copy of the **Bournemouth Times and Directory** of
Saturday, 19th September, 1925

3. A copy of the **Bournemouth Guardian and Hants and Dorset Advertiser**
of the same date

4. A copy of the **Bournemouth Daily Echo** of the same date

5. A copy of the **Bournemouth Graphic** of Friday, 18th September, 1925

6. A copy of **The Radio Times** of Friday, 18th September, 1925

7. A copy of **The Architects' Journal** of 9th September, 1925,
containing copies of the architects' drawings and plans of the Pavilion.

8. A copy of the **minutes of the Council and Pavilion Committee**
of 1st September, 1925,
containing the resolution of the Council
to lay the foundation stone on
Wednesday, 23rd September, 1925 at 3. p.m.

9. A copy of **The Bournemouth Municipal Orchestra -**
Twenty-One Years of Municipal Music, 1893-1914
published for the Winter Gardens Committee in May 1914

10. A copy of **Bournemouth, 1810-1910** by Charles H. Mate, J.P., F.J.I.,
and Charles Liddle, Borough Librarian

11. A **record on vellum of the laying of the foundation stone**
under the seal of the Council.

12. A **copy of the contract** for the foundations between
Messrs. Jones and Seward, Ltd., and the Corporation, together with the
specifications, schedule of prices and form of tender.

13. **Silver coins** representing the following values: 5s., 4s., 2s. 6d., 1s., 6d., 3d

14. **Bronze coins** of the following values: 1d., halfpenny, farthing.

15. **Treasury notes** of the following values: £1, (J I/57, 124,000) 10s. (N/46 288,360)

Dated this 22nd day of September, 1925.

FACT

MORE THAN YOU'D EVER WANT TO KNOW!

ROOFING

Over **7,000 square yards of asphalt** roofing and damp-course from the mines in the Val de Travers in Switzerland were used. *(Suppliers: Val de Travers Asphaltic Paving Co., Ltd, Bournemouth)*

PLATE AND CUTLERY

The entire plate and cutlery came from *Mappin & Webb at their Royal Works in Sheffield*. Restaurant equipment included **£3,000 worth of silver and cutlery**.

EMPIRE STONE

The whole of the stone-work to the superstructure was built in Empire Stone, a **re-constructed Portland Stone**. *(Suppliers: Empire Stone Co. Ltd., Strand)*

BAR EQUIPMENT

The counters were inlaid with "Dalex" (pre-Doctor Who!), and the cellars were fitted throughout with **glass beer pipes and "Optic-Pearl" measuring taps** for hygiene. *(Suppliers: Gaskell and Chambers)*

PIANOS

Chappell pianos were used throughout the building. *(Suppliers: Messrs. E. Price and Sons, Gervis Place)*

```
NEW  PAVILION   -   BOURNEMOUTH

Pianos  exclusively  by
C H A P P E L L

Sole  Agents
E. PRICE & SONS, LTD.
Handel House
5 & 7, GERVIS PLACE, BOURNEMOUTH
```

STONE

The balustrades were in **Portland Stone**, and the stone steps of the entrance were artificial. *(Suppliers: Stroncrete Manufacturing, Ltd, Bournemouth)*

STAGE EQUIPMENT

The **safety curtain** has a solid mild steel plate back weighing over **eight tons** and could be lowered in half a minute. (The original safety curtain is still in situ.) There was a counter-weighting system for the scenery. *(Suppliers: Frank Burkitt, London)*

PLASTER WORK

The whole of the interior **plaster work was ornamented** in keeping with the imposing character of the general structure. *(Suppliers: Dejong and Co, Ltd., London)*

FIRE PRECAUTIONS

The thousands of people who would use the Pavilion were to be protected by a system of **water-tanks, hydrants and sprinklers**. Automatic sprays would drench the fire and an alarm would be sounded. *(Suppliers: Mather and Platt, Ltd., Manchester)*

ORNAMENTAL IRONWORK

The building is noted for a **handsome balcony rail**, foyer balustrades and lantern lights, and richly embossed copper finial (decorative feature at top). *(Made and supplied by: Mr. J. Caslake of Malmesbury Park Road)*

FLOORS

There were hollow-block floors, **reinforced concrete staircases**, pre-cast Terrazzo tile-paving, Terrazzo wall-linings and skirting-boards. *(Suppliers: Diespeker and Co. Ltd., London)*

ELECTRICAL EQUIPMENT

"Tucker" electrical switches and accessories were installed. *(Suppliers: Messrs. Aish and Co.)*

SODA FOUNTAINS

The Pavilion boasted two soda fountains of the **very latest design** and structure. The larger one, in the cafe, was of greater dimensions than any other on the south coast. It claimed

to be capable of meeting any reasonable demands which may fall on it. Both fountains were

finished in black and white vitrolite with nickel-plated counters and draught arms, and both were **mechanically refrigerated**. Automatic electric carbonators gave a constant supply of ice-cold water. Claims about them stated, "**Ice-cream can be stored in perfect condition, being kept at a suitable degree of hardness either for use alone, or as a foundation for the many and various delicious sundaes which are now so popular.**" It was of entirely local manufacture. *(Suppliers: Bournemouth Ice and Ice Cream Factory, Boscombe)*

FURNITURE

Most of the **furniture** was designed and **made locally**. Three big carpet squares and three "runners" were laid in the first-class restaurant, where the furniture included **300 chairs** with green hide backs, and seats and oak tables with glass tops. The **specially woven carpets** were green to provide harmony with the furniture. In the second-class restaurant, the **oak chairs** had specially shaped backs, and the west lounge furniture included **four settees** in best hide. In the auditorium, the seats were all **"St. George"** theatre chairs (research has not discovered any information about this type of seat). The house tabs

- the main curtain in the proscenium arch - was a novel design in autumnal colours, the feature being a suggestion of **flames embroidered in yellow on copper background**. The carpets were again specially designed in old gold and blue. The Tea Room was in mauve - both dark and light, with yellow curtains and vivid green pelmets. *(Suppliers: Messrs. J.J. Allen, The Quadrant)*

WALLPAPER AND FRIEZES

A local supplier, who also had been honoured with orders to redecorate parts of Buckingham Palace, provided **English Gold Leaf** for the dome of the auditorium. *(Suppliers: Messrs. John Line and Sons, Ltd, Bournemouth)*

FLOWERS FOR OPENING CEREMONY

The carefully selected flowers provided imaginative colour schemes. *(Suppliers: Fruit and Flowers)*

INTERIOR WALLS

The artistic finish on the **interior wall decorations** used Walpamur Products and Thorolds Plastoline. *(Suppliers: Kennedy's (Bournemouth) Ltd., Builders Merchants.*

FIRE EXTINGUISHERS

Special care was exercised in the choice of the many fire extinguishers - in particular the Grinnell **automatic sprinkler** which is noted for the fact that it does not disfigure any interior decoration. *(Suppliers: Mather and Platt, Ltd., Manchester)*

BUILDERS

Both the **building contracts** (foundations and superstructure) were secured in open competition by *Messrs. Jones and Seward, Ltd of Bournemouth.*

FACT

What the Pavilion Contained
GOOD VALUE FOR MONEY

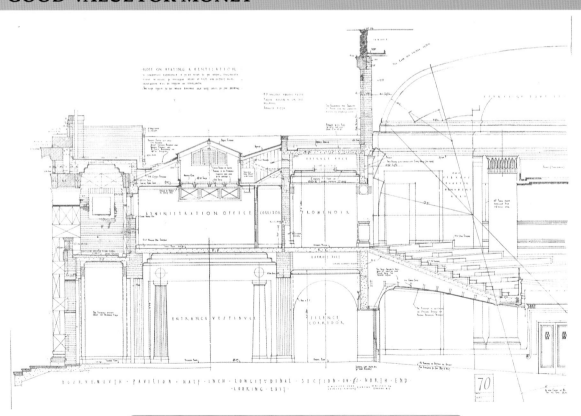

Architects' Cross-Section of Entrance and North Side of Auditorium.
The Cantilever system of construction of the Circle is made very clear

Concert Hall - 83 ft by 83 ft
(This is what we now call the Theatre)

Tea room with sprung dance floor - 134 ft by 92 ft
(This is what we now call the Ballroom)

Two lounges - 45 ft by 25 ft
(These were on either side of the building, entered from the corridors to the ballroom. There were steps which went up to the circle promenades on either side. They were demolished when the stage was enlarged and became one through-bar, which we now know as "The Phoebe". Evidence of the old lounges can be seen half way down the stairs from the west promenade (near Gentlemen's Toilet) to the top West Terrace; a small trap door is blocked in the ceiling, and above it, is a small room)

Small Hall or Lucullus Room - 62 ft by 29 ft

First-class restaurant - 100 ft by 40 ft

Second-class Restaurant - 76 ft by 40 ft
(Both these restaurants were below the Ballroom. They are currently called "Oasis", but, sadly, closed.)

The stage is 50 ft wide at the proscenium opening, and 30 ft from back to front.
The depth can be increased by 12 ft. The proscenium arch is 45 ft wide and 50 ft high.

The **Concert Hall gallery** can accommodate 700, giving a total capacity of 2,000. The construction was of a **cantilever system** of construction in reinforced concrete, which enabled an uninterrupted view of the stage from every point. A cantilever is a very large bracket for supporting balconies. This is well illustrated on the cross-section on the previous page. The Circle is just to the right of centre.

76 Years of the Bournemouth Pavilion - A CELEBRATION

Programme Advert 1968

This beautiful Rolls Royce, complete with chauffeur, is always available to take you anywhere at any time . . .

Telephone

Bournemouth Escort Service
Westbourne 61087
Craydon Lodge, Alumdale Road, Westbourne

Ghostly Tales
SIMON BAGNALL GETS SPOOKY

*Most large buildings have their fair share of ghosts! The **Pavilion** is no exception. Stage Manager **Simon Bagnall** recalls a few personal experiences.*

"**November 4th, 1992 11.40 a.m.** I remember the occasion vividly. Here's the background - there's a story that tells of an amateur dramatic lady called **Emily** who collapsed and died on stage, and who now sometimes walks round the circle promenade wearing a period costume dress and a bonnet. On the day I mentioned, I was on stage and **Barry Beresford**, who was then the Stage Manager, was in the circle. He came down for a cup of tea and said, *"I've just seen the ghost!"* He said that Emily had walked up the central aisle and passed through the curtains and the door at the back of the circle, even though the door had been chained. She was wearing a large bonnet. Barry then got a piece of paper and a pen and he drew me a picture of the lady - not casually or slowly, but with rapid hand movements in fact, the picture was finished in a flash. It looked something like this drawing on the right.

As he drew the picture, his eyes were red and streaming with tears, and the building went cold. It's claimed that a lady once spoke to Emily.

"Also, a red admiral butterfly sometimes appears and flies around the auditorium. I've actually seen it. It has apparently been stepped on but still survives. One time, it landed on one of the chandeliers in the auditorium and stayed there for weeks. As butterflies only live for a few days, we thought it was dead, but eventually it flew away.

"There are other strange things, too - one morning, I was in to work early and went to the property room at the back of the stage to make a cup of tea. The Safety Curtain was down, and I heard **footsteps on the stage**, but when I went to see who it was, I saw no one. I've quite regularly heard footsteps on stage even when it's locked. And believe you me, it's **an eerie building** in the dark."

"Emily"

Bournemouth Pavilion Theatre

Week commencing Tuesday 1st April

THE LION, THE WITCH & THE WARDROBE

£5, £3 Child, with generous party concessions

Theatre Royal Hanley plc presents

CABARET

with
WAYNE SLEEP as the Master of Ceremonies
Produced by **PAUL BARNARD** Directed and Choreographed by **GILLIAN LYNNE**

Opens Saturday 28th June at 8.00pm

THE GRUMBLEWEEDS

Holiday Showtime

STU FRANCIS, Teddy Peiro and Patricio,
Cathy Peters Hotline Dancers, FAITH BROWN,
Produced by **Peter Sontar**, Choregraphed by **Cathy Peters**
Pavilion Theatre Orchestra

1986

Some Miscellaneous Facts
MISSING SEATS, A CHATTY ORGANIST and A PASS DOOR

Old Square!

Around the **Circle Promenade**, there are eighteen perfectly square windows with views across the Pleasure Gardens to the west, with the Car Park, the Imax Building and the sea to the east. The nine windows on the east side can be seen below.

Good Seats Not to Book!

Six **Circle** seats in the back row - **32 to 37,** have been removed to house the lighting and sound controls.

Poster Sights!

The Pavilion has 35 Poster sites across the Town Centre and the Suburbs, given a capacity for displaying 200 posters.

Office Pass Door

At the back of the Circle, on the north-west Promenade, and next to the enormous fire hydrant, is a door which allows access to the offices on the West Side of the Foyer. This was not put in place when the offices were built in the 1950s, but is a later addition, which allowed the manager to pop into the Theatre to see how the show was going without having to cross the Foyer. Folk lore suggests that two department managers were not too keen on each other, and this door allowed them to keep a reasonable distance between them! I have found no proof of this!

A Chatty Organist

Borough Organist, Harold Coombs *(See Page 69)* used to amaze members of the audience in the front rows, by turning round and having a conversation with them while he was playing!

The rather stern east side of the Auditorium, well illustrating the art-deco features. Note the nine square windows in the Circle Promenade.

1929

March 19th - Pavilion opened by **Duke of Gloucester**.

There was a wealth of **alternative entertainment** on offer, and this was expanding by the month, an indication of how Bournemouth was growing; and **Westover Road** was becoming the hub of entertainment. Here are some examples: *(see also Page 84)*

Pavilion - 2,000 people in Concert Hall
Pavilion Ballroom - 1000s coming and going
New Regent Theatre (opposite Pavilion and still to come) - now **Odeon** - 2,300 people (with a small **Mighty Wurlitzer**)
The new **Westover Cinema** (almost opposite Pavilion and still to come) - 2000+ people (with a small **Compton Organ**)
Westover Ballroom (behind Cinema) - 750 people
Proposals for **a Little Theatre** in Hinton Road (this would later become the Palace Court Theatre)
Proposals for an **Ice Rink** (opposite Pavilion)
St. Peter's Hall in Hinton Road - plays and concerts and **"even gayer events"** (Bournemouth Daily Echo)
Winter Gardens (old conservatory building - former home of **Municipal Orchestra**) - up to 2,000 people
(What we now call the Winter Gardens was built as an indoor-bowling-green in the mid 1930s)
Other cinemas, including **Electric** (with a small **Christie Organ**) on Commercial Road (where Marks and Spencers is now)
And to accommodate these places of entertainment, a proposed **1,000 car garage car-park** in Hinton Road - on four floors - Bournemouth's first multi-storey car-park. And it's still there!

And so, back to the Pavilion -

Shows at the Pavilion in 1929 included popular singer **John McCormack** and **The Review of Revues**. **Paul Robeson** gave two shows, the only ones in the provinces.

Philip Dore was appointed as Borough Organist. The **Compton Organ** was the biggest the company had built to date.

October - the **Regent Theatre** opposite opened. This had over 2,000 seats, a magnificent internal decor with marvellous decorative dome, a full-stage operation and a nine-rank **Wurlitzer Organ**. Architecturally, it was **Italianate** in style, rather like a 15th century Italian covered open arcade.

This was to be used for cine-variety, where a film would be shown and a star would appear on stage for the second half. Although not used at all in 2005, the stage and its facilities are still there.

October - Pavilion forecourt **fountain** inaugurated. This was to be tremendously popular and a later cause of considerable discontent!

November - First stage show was 'The House Agent'.

1930

With the Pavilion now settling in as the **premier entertainments and leisure centre** for the town, this year saw the beginnings of more rival ventures.

First, the opening of the **Westover Ice Rink**, just above the Westover Motors showrooms which would pave the way for a new type of variety show **on ice**! The building was another brave new departure in Bournemouth's architecture which added still more character to Westover Road. Like the Pavilion, it used **Art Deco** style and the windows facing towards Westover Road are said to represent

icebergs.

December - foundation stone of the **Little Theatre** almost opposite the Pavilion was laid. Although facing Hinton Road, the back of the theatre was visible from Westover Road. This was pre-Palace Court Hotel days.

All Year - regular concerts with the **Bournemouth Municipal Orchestra** and many guest conductors and soloists.

1931

June - **Little Theatre** opened by **Sir John Irvine**. This is a 600-seater compact theatre, almost perfect in design, with full stage workings. Owned by **The Bournemouth Little Theatre Club**, it hosted professional companies, too, especially in later years, and for many years showed weekly repertory, notably with the **Barry O'Brien Company**.

July - **Lawrence Harker**, the Pavilion Manager, was refused structural alterations.

All Year - Bournemouth Municipal Orchestra concerts.

1932

Percy Whitlock was appointed as **Borough Organist**. In the early days, he was not at home with the instrument but mastered it within months. He played solo concerts, solo items and worked with the Bournemouth **Municipal Orchestra**. Often, there would be no organ score for him to follow, so he would 'busk' along with the orchestra.

February/March - Legendary actor **James Mason** played twice in two separate plays.

September - '**The Bouquets**', a variety concert party played in the Concert Hall.

October - the world-famous '**Twinkle**' revue with **Clarkson Rose**. This was very popular and light-hearted and played to packed houses wherever it went. The show regularly visited Bournemouth well into the 1950s, when the New Royal Theatre closed.

1933

May - Bournemouth Municipal Orchestra's 40th Anniversary Concert. This was **broadcast by the BBC** and played to a full house. The orchestra was augmented by some of the original members who had played in the first concert in 1893. The concert is notable in that **Sir Dan Godfrey** made a faux-pas after the playing and singing of Elgar's **Pomp and Circumstance March No. 1** (Land of Hope and Glory), he spoke to the radio audience and said that he hoped they would all come to Bournemouth for their holidays. He was severely admonished for advertising!

Stars appearing this year included **Jack Payne and his Band** with the comedian **Ted Ray**, later to be famous for his radio show '**Ray's a Laugh**'. **Flotsam and Jetsam**, and **Rex Harrison** also appeared. **Jack Hylton and his Band** and **Ballet Russes de Monte Carlo** were among other famous names to grace the stage.

July - The **1933 Continental Nights**, a variety show starring **Wee Georgie Wood** was presented by **Ivan Kotchinsky**, an impresario who seemed to be just starting a long relationship with the Pavilion.

July - There was an unusual drama called '**Children in Uniform**', a German play foreshadowing the **Hitler Youth Movement**.

Boxing Day saw the first pantomime, in which **Mona Magnet** starred. This was a touring pantomime which played for two weeks, and was followed by another touring pantomime, **Robinson Crusoe**, which also played for two weeks. These should not be considered as the first of the big production pantomimes which started a year later.

December - a large children's party featured a film or films about **Mickey and Minnie Mouse**, and other characters.

1934

There was **more development** in Westover

Road this year with the building of the **Palace Court Hotel** (which has, in recent years, had several name changes!). This is **Art Deco** with the front aspect designed to look like the side of **an ocean liner**. The hotel had the country's first ever multi-storey car park which is still there, is very tight for parking and is still very expensive!

This year saw the **Russian Ballet**, a **Shakespearian Festival (**with special terms for school parties!) and six conductors took part in Municipal Orchestra Concerts as **possible successors** to Sir Dan Godfrey.

Two international stars appeared, namely the return of **Paul Robeson**, and the composer/piano recitalist **Sergei Rachmaninov**, who gave a solo concert. Folk law suggests that after the recital, he crossed to the **Royal Bath Hotel** and sat in the lounge to hear what type of music the British people were listening to. The leader of the band/orchestra at the Royal Bath was **Montague Birch**.

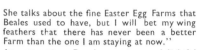

CONCERT HALL

TUESDAY AFTERNOON, MARCH 13th, at 3.0

Special Recital by

RACHMANINOFF

(The World-renowned Composer-Pianist)

1. Variations in C minor .... *Beethoven*
2. Nachtstück in F major ... *Schumann*
3. Impromptu in F minor, Op. 142 *Schubert*
4. Sonata, B flat minor, Op. 35 ... *Chopin*
   Allegro Agitato—Scherzo—Marche Funèbre—Finale

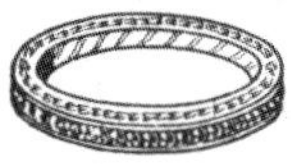

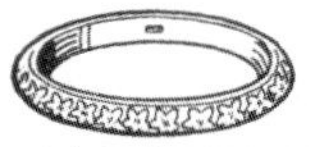

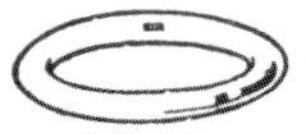

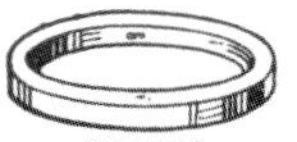

Interval

Tea, Coffee, and Ices may be obtained from all Attendants

5. Children's Corner Suite ... *Debussy*
   Doctor Gradus ad Parnassum—Serenade for the Doll—The Snow is Dancing—The Little Shepherd —Golliwog's Cake-Walk
6. (a) Two Preludes
   (G major, A minor)   }
   (b) Moment Musical   } *Rachmaninoff*
   (E flat minor)   }
7. Scherzo in A flat major ... *Borodine*
8. Invitation to the Valse *Weber-Tausig*

Steinway Piano

TO LET

April to July - Theatre/Concert Hall was closed for stage enlargement. Although the early claims suggested that the stage and equipment could cope with big London shows, the truth was that much more space and technical equipment were needed. This enlargement saw the fitting of the theatre's famous **revolving stage**, which was to be used for over fifty years in pantomimes and variety shows.

July - The first show on the new stage was 'White Horse Inn', an enormous musical in its day! The Company Stage Carpenter was **John Laurie**, who, after the tour, was appointed as **Pavilion Theatre Stage Manager** and he stayed until his retirement in 1972. He was one of the legendary stage managers in British theatre history, renowned for his firmness, his unquestioned ability and his determination to overcome all problems with solutions which weren't always conventional. *(See also Page 224)*

August - **Gertrude Lawrence** and **Douglas Fairbanks Jnr.** played the Pavilion. They were known to be 'an item' at the time.

September - **Sir Dan Godfrey** retired in an emotional ending to his career. He was so upset that he had to be helped down by leader **Montague Birch**. (Birch was a faithful servant of the Bournemouth Orchestra, taking over the baton during the Second World War, and playing piano and violin. He was also a light music composer.) At the end of the concert Godfrey and his successor **Richard Austin** stood with arms linked as the whole audience joined with **Auld Lang Syne**.

December - The first-ever specially designed pantomime for the Pavilion's enlarged stage was presented by impresario, **Harry Benet**. 'Cinderella' was one of four pantomimes in Bournemouth this year. Others were at the **Theatre Royal** in Albert Road, the **Boscombe Hippodrome** and the **Westover Ice Rink**. How quickly Bournemouth was growing, and how quickly was the entertainment scene keeping up with it!

1935

March - First **Music Festival** brought distinguished conductors to the Concert Hall.

April - The **Bournemouth Little Theatre** changed its name to the **Palace Court Theatre**.

Shows this year included 'Lilac Time' and a play called '**The Shining Hour**' starring **Gladys Cooper**.

The **Ballroom** hosted such big names as **Roy Fox**, **Jack Hylton** and **Geraldo**.

The development of Bournemouth and its entertainment facilities continued with the laying of the foundation stone for the **Pier Approach Baths**. These would later be providing shows in opposition to the Pavilion.

The year saw the end of the **old Winter Gardens** with a final concert from the Orchestra and a **Pageant of Wessex History**. The building was dismantled immediately afterwards.

The Pantomime was '**Dick Whittington**', again presented by Harry Benet.

1936

February - There was yet another appearance by **Paul Robeson**. The month also saw the first ever **Children's Choral and Orchestral Concert** at the Pavilion, organised by the **Schools Orchestral**

Reproduced by kind permission of the "Daily Sketch."

Organisation.

Other stars this year included **Marie Tempest**, **Sybil Thorndike**, **Diana Wynward** and **Seymour Hicks**.

The **Vic-Wells Opera Company** ("bringing culture to the masses!") and **Markova-Dolin Ballet** added culture to the concert hall, and on the other side of the coin, **Billy Cotton and His Band** played, no doubt with those white paper balls!

July - **Gracie Fields** appeared. *(See P. 61)*

July - the BBC transmitted what must have been a very progressive outside broadcast featuring music from the **Pavilion Ballroom**, **Boscombe Pier Concert Hall**, an organ recital on the **Wurlitzer in the Regent Theatre** and band music from the Irish Guards on **Bournemouth Pier**.

December - Plans were announced to form a **pit orchestra** for the Pavilion.

December - The pantomime was '**Jack and the Beanstalk**'.

Also, **Matheson Lang** appeared in '**The Wandering Jew**'. During one performance, the show was paused so that the audience could hear the abdication speech of King Edward VIII. Folk lore suggests that Lang listened to the broadcast on a wireless which was balanced on a beer crate back stage. (Wonder why there was a beer crate backstage?)

In this year, the Corporation built the country's largest indoor bowling green on the site of the old **Winter Gardens**. The name stayed the same, and this hall was to have a great influence on the Pavilion in the future when it became a concert hall.

1937

During this year, the new **Westover Cinema**

opened opposite, boasting an auditorium for 2,000+ people, and the Pavilion fought back with a summer season of **Vaudeville**. This show was probably the **first twice-nightly show** at the Pavilion.

March - **Sybil Thorndike** appeared in the play 'Six Men of Dorset', by Miles Malleson, highlighting the events which led to the **Tolpuddle Martyrs**. It's not clear whether her husband **Lewis Casson** was in the production, although they acted in the play together for many years.

April - **Sir Thomas Beecham** conducted the **London Philharmonic Orchestra** in the Pavilion Concert Hall.

October - The first concert by an enlarged Municipal Orchestra was broadcast from the Pavilion.

November - New Indoor Bowling green was officially opened at **Winter Gardens**. The cost was **£30,000**.

December - 'Cinderella' was the pantomime.

1938

This was the year that saw the amazing **Ivor Novello** musical, 'Crest of the Wave' at the Pavilion. The production was noted for its realistic 'train crash' which required one of the carriages to swing out over the orchestra pit and stalls. For this sort of staging, special safety licences had to be obtained.

December - The pantomime was 'Aladdin'.

1939

This was an important and landmark year in history, and the outbreak of war caused many changes in routine and entertainment. Before the war, every weekday afternoon there was a **Tea Dance** from 4 p.m. to 6 p.m., costing 1/- on Monday to Friday and 1/6 on a Saturday. **Evening Dances** cost 1/6 except on Saturday when 2/6 was the price.

There were some considerable restrictions on making advance bookings and Thursday afternoon concerts; **Travelogues** (of which there were many) and Sunday concerts could only be booked one week ahead. The lowest seat prices in Stalls and Circle at any performance could not be reserved. This indicates the overall success of the Pavilion.

March - A Music Festival included Beethoven's 7th **Symphony** conducted by **Sir Thomas Beecham**.

July - This month saw the inauguration of the **Bournemouth Telephone Area**. The official ceremony was followed by tea-table hospitality at the Pavilion for all members of staff. **Beales** Store had the prestigious telephone number of **Bournemouth 1**.

July - **Sir Dan Godfrey died** following a brain spasm during a rehearsal at the Pavilion.

July - the first of many productions at the Pavilion of '**Me and my Girl**'.

July/August - there were star-studded variety shows with such names **Nosmo King** (name from seeing two doors with the words 'No Smoking'!), **Billy Cotton**, **Wee Georgie Wood**, **Norman Evans**, **Elsie and Doris Waters**, **Ted Ray**, **Issy Bonn** and the **D'Oyly Carte Opera Company**. **Max Miller** also made an appearance, but had the curtain rung down on him because his act was so filthy.

Planned for **September 4th** was a vaudeville show with **Mantovani and his Orchestra** and **Tommy Handley**. Mantovani was well known locally because he had played with a smaller group in a cafe/restaurant in Westover Road, and Tommy Handley was later to be extremely popular with his radio programme **ITMA** - 'It's That Man Again'.

September 3rd - **War broke out** and the Home Office ordered the immediate **closure of all forms of entertainment**, both indoors and out. This affected 19 cinemas in Bournemouth and Poole, as well as the Pavilion, although the ballroom was allowed to open as a cafe until 8 p.m. each evening. Both piers remained open until 8 p.m. but the concert parties and band performances on the piers were cancelled. The government feared that if a bomb should hit a place of entertainment, there would be much loss of life. Then it was soon felt that morale would be lessened without the escapism of cinema and other forms of entertainment, and the **cinemas began to open again by September 9th**, following a lifting of the ban by the Home Secretary.

September 11th - The Pavilion Concert Hall gave an extended evening of entertainment, featuring the full Municipal Orchestra, the Organ, a Conjurer called **Chris Carlton**, and the **Sim Grossman** Stage Band.

The Orchestra was severely reduced in size, including **dismissal of all women players**. **Richard Austin** resigned and **Montague Birch** took over as conductor.

After the quick re-opening of the Concert Hall, a full programme of entertainment followed, including the familiar **Travelogues** and **Orchestral Concerts** and a series of plays with famous artists. **Robb Wilton** (whose catch-word was 'The day war broke out....'), **Robertson Hare**, **Phyllis Neilson-Terry**, **Fay Compton**, **Jessie Matthews** and **Sonny Hale** are just a few of the names.

Afternoon Travelogues included '**Adventures with Eagles**' with **Capt. C W R Knight**, and '**Life in the Wilds**' with the original naturalist film-maker, **Cherry Kearton**.

The Municipal Orchestra featured many top-line soloists including **Myra Hess**, **Solomon**,

Pouishnoff and **Ida Haendel**.

As the war progressed the **theatre in general began to decline**. The popular handsome male leads were being called up to the armed services (such as **Richard Todd**, who had been brought up in Wimborne), and money was so limited that impresarios couldn't afford to build scenery for lavish productions. This meant that a good number of older musicals using lesser known artistes were put on tour. At the Pavilion, these included '**The Belle of New York**' and '**No, No, Nanette**'.

Interval refreshments were priced as follows: Ices, 6d; Coffee, 4d a cup; Tea, 4d a cup; and the

programme announced that "*Horlicks deliciously mixed is served throughout the Pavilion and all Beach Cafes*".

December - To conclude the year's entertainment, Harry Benet presented his annual pantomime for five weeks - **Babes in the Wood**. There were daily matinees except on Thursday, and the seat prices were 3/6, 2/6 and 1/6.

The Pavilion had coped well through those early months of the Second World War, and had provided **comfort and joy** to a population deeply depressed.

CLASSIC PICTURE

A very clear photograph from the air of the Pavilion complex sometime in the early 1930s. The Ice Rink is complete, as is the Regent Theatre (Gaumont/Odeon), with its dramatic and distinctive dome, and the Little Theatre. But the Pavilion fly-tower is still in the original smaller format. This dates the picture probably in 1933. Note the Y.M.C.A building to the right of the Little Theatre, and the garage to the right of the Pavilion. This was later to become a small bus depot for Hants and Dorset Motor Services.

BRIGHTEN A DULL DAY
AND PAY A VISIT TO

W O O L C O

Enjoy one stop shopping on one floor, no long walks, no climbing stairs. 40 departments to choose from, everything from food to fashion to furniture and tyres. Something for everyone and every taste, at very keen prices.

FREE! CAR PARKING FOR 2,300 CARS

Don't go on any rushed, wild shopping sprees. Take your time, shop in comfort. Enjoy a rest, a meal or a snack in our self selection restaurant.

75,000 SQ. FT. OF Air Conditioned LUXURY

We are also open most bank holidays. THE LARGEST STORE ON ONE FLOOR IN BRITAIN!

WOOLCO DEPARTMENT STORE
THE HAMPSHIRE SHOPPING CENTRE
CASTLE LANE WEST · BOURNEMOUTH
TELEPHONE 56201

SHOPPING HOURS
MONDAY 10 a.m. 6 p.m. THURSDAY 10 a.m. 8 p.m.
TUESDAY 10 a.m. 8 p.m. FRIDAY 10 a.m. 8 p.m.
WEDNESDAY 10.15 a.m. 8 p.m. SATURDAY 9 a.m. 6 p.m.

MERLEY TROPICAL BIRD GARDENS

MERLEY · POOLE · DORSET
(Entrance near Willett Arms on the A.349 Wimborne, Poole Road)

DORSET'S FINEST COLLECTION OF BIRDS
in 3½ acres of lovely gardens

OPEN DAILY
10.30 a.m. - 7 p.m.
Dogs not admitted to gardens
Tea Room
Car Park
Wimborne 3790

Apr. to Oct.

Left: "The largest store on one floor in Britain"
Woolco were regular and loyal advertisers in the Bournemouth Pavilion programme. They often took the whole of the back page.
The store has now been demolished and rebuilt in a new complex called Castle Point.

Above: Much loved and long-gone, the Merley Bird Gardens advertised frequently.

Right: Eldridge Popes were also regular and loyal advertisers, and operated the Oasis Bar at the Pavilion for some time. Sadly, they no longer brew their own beer, and many beer-drinkers still miss their IPA

MAKE HOLIDAY FRIENDS WITH A

Huntsman

THE BEER OF WESSEX
'Your Idea Of Beer'

Brewed by Eldridge Pope & Co. Ltd. of Dorchester

Eldridge Pope also have one of the largest stocks of fine wines and spirits in the South of England.

Available in the Bournemouth area from

Eldridge Pope Wine Shops at:
799 Christchurch Road, **Boscombe**
13 Grand Parade, **Canford Cliffs**
1 Alumhurst Road, **Westbourne**
457 Wimbourne Road, **Winton**
29 Catherine Road, **Southbourne.**

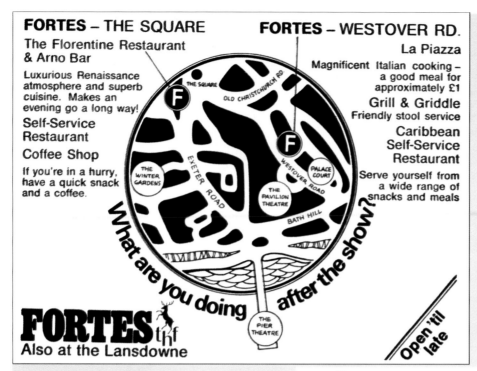
Left: Happy memories! Italian meal for £1! All the Fortes shops have now disappeared from Bournemouth, the Square branch having been totally destroyed in a disastrous fire. All buildings still operate as food and drink outlets.

Below: Beales would have to take the prize for being the most loyal advertiser in the Pavilion programme. For many years, they had the title page, under the name of the play. As their new store was being built, following a bombing raid in 1943, when their lovely art-deco shop was totally destroyed, the adverts kept the audiences up to date with building progress

The centre of interest for shoppers with its Restaurant high above the town, and six selling floors of Fashions, Furniture, Gifts and the Man's Shop through which the shopper can wander at will.

Left: This 1965 advertisement reminds us of another Department Store. There was a top-floor restaurant with views over the Square, and an afternoon music recital. The store is still in existence but it's called Debenhams nowadays.

Always plenty to drink in the Pavilion programme

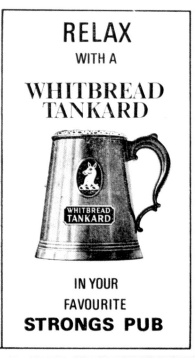

Enjoy a real <u>country</u> beer in the STRONG country

These are just a few of the famous names to advertise in the Bournemouth Pavilion programme over 76 years. Strongs, the Brewers from Romsey were taken over by Whitbread, but Badger Beer is still brewed at Blandford by Hall and Woodhouse

Betty Mark - Staff Canteen

As told by her daughter PAT BOND

Every theatre has its characters, and one of the most delightful people ever at the Pavilion was **Betty Mark**, a former housekeeper at **St. Katherine's Vicarage** in Southbourne, who for eighteen years from 1955, was the **manageress of the Stage Canteen**, situated underneath the stage and right below the west organ chamber of the auditorium. All those years she served teas, coffees and snacks to the most famous of stage artistes and to the humblest of casual stage staff - and always with a smile and chirpy comment. She enjoyed a laugh, and loved her work deeply - refusing to take time off even when she wasn't too well. She skilfully juggled her job and her home life, pleasing her family and her customers - in fact, her work wasn't just a job, it was a total way of life.

Her work there is vividly recalled by her daughter, **Pat Bond**, who remembers her mum running up the road each day - twice, because, like most theatre staff, she was on a split shift - cheerfully waving as she went to catch the bus. A real happy personality, she wooed hundreds of customers with joy and with cups of tea. **Ken Dodd**, on the photo he signed for her wrote, "Thank you for the teas(e)!" and he had always called her his "teas(e) lady". **Freddie Starr**, Betty recalled with a wry grin, asked her to take him a cup of tea into his dressing room, and when she got there he stood up, totally naked, in the bath! **Danny La Rue** had a particular affection for her, and the **Barron Knights** gave her a table lamp as a thank you gift after their pantomime season - a lamp which she kept until she died as a valued memory. The cast of '**My Fair Lady**' gave her a

basket of artificial flowers and she refused ever to throw them away. **David Whitfield**, at her behest, sang his famous song **"Cara Mia Mine"** especially for her mum and dad, Pat and Harry, during a performance.

Sadly, at only 57, she died, but her photograph stayed hanging in the canteen for many years afterwards, until it was closed for safety reasons in the 1990s - a tribute to her memory and popularity. Working with some of the biggest names in show-business never went to her head - she remained a very ordinary person, but was often a shoulder to cry on for the big, the small, the famous and the not-so-famous. Those who knew her will always think about her whenever they walk towards the room that housed the canteen. It's now an electrical workshop, but those who remember still envisage the hatch, with the smile and the teapot, always throwing out a welcome when the performance was dragging and the day was long. When she went into hospital not long before her death, the cast of '**Robinson Crusoe**' visited her, a fitting tribute to a fine lady. Her autograph books read like a who's who of stars; this list is merely a few of the hundreds she had:

Betty with Chief Stage Electrician Alec Holland, in about 1960

Bruce Forsyth, Don Rivers, Kaye Sisters, Simon Oates, Gladys (Mrs) Mills, The Shirelles, Dawn Addams, Lance Percival, Danny La Rue, Dallas Boys, Edmund Hockridge, Kenneth MacKeller, Vera Lynn, Jimmy Tarbuck, Arthur Haynes, Lionel Blair, Cecily Courtneige, Rawicz and Landauer, Margaret Lockwood, Robertson Hare, Dora Bryan, Richard Todd, Joan Regan, Barry Sinclair, Mr Pastry (Richard Hearne), Des O'Connor, Alfred Marks, Freddie Starr, Marty Wilde, Frankie Vaughan, Norman Wisdom, Dickie Valentine, Marlene Dietrich, Flora Robson, Ivor Immanuel, Pearl Carr and Teddy Johnson, Norman Collier, Harry H Corbett, George Chisholm, Leslie Crowther, Alma Cogan, Tommy Trinder, Winifred Atwell, Terry Hall and Lenny the Lion, Dick Emery, David Nixon, Shirley Bassey, Billy Burden, Zena Martell, John Gregson, Adam Faith, Tommy Trinder, Irene Handl, Eddie Calvert, Ruby Murray, Flora Robson, Margaret Lockwood, Julia Lockwood, Brian Bennett, Tommy Cooper, Dusty Springfield, Spike Milligan, Sybil Thorndike, Diana Dors, Ted Rogers, Billy Dainty, Al Read. And many, many more! A real hall of fame.

Just two of Betty Mark's fans!
Margaret Lockwood
and
Richard Todd

35

So Much to Remember
BOB BOLLOM

*Bob Bollom was born in the same year that the Pavilion opened, and his earliest memories concern the **British Restaurant**, the name given to the Popular Restaurant during the Second World War years.*

"It was a good and reasonably-priced place to eat, and although there was food rationing in place, you always got a good meal. It was open to the general public and a three course meal cost half a crown - that's twelve and half pence in new money! I was totally overawed by this restaurant at first because it seemed very high class. *(There are more facts and details about the British Restaurant on Page 47)*

" My first theatre memories are towards the end of the war when I was about 16 or 17. Mum was a great theatre fan and she used to take me to see some of the really big American stars. I can remember **Alan Jones** - he

This is the Buffet Bar on the bottom floor of the Pavilion in 1929. For details of the Popular/British Restaurant, see Page 117

was the man who made the song "**Donkey Serenade**" famous and was the father of singer **Jack Jones**. I recall, too, **Peggy Ryan**, the dancer and film-star who played many films with **Donald O'Connor**. She danced on the stage and also told jokes. Over the

years, I can remember seeing the **Billy Cotton Band Show** and a special treat was seeing the great film-star **Tyrone Power** in a melodrama. **Douglas Montgomery** also played the theatre, and at the same time he was appearing as the villain in the **Bob Hope** film "**The Cat and the Canary**" at the **Astoria Cinema** near Pokesdown Station. I was the projectionist there at the time, and our manager managed to persuade Douglas to come along to the cinema and make a public appearance.

"I recall, too, **Dirk Bogard**e and **Geraldine McEwen** in a play called "**Summertime**" which was directed by **Peter Ha**ll. Sadly, in more recent years, my big regret has been that there are very few plays at the Pavilion. But I like musicals, and we're quite well catered for with those. I loved **Max Wall**, and **Chris Barber** was brilliant - and the revitalised **Bert Kamphfert** orchestra was good. Of the big shows, I loved "**Hi-Di-Hi**" - I remember a lot of ad-libbing in that, which was fun.

"**Frankie Laine** was absolutely wonderful, but he had put on rather a lot of weight and this made his voice better and more powerful. And I'll never forget **Morecambe and Wise**, especially that sketch when they play ventroliquist and dummy - quite unforgettable. Yes, I have some really brilliant memories of the Pavilion, and it's a shame that the seats aren't too comfortable, and I often feel that the theatre is neglected at the expense of other parts of the building."

Bob Chapman

LIFETIME SUPPORTER OF PAVILION

Bob Chapman has been a Bournemouth Council member for the Central Ward since 1981. He was the leader of the Council for four years and, prior to that, led the Conservative Group for a number of years.

"The Pavilion is very close to my heart because it's right in the centre of my ward, and I have always done my best to support the complex. I've lived in Bournemouth since 1949 when my parents moved from Leicester to open a haberdashery shop in Pokesdown. My dad was disabled and he always insisted that mum went out for one night a week, and she always took me with her. In those days, it cost 3d to travel from outside the New Bell Inn to the town centre, by fast and smooth-running trolley-buses. Within fifteen minutes we could be outside the Pavilion, and we had no parking problems. We mostly went to the theatre, sometimes to the New Royal Theatre in Albert Road and sometimes to the Palace Court Theatre in its days under the Bournemouth

Little Theatre Club. But usually, we found ourselves in the Pavilion; we preferred it to the others and there was a very wide variety of shows on offer.

So Many Excellent Musicals

I can remember musicals such as '**The King and I**', '**Carousel**', '**My Fair Lady**' and '**The Sound of Music**', and some excellent variety shows. The one which really sticks in my memory was **Jimmy Tarbuck**, who was absolutely hilarious.

"One of my great friends when I was at School at St. James' Pokesdown was **Brenda Childs** (later **Brenda Baker**) who became a leading member of the **Bournemouth and Boscombe Light Opera Company**, and I have seen virtually all their shows since the first one in the old **Boscombe Hippodrome** in 1954. I've always much appreciated West End musicals, opera and ballet, being a regular patron since my early teens, and I've always regretted that there were so few opportunities to soak up this sort of culture. Now, on a somewhat different level!, I'm a regular Thursday night visitor to the Ballroom for **Mojive**. This used to be called **Ceroc** and it's a wonderful evening of fun dancing arranged by **Phil and Elaine Rees**, and there are usually between two and three hundred people there.

There have been so many good shows at the Pavilion that it's difficult to single out a few which were special, but I particularly recall 'Buddy' - such a happy show - and Tommy Steele, who was for ever memorable. He was such a lovely personality with his singing and his dancing, and although we'd heard him on radio and seen him on television, we saw the truly vibrant and brilliant man that he was in a 'live' show. More recently, we have seen Michael Ball, who gave great performances and certainly brought out the HOUSE FULL signs.

"The Eastern European Opera Companies are superb and it's very sad that the theatre isn't full when they play, because it should be. The Ukranians and the Moldavians give performances far better than our own opera companies. They get no subsidies and so the only way they can make themselves pay financially is to ensure a top-rate show. You can hear every word and you'll never hear better singing. On the general entertainment level, 'That'll Be the Day' is an excellent show with an extremely talented cast. And mentioning all these shows illustrates what a flexible building the Pavilion Theatre is - just as much at home for variety as it is for the Mayor Making Ceremony, or for the Salvation Army's performances for Remembrance and Christmas.

The Remembrance evening is always a time to reflect and is very moving, and at Christmas, the theatre's magnificent Compton Organ comes into its own for congregational carols. The Theatre has such good stage facilities and the excellent stage crew, under Christian Knighton, are just second to none. The staging and lighting are always impressive.

Paul Slickey not really so slick

"Looking back, I remember in 1959 coming to see a show called 'The World of Paul Slickey', an avant-garde musical which raised quite a few eyebrows and was one of a series of shows which changed the whole face of entertainment at that time. It was described as 'a play of manners with music', and was written by the angry-young-man playwright, John Osbourne. There were some choice words and risque ideas. I went with Hugh Ashley, and neither sets of parents were happy that we were there - I think they felt we would be corrupted, but we were young and in the sixth form and we felt we had to. And I don't think it did either of us much harm! To be honest, neither of us can remember very much about it, but Hugh seems to recall that the central character wore a black hat with a very wide brim. It was one of the first plays at the Pavilion which caused controversy in town, many residents thinking it should never have been performed. I suppose it was a little bit like an early

'Jerry Springer - The Musical' show. Others to follow it in later years would be **'Billy Liar'**, **'Hair'**, and **'Fings ain't what they used to be'**. There are always plenty of playwrights with something to say, but sometimes many people don't want to hear it. But the Pavilion has never shirked its responsibility to keep abreast of modern theatre.

"I'm a member of the **South West Arts Council**, and here, Bournemouth is renowned for not subsidising artistic shows. I can see both sides of the argument - if the Council uses rate-payers money to give subsidies for touring shows, then there is still no guarantee that the Bournemouth people will attend. We certainly attract some first-rate shows, but we

The World of Paul Slickey

CAST (in order of appearance) :

Copy-boys	DAVID HARDING
	JULIAN BOLT
Jo, the secretary	IRENE HAMILTON
Jack Oakham, alias Paul Slickey	DENNIS LOTIS
Common Man	KEN ROBSON
1st Naval Man	BEN ARIS
2nd Naval Man	GEOFFREY WEBB
Deirdre Rawley	MAUREEN QUINNEY
Lady Mortlake	MARIE LOHR
Trewin	AIDAN TURNER
Michael Rawley	JACK WATLING
Mrs. Giltedge-Whyte	JANET HAMILTON-SMITH
Gillian Giltedge-Whyte	JANET GRAY
Lord Mortlake	HARRY WELCHMAN
Lesley Oakham	ADRIENNE CORRI
Father Evilgreene	PHILIP LOCKE
Guide	GEOFFREY WEBB
1st Girl	NORMA DUNBAR
2nd Girl	PAM MILLER
3rd Girl	ANNA SHARKEY
1st Man	KEN ROBSON
Lady Photographer	STELLA CLAIRE
Photographer	CHARLES SCHULLER
Journalist	GEOFFREY WEBB
Wendover	BEN ARIS
George	TONY SYMPSON
Terry Maroon	ROY SONE

Dancers :—

GEOFFREY WEBB	STELLA CLAIRE
BEN ARIS	PATRICIA ASHWORTH
JULIAN BOLT	NORMA DUNBAR
DAVID HARDING	PAM MILLER
KEN ROBSON	ANNA SHARKEY
CHARLES SCHULLER	JANE SHORE

Time : THE PRESENT

The entire action of the play takes place between the office of Paul Slickey, Gossip Columnist for the "Daily Racket", and Mortlake Hall, a stately home somewhere in England

ACT ONE

"Seen through the key hole"	Dancers
"Don't think you can fool a guy like me"	Jack and Dancers
"We'll be in the desert and alone"	Jack and Deirdre
"It's a consideration we'd do well to bear in mind"	Michael
"How do you occupy a man ?"	Deirdre
"Tell me later"	Jack
"The Income Tax Man"	Lesley and Michael
"The Mechanics of Success"	
"Bring back the Axe"	Mrs. Giltedge-Whyte
"I want to hear about beautiful things"	Mrs. Giltedge-Whyte
"If I could be"	Jack, Jo and Dancers

ACT TWO

"On Ice"	Jo and Dancers
"You can't get away with it"	Father Evilgreene and Dancers
"The World's going bust"	Jack
"A Woman at the Weekend"	Lesley, Jack, Deirdre and Michael
"I'm Hers"	Terry
Reprise—"I want to hear about beautiful things"	Mrs. Giltedge-Whyte
"Them"	Jack and Dancers
Reprise—"Tell me later"	Jack
Reprise—"Don't think you can fool a guy like me"	Ensemble

Sound equipment by Stagesound (London) Ltd. Lighting equipment by Strand Electric and Engineering Co., Ltd. Telephones supplied by the G.P.O. Costumes for Miss Lohr, Miss Corri, Miss Quinney and Miss Hamilton-Smith by M. Bermans Ltd. All other ladies' costumes by Elizabeth Curzon Ltd. Wigs by Wig Creations. Shoes by Dolcis Ltd. and Anello & Davide. Stockings by Bear Brand. Leotards by Anello & Davide. All satin supplied by West Cumberland Silk Mills Ltd. Miss Corri's and Miss Ashworth's spectacle wardrobe by Oliver Goldsmith. Shirts and pyjamas tailored by Bonsoir. Hats by Patrick Summer. Furs by M. Prager Ltd. Gloves by R. & J. Pullman Ltd. Silverware supplied by Richard Ogden Ltd. Kingsway and Woodbine cigarettes by W. D. & H. O. Wills Ltd. Lighters by Ronson. Built furniture by Stuart Stallard. Cameras and photographic equipment by Kodak Ltd. Potato Crisps by Smith's Potato Crisps Ltd. Schimmelpenninck Duet cigars supplied by Joseph Samuel & Son Ltd. Pale Ale by Watney Combe & Reid Ltd. Binoculars by Negretti & Zambra Ltd. Watches by Austin Kaye. Wardrobe care by Lux. Heat controlled steam iron by Morphy Richards. Sewing machine supplied by Singer Sewing Machine Co. Ltd. Vodka by Smirnoff.

Attractions appearing at the Pavilion Theatre are booked in conjunction with Howard & Wyndham Ltd., 9 Grafton Street, London, W.1.

Staff for Production		Staff for DAVID PELHAM	
Deputy Stage Manager	JOHN COPLEY	General Manager	ANTHONY PELLY
Assistant Stage Managers	MINETTE CLARE	Assistant to David Pelham	ANNETTE TUTE
	J. COLIN DUDLEY	Art Director	ROGER RAMSDELL
Ballet Mistress	JANE SHORE	Production Stage Manager	DIANA WATSON
Carpenter	FRANK NEWELL	Production Secretary	CAROL WALTON
Electrician	FRED WEBB	Press Representative :	
Wardrobe Mistress	MRS. DOUGHTY	DEANE & PHILLIPS	TEM 6443
Press Representative :			
DUNCAN MELVIN	REG 4562		

"One of the most spectacular shows of all time was the ballet **'Don Quixote'** with the **Royal Ballet of Flanders**. It's one of the highlights of my theatrical memories and sadly there were only about two hundred there to see it. I can never understand why so many Bournemouth people complain that there's not enough culture in the town, but when there is something really worthwhile, they ignore it. It's not because of bad advertising, but purely through lack of interest. In all my years as a patron at the Pavilion, I've seen some top quality entertainment with so few supporting it. It reminds me of the **Palace Court Th**eatre which had so much money spent on it by **Louis Michaels** and which had such wonderful pre-London shows with big star names, but support by audience was small and so, in the end, it closed as a theatre, a great loss to the Bournemouth entertainment scene.

can't guarantee an audience. Perhaps we should accept that Bournemouth, Poole and Christchurch as an area is regarded by all government organisations and regional agencies as one urban area. Thinking of the entertainment situation with that in mind makes sense. Poole has a splendid medium-sized theatre for plays, it has a wonderful concert hall for orchestra and choral concerts, and Bournemouth has a larger theatre for musicals, operas and ballets, as well as the biggest hall in Southern England in the Windsor Hall of the Bournemouth International Centre (up to 7,000 people!) for large popular music concerts. The area is further complemented by the lovely Regent Centre in Christchurch for smaller shows. I fear that the deeply routed and spirited rivalry between the towns is detracting from a sensible usage of all the available facilities. Perhaps we don't need to see ourselves as competitors, but as colleagues.

The Bournemouth Pavilion is a perfect theatre for ballet, musicals and opera. In any other town it would be **a resource regarded as a treasure**. Part of the town's history, its ballroom and theatre are wonderful and without equal; Bournemouth would be a much poorer place without them. During my time as leader of the Conservatives on the Bournemouth Borough Council, I spent four years trying to get a government loan of nearly ten million pounds and much discussion with **English Heritage** to get the **Shed** *('temporary' building on West Terrace)* pulled down. Regrettably, the scheme did not proceed. The actual structure of the Pavilion is massive, and it couldn't be built today. Whatever the future holds for the complex, let's hope it survives and continues to provide entertainment for many more years to come."

Canopy in 2005

Warning sign at top of stairs from dressing rooms to stage. There is one on each side. They were painted by John Ralls, Property Master in the 1950s and 1960s.

Three Men in a Week!
BRENDA BAKER

Bournemouth and Boscombe Light Opera Company

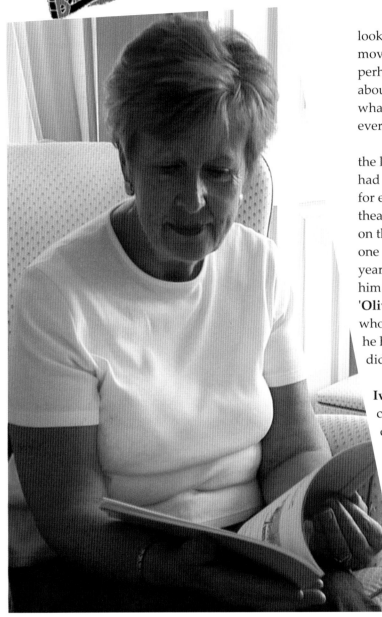

The Bournemouth and Boscombe Light Opera Company have performed their shows at the Pavilion for all but fifty years, and are the longest-running company ever to tread the theatre's stage. Brenda Baker, the current Chairman, has been a member since 1960.

"I've lived in Bournemouth virtually all my life, and I went to St. James' School in Pokesdown as well as joining the church choir. I was invited to join **BBLOC** in 1960 and my first show as a member of the company was '**King's Rhapsody**' in 1960. Since then, apart from a couple of shows in the 1960s, I've been involved with all the shows. The company is like a large family where we all work together and

look after each other. Many of the principals tend to move on, but others stay within our ranks and perhaps help us make the tea. The wonderful thing about the members is that we all chop and change in what we do - it's a real community effort where everyone pulls together.

"Particular incidents I can remember include the lovely donkey we used in '**The Desert Song**'. He had to be walked through town from where he lived for every performance, and when he got to the theatre, he was kept downstairs. He was brought up on the stage scenery lift when he was needed, and one of our members, **Leslie Moore**, who was fifteen years old at the time, was responsible for following him around the stage with a shovel! Then, in '**Oliver**', we had a super little dog (Bill Sykes' dog) who had been specially trained for theatre work, but he had become rather lazy as he got older and he didn't always do what he was told.

"In '**King's Rhapsody**', I had lots of songs. **Ivor Novello** was always my favourite light-opera composer. It's worth noting that in those early days, we didn't use any microphones. There's an amusing story from our 1986 production of '**The Student Prince**'. I was the leading lady, and my opposite male singer was **Malcolm Cuthbert**. Just before we came to final rehearsals, he lost his voice and so we had to book a professional but he, sadly, just couldn't do the part. We were helped out by a local professional opera singer called **John Andrew** who sang the songs from the orchestra pit, while Malcolm mimed on stage. After two nights, John seemed to get the same throat infection as Malcolm. Malcolm managed to sing for two nights but was still not one hundred percent fit. So, enter our good friend, the late **John Lawrenson** (who so often appeared on BBC Radio 2's 'Friday Night is Music Night') who kindly jumped in for the Saturday performance. We got there in the end, and the *Daily Mail* picked up the story under the headline, **'Leading Lady Gets Through Three Men in a Week'!**

"We were very pleased in '**My Fair Lady**' in 1995 to use the revolve at the Pavilion. It was a great effect where we were able to change scenes from Higgins' study to the street outside. It's a great shame that that lovely revolve has been covered over. We also used it effectively in 'Carousel'. Then, in the first time we performed 'Hello Dolly', in 1972, we built a passarella right round the front of the stalls, just outside the orchestra pit, and we were all able to dance around - truly wonderful. The show 'Naughty Marietta' in 1964 was good fun, as well; I was the lead again, and had to make an entry with the song 'Ah, sweet mystery of life, I've found you'. We'd built a well on stage, and this is where I made the entrance but there wasn't a lot of room, and had to sit crouched down out of sight until my cue, when I sprang up into view.

"One of the most amusing errors which happened was in 'New Moon' in 1962, when we had the sound-effect of a baby crying. During one performance, something went wrong and the baby came out of the speakers as a tenor crooning!

"Many of the cast of our shows joined the Welsh National Opera as supers (extras), and some even played in the Royal Ballet.

"I love the Pavilion - even though I don't take part any more, there's still the wonderful warm atmosphere to absorb. On the Sundays before our week of shows, we are allowed to 'walk the stage', just to get the feel of the boards and soak up the ethos. Whenever I walk on to the stage, even as an oldie, I feel the warmth of a real theatre, and the newcomers show their feelings by the looks on their faces as they see the 1600 seats or so, which in some ways look so intimidating but in others so welcoming and friendly. Many of them are amazed at its sheer size. In the earlier days, there were some problems with sound; there were some dead spots but all is well nowadays, and everything is so much easier with modern microphones and sound systems. It's such a shame that the big companies don't come here anymore."

FACT BBLOC Show List - 1954-2005

The first two shows were performed in the Boscombe Hippodrome, but BBLOC have played the Pavilion ever since 1956.

1954	Katinka		1979	King's Rhapsody
1955	Night in Venice		1980	The Sound of Music
1956	Magyar Melody		1981	The Merry Widow
1957	Quaker Girl		1982	My Fair Lady
1958	The Dubarry		1983	Annie Get Your Gun
1959	Waltz Time		1984	Hello Dolly
1960	King's Rhapsody		1985	No No Nanette
1961	The Gypsy Baron		1986	The Student Prince
1962	New Moon		1987	Half a Sixpence
1963	Pink Champagne		1988	The Land of Smiles
1964	Naughty Marietta		1989	Oklahoma
1965	Night in Venice		1990	Guys and Dolls
1966	The Gypsy Princess		1991	Gigi
1967	Show Boat		1992	Fiddler on the Roof
1968	White Horse Inn		1993	The Pyjama Game
1969	The Count of Luxembourg		1993	The Boy Friend
1970	The Desert Song		1994	South Pacific
1971	The Merry Widow		1994	Mr. Cinders
1972	Hello Dolly		1995	My Fair Lady
1973	Kismet		1996	42nd Street
1974	Fiddler on the Roof		1997	Me and My Girl
1975	Mame		1998	Carousel
1976	Carousel		1999	Singin' in the Rain
1977	The Card		2000	Hello Dolly
1978	White Horse Inn		2001	Oliver
			2002	Wizard of Oz
			2003	Kiss Me Kate
			2004	My Fair Lady
			2005	Me and My Girl

Many people who visit the Theatre are unaware of an extensive and interesting archive of photographs and other memorabilia in the two corridors (east and west) from the Foyer to the Ballroom. Sadly, security restrictions make it impossible to keep these two corridors open, but it's worth the trouble to ask, because there is some fascinating material to absorb.

In the East Corridor - to left of Foyer:

On the left, before the Ice-Cream kiosk, is a case of pictures featuring the **Revd. William and Mrs. Frances Yorke-Batley**, who for decades invited members of the casts of shows playing all the **Bournemouth Theatres** for afternoon tea at their home in Southbourne. Revd. Yorke-Batley was the **theatre chaplain** for many years in the 1950s and 60s, and there are pictures which show **Leslie Crowther**, **Hinge and Brackett**, **Rolf Harris** and many more. When William died, his wife continued the tradition until her death.

Almost opposite is a tribute, by local hairdresser and impresario, **George Fairweather**, to **Tony Hancock** who, it's said, as a Bournemouth man, played the Pavilion many times.

Stewart Granger also played here in 1949, with **Jean Simmons**. His family lived on the East Cliff, and there is a letter to the people of Bournemouth from **MGM - Metro-Goldwyn-Mayer**.

Posters along both sides of the corridor remind us of shows by **Frankie Howerd** (1991), **Norman Wisdom**, **Victoria Wood** (1988) and a host of others, including the production of '**Brideshead Revisited**' in 1995, and starring **Richard Todd**.

Half way down is the only known copy of the architects' original plans for the building *(see picture on page 4)*, some information about the opening of the **Little Theatre** (Palace Court Theatre), and some memories of the **Pier Theatre**.

WEEK COMMENCING MONDAY, MARCH 14th   NIGHTLY at 7.30
Matinees : Wednesday, Thursday and Saturday at 2.30

STEPHEN MITCHELL
(for London Theatrical Productions, Ltd.)
presents

The Power
of Darkness
by
LEO TOLSTOY

English Version by Peter Glenville

Characters
in order of their appearance :

Peter Ignatych	HERBERT LOMAS
Anisya, his second wife	... SONIA DRESDEL
Akulina, Peter's daughter by his first marriage (aged 16)	JEAN SIMMONS
	(by permission of the J. Arthur Rank Organisation)
Anukta, daughter of Peter and Anisya (aged 10)	PERLITA NEILSON
Nikita, their labourer	STEWART GRANGER
Matrena, Nikita's mother	MARY CLARE
Akim, Nikita's father	... HAROLD SCOTT
Marina	MARY HORN
A neighbour	... DEIDRE DOYLE
Marfa, Peter's sister	BERYL EDE
Mitrich	FREDERICK VALK

In the West Corridor - to right of Foyer:

Here are dozens of handbills, posters and programmes from across the years and especially the **1940s** and **1950s**, including many of the pantomimes. There is also a copy of the programme printed for the **Opening Ceremony** in 1929 *(pages 13-17)*, and a photograph of the **complete staff** taken as the building opened. The entire archive is well worth more than just a passing glance.

76 Years of the Bournemouth Pavilion

Author Memory: In the days when the pit orchestra played for twenty minutes or so before the shows and during the intervals, the players were brought up on the orchestra pit lift to about half way. This meant that their heads could just be seen, and Byron Brooke, the Conductor, would be seen above the waist. I used to start the motor for the lift, and usually manage to stop it at the correct mark. Sometimes, the lift would come too high, and Byron would make grimaces at the Prompt Corner, and signal - while still conducting! - to take the lift down a little. The reason? As the lower part of his body couldn't normally be seen, he wore only the top part of his evening suit, with a any old pair of trousers!

A Journalist's View
A PRIVILEGE TO VIEW THIS NEW BUILDING

By the time the Pavilion had been officially opened, many residents had already absorbed the pleasant exterior of the complex, but most had not been able to go inside. There's no doubt that the building was nothing short of wonderful - warm, inviting, colourful and fitting for entertainment. How exciting it would have been to be among the first to experience the concert hall and ballroom!

A *Bournemouth Daily Echo* reporter was "privileged" (his word!) to be shown around the building by one of the architects, and wrote in glowing terms about what he saw. He speaks of the spacious vestibule, with a pair of Doric (Greek architecture, distinguished by simplicity and massive strength) columns at each end. Electric light fittings take the form of torches, which throw the light up to the ceiling, from which it is flooded downwards. "The principle, known as the semi-indirect, is in operation inside the concert hall and in various other parts of the building."

Attractive Range of Samples

"The floor of the vestibule is laid with polished terrazzo, the design consisting of five-pointed stars. From either end there rises a circular staircase, leading up to the concert hall balcony and "promenade" above." Mention was made of some uncommon effective metal work on the stairways. Either side of the three arches which are directly in front of the main entrance, there is a corridor for entrance to the auditorium and which then runs right round the building, linking almost directly with every other section. "In this corridor, by the way, are conveniently appointed kiosks for the sale of chocolate, tobacco, cigarettes, etc., other show-cases having been let to well-known local business houses for showing attractive ranges of samples.

"On entering the auditorium, one appreciates the fact that, in deciding their colour-scheme, the architects have not been unmindful of psychological possibilities" - *(not quite sure what that means, and why*

the double negative?). "Terra-cotta rose and old gold are among the shades happily employed; the composition as a whole being calculated to put audiences into the mood for listening to good music or enjoying any of the other forms of entertainment. Among other things ministering to the physical comfort and well-being are the 1,600 tip-up chairs. The upholstery throughout is most luxuriously sprung, while auxiliary springs have been fitted beneath every seat. Special care has been exercised with regard to the sight-lines. The seating is so arranged that unobstructed views of the stage are enjoyed from every part of the house. The promenade encircling the balcony is furnished with elegant settees. High overhead, in the centre of the ceiling, is a large decorative device in the form of a 'sunburst', surrounded by a wide-spreading group of golden stars.

Tiers of Silver for the Municipal Orchestra

"The stage has been fitted up as adequately as any city in the country and includes a complete three-colour lighting installation. A new arrangement has been devised for seating the Municipal Orchestra. The musicians occupy tiers effectively treated in silver, and beyond them through a row of silver columns, one sees a wonderful cyclorama so ingeniously constructed as to give the impression that the view is absolutely unlimited." The reporter then mentions the versatility of the orchestra lift, to be used by the strings and soloists.

"Acoustics are assisted by curved resonators at either end of the proscenium opening. The divided organ stands behind these, but the console (keyboards and pedals) is on a lift by means of which the player may be raised to a high level, thus being brought within the effective radius of limelight shining down from a circular grating in the roof." Praise is given of the wonderful stage curtains, in bold design with an old-gold background and crinkly, multi-coloured flames shooting upwards.

Sprung Floor

The lounges, to east and west of the corridor are "pleasant and commodious, intended as meeting places where patrons of the concerts and entertainments may foregather for social intercourse and refreshment. Just beyond is the enormous tearoom and dance-hall, where the specially sprung floor will dance three-hundred people. This rendezvous looks like easily justifying its claim to be one of the most beautiful of its kind in the country. Everybody will admire the mural decoration behind the band recess, representing a pageant of dancing and painted by Miss Sydenham from the local school of art."

Sumptuous Chamber of Mirrors

The reporter continues his perambulation downstairs to the mezzanine floor and to the 100-seater Lucullus restaurant - named after a famous Roman epicure. "Its curtains are richly coloured and of artistic design, the cane-back chairs surrounding the circular tables fitting pleasantly into the scheme, as do the numerous ball-like lights arranged in practically oval formation overhead. Descending another short flight of stairs, we arrive at the main restaurant. One notices straightaway the striking way in which the walls of this sumptuous chamber have been treated with mirrors. The design is very modern in character and contains a suggestion of French influence. Contrasting with the soft cinnamon colouring of the walls is the pretty green of the hide upholstering the chairs, while the green and gold of the squares of carpet lend additional distinction to the place.

"Close to the main restaurant is the buffet; this is floored with polished terrazzo in broad panels, and while the treatment is quiet and simple, a feeling of cheerfulness is imparted by the general colour scheme and a note of richness by the very elegant electric light fittings. Especially notable are the buffet fittings, refined in detail and beautifully executed in Austrian oak." His final comment suggests that the room is not unlike the lower parts of an Atlantic liner.

This description is so clear and detailed, that we can all imagine and share the excitement of those privileged guests who attended the opening ceremony, and gasped spontaneously at the splendid new centre of entertainment. Styles of journalism have undoubtedly changed, and it's interesting to note that no reporter ever claims that the Pavilion is 'the best' only that it is 'one of the best'.

The Bournemouth Pavilion (1929-2005) - A Celebration

FICTION

The Unofficial Bournemouth Guyed

*This amusing extract comes from an unofficial Bournemouth guyed (guide) published in 1935 by **The Town's Appeal Fund for the Royal Victoria and West Hants Hospital and the Eventide Homes**. The Guyed describes itself as 'The Truth, the Whole Truth and Nothing Like the Truth'.*

"One approaches (metaphorically speaking of course) this Palace of Majesty with a certain amount of nervousness. How can an innocent little Guyed like this attempt adequately to describe this wonderful Temple of Music, when the whole of the London Press have devoted pages to this marvellous institution. There is only one Pavilion like Bournemouth's (I mean the one on the sea front, not at King's Park). We proudly claim there is no Municipal Orchestra quite like Bournemouth's. Our famous Orchestra has been heard in all parts of the world, yea, even when the wind has been blowing Springbourne way. It is stated that the visits and promised visits of eminent conductors to Bournemouth Pavilion exceed the number of concert lovers attending the Albert Hall on a big boxing night. Its happy-looking General Manager, Mr. L.H. Harker, believes in round figures. (Nothing personal, believe me!) For this reason he induced his Committee to provide the Pavilion with a wonderful revolving stage. Now he has round figures on the stage, in the box office and the ballroom and leaving the restaurant. Yes, everything is an all-round success at the Pavilion."

The 'Difficult' Get-In
FROM LORRY TO STAGE

Scrap-book of big get-in

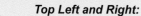

Top Left and Right:
The lorries arrive and wait to be unloaded. Small shows may have just one load, while big musicals will have dozens
Centre Right:
A lorry waiting to be unloaded at the Stage Door
Centre Left:
The lift which takes the scenery, lighting and props from Stage Door level to the Stage above. Pavilion Stage Manager Simon Bagnall is on the right
Bottom Right:
The Stage gradually filling as the lorries are unloaded
(These pictures were taken during the get-in and fit-up for the musical 'The King and I' in the Summer of 2005.)

1940

January - During the pantomime run, Sunday entertainment included Handel's 'Messiah', a special concert organised by the Mayor for ARP workers, and the ballroom hosted several events, including a **Grand Children's Party**.

Stars to appear this year included **Marie Tempest, Sir Henry Wood, Sir Hamilton Harty, Solomon, Hermione Baddeley, Eddie Gray** and the **Henry Hall Orchestra. Joan Hammond** and **Dino Borgioli** played in a gala concert in aid of the appeal for **Women in Uniform** - top seat price was 7/6d.

March - seven hundred people attended the **Annual Ball of the Bournemouth Fire Brigade** and **AFS**.

April - It was decided to cut the Municipal Orchestra from **35 members to 24** and they were to provide more outdoor music; the final concert of the larger group was in May. The **Boscombe Hippodrome** put on 'Strip Ahoy', which was probably the **first recorded nude show** in the town. Women were allowed to appear naked, but only if they were perfectly still and only for a few seconds. This sort of entertainment was prevalent during the wartime years in some provincial theatres and at the London Windmill.

April/May - In the spring, the Council cancelled the long-established **Willie Cave Concert Party** on the West Beach, because it had been losing money for years, although it appears that his show moved to the **Boscombe Pier Pavilion**. When the pier was blown up for defence reasons, he, with his troupe, came to the Pavilion.

May - Pavilion hosted a commemorative **Stamp Exhibition** for the first postage stamps, and there was a talk by the grandson of **Sir Rowland Hill**.

May - 4,000 delegates attended the **Labour Party Conference** in the Pavilion and in the Regent Theatre opposite. **Clement Atlee** pleaded with the Party to allow him into government. (Some sources claim that Atlee did not attend this conference at all.) Another highlight was when **M. Leon Blum**, the former **Socialist French Premier** spoke in French (with a translator!) and **Percy Whitlock played** '**Marseillaise**' on the organ. This conference was a crucial point in the war and it's thought that the delegates agreed to power-share with the Conservatives if Neville Chamberlain was replaced by Winston Churchill. It's arguable, in this case, that the **whole course of the Second World War was decided at the Bournemouth Pavilion.**

May - A lecture by **Jan Masaryk**, son of the first President of Czechoslovakia was entitled '**Why we must win this War!**'

June - A mass meeting of the Bournemouth **Hotel and Boarding House Association** complained of four bad seasons, with the war further restricting visitor numbers and many places were closing. **December** - 'Dick Whittington' was the pantomime, presented once again by Harry Benet.

1941

January - cinemas were allowed to be open on Sundays, and Harry Mears' Palladium was the first to do so. *(In Southbourne, later the Embassy)*

April - over Easter, the Lucullus Room was open for lunches and dinners until 10.00 p.m.

April - **Richmond Hill Congregational Church** (now URC) was damaged by bombs, making the building unusable for several months. The Corporation allowed the church to hold their morning services in the Pavilion Concert Hall. **Dr. John Short**, the Minister, quoted by **J. Trevor Davies** in his book **"Richmond Hill Story"** in 1956, commented that "bigger congregations than ever assembled there, many who seldom, if ever, entered a church. They were greatly helped in these grim days." The services returned to the church in June.

June - An officer from **Provost Marshall HQ**, with a number of NCOs visited the ballroom to obtain names of commissioned officers who were dancing there, and informed them that they could not be permitted to remain or in future use the ballroom. The General Manager was told that officers would not be permitted to use the ballroom, and, later, the Council had a rather sharp debate.

July - Member of Parliament, **Dingle Foot**, gave a lecture on '**Inside Europe**', and in August, **Bernard Newman** spoke on '**How Goes the War?**'

September - the King asked for a **National Act of Intercession** to mark the opening of the third year of war, and the **Service for National Day of Prayer** was held at the Pavilion, conducted by the Rural Dean, Canon H. R. Burrows, and Revd. Ernest Coltman, President of the Free Church Council. The prayers looked back, thanking God for deliverance from the enemy, for the determination of the people and for great leadership at home.

Winter - During the winter of 1941 and the early part of 1942, the **Popular Restaurant**, which had been taken over by the **Food Control Office** at the beginning of the war, became a **British Restaurant**. These were very ordinary restaurants, often rather like staff canteens, where people could have a good quality and wholesome meal without having to give up coupons from their ration book. They were not commercial, but were open to all. At the Pavilion, the British Restaurant was to serve 1500 to 2000 luncheons a day; but there was a difference here, not seen elsewhere in the country. The **Lucullus Room** was allowed to serve exactly the same meals as in the Popular restaurant, but with silver service, offered at an increased charge, and having waiter service as opposed to self service.

October - King George VI and Queen Elizabeth visited the Pavilion to inspect Dominion airmen - the first-ever visit of a reigning sovereign to the town.

November - Bournemouth Home Guard held a concert.

November - another Ivor Novello show, '**The Dancing Years**', played in the Concert Hall. This show had a theme dominated by the rise of Nazism. The Ballroom and the Concert Hall were to close at 9 p.m., the last trolley buses leaving the Square at 10.15, and the last motor buses at 9.30.

Boxing Day - there was not enough room in the Ballroom to accommodate all those who wanted to dance, and the Pantomime, '**Robinson Crusoe**', was completely sold out.

1942

January - a special performance of 'Robinson Crusoe' was given for 1800 children of servicemen.

The year was packed with a variety of shows, including **Vivian Leigh** in '**The Doctor's Dilemma**', **Sadlers Wells Ballet**, **Bobby Howes** in '**Lady Behave**', '**Chu Chin Chow**', '**Blithe Spirit**' with **Ronald Squire** and **Ursula Jeans**, an **International Circus** with horses and pigeons, **Sadlers Wells Opera** and **Diana Churchill** in '**Stranger's Road**'.

March - Municipal Orchestra gave a concert in aid of Bournemouth **Warship Week**.

Programme notes gave this information: *Air raid warnings given by means of four flashes of three seconds each on electric signs each side of proscenium arch. Red flashes for 'Alert'; Blue for 'Raiders Passed'.* (The housing for those signs are still on proscenium arch**!**) *If warnings are given during the interval, the appropriate sign will be left on until immediately before the rise of the curtain.*

May - An **RAF Re-Union Rally** was held for the **RAF Benevolent Fund**. The Orchestra was joined by **Flotsam and Jetsam**, given their first public

performance together for well over a year.

October - There was a special broadcast from the Pavilion transmitted on wavelengths for comrades at home and overseas. Artistes included the **Southern Command Broadcasting Orchestra** and the **Household Cavalry Male Voice Choir**.

October - Commander Stephen King-Hall, M.P. gave a lecture entitled '**Total Victory: Its Meaning and Way of Achievement**'. King-Hall became well-known later as a broadcaster on children's radio and television. Other lectures had a similar war theme, such as '**Soviet Russia at Peace and at War**', and '**Norway Fights On**'.

December - Nellie Wallace, who came to live at Wick, starred in '**Mother Goose**'. On Boxing Day, she injured her wrist (or was it her leg?) while curtseying, but still went on stage. *(See Page 167)*

1943

Programme notes at this time gave this announcement: *Will Patrons kindly note that the special service of buses hitherto leaving Pavilion forecourt at the termination of evening performances is now suspended. Last buses for all destinations leave Square at approx. 9 p.m. and performances terminate early enough for Patrons to use the normal services from the Square.* Many Bournemouth buses were on loan during the war to other parts of the country. The *Daily Echo* reported in February, 1944, that in pre-War days, buses used to wait outside the Pavilion in the forecourt for the theatre crowds. Theatre and Cinema goers were causing congestion in Westover Road.

January - Margot Fonteyn, **Robert Helpmann**, **Beryl Grey** and **Moira Shearer** in the chorus, all appeared with the **Sadlers Wells Ballet**. '**Swan Lake**' was performed in full. Other star names to come to the Pavilion this year were **Esmond Knight**, **The London Symphony Orchestra**, **Constance Cummings**, **Arthur Lucas**, and **Michael Redgrave** played the lead in '**A Month in the Country**'. '**Chocolate Soldier**' and '**No, No, Nanette**' also played.

There were public meetings on **Road Safety** and **Aid to China**, **Daphne Spottiswoode**, aged only twelve, **played Beethoven's 3rd Piano Concerto,** and lectures included '**The Life of a Coalminer**'.

April - Oscar Rabin and his Band, with supporting acts, played a successful concert.

May 23rd saw the biggest bombing raid of the War on Bournemouth's Town Centre. **Punshon Memorial Church** at the bottom of Richmond Hill, **Woolworths** on the other side of the Square, **Beales'** store and the **Metropole Hotel** at the Lansdowne were all destroyed. The Sunday afternoon concert went on as advertised with the Bournemouth Municipal Orchestra conducted by **Adrian Boult**. He altered the programme slightly to fit in with the mood of the town. *(See Page 102)*

(See Page 102)

SUNDAY AFTERNOON, MAY 23rd, at 2.45

THE MUNICIPAL ORCHESTRA

Leader : **Byron Brooke**   Solo Organ : **PERCY WHITLOCK**
Conductors : **SIR ADRIAN BOULT** and **MONTAGUE BIRCH**

The First of Two Concerts to Commemorate the 50th Anniversary of the Formation of The Bournemouth Municipal Orchestra

GOD SAVE THE KING

1. Overture "Cockaigne" ("In London Town") ... ... *Elgar*
2. Rhapsody "A Shropshire Lad" ... ... *Butterworth*
3. Theme and Six Diversions ... ... *Edward German*
   - (a) Theme : Andante con moto
   - (b) Allegro ma non troppo (Maestoso)
   - (c) Allegro molto (Scherzando)
   - (d) Allegro vivace (Gipsy Dance)
   - (e) Andante con moto (Tranquillo)
   - (f) Allegro (a la Valse)
   - (g) Andante con moto ; Allegro brillante

   (Conducted by **Montague Birch**)

   This work is being played as a tribute to the first British composer represented at the inception of The Municipal Orchestra on May 23rd, 1893

4. "Conversation Piece" for Organ and Orchestra ... ... *Whitlock*
   Soloist : **PERCY WHITLOCK**
5. Symphony (No. 2) in D ... ... *Brahms*
   - (a) Allegro non troppo
   - (b) Adagio non troppo
   - (c) Allegretto grazioso quasi andantino
   - (d) Allegro con spirito

Elgar's **"Cockaigne"** Overture was replaced by **"Nimrod"** from the Enigma Variations. Because of reporting restrictions, The *Bournemouth Daily Echo* referred to Bournemouth as 'a south coast town', and reviewed the orchestral concert without mentioning programme changes.

June - Running until September saw '**Come to the Show**', produced by Walter Paskin. The programme and scenery changed every week and the spectacular scenes were beautifully dressed. On one evening, the company repeated an entire performance during an 'alert' period, not finishing until the early hours of the morning. This year, the show created new records.

July - A new floor was laid in the Ballroom. This took six workman two days to complete, using twenty tons of wood - some 4,200 square feet of American oak grooved flooring. Each end was mitred and no nails were used. The floor was placed on metal 'shoes' supporting the steel joists. The timber came from **Sherry and Haycock**, and the floor was surfaced and polished using 28lbs of wax. The entire cost was £700.

July - The **British Restaurant** reported its first year's success by announcing that it had served 932,807 main and subsidiary meals and 908,484 beverages.

August - **Vilem Tausky** joined Montague Birch for concert by the Municipal Orchestra.

November - An **Armistice Concert** featured '**Home Guard March**', by **Montague Birch**. Also, there was a rare performance of **Elgar's 'King Olaf'**.

December - The **Royal Canadian Air Force** held a concert entitled '**Victory Roll**', and the songs were performed by L.A.C. **Ted Hockridge**, who would, in the summer of 1957, appear as top of the bill at the New Royal Theatre in Albert Road as **Edmund Hockridge**!

December - 'Jack and the Beanstalk' starred **Dick Tubb**, who on one day, when an extra matinee was required, undertook 38 costume changes. The pantomime was twice nightly.

1944

'I'll See You Again' starring **Glynis Johns**, 'The Student Prince' with **Bruce Trent**, 'Tomorrow's Eden' with **Diana Churchill**, 'The Last of Summer' starring **Fay Compton** and 'Love for Love' starring **John Gielgud**, who also produced, were just some of the shows on offer in 1944.

Music came from **Kathleen Ferrier**, making an early appearance in her career, the R.C.A.F. Band with **Irving Berlin** singing '**My British Buddy**'; at the end of the show, there was a moving moment when from each side of the ballroom, British and American flag parties marched in. Cabaret was provided by the pantomime stars and the organiser, Lt. W.H. Howard-Appleton, RAPC said: "We again record our gratefulness for the help which Uncle Sam gave us in the dark days of 1940. Today we are together and we are stronger and more powerfully armed than ever before. Irving Berlin's new show, '**This is the Army**', was at the **Boscombe Hippodrome** the same week and he took every opportunity to perform its songs. **Henry Hall and his Orchestra, Billy Cotton and His Band**, including singer **Alan Breeze**, and the musical 'The Arcadians' made for some lighter moments.

January - Mendelssohn's Violin Concerto was played by the Polish violist, **Fryderyk Herman**, and the 8th **US Army Air Force** staged a musical entitled 'Skirts'.

February - The council decided not to have a Municipal Orchestra of 100 players, but reduced the number to 24.

April - Two **Agatha Christie** plays played in the town, '**Ten Little ......**' at the Pavilion, and '**Love From a Stranger**' at the **Palace Court Theatre**.

May - **Robert Helpmann** and **Beryl Grey** appeared with **Sadlers Wells Ballet**.

July - The **Western Brothers** appeared in International Vaudeville.

August - The Bournemouth and District Anglo-Polish Society organised a concert by the **Polish Army Choir** and songs included the '**Polish Underground Hymn**'.

September - 'Private Lives' starred **Raymond Huntley**, who later went on to be a well-known film and television actor, appearing in a least 70 films, including 'Passport to Pimlico', 'The Admiral Crichton', and 'Carleton-Browne of the FO'. He also will be remembered for his performances in the television series, 'Danger Man' and 'Upstairs, Downstairs'.

November - **Bernard Miles** appeared in a play about the Home Guard set in the summer of 1940 - **'They Also Serve'**. Also, **John Heddle Nash** sang with the Municipal Orchestra in a performance of **Elgar's 'Dream of Gerontius'**. The pantomime was **'Red Riding Hood'**, starring Betty Huntley Wright.

1945

February - Sadlers Wells Opera, 'While the Sun Shines' starring **Ronald Squires**, and 'Desert Rats' with **Richard Greene** (later to be ITV's original black and white Robin Hood) got the year off to a good start.

Other plays throughout the year included '**Arsenic and Old Lace**', J.B. Priestley's '**How Are They At Home?**' and two plays by **Edgar Wallace**.

March - **Celia Lipton** in 'Peter Pan'

May - **VE Day**, for which the Pavilion was to stay open with full catering and entertainment available. The Mayor of Bournemouth, Councillor H C Brown, after a short 'broadcast' from the balcony of the Town Hall and a service at St. Peter's Church with community singing, once again switched on the illuminations of the Pavilion fountain. However, this was only for a limited period, as black-out restrictions had not yet been lifted.

July - A whisky racket was discovered.

December - 'Humpty Dumpty' with **Albert H. Grant**.

1946

Percy Whitlock died in May.

The Air Ministry released the **Winter Gardens** which they had requisitioned at the beginning of the War. Council decided to convert the premises into a Concert Hall for the Bournemouth Municipal Orchestra.

December - 'Cinderella' starred **Freddie Foss**.

1947

October - Bournemouth Municipal Orchestra has its first concert in the **Winter Gardens**, its new 'home', with new conductor, **Rudolf Schwarz**, and 47 players. The Orchestra was renamed **Bournemouth Symphony Orchestra** in 1954 with **Charles Groves** as conductor.

December - 'Goldilocks and the Three Bears' with **Dorothy Ward**.

1948

December - **Binnie Hale** starred in 'Little Miss Muffet'

1949

In this year, the **Regent Theatre** opposite became the **Gaumont Cinema**. It changed its name

FOR TWO WEEKS COMMENCING MONDAY, APRIL 11th   NIGHTLY at 7.30
(Good Friday excepted).
Matinees : Wednesday, Thursday and Saturday at 2.30

Leslie Henson & John Buckley, Ltd.
present
The Musical Farce
entitled

'Bob's Your Uncle'

Book by **Austin Melford**   Music by **Noel Gay**   Lyrics by **Frank Eyton**

with

LESLIE HENSON   VERA PEARCE

Valerie Tandy

Settings by Caroline Scott Plummer.   Costumes by St. John Roper
Directed by **Leslie Henson and Austin Melford**
Ensembles staged by Beatrice Appleyard

AFTER A YEAR'S LONG LAUGH AT THE SAVILLE THEATRE, LONDON

again in 1986, when it became the **Odeon Cinema**.

April - **Leslie Henson** and **Vera Pearce** appeared in the musical, '**Bob's Your Uncle**', and **Fred Emney**, the actor/comedian who was big in both meanings of the word, was in Strauss' romantic musical masterpiece, '**The Chocolate Soldier**'.

July - General Manager **Lawrence Harker** retired.

August - An enormous booking from America came with a week's variety starring **Alan Jones**, the singer who made a fortune with the song 'Donkey Serenade' and who was also the father of **Jack Jones**, the ballad singer. On the bill too was comedian **Joe Black** who appeared in the 1957 summer season at the New Royal Theatre.

August - More entertainment from the states with "Hollywood's Famous Film Star", **Peggy Ryan** with her new film partner, **Ray Macdonald**. It would have cost you at least 3/- to get in.

December - 'Mother Goose' with **Tommy Fields** and **Eve Lister**.

Two Places you won't see

Lift Motor at Ballroom Roof level

Outside the lime/projection box. This is directly above the Foyer and the back of the Circle Promenade. It was built in 1934 when the stage facilities were enlarged and improved. This is not a good place to work when the weather is wild - the only access is across the roof.

The Pavilion's Art Deco

SOME IMAGES OF A GLORIOUS PAST

The Bournemouth Pavilion is built in art-deco style. A concise definition of the term 'art-deco' is almost impossible. Its influence started in about 1900, but the real beginning of the art-deco period is said to be about 1920, and was described as a 'controversial new style'. The movement continued up to the beginning of the Second World War in 1939, and then began to drift away, absorbed by other influences. Art-deco had a substantial impact on jewellery, sculpture, furniture, glass, architecture and graphic design. Classical influences, such as Egyptian, Greek and Roman, were coupled with modernism. Art-deco offered elegant environments of a cool sophistication, creating objects from new man-made materials like plastic and bakelite, and using exotic woods and inlays in furniture. (see: *www.collectics.com/education_deco.html*) The Bournemouth Pavilion is said to have Egyptian influences, and it's interseting to walk around the building to see if they are still evident. These photographs illustrate some of the features of building and its fittings.

Original brass display case - there are several in foyer

Recess in corridor walls. There is one in each corridor. Notice the glass 'fluting'

Detail of brass railing in Circle

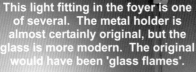

This light fitting in the foyer is one of several. The metal holder is almost certainly original, but the glass is more modern. The original would have been 'glass flames'.

Lovely archway, echoed in second arch in corridor. Also, elegant pillars.

Top Left: Elegant pillars in Main Foyer

Top Right: Ceiling in Vestibule with Chandelier

Bottom Left: Opening Plaque in frame in Vestibule

Bottom Right: Ceiling in Main Foyer

n.b. these pictures were taken in 2005 and do not represent the original colours. These have changed over the years.

Two photographs which well illustrate the elegance and charm of the original Pavilion.
Top: The graceful wrought-iron and wooden handrail on the West Staircase from the Corridor down to the Lucullus Room level, with the distinctive original terrazzo flooring
Bottom: The South-east corner of the square auditorium, with the gentle art-deco designs above the organ chamber. n.b. the chandelier is not original

Above: The distinctive sunburst design at the centre of the auditorium dome. n.b. the chandelier is not original

Right: A somewhat humble window above the West Foyer Staircase. It is replicated on the East side.

Right and Left: Something that only 'Ladies' know! On the doors to the ladies' toilets on the East Side of the Circle Promenade, the original 1d slot machines are still intact!

You Won't Believe It!!! Bloomers!

Herewith a short selection of conversations held between staff in the Box Office and patrons - truly, you won't believe it!

Patron: How much are the seats?
Staff: £7.50, £8.50 and £9.50.
Patron: So which seats are the most expensive?

****

Staff: I can offer you 'C' row.
Patron: I'm very short and a bit worried about seeing. Have you anything further back?

****

Staff: Would you like stalls or circle?
Patron: Is the circle upstairs?
Staff: Yes.
Patron: Could I have the £8.50 seats in the stalls, in the circle?

****

Staff: I'll seat you over the doorway so no one will be in front of you.
Patron: Won't that be dangerous. We don't want to fall out of our seats.

****

Patron: I bought a Gary Glitter ticket in Peterborough, but I've recently moved here. Can I use my ticket here?

****

Patron: Where is the David Essex show tonight?
Staff: In the Windsor Hall of the B.I.C.
Patron: Which town is the B.I.C. in?
Staff: Bournemouth.
Patron: O.K. It's just that we've bought tickets and we are half way to Brighton and just thought that the B.I.C. might not be in Brighton.

****

Staff: Are you senior citizens?
Patron: No, we're holiday makers.

****

Patron: Do you sell tickets?

****

Staff: Could I have your surname please?
Patron: Mastercard.
Staff: No, your name, please.
Patron: 4929 571..........

****

Patron: Is the Box Office open all afternoon, or just parts of it?

****

Patron: How much are the £6 seats?

****

Staff: Have you booked before?
Patron: Yes, several times.
Staff: Can I take your postcode, please?
Patron: B37 17YN Birmingham.
Staff: There isn't anything listed under that post code.
Patron: That's because my friend used to book the tickets and now he's dead.

****

Patron: I thought that two for one on Edwina Black meant that I had to book for two shows and get one lot free. So I booked for 'Murder by Sex' as well, but I don't want to see that, I want to see 'The Case of the Frightened Lady'.

****

Patron: I'm not ringing to book tickets. I want to sell my piano.

****

Staff: We only have seats available for the 5.45 performance.
Patron: Is that the quarter to six show?

****

Patron: Can we get a drink in this building?
Staff: Alcoholic?
Patron: No, I'm NOT an alcoholic!

****

Staff: Are there any senile citizens in your party?
Patron: Yes, all of us!

****

Staff: What name shall I reserve the tickets in?
Patron: My name, please.

****

Staff: What's the name on the credit card?
Patron: Mine.

****

Patron: Have you got tickets for Daniel O'Donnel?
Staff: Only restricted view - you can't see the whole of the stage.
Patron: What time can we go in?
Staff: Well, the theatre doors will open at seven, and the show starts at half past seven.
Patron: So, we can only see half an hour?

Staff: What?
Patron: Restricted viewing - is it for half an hour?
Staff: No, you can't see the whole of the **stage** not the whole of the **show**.
Patron: Sorry, love, you'll have to excuse me. I'm old and I like Daniel O'Donnel.

****

Staff: The seats are half way back in the middle.
Patron: Half way back from the front, or half way back from the back?

****

Staff: Can I help you?
Patron: No, I'm just looking at the Box Office.

****

Patron: Now, this two for the price of one offer. What does that mean?

****

Staff: Would you like to sit in the stalls?
Patron: Well I'd prefer a seat.

****

Staff: The B.I.C. has a car park for 700 cars.
Patron: But I've only got one car. Does that matter?

****

Patron: Is it all right to wear my blue trousers in the B.I.C.?

****

Patron: Is row M in front of row L or behind it?

****

Patron: Can you tell me how tall the person sitting in front of me will be?

****

Patron: Does the flat floor slope?

****

Patron: What does the swimming pool have in it?

****

Patron: I'd like to book some tickets, please.
Staff: What for, madam?
Patron: Because I'd very much like to see the show.

****

Staff: It's on at the Pier Theatre.
Patron: Does that mean I need to bring a life jacket?

****

Patron: Is there a pillar there?
Staff: No, Sir - not in the middle of the front row of the stalls.

What a Silly Language!

Staff: **I'd just to like to warn you that there is a bar in front of these seats.**

Patron: **Will people still be served during the performance?**

Well, that's common sense - isn't it?

You Won't Believe This, Either!

When Max Bygraves gave his 'farewell' concert in the Bournemouth Pavilion in 2004, he made it clear that it was merely a farewell to the country, and that he would be back. In 2005, he gave another performance which was heavily advertised on posters across the foyer and forecourt. After one of the lunchtime organ concerts, a couple were seen staring at his picture on the poster, and their conversation was something like this.

Woman:	Oh, look, Max Bygraves is here next week.
Man:	No. It's not really him.
Woman:	Well, the poster says he's here.
Man:	No. Max Bygraves wouldn't play in a theatre like this.
Woman:	But that's his picture.
Man:	Must be someone who looks like him; you know, what do they call them? Tribute artists.
Woman:	Well, that's a shame - I'd really like to see him.

Max did play here as advertised, but this poor couple must have missed him!

BECKY WEEKS

Becky Weeks is a Ticketing Office Cashier who for a while was in a job-sharing scheme working on group bookings.

"I've got the theatre and entertainment in my blood and I when I was looking for a Saturday job, I met the Pavilion Theatre Manager, **Bob Bentley**, and got a job initially as a '**Bluecoat**' - those are the people who stand at the doors for performances and take tickets and show people where seats are. At first, the work was only seasonal, but then I was asked to become a permanent part-timer. While this was happening, I was also taking part in amateur shows. At the age of nine, I had appeared as Gretel in '**The Sound of Music**', and I worked with **Bournemouth Theatre Promotions** who, in '**The King and I**', used professional principals in the amateur company. I loved all this, and really wanted to work here on a full-time basis, and eventually I was appointed to the Ticketing Office.

"As an aside, I took part in the ITV '**Soap Stars**' contest where many actors and actresses 'fought' it out for the parts in a new family in 'Emmerdale'. I didn't make it to the Soap, but it was really good fun. Professionally, I was the 'young' Prunella Scales in the television drama '**The Ghost of Greville Hall**', a lovely period drama. Then in 1992, I appeared with BBLOC in '**Fiddler on the Roof**' and in 2005, I was Sally in '**Me and My Girl**'.

"I feel very emotionally attached to the Pavilion; having worked here and appeared here, I feel it's my real home. For a while, my job was concerned with the Group Bookings through the Ticketing Office. I discussed special rates, promotions and deadlines in schools. Part of my work was to advise schools on how to collect the money and how to ensure that they met their deadlines - I became quite good at chivvying customers on!

"Some of the phone calls we receive are very rude - just people who treat us as if we're not important, and others are rude in the 'naughty' sense, patrons who seem to want to be too friendly. Being up front in the small Office in the foyer can be very frustrating on occasions, because everyone expects you to know everything. We can be selling tickets for up to one hundred shows, but each individual patron imagines that we can know all the facts about all of them. Regular customers often get offended because you want to see their debit or credit card - they feel that as regular visitors they deserve

special treatment, but we have to stick to the rules.

"We have a shortcut system on the computers where we put a person's surname, say 'Smith' and then 'cash' or 'card' according to how the customer pays; so it would be, 'Smith Card". We have one lady who always pays by cash, and as her name is Mrs. Cash, the code appears as 'Cash Cash'. You can see why we always refer to her as Mrs. Cash-Cash!

"Obviously, we are always very careful not to say anything which might upset or annoy the patrons, but what we say behind the glass can't be heard from outside, so often, if someone's being really awkward, we can say what we are thinking. But the nature of our job is such that we should just grin and bear it.

"We have two twins who come regularly - they're aged about fifteen and always come with their dad, but they always book the seats. They're lovely and polite. We have one patron who really has a body odour problem. In the past, other customers have asked to be moved away, so I can't put this person close to anyone else. When this patron's been in the theatre, we have to use some Fabreze on the seat! Another patron has an extremely loud voice and literally shouts at you through the glass, so that no one else can hear anything. We all try to avoid this one! But, it's a grand job, doing something worthwhile in a building you love and with people who are great."

Pavilion Manager
BOB BENTLEY

"I was born in Dublin, although my dad came from Worbarrow in the Purbecks, close to the now lost village of Tyneham. At the age of 15, I hadn't done particularly well at school and, importantly, I didn't speak Gaelic, so the obvious career to take up was the army. In 1963, I found myself stationed at Wool, a mere stone's throw away from my dad's old home, and I was later transferred to Bovington. It was almost by accident that I found my way into theatre work; when I left the army, I worked for a computer software company in Poole - a job I was never very happy with - and, as fate would have it, in 1991, I was laid off during the recession, but was offered a job through the Regular Forces Employment Agency (R.F.E.A) at the Bournemouth International Centre as a House Manager. The General Manager at that time was Luis Candal, and he knew that I much preferred the atmosphere at the Pavilion. Luis was not always the most conventional of managers, and one day, as I passed him in a corridor at the B.I.C., he casually mentioned "Oh, Bob. You start at the Pavilion on Monday!"

Impossible to Plan a Day

"So here I am, and my official title is Pavilion Manager, where I am responsible for the entire complex. If you like, I'm the operations manager, making sure that we provide the service we should to the public. That means that any carefully planned days are virtually impossible and that no two days are ever the same. One unexpected day came when I was duty house manager at the B.I.C. There was a big conference taking place for one of the large communications unions, and we had been receiving regular bomb hoaxes by telephone on Thursdays. On the Thursday, we received the hoax call, and discussed it with all the various agencies and eventually decided to ignore it. The hoax claimed that there would be two bombs, one at 10.30 and the other at 4.00 p.m. There were 4,000 delegates in the Windsor Hall, and after discussion with the conference organisers, we decided to check the hall when they all went off to lunch. There had, of course, been no bomb in the morning, but we felt it right to act on the side of caution. But we couldn't do a check, because the delegates had left their bags in the hall, so the Conference President suggested that we should 'treat the delegates like grown-ups' and inform them of the situation. Oh dear! This is what we did and I was summoned to appear on the platform to state my case and my reasons. I was subjected to very heavy questioning about why their bags hadn't been checked and so on. A so-called 'spokesman' for the delegates voted for an adjournment, and in fact there was no choice, because one group of delegates decided they would leave the building anyway, which meant that no voting could take place. The irony in the situation was that the Smugglers' Bar in the same building was filled all afternoon!

A Difficult and Special Announcement

"I was on duty at the Pavilion at the weekend that Princess Diana was killed. She died early on Sunday morning, and we were showing our regular rock-show 'That'll Be the Day'. We all felt that we should do something to mark the sad occasion, so we had a meeting to discuss what announcement should be made, what wording to use, who was to do it and what tone it would take. It was decided that I would make the announcement as a disembodied voice through the public address system from backstage. I had a carefully worded cue-card and this was one announcement I couldn't afford to get wrong. It was very dark backstage and I was given an angle-poised lamp which was at the extreme limit of its cable and hardly reached me at the microphone - and what's worse, it kept collapsing! I can remember thinking,

'Please don't collapse when I'm speaking'. Mercifully all was well, and this was one of the most powerful two minutes I can remember. Then the show went on, with the cast very respectful and very careful.

Sad and Tragic Things Happen

"Sometimes, the most unlikely and sad things happen. One night, a patron already seated on the aisle for the Joe Pasquale Show quite suddenly

at the back of the circle couldn't hear and continued to let people in until those going out explained the situation. When we eventually did get the show started, some patrons decided to get a refund and go home, but others came back in. Joe Pasquale was absolutely brilliant, and wonderfully worked his way through the stage routine, changing his script as necessary to avoid unfortunate comments.

PAVILION OPERATIONS STAFF
SUMMER 2004

keeled over and died, falling into the aisle, just a quarter of an hour before the curtain went up. St. John's Ambulance crews were on the scene, and one of my front-of-house assistants, Eileen Baker, stayed with the person while we waited for the paramedics. As Eileen was there in this obviously tragic situation, another patron came down the aisle, tapped her on the shoulder and asked where seats B34 and 35 were. Eileen explained that this wasn't the best moment, but the patron insisted on being told where their seats were. Many others patrons in the theatre were, for obvious reasons, a little uneasy, but they couldn't get out because of the person in the aisle. So, I organised a quiet evacuation, making a gentle announcement - with no microphone - from the orchestra-pit rail, asking people to leave the auditorium quietly. I had to be reverent and forceful at the same time. Unfortunately, the ticket-collectors

A Master of Spoonerism

"So, as you can see, I often have to make announcements about all sorts of things, and they can be very easy to mess up. One evening, there was a big function in the Ballroom, and those attending were still drinking in the Phoebe Bar before entering the Ballroom. I was asked to tell them that the ballroom was open and ready. I made an announcement from the reception desk and was, of course, unable to hear what I was saying. I was supposed to say, 'THE DOORS TO THE BALLROOM ARE NOW OPEN.' What I actually said was, 'THE BALLS TO THE DOOR-ROOM ARE NOW OPEN.' I was told afterwards that a lady Phoebe Bar was seen to splutter and spray her drink all over the table! Strangely enough, I made exactly the same error more recently when I was standing in the corridor talking to some patrons. I said, 'The balls to the door-room are now open', but nobody even noticed. Probably no one was listening!

"My job is one which puts me in a very special situation with the customers - my relationship becomes quite intimate. When I'm on duty, I always wear an evening suit with a black tie - it's the right thing to do. When people go to the theatre they want to have a special experience, and also if I'm dressed properly, patrons can easily identify me as the manager. It's a lovely job, because I really enjoy talking to people, and I meet some interesting and special folk. The weather and parking problems are common talking points, though the parking is a lot easier now. In the days when stewards let cars in through the barriers, some people felt cheated, but now that the car park is open all the time, drivers can see if there are any spaces and life is a lot easier. Probably the most common question is, 'What time does the show end?'

Complaints are Carefully Considered

"I get a fair share of negative comments, and many complaints are concerned with the sound levels, most commonly that the sound is too loud. Most of us nowadays control the sound levels ourselves on our televisions, and that makes it more difficult to accept a level which to us is too high. There's no doubt that over the years, the sound levels have improved in all theatres, and the engineers involved with each show are very keen to please their audiences. Modern technicians and engineers can conquer all problems if they wish to. Many of our audiences don't realise that if the sound is unacceptable, then it's not our fault. The company always decides and often works the controls. If the star of the show - the artist who's attracted the audience to the show - wants it loud, loud it will be. A good example of how a situation can be improved is with the quartet G4, a group which sings both pop-orientated music and opera. When they played the Pavilion in 2005, after the first number, we were inundated with complaints that the sound level was grossly too high. The Company Manager, working with me and with their own sound engineer, set to

work to improve the situation. There was a determination from all of us to get it right. By the end of the third number, levels were greatly altered and improved, and there was definitely less bass pounding against our chests! This situation proved that we do listen and that we are prepared to get it right; but a problem is that what one patron thinks is right, is dreadful to the person sitting next to him. We have to compromise and usually, we get it right.

"It is very important that we listen to what the patrons tell us, and to help with this we have a long-running customer survey process. As audiences leave the theatre, we give them a short questionnaire with a pre-paid postage stamp; this was my idea to improve customer relations. We seemed to get so much bad press and we found that staff carrying clip-boards after the show were ineffective, because no one wanted to stop and answer questions. We're pleased to say that about fifty-percent of them are returned with some very helpful comments. Most patrons pay tribute to the staff at the Pavilion - we get many notes of praise. In 2005, we had a glut of praise about staff from the **Bournemouth Music Festival** who held a series of shows here. *(A copy of part of the Questionnaire is printed on the next page.)*

Every Individual is Important

Each individual is very important - one evening we had a patron in the theatre who had had a serious leg operation; I had spoken to them about it and we had arranged a special seat, organised an early arrival and fixed up special parking arrangements. When the patron arrived, we realised that seating him early would mean that other patrons couldn't get in. So the staff organised better seats in a more appropriate situation, and everyone was very happy. What the staff did was instinctive, and that shows the true quality of staff members at the Pavilion. We have a small nucleus of between 20 and 30 permanent full-timers, but casual staff can push the number to between 100 and 150 on a night when we have a theatre show and a function in the ballroom.

"It's a good job and I love it and I pay tribute to the loyal and excellent staff."

Gracie Fields - Right up OUR alley

I am grateful to local historian **John Walker** who gave me details of the appearance of **Gracie Fields** at the Pavilion in July 1936. On the same day, the **paddle steamer** named after the singer came to Bournemouth Pier. The paddle steamer was later to be one of the large flotilla of boats involved with the evacuation of Dunkirk in 1940, where, sadly, she was sunk. **Gracie Fields** - the singer! - gave a cracking performance on stage and lived on long after! She was just one of the country's legendary performers who trod the boards of the Bournemouth Pavilion.

CUSTOMER SURVEY

1. Which venue did you visit & on what date?

Bournemouth International Centre ○
Pavilion ○
Pier Theatre ○
Date: _____

2A. What event were you attending?

_____

2B. What was your seat number?

_____

3. Is this your first visit?   Yes ○   No ○
Will you visit again?   Yes ○   No ○
How many times a year do you visit us?

_____

4. How did you find out about the event?

Local press ○   TV ○   Radio ○   National press ○
Hotel/guest house ○   Conference brochure ○
Local posters/banners ○   Visitor Information Bureau ○
From venue reception desk/Box Office ○   Direct Mail ○

Other ○ _____

_____

5. Are you:

Under 18 ○   18–35 ○   36–55 ○   Over 55 ○

6. Please provide the first part of your postcode (e.g. 'BH4'): _____

COMMENTS

_____
_____
_____
_____
_____
_____
_____

	Excellent	Good	Average	Below average	Poor
7. How does our venue compare with others that you have visited?	○	○	○	○	○
8. How did you rate the staff and quality of service in the following areas?					
Box Office	○	○	○	○	○
Reception	○	○	○	○	○
Theatre/Hall	○	○	○	○	○
Bars/Catering outlets	○	○	○	○	○
9. In the venue, what did you think of the following:					
the event overall	○	○	○	○	○
seating and sightlines	○	○	○	○	○
the sound quality	○	○	○	○	○
catering/bar choice	○	○	○	○	○
10. How did you rate the following facilities:					
toilets	○	○	○	○	○
signage	○	○	○	○	○
access	○	○	○	○	○
car park	○	○	○	○	○

11. If you have a disability or care for a disabled person, how best could we improve the service we provide?

_____
_____
_____
_____

12. Our policy is to promote racial equality. This means trying to provide for all people, whatever their race, colour, ethnic or national origin. To do this we require to know about the people who respond to this survey. Please indicate your ethnic origin by ticking just one box below:

WHITE   British ○   Irish ○   European ○   Portuguese ○   Eastern European ○   Any other white ○

MIXED   White & Black Caribbean ○   White & Black African ○   White & Asian ○   Any other mixed ○

ASIAN OR ASIAN BRITISH   Indian ○   Pakistani ○   Bangladeshi ○   Any other Asian ○

BLACK OR BLACK BRITISH   Caribbean ○   African ○   Any other black ○

OTHER ETHNIC GROUPS   Chinese ○   Korean ○   Any other ethnic ○

Ticketing Office

ANGELA BURGESS
GAIL COLLINS

For most theatre-goers, the Ticketing Office at the Pavilion is the small set of grilled windows to the right of the main entrance, hiding round the corner next to the Coffee Bar. In reality, this represents only a small fraction of the operation; the Ticketing Office has a large cluster of rooms above the foyer to the left of the entrance and is a lively and extremely busy work-place. **Angela Burgess** *and* **Gail Collins** *are Ticketing Managers; Angela has always lived in Bournemouth and has worked in the Ticketing Office for fourteen years, and Gail has lived in the town for fourteen years, having worked in similar jobs elsewhere. Their job is a senior management position and they deal directly with the major outside promoters. They explain what goes on.*

"Our job description is 'to provide effective control of all ticketing staff'. Some thirty-seven staff work in the Ticketing Office Department, including full-timers and casual part-timers; working out the staff rotas each month is a job which takes three or four hours. We don't sell tickets only for the Pavilion, but for all Bournemouth Entertainments and also for external shows - for example, we sell Condor Ferry Tickets for Poole and Weymouth, we sell tickets for local mini-bus tours, for Community events, for the Dorset Steam Fair, sometimes for the New Forest Show, and for AFC Fitness First Stadium Shows, events at Somerley House and many other outside venues, including the Isle of Wight Music Festival; we even sold 500 tickets for the prestigious Robbie Williams Show at Knebworth. As soon as it was made known on the internet that we had them, they sold almost immediately. We are in regular contact with promoters of all sorts of shows, and they frequently contact us. To sell their tickets is good for the Pavilion because a small percentage of each ticket price comes to the Ticketing Office, so it's in our own interests to sell as many as we can for as many shows as we can. We have a small satellite Office at the land end of the Pier and the new B.I.C. Ticketing Office will have five windows, but will still remain under our control.

Angela Burgess and Gail Collins

Big Operation

"In our offices, which overlook the fountain in the forecourt, we have staff working on block bookings, on postal bookings and on up to seven phone-lines working for twelve hours a day. As we are the hub of ticket selling for the whole of the Bournemouth area and well beyond, the phone lines are always very busy.

"Part of our work is to design the overprinting of the tickets for each individual show, making sure that all the relevant and necessary wording is clear and obvious. The tickets themselves are printed elsewhere but we overprint for each ticket sold for every show; this is a good system in that we only print tickets when they've been booked. The old system of a ticket pre-printed for every seat in the theatre was very wasteful, as often the show isn't sold out. With all the events we work for, we reckon to over-print not far short of a million tickets in twelve months, and we order them at 200,000 at a time!

Never a Dull Moment

"All tickets ordered by post or by phone are sent out in colourful wallets, which we design and which are printed free by a local printer. The job is wonderful, and really hard work - we're kept very busy throughout all the day, and someone has to be on duty for all the shows. We're also responsible for the configuration of seating plans, which we do on a very useful computer programme - it's a far cry from the old bird's-eye-view plans in black and white where each seat was a numbered square. So there's never a dull moment, and we wouldn't have it any other way!"

Unseen but Often Heard

If you call the Box Office by telephone, you'll be answered by one of large team of operators. Here are just three of them, **Joy Cox**, **Michael Bevan** and **Jonathan Wilton.**

Pavilion Theatre

BOURNEMOUTH

Terrorist on the Roof?

GAIL COLLINS recalls an unusual incident with some embarrassment!

"Although I'd done other jobs, I hadn't ever worked in a theatre before and was very conscious that I had a lot to learn, and I learned very quickly indeed. When you're in a new job you have to keep your wits about you and hope you get everything right. One evening, very early on in the job, I was left to look after things on my own; they said it was all part of the learning process. I was working in the office just above the east side of the foyer, when I saw a lady with a long bag shoot past me going upstairs. We were showing 'Jesus Christ Superstar' at the time, and I convinced myself that the lady was a sniper getting up onto the roof. I had visions of a terrible incident and seeing the whole story told in the papers. I could see that I would be asked why, if I'd seen the woman - I hadn't done anything about it. So I just reacted in what I thought was the correct manner - I didn't panic but desperately wanted to do the right thing. I immediately reported what I'd seen to senior management, but they didn't seem at all concerned; on the contrary, they seemed to think it all rather funny. Then they told me that the staff who worked in the follow-spot/projection room had to go up the same stairs and past our office. The lady I had seen had merely been one of the staff going up to work."

BOURNEMOUTH ENTERTAINMENTS
PAVILION THEATRE
MEASTRO MUSIC INTERNATIONAL PRESENTS
ROYAL MARINES CHRISTMAS SPECTACULAR
THU 2nd DEC04 7:30 PM
£10.50
CIRCLE B77
TO BE RETAINED - Tickets cannot be exchanged or money refunded once purchased - TO BE RETAINED

The Magnificent

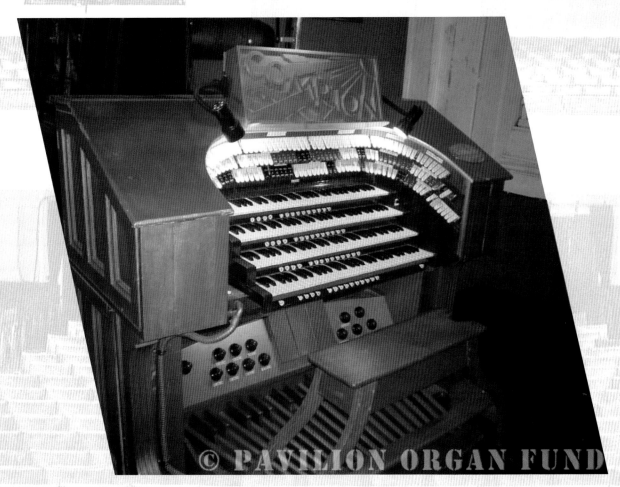

© PAVILION ORGAN FUND

COMPTON ORGAN

The specifications of the organ are very complicated, and are probably of interest only to organists themselves. Below is a vastly simplified list of what's available. For a complete and detailed list of the organ pipes and layout, please log on to www.pavilionorganfund.org.uk and click on the 'History' icon.

Chamber A

Diaphonic Diapason	16, 8, 4, 2
Diapason	8, 4, 2
Viole	16, 8, 4, 2
Celeste	8, 4, 2
Stopped Diapason	16, 8, 4, 2
Harmonic Flute	8, 4, 2
Salicional	16, 8, 4, 2
French Horn	T.C. 16, 8, 4
Bombarde	32, 16, 8, 4
Harmonics	5 Ranks

Chamber B

Diapason	8, 4, 2
Tibia	32, 16, 8, 4, 2
Concert Flute	8, 4, 2
Viole	8, 4
String	8, 4
Clarinet	8, 4
Vox Humana	T.C. 16, 8, 4
Oboe	16, 8, 4
Trumpet	16, 8, 4

The easiest way to describe the numbers is that they refer to **pitch**; e.g. an **8' pipe** will sound at the same pitch as the note the organist plays. A **16' pipe** will play **one octave below** the pitch being played, a **4' pipe** will be **one octave above** the pitch being played, and a **2' pipe** will be **two octaves higher**. Confused? Don't worry! Mix them all together and what do you get? A lot of very good sounds! By using, say, seven different stops and having them on 2', 4', 8' and 16', you could, by playing just one single note on the manual, hear 27 pipes sounding! So, play a chord of four notes and hear 108 pipes sounding. You can keep on working it out!

The organ also has many **special sound effects** which would have been used in the accompaniment of silent films (such as a **train whistle** and a **steamer horn**), and a great deal of percussive instruments, such as **Chime**s, **Xylophone**, **Glockenspiel**, **Sleigh-bells**, **Carillion**, **Bass Drum**, **Snare Drum**.

Each of the two chambers has a sound control, operated by the organist by a **balanced foot pedal**. These control a series of **wooden shutters**, rather like venetian blinds, which open to allow more sound to be released from the top of the chambers to be 'thrown' back by the dome into the auditorium. The third large foot pedal is effectively a **crescendo pedal**, which, as it's pushed forward, brings into operation more and more stops, thus increasing the volume of the instrument. When this crescendo pedal is fully forward, the organ will be at full blast, and extremely loud to anyone sitting in the Circle. (Perhaps that's why Sean and Ryan wear headphones as they operate the lighting and sound for the concerts!)

The Organ - History and Design

FACT

FROM 1929 to 2005 - and still playing!

The **Organ** was installed in 1929 for the opening of The Pavilion, and folk lore suggests that there was some apprehension on the day before the official Royal opening, because claims were made that the organ would not work. These were totally unfounded.

A **Civic (Borough) Organist's post** was created by the Council and this remained until 1978, with the following organists:

1929 - 1932	**Philip Dore**
1932 - 1932	**Herbert Maxwell**
1932 - 1946	**Percy Whitlock**
1946 - 1962	**Harold Coombs**
1962 - 1978	**Reginald Hamilton-White**

*(More information about the organists appears in **The Organists** section on Page 68)*

The **John Compton Organ Company** were given the contract to build a Concert Organ able to play the most complex pieces of classical music and also the latest "pop" music of the day. John Compton had already had some success with his installations in major Concert Halls and Churches throughout England. **Two concrete chambers** both 48 feet high were constructed either side of the proscenium arch to house the **1852 metal pipes**, stacked on various levels in the chamber. At the top, a system of horizontal wooden shutters controls the volume of sound that bounces off the dome into the auditorium below. A teak four manual console was placed on a small lift just to the left of the right hand chamber, known as Chamber A.

The **Municipal Orchestra** played frequently with the Compton Organ and it was used in their programmes as a solo instrument. John Compton's design was fascinating, especially his extension principles and (at that time) modern electric action. The extension system means that, instead of the traditional idea in organs that each note had its own pipe, each rank of pipes could be used to support several stops at the same time; i.e. one rank of pipes could be playing several notes at the same time. *(See Page 66)*

By 1978, the organ, which had suffered years of neglect, became in such a poor state of repair that it was virtually unplayable. So it was that a small group of volunteers, led by **Christian Knighton**, a young member of the stage crew, and **Len Bailey**, a local organist, took over the maintenance of the Compton. Since then and with the help of the **Bournemouth Council Lottery** and **public donation**, many maintenance projects have been completed. Every one of the 22 Ranks of pipes is working and the organ sounds exactly as it would have done in 1929 - in fact, probably better. Both Chambers have been cleaned and painted, and modern lighting and

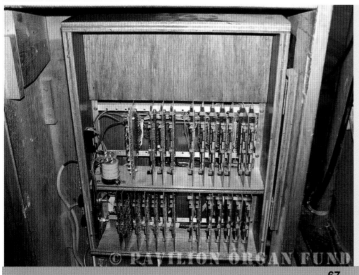

AN INSIDE VIEW

This picture shows the Inside of the console, illustrating the piston setting workings. A piston is an automatic push-button 'switch' which enables the organist to choose a selection of stops. They are the little white round buttons between the manuals (keyboards) of the console. The Pavilion Compton has all but sixty of them, and a further thirteen foot pistons, which are large buttons just above the pedal board. The advantage is that organists can select preset sounds across the entire instrument literally 'at the touch of a button'. For the further confusion of the organist, some of the pistons have 'double-touch' where a soft press creates one set of sounds, and a hard push yet another! It's also possible to store the organists' presets so that when he/she returns, they can be instantly reinstated.

communication have been fitted. The organ retains the original Compton action and some cotton covered wiring.

The work, interest and dedication of Christian Knighton, who is now the Technical Co-ordinator for Bournemouth Pavilion and BIC, cannot be over emphasised. Without his charisma and his strong determination, the organ would have fallen into total disrepair and would, by 2005, probably have been destroyed. Christian and the **Pavilion Organ Fund** continue to make the public aware of the instrument by weekly lunchtime concerts through most of the year. These concerts are free, but the collection taken - in old organ pipes! - provides the funds that go towards the seemingly endless list of repairs. Dorset organ-builder **Derry Thompson**

looked after the repairs and maintenance for many years, and now **Tim Trenchard** from Shillingstone, spends endless hours of work in tuning and repair projects, with **Phil Burbeck**.

A team of the finest organists provides a wide range of light and classical music at the weekly concerts. In recent years, the organ has been used to accompany silent films, and this has proved immensely popular. There are few theatre organs which survive in their original environment, but the Bournemouth Pavilion Compton still sounds beautiful in its un-altered original home. The long-term aim is to keep the instrument running forever as a tribute to John Compton's organ building skills. The Organ is now a **grand old lady of 76,** and she's sounding good!

The Borough Organists

1929 - 1978

The first appointment as Borough Organist was **Philip Dore**, but he was never completely at home with the Compton Theatre Organ, finding it quite difficult to play. Nevertheless, he gave outstanding performances as a soloist and as accompaniment to the Bournemouth Municipal Orchestra. Philip who was an F.R.C.O., was born in Portsmouth where he became organist at a Calvinistic Chapel at the age of eight. He was a chorister at **Chichester Cathedral** and was appointed as sub-organist there in 1922. He was also organist at **Portsmouth Cathedral**.

In 1932 **Herbert Maxwell** took over as organist for a very short period.

Percy William Whitlock became **Borough Organist** in 1932 and remained in the post until his early death, at the age of 42, on May 1st, 1946. He had

been turned down for the post of organist at **Rochester Cathedral** and came to Bournemouth as organist at **St. Stephen's Church** in town centre. He was not entirely happy with the Pavilion Compton Organ to start with, but spent several months learning how to get the best out of it. Not only was he a brilliant organist, but also a composer of real merit. His compositions for the organ were widely known and played, and there has been something of a revival in interest in his work in the late 1990s and early 2000s. His music included some choir anthems and church services. He was known for his endearing personal qualities, such as a wit and sense of fun, coupled with an atmosphere of gentleness. He managed his dual role at Church and Concert Hall between 1932 and 1935 professionally.

Plaque unveiled on Pavilion Entrance wall in 2004 to the memory of Percy Whitlock

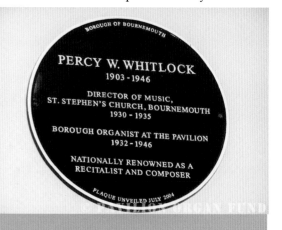

PERCY W. WHITLOCK
1903 - 1946

DIRECTOR OF MUSIC,
ST. STEPHEN'S CHURCH, BOURNEMOUTH
1930 - 1935

BOROUGH ORGANIST AT THE PAVILION
1932 - 1946

NATIONALLY RENOWNED AS A
RECITALIST AND COMPOSER

PLAQUE UNVEILED JULY 2004

Whitlock Plaque unveiling: **Left to right:** Tim Trenchard, Christian Knighton, Len Bailey, Malcolm Riley, Daniel Campbell, Richard Hills, Simon Lindley.

His musicianship, sincerity, charm, enthusiasm, and sense of humour made him a unique and delightful character. There is little doubt that his work at the Pavilion increased the reputation of the orchestra, and of the town.

Percy Whitlock

In 1946, a change of style was created with the appointment of **Harold Coombs** as Borough Organist.

Whereas both Dore and Whitlock had been 'classical' organists, Coombs was definitely of the cinema age and genre. Born in 1902, he was a delicate child, prone to illness, and educated at home by his parents. He was appointed as assistant organist at the **Church of St. Oswald in Sheffield** at the age of ten. In 1933, he became the first resident organist at the **Capitol Cinema** in **Aberdeen**, following on from **Edward O'Henry**, who co-incidentally played for a while at the Electric Cinema in Bournemouth. He had several moves before coming to the Pavilion, including much playing to

military audiences and with symphony orchestras, and his appointment to the largest extension organ in Bournemouth was an acknowledgement of his adaptability to all types of music. He played solo, with the **Bournemouth Symphony Orchestra** under **Rudolf Schwartz** and with the **Pavilion Theatre Orchestra** under the baton of **Byron Brooke**. During his time at the Pavilion, he broadcast regularly from the theatre and from the BBC Theatre Organ in London. He was dogged throughout his career by poor health and had to resign from the post in 1962, dying two years later. The author had the privilege of knowing him during the late 1950s, and remembers him as a cheerful and bouncy character, with always a smile and a frequent little moan about some stop on the organ which wouldn't sound properly. His fingers literally danced on the manuals, reflecting the movement of his dancing feet on the pedals. He was a real character with a tremendous sense of musical fun and a musical ability second to none.

Harold Coombs

On Coombs' retirement, **Reginald Hamilton-White** (seen below with **Betty Mark** in the stage canteen) took on the role as organist but was far happier when playing his real instrument, the piano. When he finally disappeared from the console in 1978, no Borough Organist was appointed, and the organ began to fall into disrepair.

Locked in the Theatre
GEOFFREY YARWOOD

"During the 1970s, I was one of a small team of organists who gave regular Wednesday lunchtime concerts on the Compton. One week, the two corridors either side of the auditorium, which lead from the foyer to the ballroom were being decorated and so access was somewhat limited. After the concert, I entered through the Stage Pass Door on the west side, changed into my smart playing clothes and played for an hour. At the end of the concert, I took the organ down on its lift, and went back to the dressing room, and after changing went, as ever, back to the pass door to get off the stage. But, during the concert, the decorators' gantry had been moved and was totally blocking the door. The men seemed to have gone off for lunch, so I couldn't get out. My only exit, as far as I could see, was to go back up on the organ, climb over into the auditorium and leave by the exit doors. No go! These had all been chained and padlocked, so here was I in a dimly-lit theatre with nowhere to go. Eventually, by banging on the auditorium doors into the foyer, I managed to attract the attention of my wife who, by this time, was getting a little worried about me. She heard me through the door, and contacted the front-of-house manager, Chris Baldwin, who was able to 'release' me! It was a worrying few minutes, and although I was never in any danger, it was really quite frightening."

Semprini and Ivor Emmanuel
LEN BAILEY looks back

The name of **Len Bailey** has been to the forefront in the story of the Bournemouth Pavilion's famous **Compton Theatre Organ**. In 1945, he came to live in the New Forest, and travelling to the Pavilion to hear **Percy Whitlock**, the Borough Organist, play, Len was fascinated by the melodious music and this gave him a real yearning to become a theatre organist himself. The late 1950's saw **Harold Coombs** as the regular organist and Len was asked to deputise for him during show-intervals, and when the post of Borough Organist was discontinued, Len was asked to be on stand-by in case any of the visiting shows required the organ.

He began to play regularly for Sunday evening shows, and two stars remain as highlights of Len's work. The gentle pianist **Albert Semprini** - star of 'Semprini Serenade' on the BBC Light Programme - appeared on several occasions and Len was asked to play duets with him, thus beginning a firm professional friendship; Len recalls that he and Semprini were always the first two people to arrive at the theatre for the shows.

Another star to work with Len was Welsh singer **Ivor Immanuel**, who asked for the organ to accompany him on Arthur Sullivan's well-loved song '**The Lost Chord**'; afterwards Ivor confided in Len that he had never before received such wonderful and warm applause. Len also recalls working with some of the stars from the BBC's successful light entertainment programme, '**The Black and White Minstrel Show**' who often performed on Sunday evenings.

Then, in the mid-1970's, the bellows on the organ became so worn that they needed replacement. The large cost of repair could not be borne by the theatre's management, and so they suggested that the **organ be closed down**. But Len was able to obtain the services of a local organ builder from Maiden Newton, **Derry Thompson**, who agreed to carry out the work in situ, and thus save the Pavilion many hundreds of pounds. But that was only one crisis; later, Len heard a rumour that the console was to be removed to enlarge the orchestra pit in order to cater for the large number of musicians needed in some of the touring shows. He had to act quickly - immediately booking a future date for a public organ concert, and succeeded in obtaining the services of the organist **William Davies**, one of the big theatre organ stars of the day - *'a real big-ee'*, as Len calls him. The concert was a great success, and so Len, encouraged by this and also by **Christian Knighton**, a new casual stage-hand, who had started to show an interest on the electrical side of the organ.

So a whole series was arranged with tip-top organists and a charge of £1 per seat. In those early days, the concerts were presented by **B.K.T. Productions**, the letters being the initials of the three people - Bailey, Knighton and Thompson, but this label did not last for long. It was later that Christian suggested that the concerts should be free, and from then on the events became even more successful. During all this time, the Pavilion's Musical Director,

Byron Brooke, encouraged Len to play for pantomimes and musicals. When Derry Thompson left the scene for other projects, another local organ builder, **Tim Trenchard** took over the mantle, and he's still there today.

Len says that he never suffered any real nerves before playing - 'there isn't time,' he says, 'just push the button which starts the lift to bring the organ up from the pit and start playing.' He reminisces about how on one occasion, while playing the organ, someone backstage inadvertently switched off the lights on the organ console and left him playing the dark. In 2004, Len had what he describes as *'a great privilege and honour'* to help unveil the plaque, on the front of the Pavilion, to Percy Whitlock, the organist who had started Len's real interest. It's certain that, had not Len shown the first drive and felt the real need to preserve the organ, that by now it would have declined to the state of uselessness. As the weekly concerts continue, playing to four and five hundred people, Len, and his colleagues, can be gratified that his work has been worthwhile.

The Pavilion Forecourt bearing details of one of Len Bailey's Concerts. "in these days," says Len, "the front of the Pavilion looked sensible!"

More facts about the Magnificent Pavilion Compton Theatre Organ >>>>>

FREQUENT CONCERTS

Some of the regular organists visiting in 2005, are: **Nicholas Martin**, **Len Rawle**, **Paul Roberts**, **Ian Flitcroft**, **John Mann**, **Penny Weedon**, **Richard Hills**, **Byron Jones** and **Michael Maine**. Also, **Donald Mackenzie** - who is the resident organist at the Odeon in London's Leicester Square, where he plays a slightly smaller Compton Organ - not only gives concerts at the Pavilion, but accompanies the silent films. When **Nigel Ogden** gave a concert in 2004, all but 800 people came into the Theatre, and when the Pavilion has its annual **Christmas Cracker Carol Sing-Song** in December, there'll almost certainly be 1000 people who come to enjoy the music and join in. This is an unusual occasion in that **members of the staff** of **Bournemouth Entertainments** come and take part, and **Bob Wetton**, the Stage Manager of the Pier Theatre, plays the organ.

MEMORY

Len Rawle
First Theatre Organ I ever played

Len Rawle is one of Britain's best-known and best-loved theatre organists, who for forty years has maintained a fresh sense of enthusiasm for both playing and maintaining theatre organs. This has resulted in him becoming a much travelled organist who seems always to extract something new from whatever organ he plays. When he played the Pavilion Compton in 2005 - the first time in some fifteen years - he was enchanted by what he described as a "**wonderful, wonderful instrument**". He spoke of it lovingly, as if it were an aging old lady, and he said that it was a "**privilege and honour to be invited to play it and to experience the remarkable atmosphere of the Bournemouth Pavilion**". He says that this Compton is unique, built for special circumstances for use with the Bournemouth Municipal Orchestra, and he gave praise to those who maintain the instrument. At the end of his concert, where he had produced sounds not heard before, he patted the console and thanked the organ for the pleasure it had brought him. He was pleased to tell the story that this was the **first-ever theatre organ** he played - back in the early 1950s when on holiday in the town, he had been allowed to play the organ under the watch of the then Borough Organist, **Harold Coombs**, a man he described as a brilliant musician. Len didn't understand the workings of the pedal notes and Harold said, "If you don't know what they are, don't play them!" He then gave Len a book about the techniques of pedalling, a book which Len still has to this day. And Len certainly has no problem with the pedals now! Len also reported that he proposed to his wife in the Pleasure Gardens in Bournemouth, beneath the shadow of the Pavilion.

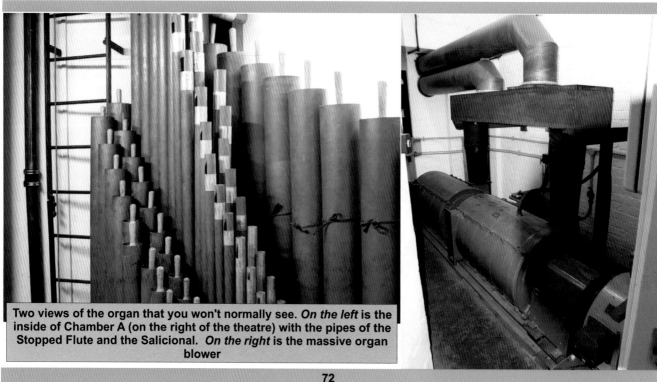

Two views of the organ that you won't normally see. *On the left* is the inside of Chamber A (on the right of the theatre) with the pipes of the Stopped Flute and the Salicional. *On the right* is the massive organ blower

The Pantomimes

1934 - 2005

Virtually every resident of Bournemouth has some memory of a pantomime. Cast your eye over the list and see how many you can recall. Michael Lunn has kindly produced the list of shows, but in some cases it has been impossible to find the names of the stars.

From 1934 until 1947, the pantomimes were presented by impresario Harry Benet; from 1948 until 1961 (except 1960 when the theatre was closed for repair), Emile Littler provided the shows, and he was joined for two years in 1962 and 1963 by Tom Arnold. Derek Salzberg took on the role from 1964 to 1976, and from then a variety of impresarios have been involved, including many shows by Paul Elliott, the impresario who comes from Bournemouth.

The List

Christmas 1934
Cinderella
Christmas 1935
Dick Whittington
Christmas 1936
Jack and the Beanstalk
Christmas 1937
Cinderella
Christmas 1938
Aladdin
Christmas 1939
Babes in the Wood
Christmas 1940
Dick Whittington
Christmas 1941
Robinson Crusoe
Christmas 1942
Mother Goose
(Nellie Wallace)
Christmas 1943
Jack and the Beanstalk
(Dick Tubb)
Christmas 1944
Red Riding Hood
(Betty Huntley Wright)
Christmas 1945
Humpty Dumpty (Albert H. Grant, Kiki Reedy
Christmas 1946
Cinderella (Tessa Deane, Freddie Foss)
Christmas 1947
Goldilocks and the Three Bears (Dorothy Ward)

Christmas 1948
Little Miss Muffet
(Binnie Hale)
Christmas 1949
Mother Goose
(Tommy Fields, Eve Lister)
Christmas 1950
Aladdin
(Nat Jackley)
Christmas 1951
Goody Two Shoes
(Sonny Jenks, Jerry Desmonde)
Christmas 1952
Cinderella
(Jean Kent, Roy Barbour)
Christmas 1953
Jack and Jill
(Charlie Chester, Sid Plummer)
Christmas 1954
Babes in the Wood
(Reg Varney, Cardew Robinson)
Christmas 1955
Dick Whittington
(Tommy Fields, Adelaide Hall)
Christmas 1956
Little Miss Muffet
(Charlie Cairoli)
Christmas 1957
Mother Goose
(Max Wall, Billy Dainty)
Christmas 1958
Puss in Boots
(Reg Varney, Tommy Cooper)
Christmas 1959
Cinderella
(David Nixon)
Christmas 1960
Theatre Closed for Repair
Christmas 1961
Goody Two Shoes
(Mr. Pastry, Kenneth MacKeller)
Christmas 1962
Aladdin
(Adam Faith, Tommy Fields)
Christmas 1963
Cinderella
(Danny La Rue)
Christmas 1964
Puss in Boots
Christmas 1965

Mother Goose
(Freddie Frinton, Braemar Pipers)
Christmas 1966
Jack and the Beanstalk
(Diana Dors)
Christmas 1967
Robinson Crusoe
Christmas 1968
Aladdin
(Harry H. Corbett)
Christmas 1969
Cinderella
Christmas 1970
Dick Whittington
(Barron Knights, Reg Dixon)
Christmas 1971
Puss in Boots
Christmas 1972
Robinson Crusoe
Christmas 1973
Aladdin
(Roy Castle)
Christmas 1974
Cinderella
(Arthur Askey, Dickie Henderson)
Christmas 1975
Jack and the Beanstalk
Christmas 1976
Robin Hood
(Jack Tripp, Leslie Crowther)
Christmas 1977
Aladdin
(Lenny Henry, Don Maclean)
Christmas 1978
Dick Whittington
(Peter Glaze, Jan Hunt, Ed Stewart)
Christmas 1979
Babes in the Wood
(Matthew Kelly, Elizabeth Estensen, Bill Pertwee)
Christmas 1980
Sleeping Beauty
(Arthur English, Billy Dainty, Jack Douglas)
Christmas 1981
Aladdin
Christmas 1982
Cinderella
Christmas 1983
No Pantomime

Christmas 1984
Goldilocks and the Three Bears
(Ted Rogers)
Christmas 1985
Cinderella
Christmas 1986
Aladdin
(Anita Dobson, Derek Griffiths, John Boulter)
Christmas 1987
Jack and the Beanstalk
(Lorraine Chase, Michael Elphick, Matthew Kelly)
Christmas 1988
Dick Whittington
(Paul Shane, Derek Martin, Peter Goodwright)
Christmas 1989
Snow White
(Marti Caine, Karl Howman)
Christmas 1990
Aladdin
(Sue Pollard, Matthew

Kelly, Gordon Honeycombe)
Christmas 1991
Jack and the Beanstalk
(Max Boyce)
Christmas 1992
Cinderella
(Stefan Dennis, June Brown, Windsor Davies)
Christmas 1993
Babes in the Wood
(Roy Hudd, Geoffrey Hughes, Jack Tripp)
Christmas 1994
Robinson Crusoe
Christmas 1995
Cinderella
(Les Dennis, Kathy Staff)
Christmas 1996
Dick Whittington
(Paul Daniels, Peter Byrne)
Christmas 1997
Peter Pan
Sean Canning, Andy Ford)
Christmas 1998

Beauty and the Beast
(Robin Coussins, Buster Merryfield)
Christmas 1999
Robinson Crusoe
(David Essex)
Christmas 2000
Aladdin
(Jeremy Beadle, Gareth Hunt)
Christmas 2001
Dick Whittington
(Wayne Sleep, Sid Owen)
Christmas 2002
Cinderella
(Ruth Madoc, Chris Jarvis)
Christmas 2003
Snow White
(Marti Webb)
Christmas 2004
Jack and the Beanstalk
(Chris Jarvis, Chris Ellison)
Christmas 2005
Aladdin
(Chris Jarvis, Ray Meagher)

Paul Elliott is an old boy of Bournemouth School and has been for many years one of the most successful impresarios in Britain. He presented shows at the Palace Court Theatre for a short time (and starred in his own production of 'Lock Up Your Daughters' at that theatre, replacing Bill Maynard in the lead role in the 1960s. This was one of his bigger shows - the London Palladium Production of the most famous of all Pantomime stories. It was an interesting cast - designed to appeal to virtually everybody - an Australian Soap Star, a British Soap Star and a well-loved actor from television comedy shows. Stefan Dennis is now back in 'Neighbours', currently wreaking havoc on the poor folk of Erinsborough - with only one leg! June Brown is still the most popular comedy actress in the BBC's often depressing Soap. Christmas 1992 and New Year 1993 were bound to be winners at the Bournemouth Pavilion.

Left: The latest fountain (2005), cause of pleasure and anger. Many motorists don't like their cars being sprayed when the wind blows. It's a hard life!

Right: The Canopy on the main frontage in 2005. This is thought by some to be a monstrosity, and reminiscent of a building site's scaffolding. It certainly does detract from the original design, even if that was rather bland.

Left: The wonderful, warm Foyer, with the gentle arches, the fluted pillars and the terrazzo floor. Pure elegance!

Three Splendid Views of the Corridors either side of the Auditorium, both leading to the Ballroom.

Top Left: West corridor with Ballroom entrance in distance. Note Archive pictures on left wall.

Top Right: Entrance to West Corridor from Foyer - almost grotto-like.

Right: East Corridor with afternoon sunshine creating dramatic but warm shadows

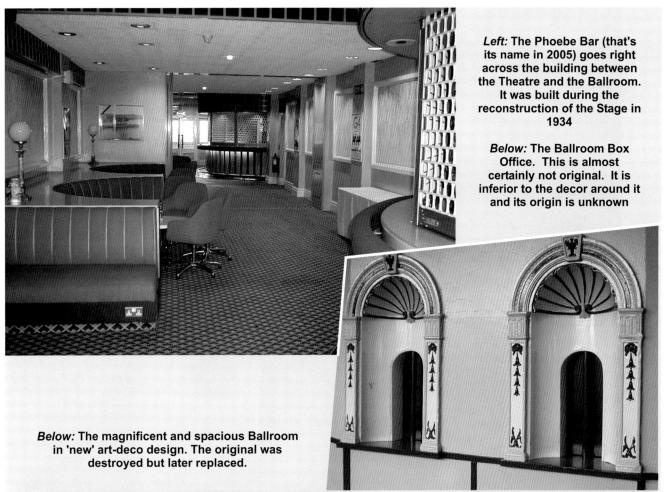

Left: The Phoebe Bar (that's its name in 2005) goes right across the building between the Theatre and the Ballroom. It was built during the reconstruction of the Stage in 1934

Below: The Ballroom Box Office. This is almost certainly not original. It is inferior to the decor around it and its origin is unknown

Below: The magnificent and spacious Ballroom in 'new' art-deco design. The original was destroyed but later replaced.

The Ballroom

The Lucullus Room. This name has been with the restaurant since the opening in 1929, although other names were tried unsuccessfully. e.g. Captain's Table

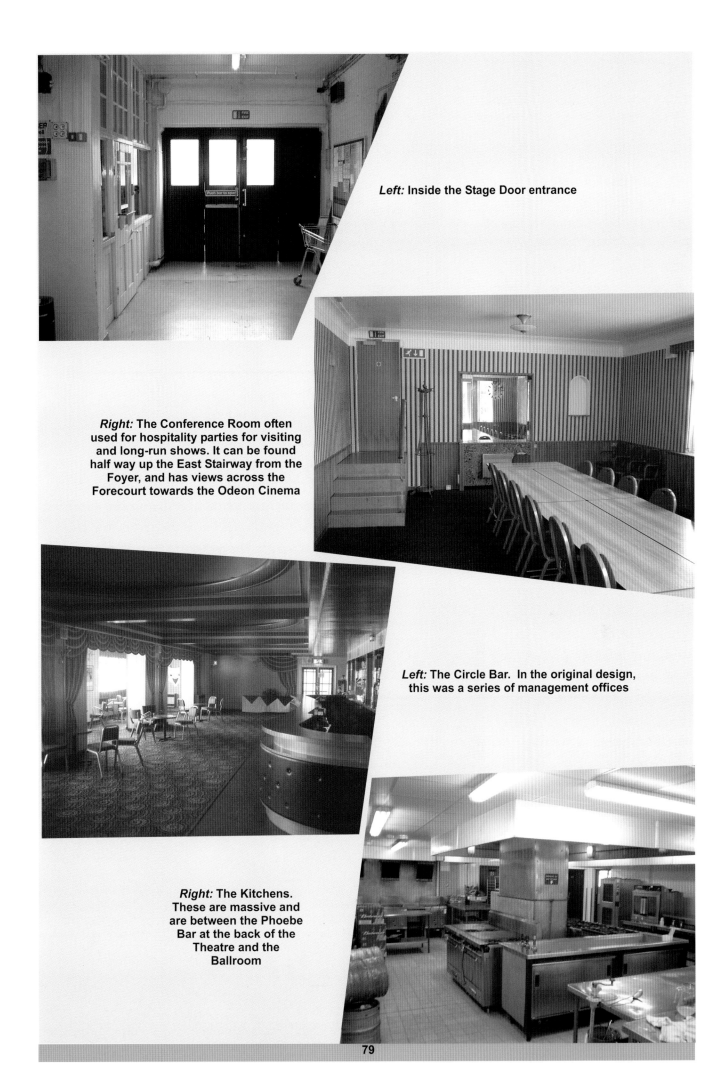

Left: Inside the Stage Door entrance

Right: The Conference Room often used for hospitality parties for visiting and long-run shows. It can be found half way up the East Stairway from the Foyer, and has views across the Forecourt towards the Odeon Cinema

Left: The Circle Bar. In the original design, this was a series of management offices

Right: The Kitchens. These are massive and are between the Phoebe Bar at the back of the Theatre and the Ballroom

National Union of Teachers Annual Conference - 1930

One of the first conferences in the Pavilion was the Annual Meeting of the National Union of Teachers in 1930. In a large promotional book given to all delegates, an unknown author spoke mellifluously of the building. The Pictures come from the brochure.

"One of the things which will impress the visitor whose previous acquaintance with Bournemouth was prior to the summer of 1929, will be the splendid advance which has been made in the provision of places of entertainment. Not only does the Pavilion concert hall provide a much more worthy setting for the Municipal Orchestra than was previously available, but the programmes also regularly include a variety of stage attractions, both brave and gay, by artistes of international repute. No expense has been spared in the attainment of an ideal concert hall, both from the point of view of the entertainments given, and the comfort of the patrons. It was designed under the supervision of a noted authority on acoustics, and the elaborate stage settings and equipment are such to facilitate the presentation of attractions of special charm. It is furnished with a magnificent organ, which combines the characteristics of a great cathedral organ and the finest theatre instrument. The Pavilion Tea Lounge and Dance Hall is ideally situated with a wide sweeping outlook across the Bay and Gardens. The dance floor is laid on springs, and the scheme of decoration and multi-coloured lighting effects achieve at once an atmosphere of brightness and refinement. In common with the remainder of the building, the ventilation of the Dance Hall is controlled by an installation which propels purified air through the hall and extracts the vitiated air."

Sounds like a pretty good place!

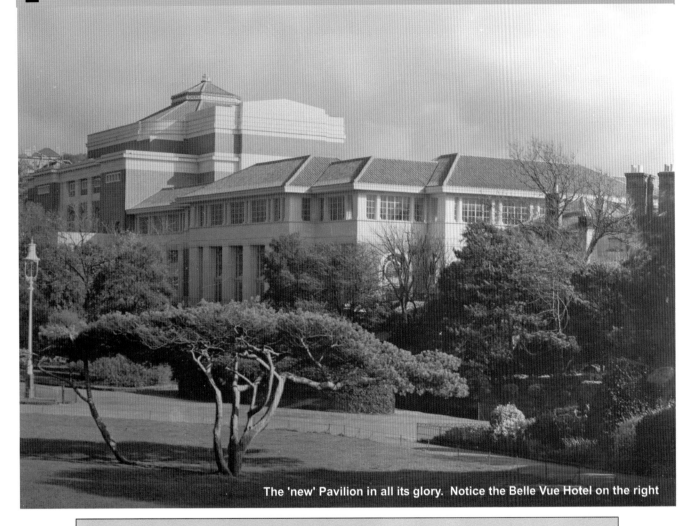

The 'new' Pavilion in all its glory. Notice the Belle Vue Hotel on the right

The Regional Press

When the Bournemouth Pavilion opened, the news was of importance to almost every national, regional and local newspaper in the country, all of which had editorial coverage. Readers in Bristol, Yorkshire, Birmingham, Sheffield, Nottingham, Manchester and Liverpool are just a few which became aware of the growing importance of Bournemouth as a sea-side resort.

The Daily Telegraph reported that: *We often hear complaints, not without*

justification, that English holiday towns neglect to compete with Continental resorts in their provision of amusement and pleasant places in which to idle the hours away. Bournemouth has shown what can be done in England. The Pavilion, in five years, has grown up opposite the entrance to the pier in a place Nature apparently designed for it. Observing it from the seafront, one gets the impression of a balanced, square-looking structure, rising in three well-proportioned, shallow terraces, one behind the other, and when time has a little softened its

present tone of newness, it will present a seemliness and dignity which Bournemouth will observe with quiet satisfaction and other seaside towns with secret envy. The building is more than an imposing addition to the town's architecture; it is a social portent, a tribute to the sagacity of the municipal fathers.

The Daily Mail decided that the most important part of the **Duke of Gloucester**'s visit was that he went to Christchurch Priory, while the **Morning Post** reported the Duke's comments that seaside resorts had a part to play in the life of the nation, for they took upon themselves the pleasant duty of acting as physicians to the industrial towns, offering health to the sick, renewal of vigour to the convalescent, and a playground to those in full health. They also carried a picture of the Duke with the Mayor of Bournemouth. *(This can be seen in the Opening Ceremony report on Page 7)*

The Times described the building as an *imposing building facing the pier, claiming to be the finest building of its kind in the country*, **and The Nottingham Journal** found *the ballroom to be palatial and very handsome.* In the late 1920s, cinemas showed news reels as part of their programmes of entertainment, and the opening of the Pavilion was shown by the following: **Gaumont Graphic**, **Topical Budget**, **British Screen News**, **Pathe Super Gazette** and **Empire News Bulletin**; this means that virtually everyone who visited the cinema that week anywhere in the country would have been made aware of this wonderful new Pavilion!

The Bournemouth and Southampton Graphic printed a cartoon about the Pavilion from much earlier in the century. **The Daily News** also reported the closure of the old **Winter Gardens**: *No tears will be shed at the passing of the Winter Gardens, for there is no comparison between* the two buildings. This great enterprise has not been carried on during all these years for nothing, but the cost to the rates must have been more than repaid by the advertisement of the town as a health and pleasure resort. For **The Birmingham Gazette** there was *a frantic last minute rush to complete the building for the opening by the Duke of Gloucester. Dismay was caused by a rumour that the organ would not work, but on trial it proved to be satisfactory.* **The Yorkshire Post** described the new Pavilion as *the last word in luxury, comfort and pleasure. Its white stone walls and red tiled roof form a striking contrast to the dark green of the surrounding trees.* Even the **News of the World** found the story important enough to report, and they remarked that *the Duke was presented with a gold cigarette box by the Mayor.* An unusual report in the **Bexhill-on-Sea Observer**, seemed to indicate that the writer was rather more fond of Bournemouth than he was of Bexhill! *Bournemouth, with its long and successful record of municipal music does provide an example of a seaside town with a policy which other holiday and health resorts might emulate in some respects with advantage. It has determined to have the best and has not hesitated to spend money on getting it. Bournemouth has shown the way for municipal music and achieved success. Bexhill has gone the other way and the result is what we all know and deplore.*

The designers, the builders and the people of Bournemouth must have felt very happy about all the publicity given to their new building right the way across the whole country, and there appears to have been no criticism from any quarter. **This was certainly a good beginning.**

TWENTY-SEVEN YEARS AGO

This is a reproduction of a Cartoon dealing with the proposed Pavilion which appeared in "The Bournemouth Graphic" on May 29th, 1902.

"THE PIER PAVILION"

Song and Chorus—"Come under my Um, Come under my Um, Come under my Umberella."

1855

1938

2005

The Changing Face of Westover Road

A ROAD IS REBORN *(See also Page 25)*

The building and opening of the **Bournemouth Pavilion** was only one of several changes being made in the town centre area in **1929**. Some residents were pleased at the fast-moving development, while others were worried about how the changes would affect their lifestyle.

The area **between the Arcade and the Pier** - largely what we would call Westover Road and the Pleasure Gardens - was described at the time as *'a great pleasure highway, with a concentration of attractions unrivalled on the south coast'*. There would soon be enough spaces to accommodate nearly **twenty-thousand people** in the pursuit of fun and pleasure. Local churchmen were divided in their feelings about the development - the **Vicar of St. Peter's** claimed that the area where his congregation lived had become a **pleasure mile**, and the Vicar of a nearby church called for the **demolition of all the entertainment places** - including the Pavilion.

Many residential properties had become - or were becoming - **hotels and guest-houses** and there were hopes for a line of shops to support the area. Before the First World War (1914-1918), the only fun place was the **Westover Ice-Rink** *(not the current building)* which had since become the **Westover Palace, Ballroom and Cinema**. Parts of this can still be found behind the 'new' **Westover Cinema** in Hinton Road. In 1929, the **Pavilio**n, the **Westover Palace** *(again, not the current building)* and the new **Regent Cinema**, opened a few months later, could provide entertainment for **ten thousand** people at the same time if they were at full capacity. The Regent, later the Gaumont and now the Odeon, was a 2,300-seater and the new Westover could seat 2,000. The **Westover Ballroom** could cater for 750. There was a proposal for a new **Little Theatre** in Hinton Road (this would become the Palace Court Theatre) and yet another idea was to build a large Ice Rink (this would be the current Westover Ice-Rink, now closed). Then **St. Peter's Hall** in Hinton Road was used for stage plays, concerts and "**even gayer events**"! (so said the *Bournemouth Daily Echo*! How language changes!) On the other side of the Pleasure Gardens was the old **Winter Gardens**, previously the home of the **Bournemouth Municipal Orchestra**, and this could cope with nearly 2,000 people. These numbers don't include the folk who were enjoying **Pier and Beach Shows**. To help with parking problems, a new car park - the town's first multi-storey - was to be built in Hinton Road almost next to the Regent. This still exists today, with a single entrance in Hinton Road, but when first built, it had an entrance in Westover Road as well.

So this was an exciting era of growth for **Bournemouth's entertainment** scene - and right at the heart of it was the very **prestigious Pavilion**.

(n.b) This is a difficult decade to be sure about the shows which played at the Pavilion. It was an age when no dates were put in programmes, and the calendar was such that both 1951 and 1956 share the same dates. The shows here are thought to be correct, but there is doubt and some may be displaced. But any names and shows mentioned certainly did play the theatre some time in the 1950s!

During the **early 1950s**, the legendary **Greta Garbo** attended a show at the Pavilion with her photographer friend, **Cecil Beaton**.

1950

February - 'One Bright Day', a play starred **Derek Farr** (very popular male lead in films and on stage), **Renee Asherson** and **Naunton Wayne**.

18ᵗʰ March - 21ˢᵗ Anniversary Dinner for the opening. A special menu included *Supreme de Poulet* for *l'Anniversaire de Pavilion*. No idea why French was used instead of English.

18ᵗʰ March - In the Theatre - **A Coming of Age Gala Performance** which featured the **Bournemouth Municipal Orchestra, Harold Coombs** and **International Ballet**. Also on the bill were **Geraldo and His Orchestra, Ethel Revnell** and **Stanley Holloway** (who had appeared in the opening show in 1929). Note, too, singer **Eve**

Boswell.

April - play called '**Madame Tic-Tac**' which is apparently slang for sign language. Also this month, **Anton Dolin** and **Alicia Markova** (two ballet stars who had spent most of their working lives working together) appeared, as did **Gladys Cooper**. There was also a rare showing of an Ibsen play, '**Rosmersholm**', a dramatic glimpse into human nature.

October - the **London Festival Ballet**, only recently formed, made one of many appearances at the theatre.

November - The Council decided **to reduce the size of the Theatre Orchestra**. This led to a three-year battle with the Musicians' Union.

December - Pantomime was '**Aladdin**' with **Jean Marsh, Nat Jackley** and **Millicent Martin**.

1951

This year saw some really big names in the theatre including **Martin Green** with the **D'Oyly Carte Opera Company**, the **Old Vic Company** in '**Captain Brassbound's Conversion**', starring **Ursula Jeans** and **Roger Livesey**, and **Moira Lister, Peter Ustinov** and **Gwen Cherrell** starred in '**The Love of the Four Colonels**'.

If those names aren't enough, the following stars played the Pavilion this year; **Max Adrian, Rose Hill, June Whitfield, Elizabeth Welch, Joyce Grenfell, Moyra Frazer, Derek Bond** (big 'heart-throb' of the 40s and 50s), **Jimmy Hanley, Barry Sinclair, Douglas Wilmer, Rupert Davies** and **James Grout**. Wow!

Still more - the list continues with **Jeremy Hawk, Ian Carmichael**, and **Dora Bryan** in '**The Lyric Revue**', **Jane Baxter** and **Herbert Lomas** in '**The Holly and the Ivy**', and **Francis Lister, Jack Watling** and **Joy Shelton** in '**Come Live With Me**'.

One Sunday (date unknown), the following all appeared in a gala concert: **Flotsam, Ronald Chesney** (Harmonica), **Anne Ziegler**

— INTERMISSION —
(a) Memories of great artists who have played at the Pavilion
(b) Signature tunes of famous stage and radio bands which have played at the Pavilion

HAROLD COOMBS at the Organ

★

GERALDO and HIS ORCHESTRA
with
EVE BOSWELL   MARION SANDERS   CYRIL GRANTHAM
LORNA MARTIN   NADIA DORE

ETHEL REVNELL

JANET HAMILTON-SMITH and
JOHN HARGREAVES
with
STANLEY HOLLOWAY
AS MASTER OF CEREMONIES

HAPPY BIRTHDAY — FINALE

GOD SAVE THE KING

The Management extend their thanks to Emile Littler and his Production Manager, Hastings Mann, for assistance in organising this Birthday performance

and Webster Booth, Albert Sandler, Jack Byfield and Reginald Kilbey. In its day, that would have been a top-notch concert.

June - Bournemouth and Wessex Festival held concerts, opera, ballet, drama, exhibitions, open-air and sporting events. There was a series of Band Concerts featuring H.M. Royal Marines, Central Band of the R.A.F., and the Coldstream Guards.

August - Sonny Jenks appeared in a two-week run of the musical 'Maid of the Mountains'.

September - Sunday shows were presented by 'Deep River Boys', and Edmundo Ros and his Orchestra, and The National Light Opera Company played for two weeks with 'Chu Chin Chow', 'Lilac Domino' and 'Merrie England'.

December - The pantomime was 'Goody Two Shoes' with Anne Doonan and Sonny Jenks.

Can there ever have been a year with more stars?

1952

March - Ivor Novello's 'King's Rhapsody' starring Marie Burke, Barry Sinclair, Elizabeth French, with the dramatic and massive Cathedral Scene.

May - Bobby Howes was in 'Goodnight Vienna', a show presented by two well-known names in the Big Band world - Jack Payne and Will Hammer, who were both heavily associated with the New Royal Theatre in Albert Road, which at this time it was presenting twice-nightly variety with some plays, summer seasons and pantomimes.

May - Another play, 'Adam's Apple', starred Marie Lohr, Derek Farr and Barbara Murray.

December - Pantomime was 'Cinderella' starring Jean Kent and Roy Barbour.

1953

Autumn - Erection of new lighting canopy

across proscenium arch, an addition which would alter the entire atmosphere of the theatre for ever. Suddenly, the area seemed quite different and the new canopy made the proscenium arch look unnaturally wide - it was, in fact, 45 ft. wide and 24 ft. high. The addition to the area did not affect the width of the stage. There had always been problems with lighting the front area of the stage and smaller shows had used material borders to reduce the height of the arch; these, in turn, had affected the acoustics. The idea was to construct a "fitment of full span, to be adjustable for height, and at the same time to house additional adjustable lighting fittings to deal primarily with the illumination of the forward part of the stage." *(Municipal Journal 1953)*

The building material used had to be light in weight for raising and lowering, but of sufficient strength to be rigid in its length. Aluminium alloy was used, designed in the form of a braced girder approximately four feet deep, hung from two points in its length. The whole structure was slung from existing steel roof trusses, but these had to be strengthened first. It was so big, that it had to be made in four separate sections and bolted together on site. The covering on the auditorium side of this gantry is of fibrous plaster panels which incorporate the Bournemouth Borough Coat of Arms. When first put up, the gantry housed eighteen automatic colour-changing spot-lights, each of 1000 watts. The total length of the canopy is 54 feet and it weighs approximately three tons. Messrs. Hunt and Company of Bournemouth supplied and installed the gantry. The machinery for changing the colours on the lamps was very noisy and could not be used during quiet scenes; the well-known pianist, Semprini, always asked that they weren't used during his playing. A full and detailed description of the engineering appears in "The Municipal Journal".

November - The Theatre **Orchestra was reduced** from eleven players to seven.

December - **Charlie Chester** starred in 'Jack and Jill' for the annual pantomime.

1954

February - 'Affairs of State' with **Coral Browne** and **Hugh Williams**. Robertson Hare returned in November with **Ralph Lynn** in 'Three Times a Day'.

March - a busy month which saw **Robertson Hare** and **Ralph Lynn** in 'Liberty Bill' before it went to London, **Vanessa Lee** in another pre-West End offering, 'After the Ball', and 'Hippo Dancing' starring the great **Robert Morley**; he also wrote the play which is described as a murder mystery.

April - **Edith Evans** appeared in a play directed by **Peter Brook**, 'The Dark is Light Enough', by **Christopher Fry**. Edith Evans played a divinely virtuous countess who attempts the moral rehabilitation of a nihilist revolutionary. I'm glad I was too young to go and see that - I think I probably am still too young! But who says there's never any culture at the Pavilion!

June - The musical 'Paint Your Wagon' came straight from London with **Sally and Bobby Howes**.

August - In a good year for musicals, **Sean Connery** (yes, Sean Connery!) appeared in a production of '**South Pacific**' *(see programme below)*. He was half way down the cast list. His biography states that this tour led him into greater things, and that it was a very important part of his phenomenal rise to stardom as **James Bond** and what happened afterwards. **Richard Shaw** was the named star of the production.

August/September - Even more big musicals followed with 'The Quaker Girl' starring **Betty Leslie** and **Sonny Jenks**, and 'Love from Judy'.

Sundays included **Rawicz and Landauer** and **The Central Band of the R.A.F.**

September - A week of **Italian Opera** played with '**La Boheme**', '**Il Travatore**', and '**La Traviata**'.

November - what must have been a memorable evening entitled '**Time Remembered**' starring **Margaret Rutherford** (aged 62 and before she was knighted) and **Paul Schofield**, who's perhaps best remembered for his stunning performance as Sir Thomas More in the film of '**A Man for All Seasons**'.

SOUTH PACIFIC

Cast in order of their appearance :

Ngana	SHIRLEY EMERY or YVONNE WALTON
Jerome	ALAN SAUNDERS or RAYMOND PAVETT
Henry	CHICK ALEXANDER
Ensign Nellie Forbush	PATRICIA HARTLEY
Emile de Beque	NEVIL WHITING
Bloody Mary	HELEN LANDIS
Bloody Mary's Assistant	JUNE PHILLIPS
Stewpot	RICHARD SHAW
Luther Billis	EDDIE LESLIE
Professor	PAUL DOBSON
Lt. Joseph Cable, U.S.M.C.	DAVID WILLIAMS
Capt. George Brackett, U.S.N.	ROBERT HENDERSON
Cmdr. William Harbison, U.S.N.	STANLEY BEARD
Yeoman Herbert Quale	FRANKLIN FOX
Abner	ABE ELLIS
Sgt. Kenneth Johnston	SEAN CONNERY
Seabee Morton Wise	PETER WHITAKER
Seaman Tom O'Brien	GORDON DOBSON
Radio Operator B. McCaffrey	ROLAND GREEN
Marine Cpl. Hamilton Steeves	CLEMENT HARDMAN
Staff Sgt. Thomas Hassinger	STANLEY HOWLETT
Pt. Sven Larsen	PETER EVANS
Pt. Victor Jerome	PETER MILLARD
Seabee Richard West	JAMES ARMSTRONG
Lt. Genevieve Marshall	BRENDA BARKER
Ensign Dinah Murphy	MELA WHITE
Ensign Janet McGregor	TERRY HOWARD
Ensign Cora MacRae	MAUREEN GRANT
Ensign Sue Yaegar	JANE HILL
Ensign Lisa Minelli	CAROLE LYN LESLIE
Ensign Connie Walewska	VALERIE WALSH
Ensign Pamela Whitmore	CAROLE BRENT
Ensign Bessie Noonan	JANE BOLTON
Ensign Betty Pitt	ROSALIE WHITHAM
Liat	CAROLE SOPEL
Marcel (Henry's assistant)	JACK SOO
Lt. Buz Adams	COLIN CROFT
Marines	ADRIAN DESMOND, BOB MARTIN

THE ACTION OF THE PLAY TAKES PLACE ON TWO ISLANDS IN THE SOUTH PACIFIC DURING THE RECENT WAR

There is a week's lapse of time between the two Acts.

INTERVAL OF 15 MINUTES

MUSICAL NUMBERS

ACT ONE

Dites-Moi Pourquoi	Ngana and Jerome
A Cockeyed Optimist	Nellie
Twin Soliloquies	Nellie and Emile
Some Enchanted Evening	Emile
Bloody Mary is the Girl I Love	Sailors, Seabees, Marines
There's Nothing Like a Dame	Billis, Sailors, Seabees, Marines
Bali Ha'i	Bloody Mary
I'm Gonna Wash That Man Right Outa My Hair	Nellie and Nurses
I'm in Love With a Wonderful Guy	Nellie and Nurses
Younger Than Springtime	Cable
Finale	Nellie and Emile

ACT TWO

Soft Shoe Dance	Nurses and Seabees
Happy Talk	Bloody Mary, Liat and Cable
Honey Bun	Nellie and Billis
You've Got To Be Taught	Cable
I Was Cheated Before	Emile
This Nearly Was Mine	Emile
Reprise : Some Enchanted Evening	Nellie

FINALE

Scenery painted by Alick Johnstone. Built by Theatre Royal, Drury Lane Workshops under the direct supervision of Louis Walton. Properties constructed by E. Boxall. Girl illustrations on men's costumes used in "Thanksgiving Follies" from Esquire Calendar 1949. Sunday comic costumes worn in "Thanksgiving Follies" printed by New York News. These costumes made by Theatre Royal, Drury Lane Wardrobe. Additional uniforms supplied by U.S. Marine Corps, U.S. Navy and U.S. Army. Shoes by Gamba. Stockings by Kayser-Bondor. Mr. Leslie's native necklace and bracelet designed by Guglielmo Cini, of Boston, Massachusetts, U.S.A. "Anchors Aweigh" played through the courtesy of Francis, Day & Hunter. The children appear by arrangement with Miss Terry. Cognac by Martell & Co., Cognac, France. Lighters by Ronson. Special make-up by Leichner and Elizabeth Arden, Nylon-Tricot "Twin Skin" Briefs by Yolande. Bristows' Lanolin Shampoo used in Act One, Scene 7, kindly supplied by T. F. Bristow & Co. Ltd. Virginia Cigarettes by Abdulla. The music from South Pacific is published by Williamson Music Ltd., 14 St. George Street, W.1.

Attractions appearing at the Pavilion Theatre are booked in conjunction with Howard & Wyndham Ltd., 9 Grafton Street, London, W.I.

Company Manager for Williamson Music Ltd.			WILLIAM STILES
Business Manager	} For		ARTHUR MELVILLE
Stage Director	SOUTH		JOHN MOORE
Stage Manager	PACIFIC		GEORGE EGAN
Assistant Stage Manager	}		JOHN EADES
Musical Director for South Pacific			CHARLES PRENTICE, Mus. Bac.
Press Representative			DAVID FAIRWEATHER (TEM. BAR 9885)

The Management respectfully invite patrons of this theatre to be seated before the rise of the curtain, and so avoid disturbance to others during the performance.
The right is reserved to refuse admission, and to make any changes in the cast necessitated by illness or other unavoidable causes.

December - 'Babes in the Wood' with **Reg Varney** from 'On the Buses') and **Cardew Robinson**, the only man in the world who could have dared record a song called '**Someone Stuffed a Crumpet up my Trumpet**'.

1955

May - **Evelyn Laye** was making a comeback after some years away from the business and she appeared in '**Wedding in Paris**'.

Sunday shows were proving successful and boasted such names as **Ken Mackintosh**, **Sid Phillips**, **Eric Delaney** (who had the biggest percussion set-up I've ever seen!) and **Frank Weir**. At this time, Sunday shows were - in theory! - forbidden to have dancing, and all artistes were prohibited from moving!

May - **Albert Modley** made his first visit to the Pavilion in variety with **Terry Hall and Lenny the Lion** (to return in summer season in 1962), and other stars appearing included **Patience Collier**, **Nigel Stock**, **Ronald Shiner** (the chirpy Cockney actor who laughed his way through so many war-films), **Hugh Manning**, and **Gladys Young**. These were all big and popular star names.

June - **London Festival Ballet** paid their annual visit.

July - Three of the stars from the BBC Radio Comedy Show, '**The Goons**' appeared with **Joseph Locke** at top of bill; **Peter Sellars**, **Spike Milligan** and harmonica-player **Max Geldray**. Many felt that the show was a bit of a con, because it did not feature the stars as 'The Goons', but as solo performers.

September - 'White Horse Inn' (the show that had opened the enlarged Pavilion Concert Hall in 1934, returned, but this time was on ice!

September - Sunday shows included **Ted Heath and his Music**, featuring **Don Lusher**, and **Johnny Dankworth and his Orchestra**, featuring **Cleo Laine**.

December - 'Dick Whittington' with **Tommy Fields**.

1956

January - The original cast production from the West End of '**Waiting for Godot**' was not well received, and resulted in many complaints and many walkouts. The play, by **Samuel Becket**, revolves round two tramps waiting by a strange tree; they argue, they eat, they contemplate suicide..... Opinions vary as to what the play is trying to say.

February - One of the greatest British film stars played in '**Summertime**' . **Dirk Bogarde** (who appeared by permission of the Rank Organisation) was a real heart-throb, and he appeared in this production with **Geraldine McEwan**. Bogarde was a very nervous man and disliked being mobbed by women fans after the show, and he was petrified when women actually shouted at him during the performances of the play. This was his last tour and he retired from the stage altogether, after a short run at the Oxford Playhouse.

May - **D'Oyly Carte Opera** with **Ifor Evans**.

May - 'Kiss Me Kate' starring **Elizabeth Garner** and **James Maxwell**.

July - **Vera Lynn** in variety. *(see complete programme on next page)*

The PAVILION   Bournemouth

Telephone 2654   Box Office 5861

General Manager: ARTHUR CLEGG

WEEK COMMENCING MONDAY, 11th JULY.

Twice Nightly at 6.15 and 8.30.

Lew and Leslie Grade present

VERA LYNN

Jimmy James

and Company.   Britain's Brilliant Comedian

WILSON, KEPPEL and BETTY
Cleopatra's Nightmare

and Big Supporting Company

August - A three-week run of '**The King and I**' starred **Eve Lister**. 49 years later in 2005, this Rodgers and Hammerstein musical played again at the Pavilion in August for two weeks.

September - Concert by the **Billy Ternant Orchestra**. He was a popular broadcaster. This month also saw **John Slater** in the Whitehall farce, '**Dry Rot**', and '**Teahouse of the August Moon**' with **Albert Chevalier**.

October - **Hermione Baddeley** played '**Your Loving Wife**', and the ever-popular musical '**The Arcadians**' played for a week. Lionel Monkton wrote the music, and the musical is set in Arcadia, the land that time forgot.

November - Continuing decline in audiences at the Pavilion led to thoughts of closure.

VERA LYNN

Jimmy James

—and Big Supporting Company—

1. OVERTURE, "Opening Night" ... *Donald Phillips*

2. AVERIL and AUREL ... ... Dance Team

3. KEN MORRIS and JOAN SAVAGE Music, Mirth and Melody

4. THE MALLINI BROTHERS ... ... Acro Humourists

5. JIMMY JAMES and COMPANY Britain's Brilliant Comedian

6. WILSON, KEPPEL and BETTY Cleopatra's Nightmare

7. INTERMISSION

Selection of melodies from South Pacific *Richard Rodgers*

    „   „   „ Guys and Dolls   *Frank Loesser*

HAROLD COOMBS AT THE PAVILION ORGAN

8. AVERIL and AUREL ... ... To Entertain Again

9. RITA MARTELL ... ... Youthful Juggler

10. JIMMY JAMES and COMPANY

11. **VERA LYNN**

with BARRY GRAY at the Piano

PAVILION THEATRE ORCHESTRA *under the direction of* BYRON BROOKE

'**Chu Chin Chow**' was on the musicals list and the **National Light Opera Company** presented both '**Lilac Domino**' and '**Merrie England**'. And **George Lacy** appeared in '**The Belle of New York**'.

December - The pantomime was '**Little Miss Muffet**' starring **Charlie Cairoli**.

1957

April - '**Peter Pan**', the much loved children's fantasy, noted for its wonderful Kirby's flying scenes, starred **Margaret Lockwood**.

July - **Robert Beatty** (yet another Briish acting heart-throb) and **Eunice Gayson** were in '**Born Yesterday**'. A million dollar tycoon hires a tutor to teach his lover.

September - '**Man of Distinction**', starring **Moira Shearer**, **Prunella Scales**, **Eric Porter** and **Anton Walbrook**.

October - London Festival Ballet.

October - New Royal Theatre closed after a production by the **Wessex Opera Company** '**The Tales of Hoffman**'. Its co-owner, Will Hammer, had died in a cycling accident a few months earlier, and the theatre had stayed open in order to honour its amateur company booking. The theatre did reopen for a very short while as an opera house, but is now a casino and night-club.

There were the annual visits by the **D'Oyly Carte Opera Company** and '**The Fol de Rols**' with **Jack Tripp**. Bands included **Ted Heath and his Music** and the **Chris Barber Jazz Band** with **Ottilie Patterson**, and **Paul Schofield** and **Megs Jenkins** appeared in '**A Dead Secret**'.

December - **Max Wall** and **Billy Dainty** delighted audiences to the pantomime, '**Mother Goose**', with their particular brands of zany humour albeit some rather adult!

1958

The long list of star performers continued this year with a selection of plays featuring, among others, **Yvonne Arnaud**, **Bernard Cribbens** and **Moyra Fraser** in '**A Ticklish Business**', **Patricia Jessel** and **Gerard Heinz** in an **Agatha Christie** play, '**Verdict**', **Celia Johnson**, **Joan Greenwood** and **Hugh Williams** in Hugh's own play, '**The Grass is Greener**' (where tourists are allowed to take tours of a private castle - this later became a film starring Cary Grant) and **Noelle Middleton**, **Jack Watling** and **Claude Hulbert** were in '**Meet the Cousin**'.

October - **Amanda Barrie** (for twenty years from 1981, she was Alma in '**Coronation Street**' was in 'Grab Me a Gondola', and **Donald Wolfit** starred in '**The Broken Jug**'. *The author was working backstage for this production, and Donald Wolfit well lived up to his reputation as being a stickler for correctness. All his staff and crew called him 'Sir', and they were not allowed to speak to him unless he wanted them to. There was a strange atmosphere of fear all around, but this fear was all a part of the respect they had for him. He had not only a stage presence, but an aura - about him all the time. I was still at school - only 16 - and I can remember being extremely fearful of doing something that would incur his wrath.*

November - **London Festival Ballet** starred **Beryl Grey**.

December - **Tommy Cooper** and **Reg Varney** starred in the pantomime, '**Puss in Boots**'.

1959

In this year, **Ralph Richardson** appeared in '**Flowering Cherry**', and **Michael Caine** and **Terence Stamp** (both to become enormous film stars) were in the war-time drama, '**The Long, the Short and the Tall**'. **Anthony Hayes*** starred in '**The Boy Friend**', the mock-1920s musical by **Sandy Wilson**, and **Dennis Lotis, Marie Lohr, Jack Watling** and **Adrienne Corri** all shocked the prudish Bournemouth audiences in John Osborne's musical, '**The World of Paul Slickey**'. *The author saw this production and found it extremely ordinary. (P.38-39)*

January - **Evelyn Laye** appeared in Noel Coward's '**The Marquise**', **Leo Genn** and **Catherine Lacey** sailed down the '**Hidden River**', and **Athene Seyler** and **Mary Merrall** took a '**Breath of Spring**'.

March - **Cecily Courtneidge** and **Nora Swinburne** starred in '**Fools Paradise**'.

May - **The Royal Ballet** played seven different shows.

December - '**Cinderella**' with **David Nixon**.

* Other names are on some handbills

Part of the Archive Material in the corridors either side of the auditorium
This is a poster from 1937

These I remember.....
CONSTANCE BROWN'S SCRAPBOOK

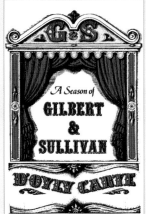

Black and White Minstrel Show was absolutely terrific. really great entertainment. I wasn't bothered by the fact that the singing was all pre-recorded - it's just political < nonsense!

I loved Dulcie Gray in this play - she was brilliant, and the play was nothing less than hilarious! >

< D'Oyly Carte are the best opera company, and it's a shame they've struggled. Gilbert and Sullivan operas are always bright and cheerful and take you out of yourself.

< This was probably the best summer season ever. I love magic anyway, and Paul Daniels is wonderful. The whole show was beautifully presented.

< What a pity this was only one night! He's one of my favourites and has an extremely good voice and a lovely personality.

Ben E King has a lovely voice > and he's a very good performer. It was amazing to hear the song 'Stand By Me' sung live.

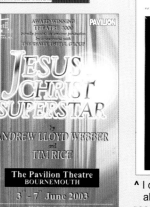

^ I really didn't enjoy this at all, and became very emotional about it all. I had to walk out. I'm not an over-religious person, but I found it very disturbing.

^ I didn't enjoy this production at all. Alfred Marks was a very good actor, but I heard him make an aside as he went off stage - apparently he wasn't happy about something, and he made it very clear!

< The only word to describe this show is SUPERB. The dancing was brilliant and we knew all the music. This was really top-line entertainment at the Pavilion.

**Constance Brown is one of the Pavilion's most loyal supporters, and attends almost every show there is.
>**

What a Wonderful Show!

DEBBIE SMITH SAYS 'WHOOPS'!

I used to work at Ladbroke's, and one of the regular customers got talking one day and he told me that he was a lighting technician for the pantomime. He said that if I ever wanted a few tickets he would arrange for them. So, I asked him for five seats for a particular performance, and he said he would ensure that they were left at the Box Office for me to pick up on arrival. When I got to the Box Office with four eager children, I was told that no tickets had been put by in my name. This was a little frustrating - imagine what the four children would have been like if I hadn't been able to get some tickets! Eventually, after much arguing and a considerable amount of pushing from me, they apologised for the confusion, and gave me **five front-row seats,** and off we went and enjoyed what was a super pantomime. When the customer concerned came back into the shop a few days later, I told him that the seats hadn't been ready but complimented him on the show, saying that **'Dick Whittington'** was brilliant. "'Dick Whittington'," he said, "that's at the Pavilion Theatre in Bournemouth. I work at the Towngate Theatre in Poole - we've got **'Jack and the Beanstalk'**!"

"WHOOPS"

Happy Times!

ROSEMARY BARNES

*Bournemouth born and bred, **Rosemary Barnes** (nee Wilton) was the grand-daughter of the man who was driving the fateful tram in 1908, which careered out of control with failed brakes at the Triangle and turned over into the gardens beneath Avenue Road. She loves Bournemouth and its history, and still looks back with affection on her days at **Winton and Moordown School** in Coronation Avenue. She has many memories of the Pavilion.*

"I suppose my earliest recollection would be of tea dances in the Ballroom - and **coffee dances**, too. In the 1940s and 1950s, the Pavilion was an important **meeting place for young people**, and most weekends there were tea dances. The tables in the centre were the best, and they were all bookable. You booked a table, had a cup of tea

and a cake, and then danced - all for 1/6d - that's less than 8p! I remember **Sid Fay's Band**, and also **Charlie Richards**, who had a trio in the late 1940s and early 1950s. We went to the dance, then across the road to the cinema, and that was the end of our week's pocket money. We always met in the Pavilion, because there was **always someone you knew** in one of the bars. In my teenage days, the **Lucullus Restaurant** was a bit expensive, but very, very pleasant and it was very exciting if you were invited to go there. I often used to go to the **Ocean Room** as well, when they held exhibitions - cake displays and students' work.

"There was a **lovely atmosphere** in the Ballroom, the architecture in there was superb - lovely **art deco**, and it seemed that **Ken Bailey** was always there - though I never remember his John Bull outfit! - and talking to everyone. He wrote a column in the **Bournemouth Times** under the name of **Genevieve**, and we used to make a point of trying to get our names in the column. Everybody knew Ken - he was part of Bournemouth and part of the Pavilion. >>

"I worked at **Kennedy's**, the builders merchants at Central Station; they've gone now, and been replaced by **Halfords** and **Staples**, but the company always hired the Ballroom for the **Annual Dinner Dance** - it was the **'done thing'** to hire the Pavilion for prestigious occasions. I used to love not only the company but especially the dances themselves; a lovely quickstep and, of course, a close waltz - that was very special. **Betty's Cafe** was almost opposite the Pavilion, and after the tea dance we would go there and meet people. It was almost next to **Fortes**.

"They were happy days and part of growing up and of living."

Lucullus Restaurant - 1950s

LUCULLUS FRENCH RESTAURANT

(Fully Licensed)

Luncheons—12 to 2.30 p.m.   Dinners—6.15 to 10.0 p.m.

The Dear Old Pav

DENNIS HALL

*Starting work at the Bournemouth Pavilion in 1965, as a member of the casual stage crew, **Dennis Hall** became the Entertainments Manager for Bournemouth Council. He is now the Chief Executive of **The Mayflower** in Southampton, but recalls that he had many happy years with what he calls **"the dear old Pav"**.*

"The Bournemouth Pavilion has played such an important part in the history of the town, and I feel privileged to have been part of its development from the 1960s until the mid 1980s. When I joined as a follow-spot operator, I thought it was the bees' knees, and it was so good to feel part of the local social scene - and there's no doubt that the Pavilion was right up there in the front line of entertainment and **the** major meeting place in town. I come from an army family and had spent all my early life with my family, where I had been involved in a lot of theatre and my uncle was a staunch member of the **Wessex Opera Company**. Although I was offered a place at RADA, I opted to work at the Pavilion and found myself in the very hot and steamy world of the lime box. This is a large room behind the back of the circle, where staff operate follow-spots. The light was produced by burning two carbon sticks at an angle, slightly away from each other (these were called 'carbon arcs' - very bright and clear), and not only were they very hot, they also produced a dreadful pungent smell. But, for me, it was wonderful to be involved in such a practical manner, helping to bring good entertainment to the people in the audience. I well remember having to 'spot' **Tommy Cooper**; his act was timed at fifty-five minutes, and the two carbon sticks would generally last about that time, so we asked Tommy if he could make sure that he didn't overrun, otherwise we'd have a moment of darkness as we changed the sticks.

Two Hundred plus a Dog!

"In 1968, I joined the entertainments department and became **Assistant Box Office Manager**, under the legendary **Sam Bell**; at this time the system was undergoing some considerable change and I was involved with the setting-up of a centralised booking system in the old Box Office at the entrance to the Winter Gardens drive - I think it's an Italian restaurant now. The summer seasons were enormous at that time, and we were still operating a manual booking system of tear-out tickets, so imagine that for a twice-nightly show with 1518 seats to fill, two full houses would need to sell well **over 3000 tickets**! There were no computers in those days - perhaps that was a good thing! And you can add the Sunday shows to that as well. In 1969, I managed the longest-ever season at the Pier Theatre and then in 1970 I became the **Pavilion's House Manager**. Although my job was primarily with front-of-house, I wanted to get involved with all aspects of the running of the theatre, so I maintained my links with the stage crew as well. These were glorious years for the Pavilion, although it must be admitted that it wasn't all **"House Full"** signs; I can remember weeks when audiences were 200 plus a dog, but generally, business was very good.

Wonderful Summer Shows

"It was the fantastic summer shows which still make me glow even today; big and popular stars, big orchestras, big stage sets, big audiences and big entertainment. Absolutely wonderful - a real example of happy and cheerful theatre - they were heady days indeed. New Year's Day 1977 saw me into the position of **Entertainments Manager**, Sam Bell having retired, and my work took me to wider and even more fantastic areas. I found myself in a

huge learning curve for the vagaries of show-business. We were much restricted by the workings of the local council, but we were also entrepreneurial, and we had some terrific years of great success.

B.I.C. Changed the Pavilion For Ever

"Then came the **Bournemouth International Centre**, and the Pavilion was, sadly, to change forever. Most of the council efforts went to the B.I.C. and this really sounded the death-knell of the Pavilion and the Winter Gardens, the **Winter Gardens** being almost completely written-off, and the Pavilion receiving less and less money. It was a new age of conferences, these enormous money-spinning affairs which brought economic stability and prestige to the town, probably at the expense of the good old holiday-maker. Here's a story to illustrate the point; we had booked the greatest star of the era to appear at the Pavilion - **Dame Edna Everage -** she was enormous in the entertainment world. On the Saturday night, following the previous show, the staff put her name up in the old familiar red letters on the gantry across the frontage; they were our letters, and we guarded them like gold. They were our main advertising ploy on the theatre. The same week, the theatre was to be used during the day by a union conference, and **Douglas Dawson**, the manager of that particular area, ordered the letters to be taken down and replaced by the name of the union in the conference. So here we were with this enormous star in the theatre but with the name of a trade union on the gantry! I mustn't tell you how I felt, but I can report that the company responsible for the Dame Edna show were nothing less than livid. Here was direct confrontation, and at the foundation of it, a symbol of the ever-continuing argument as to whether Bournemouth was a holiday town or a conference centre. I imagine it's still the same today. Anyway, Dame Edna - or **Barry Humphries** perhaps we should call him! - totally refused to appear unless his name went up on the canopy. So, mercifully, the name was changed and all was well, until the first night, when another problem arose. Dame Edna's act always finished as she showered the audience with gladioli flowers. Ten o'clock came and - oh dear! - the flowers hadn't been delivered. What was even worse from my point of view, was that no one had actually checked!

Conference or Entertainment?

"So, the conference 'boom' continued to take its toll on the entertainment scene; summer show seasons became shorter, thus changing the face of theatre in the town - not just the Pavilion, but elsewhere too. More factors also made for decline; other theatres in the area needed shows at a time when fewer shows were available, and the B.I.C. Windsor Hall would inevitably take the big popular music stars because it could cater for nearly three times as many in the audience. Put bluntly, the Pavilion became too large for the smaller modest touring plays, but too small for the big music events. The days of variety shows were obviously numbered and so there had to be big change. I saw this, and in spite of some council reservation I booked in the musical **"Annie"**, which was phenomenally successful and which proved the point that the seaside theatre tradition of comedians and singers was dying, and dying fast.

Guarantees and Percentage Splits

"All the shows which played the Pavilion were booked directly through my office (initially at the Pavilion, then later at the Winter Gardens, and later still at the B.I.C.); I would ring round various agencies or they would phone me, I would go to see shows, confer with other theatre managers about what was going down well and what wasn't perhaps as good as it might have been. If a production company called me and offered a show which I thought would be right for the Pavilion, we'd agree a date. I'd have to make sure it didn't interfere with summer shows and pantomimes and decide what time of year would be best - and then we'd pencil in a date before discussing terms, costs, guarantees, renting and percentage splits. Some shows would only appear if we could give a guarantee of takings, while others would willingly pay a rent for the theatre because they knew they could cover their own costs. All that decided, we'd need to discuss staffing for get-ins and get-outs and also for performances. And we still wouldn't be finished; it was then on to marketing with posters and newspaper adverts; perhaps I could offer three months adverts in our own theatre diary handouts and ask for a small fee towards other expenses. All this done, we would then work out ticket prices, what concessions we might offer and whether we could afford a special opening-night incentive. Sometimes we would take some of the profits from the show, but if a company rented the theatre and the staff, then they had all the takings.

"It wasn't unknown for a show to pull out after a firm booking had been made, and this could be for all sorts of legitimate reasons. If that happened, we could claim for loss of revenue by looking at the advance bookings and working out what we would lose in goodwill and sales of alcohol and confectionery. We would also be insured against such eventuality, and it was usually all very amicable. What I'd have to do then, was to try and find a couple of one-night shows to help fill the gap. If this wasn't possible, then the theatre would just have to stay 'dark' for the week.

"When I was **House Manager**, we used to have a lot of problems with the acoustics of the Pavilion. When it was built as a concert hall, there was no such thing as recorded sound, and this was often the root of the problem, because recorded sound behaves differently from 'live' sound. Sometimes, musicians and actors on stage required speakers pointing in their direction so that they could hear other people and other instruments - it's called 'foldback', and often this would be too loud, and could be heard by the audience.

Black Ties and Dickie Bows

"When the theatre orchestra was discontinued, there was a big public outcry. It wasn't a happy decision, but, quite honestly, it was an expensive luxury which required a large group of musicians to play for 20 minutes before a performance and then for two 10 minute intervals, with a quick march at the end to empty the theatre. It was a difficult case of the purse versus emotion. The orchestra, traditionally, always had to wear black bow-ties and, for that, their salary included a dress and laundry allowance. When the cut-backs began and the orchestra was made much smaller, they were allowed to wear ordinary ties. Their new contracts stated that they could be "less formally attired"! and so, at the same time, they lost their allowances. And we always had to remember that a musician who can be seen by the audience must be paid more money than one who was unseen. When the orchestra stopped altogether, **Reggie White**, or **Reginald Hamilton-White** as he was called professionally, played the organ for a while and he was followed by **Len Bailey**.

"Talking of dress allowances, the management team didn't have one until **Leslie Beresford** bought a BLUE dress shirt. His cue resulted in the 3 House Managers deciding to 'go' pastel as well! We all ordered off-white shirts because the white ones discoloured so quickly with frequent washing that we had to replace them very often. Sam Bell, the

Manager at that time, was not pleased at the idea of his managers in anything but white, so from then on, we all received a dress allowance!

Shovels at the Ready!

"I was also responsible for booking the bands which played in the Pine Walk Bandstand, and as I came from a services background, I was able to get quite a few **military bands** to play. Sometimes, if the weather was wet, they would come into the Pavilion Theatre or Ballroom to play their concerts. These bands would march round town from the Pavilion, down Westover Road, into the Square via Gervis Place and through the Pleasure Gardens to the Bandstand. One year, I even managed to get a band to bring a couple of horses who stood outside the Pavilion and we were instructed by the Musical Director to ensure that we had shovels at the ready! These marches, of course, needed traffic control from the police, and I can remember an amusing phone call with the police chief when I asked him if he could help us with a **march through town by the Red Army**! Once he'd taken the idea on board, we got them to march from the Pavilion, round the Square and back up Westover Road. There were about a hundred of them, but they couldn't march properly because they were lacking in discipline.

See Edna Everage's story on Page 95

Mind you, they were wonderful musicians and dancers, and it all brought good publicity to the Pavilion and to their show.

Oh Dear!

"There was an unwritten tradition that the Mayor of Bournemouth would invite the stars of the summer shows to a Friday lunchtime get-together with a few drinks. One year, we had **Val Doonican** at the top of the bill with a magician doing his first major booking - he was called **Paul Daniels**. Val had just picked up a brand new pale blue Daimler which he duly brought to the Town Hall and parked in the first place to the east of the main door in the horseshoe. Then Paul arrived in a 3 and a half litre Rover - the one which had a drop down bonnet rather like a wedge. He parked immediately behind Val's Daimler. At the end of the session, Paul, who was dressed - in accordance with the spirit of the era - in high platform shoes, got into his car; somehow, when he started the engine, he managed to get his foot stuck under the accelerator pedal and his car shot forward and drove straight up the back of Val's Daimler, resting on top! He couldn't get the shoe out, and eventually had to take his foot out before he could leave the car. Val, understandably, was not too impressed but he did the funny side eventually. The newspapers, of course, had a field-day!

Snow Joke!

"One of my really great memories of stars concerns **Roy Castle** in the late 1960s. It was a lovely pantomime with the evening performances starting at 7.30 p.m. Soon after the start of one show, I was down in the under-stage staff canteen having a cup of tea, when I was called back upstairs to speak to the Bournemouth Police. It was their control room, warning us that there was a severe snow-storm on the way and that many parts of Dorset were already cut off. He recommended that, as many in the audience would have come from the heart of the county, we should **stop the show and send everybody home**. I wasn't too sure, but an inspector came down and the snow started - great big flakes as big as tennis balls and they began to settle immediately. We had no choice but to stop the show and we sent the people home. Amazingly, 36 hours later, the snow had turned to rain and all the snow had completely disappeared.

Concern for Roy Castle

"It was during the Roy Castle pantomime that we had some concerns about his safety. He was a wonderful entertainer and a lovely person, and he had a great big wicker basket full of costumes which he carried onto the stage. Then he proceeded to dress up as a clown, including some enormous shoes which he used to sway about in. Then, at the end of the show, he would jump from a rostrum, wearing these shoes, into the basket. The basket would shut as he dropped in and he was completely shut inside. The trouble was the shoes caught round his ankles and they were raw.

"**Ted Rogers** was also a wonderful person. It was traditional at the end of pantomimes for the cast and staff to have a party, so I set about organising one. Ted wouldn't have it - he said, "It's my show, and I'll organise and pay for the party." Now, his favourite meal was spaghetti bolognaise, and that's what we all had, all arranged through and by him. It's sad that such a generous man should, some years later, be found destitute.

New Manager for Mike Yarwood

"When **Mike Yarwood** was right at the top of the tree, we had him for summer season - he was as big as anyone else in the country, and during his show, the Stage Doorman quite suddenly and unexpectedly quit. One of the dancers in the show said that a friend of hers was looking for a job, so I asked if he might be interested. When I'd interviewed him, I gave him the job, and he got very friendly with Mike Yarwood. So friendly, in fact, that he became Yarwood's personal agent; now he runs the biggest agency for international artistes in the country. His name is **Bob Voice**, and little did I know at the time how successful he would be.

Ouch!
Not always plain sailing!

"The job wasn't always predictable. On one occasion **I was attacked**; a very well-known and top singing group were on the bill and we were getting complaints from the audience about the sheer high level of their volume. On this occasion, I agreed with them - they **were** far too loud. I went down to the star dressing-room to have a word with them and told them that they must control the sound better and reduce it. Their manager was in the room with them and he objected. I explained that I was trying to protect their reputation and insisted that if they refused to lower the level, I would have to refund money to anyone who complained. At this, the manager told me that I had no right to do that, and took me by the lapels, physically pushing me backwards through the door. I put my fingers round the frame to stop myself from falling over, and he slammed the door shut. Mercifully my foot was in the way and this stopped my hands being shut in the door, but the door hit my nose and smashed my glasses. I immediately went to the company manager and told him what had happened and that I was calling the police. I told them I had been assaulted, that I was the licensee of the theatre and that I wanted him out. I did get a letter of complete apology, but it certainly showed me how unpredictable people can be.

Dear Old Pav is a Splendid Theatre

"I have only two regrets in my life; first that I never met **Sir Laurence Olivier** and secondly that I didn't take up an offer to be **Lenny Henry**'s personal manager. That would have been an amazing roller-coaster of a job. But I've been very fortunate, and I loved my time at Bournemouth, particularly my work for the 'dear old Pav." There's no doubt that it's a splendid theatre, and very much part of me and I hope that part of me is still at the theatre."

76 Years of the Bournemouth Pavilion

Consommé and Sherry!

EILEEN MAIDMENT

*Back in 1950s and 60s, **Flight Refuelling**, who were then based at **Tarrant Rushton**, used to hold a special Dinner-Dance each year in December for all the staff. **Eileen Maidment** of **Bere Regis** remembers them with great affection, and says that her husband used to call them "fairy-tale evenings". She tells the story.*

"They were wonderful occasions - all free, and we usually drove in and parked the car in the **Majestic Multi-Storey Car Park** in Hinton Road. The company had booked us all special spaces there, and we only had to walk through by the **Gaumont** *(now Odeon)* and across the road to the Pavilion. Sometimes, a coach would be hired and we'd all come in together. When we entered the ballroom, we were announced by a professional **Master of Ceremonies**, who was all dressed up in the traditional manner. I smile when I think about it, because he always seemed to get our names wrong! Instead of **Mr. and Mrs. Maidment**, we were always "**Mr. and Mrs. Maid-MONT**", but it really didn't matter because we enjoyed ourselves so much. Then **Sir Alan Cobham** (who owned Flight Refuelling) and his wife would personally welcome us and we were able to find our own table, with

our name cards - but not until after we'd been given a **glass of sherry!**

Then we'd notice that all the waiters were standing in the doorways, all lined up ready for action, and a **loud and ceremonial fanfare** from the dance band signalled their dramatic entrance, and in they came with the food. It was really good, all **five or six courses**, but sometimes we weren't sure what we were eating! But it all tasted fine, and there was a wine waiter constantly hovering round to fill your glass as soon as it was half empty. After the meal - and several glasses of wine! - there was **dancing and a cabaret** - usually at midnight. I particularly recall a demonstration of ballroom dancing by two local dancers, a married couple, who were stunning. The dancing was lovely, all to the sounds of the resident band of **Stanley Osborne and his Pavilion Dance Orchestra** and to **Renaldo and his Latin-American Quartet**. The evening seemed to pass very quickly, and all too soon it was time to go home, and at about 2 a.m., the waiters were all lined up again to serve coffee and consommé, which was very welcome at that hour.

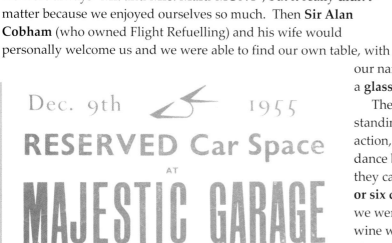

Dec. 9th   1955

RESERVED Car Space

AT

MAJESTIC GARAGE

TOASTS

"HER MAJESTY THE QUEEN"

"THE GUESTS"
Proposed by: M. J. Cobham

"THE COMPANY"
Proposed by: H. C. Harrison
Response by: Sir Alan J. Cobham, K.B.E., A.F.C.

"FOR YEARS OF SERVICE"
The Tokens of Appreciation
to be presented by Lady Cobham

DANCING
until 2 a.m.
to the music of
Stanley Osborne and his Pavilion Dance Orchestra
and
Renaldo and his Latin-American Quartet

MIDNIGHT CABARET
Emerson and Jayne
The Kendor Brothers

---

onsommé will be served in the Foyer to guests making their departure
from 1.30 onwards

MENU

Hors d'Oeuvres Variés

★

Potage Minestrone

★

Filet de Sole Bonne Femme

★

Caneton d'Aylesbury Braisé aux Olives
Petits Pois à la Mênthe
Pommes Parmentier

★

Poire de Comice au Vin Rouge
Glacé Vanille
Petits Fours

★

Café

★

THE WINES

Graves (Cruse et Fils Frères) 1949
Beaune 1947
Port: Cockburn's

They not only served, but were always ready to help anyone who was 'under the weather'!

In the theatre, I can remember pantomimes, one in particular where the fabulous scenery included some lovely lighting and some dancing waterfalls. And another show I remember was '**Evita**', which was wonderful with so much happening on stage. Both the ballroom and the theatre are lovely places and we spent some wonderful evenings in them over the years." *(Incidentally, Flight Refuelling still hold their annual dinner-dances at the Pavilion.)*

Flight Refuelling Dinner-Dance Party in the 1950s

The Bournemouth Pavilion - Celebrating 76 Years of Entertainment

Programme Cover 1950s

The Garry James Duo
DAVE NEAL and GARY MERRIMAN
relive an Ocean Room Season

*If you ever feel a little depressed about life, then give **Dave Neal** and **Gary Merriman** a call - they were the **Garry James Duo**, who played for summer season in the **Ocean Room** in 1975 for fifteen weeks and six nights a week. They, with their enthusiastic memories and joy of life, will lift you straight out of depression. They describe their music as **Country and Western** with an orientation to **middle-of-the-road** - and they played anything and everything.*

"We were based on a stage near the wall at the far end of the **Ocean Room**, looking across to the entrance to the Ocean Bar and the Pleasure Gardens. It was a brilliant atmosphere in there. When we started in May, it was rather quiet, but then, as the season progressed, there was chaos, as night after night, the room was packed full. The manager at that time was **Luis Candal**, and he used to rib us if the music got too slow. He used to say, *"You're too laid-back - up the tempo for goodness sake, they're all too relaxed and not drinking enough!"* But we did provide good quality entertainment. In those days, although there were lots of other places to go for the evening, most people used to gravitate towards the Pavilion.

"We always got good feedback from the audience - in fact, we were bought **so much drink** that we couldn't cope. Once we found that we had **fourteen pints** at the same time, so we had to enlist the help of a local boxer. He was called **Precious Mackenzie** and was one of the bouncers in the Ocean Room; he wasn't very tall, but he had enormous muscles and we made it his job to help us drink all the beer. Night after night, we were given the beer but we couldn't drink too much, otherwise our performances would have suffered. All joking apart, our job was to entertain and amuse, to give pleasure to people wanting a good night out - we weren't going to jeopardise that by drinking too much.

Miss Bournemouth Belle

"One memory will stay for ever - the Ocean Room hosted the six heats and final of the **Miss Bournemouth Belle** competition. The girls used a dressing room which we could see into! As the evening progressed, we could see all sorts of arguments going on in there, and there was talcum powder, clothes, bits of make-up - everything you can imagine being thrown about. We carried on playing 'vampy' music for them, but we could see knickers flying about and we heard strong insults

making the air blue. Then came the moment of truth - we played appropriate music for the girls as they strutted on the dance-floor, and we gave suitable dramatic drum rolls as they walked round and answered questions. The judges nearly always came from upstairs in the Ballroom - if there was a star name band up there, the leader would come down and judge - people like **Ray McVay** and so on. When the final came, it was held in the actual ballroom and we were asked to go up and play as usual.

Too Much Fun to Stop

"Over the weeks, we increased our repertoire, but some numbers were very popular and often requested, and so often repeated. One night, we forgot the words of one of the songs, but we got away with by making it into a joke and a laugh. We started each night at 8.00 p.m. and went on until 11.00. In theory, we had a twenty-minute break in the middle, but we seldom got away. **It was really all too much fun to stop**. What used to amuse us was that the girls, if they didn't have a boy friend with them, used to dance around carrying their handbags.

Adios Amigo

"We've got one very special memory which concerns the miners' hotel between the beach and the B.I.C. The people who stay there all have chest problems, something I well understood, because my dad was a miner. They all had to get back to the hotel by 9.00 p.m. and one night, just before they went, I sang Johnnie Cash's song, '**Dark as a Dungeon**'. The miners loved it, and some of them actually cried with emotion. Some nights, they were chased out of the Ocean Room by the management of the hotel!

"One night, in the height of summer, at about

nine o'clock when we were absolutely jam-packed, some fellow came in and managed to find a seat - we thought he looked a bit shifty. Then - excitement indeed! - a couple of minutes later, two of the biggest policemen we've ever seen arrived at the door with a police dog. They let the dog sniff at some clothes, let him go and he raced around the room and grabbed this man by the arm. The police cuffed him, and as the police took him out, we played '**Adios Amigo**', much to the delight of the audience who joined in with us - a totally spontaneous occasion. On another occasion, we were singing another Johnnie Cash song, '**Ring of Fire**', and the bar staff all came out with a trolley with a cake on it lit up with candles.

"We had really loved that season, but when Luis Candal asked us back for the next season, we said we could only do five nights, and he said that was no good. We've no regrets because we had a wonderful experience there and have had lots of work since. We were always very smart - clean-cut, with good suits and white shirts - and we always had to have a least one change of shirt, because the sweat used to pour off us. What we did wasn't just a performance, it was a job which required total audience participation. They sang, they clapped, they groaned - in fact, we had them exactly where we wanted them. It used to amaze us that people often wanted our autographs, but we were absolute nobodies.

"For a while, the dance band upstairs in the Ballroom was directed by **Achille Roma**, and his music had a slight Latin-American feel to it. One night, we treated ourselves to a meal in the Lucullus Room after the show, and Achille saw us there and demanded that we played a song. But we were too exhausted and just wanted to have a little relaxation. Holiday-makers often used to invite us back to their hotels for a drink where we had a laugh, and the police got to know us quite well, because we were often stopped on the way home.

"It's now thirty years on, but we still live that season. It was such fun."

*At this point in the reminiscing, **Steve Neal** entered - he's Dave's brother, and the stories kept on coming about the Ocean Room.*

"In 1968, I was the lead singer in a band called **Pendulum**, and we were booked for a show called '**Midnight with the Stars in the Ocean Room**'. **Ken Dodd**, **Des O'Connor** and **Tommy Cooper** were all there and it was a fabulous night.

"I can remember **Sunday and Tuesday Beat Nights** in the Ballroom, when we used to dance to **Tony Blackburn and the Ravers**. Tony, of course, went on to be the first DJ on Radio Caroline and recently won the ITV reality programme '**I'm a**

celebrity, get me out of here'. In those days, it wasn't considered the 'done' thing to dance to anything other than live music - oh, yes, and it cost 5/- to enter - just 25p. Then one night - here's a story to savour for ever! We were playing at a private party in the Ocean Room and it was very late at night. In the middle of the performance, **Keith Moon** of **The Who** walked in and he wanted to try out the drum kit. He said, *'I don't know how you play this rubbish drum set - I've just destroyed one upstairs better than this.'* **The Who** had been playing in the ballroom upstairs and they had somehow been smuggled down to this private party. Of course, the organisers asked them to do a number. **Pete Townsend** started to butt all the equipment, and we had to hold the drum kit down to the ground because **Keith Moon** was hitting it so hard.

"A lot of the stars came into the Ocean Room or the ballroom over the years - I can remember seeing **David Bowie**, **Dave Dee**, **Zoot Money**, **Manfred Mann**.... There were so many. **Noddy Holder** was there once. Many of them were young and hardly famous, but they all went on to become big stars. I'm really pleased to have all these memories - the Pavilion has always been a good meeting place, and I've met so many people there."

The Ocean Room was originally the Popular Restaurant, which during the 2nd World War was the British restaurant. It's now called 'Oasis', has been taken over by Beach Services and, in 2006, is closed.

Music, Bombs, Boult and Britten

GWEN CHAPMAN & ELAINE STOCK
look back on history in the making

*Gwen Chapman lives in Poole, in the same house that she was born in some decades ago, and she has many memories of the Bournemouth Pavilion. She shares them here with her friend, **Elaine Stock**.*

"I'm so pleased to add a memory or two in the book on the Pavilion. It has certainly given me very many happy hours. In my early memories, I saw it as a very **grand place** and I always felt honoured to be there. I can remember seeing **Gwen Ffrangcson-Davies** and **John Gielgud** in 'Macbeth' in 1942, and it was where I first saw an opera at about the age of 12 or 13. This was '**Rigoletto**' and I recall that the Duke of Mantua was dressed in yellow, and sung by **Arthur Servent**. Then, some time after this, in 1954, came a season of **Italian Opera**. I know we saw '**Elisir d'Amore**' on this occasion with **Kyra Vane**, **Carlo Zambighi**, **Guido Mazzini** and **Arturo la Porta**, with **Maestro Manrico de Tura** as conductor. In 1956, another visit from Italian Opera brought a host of beautiful performances - '**La Boheme**', '**Tosca**', '**Madame Butterfly**', '**Cavalleria Rusticana**', '**Pagliacci**' and '**The Barber of Seville**'.

"We didn't always sit down for the performances, but used the promenade at the back of the Circle, and we stood and watched from there, because the prices were very cheap. Also, we never thought the seats were very well arranged, and it could be very hard to see sometimes. I have lots of memories, although sometimes the dates aren't too clear, but I know that the **Welsh National Opera Company** made it's first ever visit to England at the Pavilion, and, when I saw the play '**Waiting for Godot**', many people just walked out. I didn't understand it at all and it certainly wasn't entertainment, but I'm really glad we went to see it. During the war years, there was a special printed warning in the programmes about the dangers of the war. And they proved very apposite in 1943. Our visit to the Pavilion on that day was quite momentous and totally unforgettable.

"In fact, it was an historic day - certainly the worst day that Bournemouth has ever suffered - Sunday, May 23rd. Earlier in the day, bombs had been dropped on the centre of Bournemouth. A friend and I had booked for the concert in the afternoon, and I met my friend Sheila Parkhouse at Ashley Cross to catch a **Hants and Dorset** bus into

WEEK COMMENCING TUESDAY, JUNE 2nd   NIGHTLY at 6.30
Matinees : Wednesday and Saturday, at 2.0

H. M. TENNENT, LTD.
presents
JOHN GIELGUD and GWEN FFRANGCON-DAVIES
in

MACBETH

By WILLIAM SHAKESPEARE

Characters :

Duncan, King of Scotland	...	...	...	...	...	CHARLES MAUNSELL
Malcolm) his	...	...	...	...	...	EMRYS JONES
Donalbain ...) Sons	...	...	...	...	...	JOHN SHEPHERD
Macbeth) Generals of	...	...	...	...	...	JOHN GIELGUD
Banquo) the King's Army	...	...	...	...	...	LEON QUARTERMAINE
Macduff	...	...	...	...	...	FRANCIS LISTER
Lennox	...	...	...	...	...	ALAN BADEL
Ross ...	...	...	...	...	...	ALEC MANGO
Menteith	Noblemen of	...	...	...	...	GEORGE WOODBRIDGE
Angus ...	Scotland	...	...	...	...	FRANK THORNTON
Caithness		...	...	...		FREDERICK ANNERLEY

Bournemouth. This was long before instant news and local radio, so we knew nothing about the bombing, although we had heard distant explosions. I suppose we realised that something was wrong, but we did what most people would do - went to see! When we arrived at the Square, it was visually evident that something terrible had happened. The streets were packed with fire engines, **Punshon Church** was in ruins at the bottom of Richmond Hill, and the whole area was a mess. We made our way to Old Christchurch Road, stepping over fire hoses and pavements melting in the heat and then we saw our lovely **Beales** shop in total devastation. I remember having a most peculiar feeling; there was still the concert to go to, or would it have been cancelled? That all mingled with the horror that such dreadful things could happen, and we feared that another bomb might drop on the Pavilion. But we walked on, thinking that the musicians would already have arrived. Quite honestly, our minds were in terrible torment. I can't remember if the concert hall was full or not, but I know that the conductor of the

ballet. Before we went, I made it very clear that they were under no circumstances allowed to rustle sweet papers. Then during the performance, someone behind us did just that, and one of the children turned round and asked me to tell them off!"

Bournemouth Municipal Orchestra was **Sir Adrian Boult**. As he reached the rostrum, he picked up his baton, solemnly turned to the audience and said that he had changed the programme slightly. **'Cockaigne Overture'** by Elgar was replaced by **'Nimrod'** in honour of the people who had just suffered so much. It was a great moment, bringing tears to our eyes. Somehow, all the people there and the orchestra playing on as if nothing had happened was like an act of defiance, and we were proud to be there.

"We saw many famous musicians at the Pavilion - **Benjamin Britten** conducted his own opera, **'Albert Herring'** which I hated. I didn't like **'Billy Budd'** either. But **Sir Henry Wood** was brilliant when we saw him conducting Dvorak's **'New World' Symphony**. Later, as a teacher, I took a party of Middle School children to the Pavilion to see

Gwen with Oscar, who doesn't go to the Pavilion

Early Photograph of Concert Hall with original glass chandeliers. This was the home of the Bournemouth Municipal Orchestra

Reviewing the Old

JACK and DI STRAIGHT

Jack Straight was appointed as staff reporter on the Evening Echo, Bournemouth in 1954. For many years he reviewed shows at all the Bournemouth entertainment venues, including the Pavilion, which he describes as 'the old wedding cake'! He and his wife Di have many memories of shows there. Their thoughts will remind us of so many top-rate performers which have played at the theatre.

"The display of programmes and posters in the side corridors of the Pavilion reminds us of the big names of the acting profession who appeared there in the early post-Second World War years. Even by the 1950s, when I first joined the audiences there, stars - some from Hollywood's big block-buster films - could be seen on stage. One I particularly remember was **Tyrone Power** in Bernard Shaw's 'The Devil's Disciple' - this was excellent, and who could forget a young **Michael Caine** in his early days as an actor, in 'The Long and the Short and the Tall', a wartime play by Willis Hall about group of British soldiers who captured a Japanese soldier in

the jungle?

In those days, the Pavilion was on the principal touring circuit for major companies, opera and ballet in particular. 'The Sadlers Wells Opera Company' brought some very high standard productions, and the rival London Festival Ballet had stars to match them. Headed by **Anton Dolin** and **Alicia Markova**, there was also a rising young principal, **John Gilpin** dancing the classical roles, but most unforgettable in his creation of the lead in 'Witchboy', a brilliant new work on folk lore. The

The Long and the Short and the Tall

O.8 45 Jan. 7, 1942 Security Classification Restricted	
From: 4 Inf. Bn.	
To: Main 2 Inf. Div.	
Routine Patrol.	1 Sgt., 1 Cpl., 4 Riflemen, 1 R. T Operator.
Area N. (Jahaal)	Map reference 426719 428712. Call sign "Blue".

465	Sgt. Mitchem, R.	...	...	...	...	JOHN COLIN
839	Cpl. Johnstone, E.	...	...	...	JOHN TRENAMAN
594	L. Cpl. Macleish, A. J.	...	...	HENRY CADDOW
632	Pte. Whitaker, S.	...	...	...	TERENCE STAMP
777	Pte. Evans, T. E.	...	...	...	JOHN REES
877	Pte. Bamforth, C.	...	...	...	MICHAEL CAINE
611	Pte. Smith, P.	...	...	...	LEONARD FENTON
Japanese Soldier	...	...	...	...	SAMMY WONG

Direction : JEROME BREHONY
(From a production by Anthony Page)

Decor : ALAN TAGG

Production : ANDREW BROUGHTON

PROGRAMME OF MUSIC BY THE

Pavilion Theatre Orchestra

Under the direction of BYRON BROOKE   Organist : HAROLD COOMBS

Evenings at 7.30 and Matinees at 2.15—
Intermezzo, "In Buddha's Realm" ... ... *Armandola*
Military Waltz, "The Grenadiers" ... ... *Waldteufel*
March Medley, "Passing of the Regiments" ... ... *arr. Winter*
Between Acts 1 and 2—
Descriptive Piece, "Jungle Drums" ... ... *Ketelby*
Melodies from the Musical Play, "The King and I" ... *Richard Rodgers*

The action of the play takes place in the Malayan jungle early in 1942, the Japanese were being held by British Forces 20 miles to the north.

At this time, the British Far Eastern Command was centred on Singapore, our apparently impregnable fortress, 400 miles to the south. The Malay Peninsula was occupied by British Forces, many of them inexperienced and unused to jungle warfare.

———

There will be one interval of 15 minutes

Scenery and properties constructed and painted in the English Stage's Company's workshops. Additional equipment by J. Arthur Rank Productions Ltd. Cigarettes by Players. Firearms by Bapty & Co. Sound Equipment by Stagesound (London) Ltd.

The use of the song *Bless 'Em All* is included by kind permission of Keith Prowse Music Publishing Co. Ltd.

Attractions appearing at the Pavilion Theatre are booked in conjunction with Howard & Wyndham Ltd., 9 Grafton Street, London, W.1.

Company Manager	JEROME BREHONY
Deputy Stage Manager	TIMOTHY PEARCE
Assistant Stage Manager	HOWARD DALEY

Wells' dancers later became the Royal Ballet tourers, with some fine young dancers and notable among them, one Margaret Barbieri, an entrancing star from South Africa. Later, we were to witness the sadness of **Margot Fonteyn**, in a farewell tour and the tragic end to a great career. She was a wonderful and graceful dancer.

(Memory continues on next page)

Pavilion

15 NOV 1976

Star qualities

DAME MARGOT was undoubtedly the star last night but the luminary in the ascendant was the incomparable Lynn Seymour: and one could say that even with the challenging Maina Gielgud in the company.

Dame Margot in her regal progress around her realm still commands awe and reverential treatment in any assessment of her dancing. But one sensed the poignancy engendered, particularly in the Swan Lake pas de deux, when the music is that affecting violin-'cello duet and there is the hint of parting between the Prince and his unearthly love.

Was this the swan song of Fonteyn, certainly so far as the provinces are concerned?

If so her devotees will remember her departing on a high note, thanks in no small part to the superb partnering of David Wall, clearly also a disciple.

Watching her final duet, the Romeo and Juliet to the Berlioz score and Skibine's choreography, one was tempted to think that time had indeed stood still and this was Peggy Hookham of true Juliet age. The magic had worked.

The gamine features of Lynn Seymour have matured and it is some years since we last saw her on this stage. It may be something of a cliche to say that she gives her all in whatever role she dances.

But in the two pas de deux she performed and danced with every fibre, every nerve of her supple body.

Words would have been an intrusion into the works she expressed, from the loneliness turned into joy of Solitaire to the sinuous passions of Reflections which she and her partner Robert North had choreographed. This was a bonus in all the glitter of gala ballet.

I yield to no one in my admiration of Miss Gielgud. The Sleeping Beauty pas de deux

with David Ashmole deserved the plaudits.

Circumstances, however, forced her to repeat the Forme et Ligne pas seul, which is a speciality comedy number written for her — we missed out on the Black Swan duo because Alain Dubreuil was indisposed.

To my mind the creaking door sounds and electronic burps are amusing but the joke wears a bit thin, despite La Gielgud's genius for comic expression. One almost expected her to grin broadly and perhaps wink when in the romantic mood later on.

Disappointment of the evening was the Monotones opening number. The Satie music which sounds so haunting in orchestrated form, loses such a lot even when played as well as Michael Bassett's piano accompaniment was.

Despite Alfreda Thorogood, Wayne Eagling and David Ashmole who are all excellent soloists the piece seemed to have lost the beguiling quality it had in the Royal Ballet version we have twice seen here.

Concerto — the Shostakovitch-MacMillan work — with Miss Thorogood and Mr. Eagling was pleasant with some remarkable limb sculpture. James Slater's orchestra though not overworked, played more than adequately.
— **J.S.**

Courtesy of the Daily Echo, this review of what was Margot Fonteyne's farewell provincial performance appeared in November 1976.

"New ballets which became firm favourites were 'La Fille Mal Gardee' (Ninette de Valois tried to find an English title, but it was never forthcoming!), 'Pineapple Poll' (Charles Mackerras's brilliant adaptation of Arthur Sullivan's Gilbert and Sullivan scores) featuring in a lead role, Bournemouth's **Kerrison Cooke**, and 'Elite Syncopations' to jazz tunes by Scott Joplin. This latter production involved taking the set right to the back brick wall of the stage, something the theatre-goer had never seen before. Our only other acquaintance with that particular part of the theatre was while watching rehearsals conducted by the distinguished Russian choreographer, **Vladimir Bourmeister** for his production of 'The Snow Maiden' with music by Tchaikovsky for the Festival Ballet Company. One enduring memory we have is the sight of a formidable little figure seen in the theatre foyer debating vigorously with a member of the audience the merits of her company. She was **Marie Rambert**, a pioneer of ballet in this country.

"Dancing of a different style would be featured in the importation of national dance companies from Iron Curtain countries; the Georgian State Company, the Ukrainians, Rumanians, Hungarians and the Osipov Balalaika Orchestra of Moscow. These were all enjoyed by enthusiastic audiences, but there were some token protests from dissident members of the public. Their successors in the post-Communist era are the Ukrainian Opera Company from Odessa who impressed an unusually large audience. Our own permanent import from Rumania was, of course, **Constantine Silvestri**, the brilliant little maestro who became the principal conductor of the Bournemouth Symphony Orchestra in their days at the Winter Gardens, but whose name appeared on the advertising in the Pavilion programmes.

Reporters were nameless

"My days at the Echo were before reporters names were used, so we were all virtually anonymous, but my initials J.S. were frequently seen for shows at the Bournemouth Pavilion. All the big shows came here, and we saw many pre-West End productions and many after-London tours as well. Virtually all the top names came to the theatre at some time or other. In contrast, we were privileged to see and hear **Marlene Dietrich** who had the audience eating out of her hand from the moment she appeared. Members of the audience were throwing roses on to the stage for her to pick up, and we often wondered if they were planted in the audience especially!

"As we said earlier, many of the established stars of the stage as well as the up-and-coming actors appeared on stage at the Pavilion. The Newly-formed Welsh National Opera Company did us the honour of one visit, which was not very well attended, I recall. One of our particular favourites was their performance of Benjamin Britten's 'Billy Budd' - this was powerful stuff with excellent staging and really top class singers.

Thursday 31 May

Billy Budd
Benjamin Britten

Libretto by E. M. Forster and Eric Crozier after the story by Herman Melville

Characters in order of appearance

Captain Vere	Nigel Douglas
First Mate	Ralph Hamer
Second Mate	Peter Massocchi
Mr. Flint, *Sailing Master*	Bryan Drake
Bosun	Glynne Thomas
Donald	John Gibbs
Maintop	Neville Ackerman
Novice	Ramon Remedios
Squeak, *Ship's Corporal*	Arthur Davies
Mr. Redburn, *First Lieutenant*	Julian Moyle
Mr. Ratcliffe, *Lieutenant*	David Gwynne
Claggart, *Master-at-Arms*	Forbes Robinson
Red Whiskers	Stuart Kale
Arthur Jones	Gordon Whyte
Billy Budd	Terence Sharpe
Novice's Friend	Eric Roberts
Dansker	Frank Olegario
Cabin Boy	Andrew Whitfield

Ratings, Officers, Midshipmen, Marines, Powder-monkeys, Drummers.

Conductor:	**Richard Armstrong**
Producer:	**Michael Geliot**
Designer:	**Roger Butlin**
Lighting	**Robert Bryan** and **Matt L. English**

Scenery, costumes and properties made in the company's workshops
Assistant to the Designer/George Hunt
Scenery painted by Rita Taylor and Peter Raymond

Forbes Robinson appears by permission of the General Administrator, Royal Opera House, Covent Garden.

The boys in the opera appear by permission of the Headmaster, the Summerbee Junior School, Bournemouth.
Roger Butlin is Head of Design at the Greenwich Theatre.

Albert Finney took the lead in a strange piece by John Arden, 'Armstrong's Last Goodnight'. This was paired with 'Trelawney of the Wells' by Pinero. The catalogue of stars who entertained us at the Pavilion is endless - how about these: **Gladys Cooper, Flora Robeson, Cecily Courtneidge** and her other half, **Jack Hulbert, Dulcie Gray** and **Michael Denison, Roger Livesey, Robertson Hare** (on several occasions) and **Phyllis Calvert**. And if that's not enough to make us gasp, here're a few more - **Margaret Lockwood, Julia Lockwood, Richard Todd, George Cole, Marius Goring, Joan Greenwood, Irene Handl, Leslie Phillips, Glynis Johns, Evelyn Laye, Barry Sinclair, Bernard Miles,**

Anthony Quayle, Tony Britton, Roy Hudd, Jimmy Edwards, Spike Milligan, Tommy Trinder, Richard Murdoch - the list just goes on and on.

"Our favourite pantomime was without doubt one of the later ones (1993 - 'Babes in the Wood') when **Roy Hudd** and **Jack Tripp** starred with actor **Geoffrey Hughes**, who later became Onslow in the BBC sitcom 'Keeping Up Appearances' and then Vernon in the ITV Sunday evening series of 'Heartbeat'. Jack Tripp had always been extremely funny in the days of the 'Fol-De-Rols' revues and with Roy Hudd he performed a mirror-image scene which was brilliant and hilarious.

Television Stars Galore

"My years as theatre critic were at a time when stars of television were pleased to come and visit the regional theatres, and the Entertainments Manager at that time, **Sam Bell**, was able to persuade many of the top comedians and singers to tread the Pavilion boards. As we've said, it was the big ballet and opera companies which we liked, especially Sadler's Wells Opera and the Festival Ballet. They always seemed to attract large audiences and it was very sad for the Pavilion and for Bournemouth when they stopped visiting.

"'Waiting for Godot' was quite a landmark in local theatre because it was the first time that members of the audience walked out in large numbers; this wasn't just a prudish Bournemouth audience, but they were leaving early all over the country. **Peter Bull**, who starred in the production, told us that in the north of England, they used to perform the play without the pauses so that they could get an earlier train home!

"The face of drama was definitely changing fast in the nineteen sixties and seventies; we saw the first provincial tour of the controversial musical 'Hair' when the cast took off all their costumes and danced naked. We're not prudes, but we didn't much like this so-called fashionable trend towards simulated sex and nudity, so I was quite disapproving in my review. In the same week, a large Christian convention was taking place at the old Town Hall in Braidley Road, and they wrote to me complimenting me on my stand. I heard an amusing tale from **Elaine Page** (who was in 'Hair', but not when it played the Pavilion) who told me

Vol. 3 No. 13

Entertainments Manager
for the Borough of Bournemouth :
LESLIE BERESFORD, A.I.M.Ent.(Dip.) A.M.B.I.M.

Week commencing Monday 5th March 1979

Nightly at 7.45   Matinees: Wednesday and Saturday at 2.30

MARK FURNESS for BARBARA PLAYS LTD

presents

FIONA RICHMOND

in

YES, WE HAVE NO PYJAMAS

by ANDRE LAUNAY

with

JACK CARLTON

KEVAN SHEEHAN

DEBORAH BRAYSHAW

FIONA DOUGLAS-STEWART

PETRINA DERRINGTON

GEORGIE PHILLIPS

| DIRECTED BY |
| **VICTOR SPINETTI** |

that, as is customary, for the final curtain calls, the cast were told to hold hands across the stage; she says that she reached over to the male actor next to her, but it wasn't his hand that she grabbed!

"Other shows seemed to break the decency mould of entertainment, too. **Fiona Richmond** played in show called 'Yes, We Have No Pyjamas', a show which must have encouraged the dirty mack brigade into the theatre, and I was really scathing in the review. Fiona actually phoned me the next morning and was extremely pleasant, saying that she had received a lot worse reviews, which was pretty caustic. And dear **Irene Handl** actually called into the office, complete with her little dog, a chihuahua, nestling in her bosom. She played an agony aunt in 'Dear Miss Hope'; I didn't like it and wrote a cod letter to her as my review. "And what did you want to know, dear?" she said in that famous voice. I was non-plussed, and thanked her for her concern. It was all very amicable.

107

PAVILION THEATRE
BOURNEMOUTH
Entertainments Manager for Bournemouth Corporation :
SAMUEL J. BELL
Box Office Telephone : 25861

Week commencing Monday, 9th October, 1967

Nightly at 7.45   Matinees: Wednesday and Saturday at 2.30

Frederic Piffard Productions Ltd.
present
IRENE HANDL
in

Dear Miss Hope

A Comedy by Dennis Woodford

with

ROBIN WENTWORTH
TUCKER McGUIRE   ELIZABETH TYRRELL
DUDLEY OWEN   SALLY HARRISON   MATTHEW WALTERS
and
JEREMY HAWK

Produced by ROBERT PEAKE   Designed by John C. Piper

"There were, over the years, quite a few religious-based shows, including 'Godspell' which was entertaining but in some ways flawed in its format. We also saw a stage version of the famous Oberammergau cycle of plays and this was very movingly acted indeed. Religion from another viewpoint came with the excellent productions of 'Fiddler on the Roof' - first, an amateur production by the Bournemouth and Boscombe Light Opera Company which moved the local Jewish community to block book the circle seats one night, to watch the show which was acted entirely without makeup. And then there was a professional production starring **Alfred Marks**. Going back to the Bournemouth and Boscombe Company, they achieved a unique double with their much acclaimed 'Hello Dolly', which so impressed Sam Bell, that he booked the show for a second week later in the season. An amazing and unrepeatable event took place in another of their shows 'Half a Sixpence'. At the end of a polished performance, a tall, rather military-looking elderly man appeared in front of the curtain and said how much he had enjoyed the show. He was **David Heneker**, who had written the score some twenty-five years before! Other local amateur companies included the bi-annual 'Gang Show' staged by boys and girls from the Scout Movement.

Richard Briers The Third

"A thought-provoking two-hander called 'When the Wind Blows' arose out of a cartoon character and related to the reactions of simple-minded, trusting couple to the threat of a nuclear strike when it actually happened. This was beautifully handled by husband and wife **John**

Nettleton and **Deidre Doone**. A chiller of a different era was provided by the excellent Prospect Company, offering two works by great dramatists - 'Richard III' played by another **Richard Briers**; this was unlikely casting about which he later joked that he had emptied theatres throughout the land. Admittedly, the house wasn't full but those present enjoyed his interpretation and the whole production. It was paired with a Chekhov piece with **Derek Jacobi** in the lead.

Pavilion Theatre
Bournemouth
Entertainments Manager
for Bournemouth Corporation:
SAMUEL J. BELL

Wednesday, Thursday, and Saturday, November 29, 30, and December 2 at 7.30
Matinees: Thursday and Saturday, November 30 and December 2, at 2.30

Prospect Theatre Company
Director Toby Robertson
in association with the Arts Council of Great Britain
presents
RICHARD III
by William Shakespeare

Directed by Toby Robertson and Kenny McBain
Designed by Kenneth Rowell
Music by Carl Davis
Lighting by Michael Outhwaite
Fight arranged by B. H. Barry

Friday only at 7.30
A CRISIS OF CONSCIENCE
A new version of Ivanov by Anton Chekhov

"A notable play of the 1960s was Neil Simon's 'Barefoot in the Park', prior to London and starring **Mildred Natwick** who also played brilliantly the role of the mother in the film version. Also in the cast was another actor which Hollywood connections **Daniel**, son of **Raymond Massey**. Interesting to watch but difficult to hear was the much-loved American television star, **Phil Silvers**. Sgt. Bilko became Pseudolus in 'A Funny Thing Happened on the Way to the Forum'. Other unlikely 'Romans' in the production were **Bill Kerr** and **Arnold Ridley**, who later had his greatest success of all in the wonderful BBC1 sit-com, 'Dad's Army'.

Pavilion Theatre
Bournemouth.
Entertainments Manager
for Bournemouth Corporation
SAMUEL J. BELL

Week commencing Monday 18 February 1974
Nightly 7.45.. Matinees: Wednesday and Saturday 2.30

Paul Elliott and Duncan C. Weldon (for Triumph Theatre Productions Ltd.) present

PHIL SILVERS
in

A Funny Thing Happened
on the Way to the Forum

A Musical Comedy based on the plays of Plautus
Book by BURT SHEVELOVE and LARRY GELBART
Music and Lyrics by STEPHEN SONDHEIM

with

JIMMY THOMPSON
BILL KERR

GORDON	ANTHONY
CLYDE	MORTON
TREVOR JONES	LESLEY DUFF

JOANNE WEST
and
ARNOLD RIDLEY

Directed by BURT SHEVELOVE
Designed by TERRY PARSONS

Musical Director MICHAEL REED
Lighting Designer BARRY GRIFFITHS
Original Choreography by MARC BREAUX

A Billingham Forum Theatre production
This production first staged at the Forum Theatre, Billingham, on 24th December, 1973

"Some magical effects were achieved on the Pavilion's large stage. In 1985, The Compass Company, led by **Sir Anthony Quayle**, with **Tony Britton** in the cast, staged 'The Tempest'. Despite the lack of audience support, it was a memorable experience. As was the Sadlers' Wells 'Samson and Delilah', with **Charles Craig** in fine voice but it was the final scene of a tumbling temple which stole the show. In more recent times, the Russian Supremacy in the art of ballet came in their touring show 'Stars of the Bolshoi Ballet.' As I remarked at the time, "Nobody dances quite like them." I must mention the highly popular visits of the D'Oyly Carte Opera Company presenting the Savoy Operas of Gilbert and Sullivan. Sadly all these superb moments of theatre died away as the big shows stopped playing, and there was a further deterioration when the Poole Arts Centre opened with a smaller purpose-built theatre which began to take the good quality touring plays.

Pavilion has Lovely Atmosphere

"The atmosphere in the Pavilion is very warm and it is a lovely theatre with a décor which is not too over-the-top. For a while, the ethos was almost totally destroyed by a newly-painted colour scheme of deep maroon. When the Safety Curtain came down, that too was the same awful oppressive colour, but mercifully, the scheme didn't last too long. Some parts of the auditorium are bad for hearing and also for seeing - in some seats, you couldn't see the legs of the ballet dancers which was a certain disadvantage!

Richard Baker Hiking in Shorts

"Not only the theatre played a big part in the entertainment of the town, but the ballroom did as well. Apart from the obvious dances and functions, we were very much involved with an annual Press Ball. These were really important and became big events and a major part of the town's social scene. Each year, we published a special newspaper with fun stories and silliness, and we tried to get a well-known star each year to pay us a visit. My Echo colleague, photographer **Harry Ashley**, was one of the prime movers in this, and he travelled across the country to persuade artistes to join us. One year, he succeeded in booking comedian **Benny Hill**; when he arrived, we asked him if there was anything he wanted and he said, "All I want is a girl!" By contrast, one year we had newsreader **Richard Baker** who amazed us all with an act where he dressed in shorts and sung a hiking song. Other guests included **Fenella Fielding** and **Julia Foster**. These Press Balls were designed to make money for

Richard Baker, of BBC Television, took part in the cabaret and is seen here in his sketch
" The Happy Hiker."

charities and were for many years held at the Pavilion Ballroom.

"After a few years, we found other ways of raising money for the charities; including Boxing Tournaments, again held in the Pavilion Ballroom. It was in the days when boxing was a very special sport, and all the guests used to dress in black ties and evening suits. They were very high class and they raised lots of money. But it always seemed strange to see a big boxing ring in the middle of the dance floor.

The Dear Old Wedding Cake

"Yes, we've had many, many happy hours of entertainment in the Bournemouth Pavilion - let's hope that the dear old 'wedding cake' will live on for many more notable memories."

J.S.

Just Like Dog-Racing Traps!

JEAN FRENCH and MARGARET AMBROSE
look back on the 1960s BOX OFFICE

Jean and Margaret are sisters and they worked in the Bournemouth Pavilion Box Office during the 1960s. And they seemed to be very good times.

"We sat for hours and hours in that little room just off the foyer, peeking through **the tiny windows** which had shutters on them rather like **dog-racing traps**. When you opened them, they used to shoot up, but they were necessary, even in those days, because we were totally shut away from anyone with mischief in mind. They were busy days - on a Saturday afternoon, the **queue would sometimes stretch right through the foyer** and out into the forecourt and around the fountain. We would be booking for six weeks in advance, so if every house was going to be full during a twice-

off strips. Prices varied from show to show, but the top seat would be probably **12s. 6d**, then **10s. 6d**, then **8s 6d** and then **6s. 0d** that's from about 65p to 30p. Goodness knows how we can still remember that. The **Ballet and the Opera** always did well and so did the **Black and White Minstrel Show**, but that show was a tremendous disappointment because all the music had been pre-recorded and the singers just mimed. I suppose that was an advantage in some ways, because many people used to complain about the acoustics in the Pavilion. Round about **Row J in the stalls** was very difficult and they used to call it the dip. **'Don't put us in the dip, whatever you do,'** they used to say! But there weren't usually any comments about anything behind Row J.

nightly season, we would be dealing with nearly **110,000 tickets**! It was great fun when **Ken Dodd** was appearing, because in the mornings, he would come out into the foyer with his famous **tickling stick** and pretend to tickle all the ladies in the queue with it! They loved it. **Arthur Askey**, too, used to come round, and he was a really cheeky little man - really nice.

"There were no computers in those days, but all the tickets were printed up in booklets with **tear-**

Dam Burst for Real

"Our dad - **Len Pope** - used to work on the electrics-maintenance team with the Chief Electrician/Technician who was appropriately called **Les Darke**, and I remember him coming home very late one night, because there had been a bit of a catastrophe. In the Harry Fielding Summer Shows - **'The Big Shows'** they were called - there was often a big spectacular scene. One show featured a water effect when **a dam was supposed to burst**. On this night, it wasn't only the dam which had burst, but so had the tanks of water under the stage, and the whole dressing room area was flooded. He and all the staff had to spend the night getting it all cleaned up and working again for the next evening. And in the pantomime, '**Goody Two Shoes**', with **Mr. Pastry**, the bridge over a waterfall gave way when some of the **Dagenham Girl Pipers** were standing on it. No one was hurt, though. Our dad didn't talk about his job much, but he was involved with the installation of the new carbon-arc lights for follow-spotting in the projection (lime) box at the back of the circle. But we know he loved his job.

We are the Ovaltineys

"One night, after the interval, the **Safety Curtain** wouldn't go back up, and all the audience had to be sent home. I can remember having to give refunds as they left and again in the morning. And another funny story is when we had '**The Ovaltineys' Show**' - they were, at one time, very popular in a daily early evening show on **Radio Luxembourg**. People could only buy tickets if they came in with a label from a tin of **Ovaltine!**

"We can't get used to the **Coffee Bar** in the west foyer - it used to be the **Gentlemen's Toilet** and we find it hard to accept the change. And talking of the foyer, we can remember a one-armed **commissionaire** (they call them Receptionists nowadays). He was named **Jock**, and he used to get very annoyed about the fountain in the forecourt; he used to shout, '**Turn that blooming fountain off - it makes me want to go to the loo!**' Mrs. Chandler, whom everybody called **Chandy**, was the **Head Cashier** and **Stanley Hart** was the **Box Office Manager**; he was lovely, a very quiet man, and we used to call him 'Father'. In those days, there used to be a special small box office near where the Reception Desk is today, and it was here that we sold tickets for that night's performance only. When we were in there, we used to talk to **Mrs. Thomas** - Tommy - who was the **chief usherette** and she was lovely. Of course, they're not called usherettes any more, but **Bluecoats**. Funny how things change.

Super Theatre but no end seats

"The Pavilion is a **super place**, it's a real theatre, **a proper theatre**, and for us it's just perfect. Sometimes we

didn't think so especially when we had difficult customers. Some always insisted that they must have **an end seat**, but, of course, they didn't realise that not everybody could have such a seat - there had to be someone sitting in the rows. Another problem would be if the house was nearly full, but we had groups of three seats left. We weren't allowed to sell them separately, for obvious reasons, but people used to get really uptight about it. It's like us all, really, isn't it? We all like things to be right for us and tend not to think of others. Some people wouldn't buy tickets at the extreme sides of the balcony because they complained that could see straight through into the sides of the stage.

5s. 0d taken from our Wages

"Another aspect was that we had to **pay any shortfall** there might be in the takings; there wasn't often any discrepancy, but it could happen especially as we were dealing with so much money in a short period of time. So they used to take 5s. 0d (25p) out of our weekly wages. In the summer months, when the tickets were going fast, we used to have little competitions between ourselves to see how much money we could take. We'd say, "Let's try and take £200 between 10.00 a.m. and 1.00 p.m.""

"Get me out of here!"

"They were happy days, and we enjoyed our work there. I always remember when **Russ Conway** played there, lots of women would crowd round the stage door and when he left at the Stage Door, they would scream and throw pairs of knickers at him. He used to hate this kind of adulation and would jump in his car saying to driver, 'For goodness sake, get me out of here!'"

Culinary Reminiscences - 1950s/1960s

JOHN CLARK LOOKS BACK
AS A CHEF

John Clark's memories concern the kitchens in the late 1950s and early 1960s, working there for three separate spells, twice as the Sauce Chef in the 1950s, and then again in the 1960s as the Head Chef, when he was invited back by the then General Manager, Peter Wass. He explains that the kitchens cooked for both the restaurants (Lucullus and Popular) and also the Ballroom, and so it was a busy and demanding place to work. He recalls how, for a time, the famous Lucullus Restaurant changed its name to something a little more mundane - The Captain's Table, but it wasn't long before the original name was restored, and this has remained to the present day. Incidentally, the name "Lucullus" refers to a Roman Licinius Lucullus, who was famous for his lush and expensive banquets.

During his early days, John worked with a Head Chef called Mario Leto - though everyone called him 'Jack'! - who later moved to the Bournemouth College as a Lecturer and who also wrote a book on the use of meats in catering, a book which is still an important feature in the training of chefs.

In this picture - not too clear, but taken about 1960, John is in the front row, third from left. Others in the picture include, Betty, Roy, Malcolm, Mario (Head Chef - fifth from left), Ralph, Bill, Betty, Darkie, Tom, Marcel and Margaret. The top picture represents

only part of the full team, but a complete complement working for a major function would have been about thirty staff, as seen in the picture below. This is an interesting photograph in that it shows the small white hats worn by the waitresses - the only picture we've found of them. Notice, too, the pocket handkerchiefs and the button holes!

Coyyright: Haviland Photo Finishing, Boscombe

At that time, John says, "all the soups, sauces and mayonnaises were made by the appropriate staff on the premises from scratch. Nowadays, much of the food is prepared elsewhere by caterers and brought in for the staff to complete. I think I'd find it hard working in these conditions which are so different from my days.

"In those days, the Pavilion was the **main and most important place** for functions in the area. So it was that in winter months, the restaurants and the ballroom were very busy indeed, and all the major functions were held there. **Walls Ice Cream** once held a convention there, with about 2,000 people. The whole building was taken over, and - appropriately! - the food was a cold buffet. And when **Smiths Crisps** held a special function, there were Smiths Crisps on the menu!

Menu

Assorted Hors d'Oeuvres

———

Clear Tomato Consomme

———

Fillet of Scotch Salmon
White Wine Sauce

———

Mousse of Ham in Aspic
Japanese Salad

———

Roast Chicken and Stuffing
Game Chips   Bread Sauce
Garden Peas in Butter
Olivette Potatoes
SMITH'S CRISPS

———

Sliced Pineapple
Neapolitan Ice Cream
Sweetmeats

———

Coffee

"I well remember **Peter Ward** - he was the pattiserie - and, in the late 1950s, he was asked to design a special feature for a Mayor's Reception, and he made a **complete model of Bournemouth Pier in sugar**, pastiage, sugar paste, and icing-sugar. The finished product, in white, was five feet long and accurate in design, having been modelled on the actual plans of the pier."

Coupe Florida
Mixed Fruit Cocktail

———

Crème St. Germain aux Croutons
Green Pea Soup with Sippets

———

Truite de Rivière Meunière
River Trout Fried in Butter

———

Dindonneau de Norfolk Farci Rôti à la Broche
Roast Norfolk Turkey with Chipolata Sausages and Game Chips, Bread Sauce and Stuffing

Céleris Braisés
Braised Celery

Petits Pois Fins
Garden Peas

Pommes Duchesse
Baked Creamed Potatoes

———

Gateau Glacé Elizabeth
Chocolate and Vanilla Ice Gateau with Chocolate Wafers

———

Petits Fours
Sweetmeats

———

Café
Coffee

Another Typical Menu in the 1950s

New kitchens were built in 1960, and at this time there was a problem, because the three venues stayed open during the rebuild. John tells that while the new facilities were being built, all the food had to be prepared and cooked in the Overstrand Restaurant at Boscombe. When ready, the whole meal was transported by corporation van along the sea-front. Big gas hot-plates were ready in the Ballroom - very old-fashioned by today's standards, but extremely effective. "The kitchens," *says John,* "were always too hot, not only because of the cooking, but also because of the hot air which was blown through them from the boiler below.

*One of the most important functions each year was the **Mayors' Receptions**, which varied in standard and quality a great deal according to the wishes of the Mayor in question. Some were very big and flamboyant, while others were quite modest. The young John features in this picture which was taken at the preparation of a Mayor's Reception in about 1952 or 3. The pictured waitress actually dropped her handful of cutlery just as the picture was being taken, causing some considerable noise in the ballroom. John says that all the carving was done at the actual function in the venue. Often decorative touches would have to be made to - perhaps - a boar's head, and often whole salmon, ox-tongues and lobsters were decorated too.*

"I recall on one occasion being invited by **Lyons** to a demonstration of new micro-wave ovens at **Cadby Hall**. I'm not talking about the little ovens we all have in our kitchens nowadays - these were five-foot high, and designed to reheat prepared food. They were really very good, but I didn't like the idea because it wasn't traditional cooking, and also required less skill. But it was a good day out and had a pleasant ending - during the day, we all were taken for a special meal in a **London Steak House**, and then on to a club where the cabaret was given by **Kenny Ball and his Jazzmen**. **Peter Smith**, who was

ballroom manager at the time, suggested to Kenny Ball's manager that the band should come to the Pavilion Ballroom and make a record. And he did - an EP (extended play seven-inch disc) entitled *"Ball in Bournemouth"* was recorded 'live' in the ballroom during an evening dance."

*Peter Smith began life at the Pavilion as a waiter, and during the 1958 Summer Season in the Theatre with **Bob Monkhouse**, **Denis Goodwin** and the **Beverley Sisters**, he made sure that the stars were treated to a first-rate meal each evening, cooked by John and then taken up to the dressing rooms.*

*This line of chefs was taken for publicity purposes, and as an advertisement for functions in the early 1960s.
From left to right: **Bill Smith**, **John Clark**, **Paul Dower** (Boxer Dai's Dower's cousin), **Lionel Stokes**, **Mario (Jack) Leto**.*

Peter Smith - from waiter to Ballroom Manager

"A great big stage to go on!"
CUMBERLAND CLARK

In the 1920s and 1930s, eccentric Bournemouth poet, Cumberland Clark wrote amusing and witty 'poetry' about almost every aspect of the town's life. The Pavilion did not escape! This light-hearted ditty comes from his self-published "The Bournemouth Song Book".

The Bournemouth New Pavilion
Will cater for the million,
This glorious undertaking
Shows genius in the making;
A long, long while it took to build, although no time was lost,
A quarter of a million pounds was said to be the cost.

It's built in various sections,
Sea views in two directions;
A1 for social meeting,
For drinking or for eating.
Tea rooms and beauteous balconies beset with flower and shrub.
Where roughly fifteen hundred people all can take their "grub".

For Concert, Play or Opera
No hall could be more popular;
A nice big stage to go on,
Large dressing rooms, and so on.
Of course the splendid orchestra, conducted by Sir Dan,
Remains a part and parcel of the new Pavilion's plan.

All visitors who enter
This great amusement centre
Are sure to be delighted,
Enthralled, and quite excited.
So good luck to the Corporation! May the venture pay,
And the New Pavilion meet success for many a lengthy day!

No prizes for being the world's greatest poetry, but congratulations to Cumberland Clark who succeeded in capturing the true spirit of the new Pavilion.

Theatre Tickets, designed by the Ticketing Office, as used in 2005. Only tickets purchased need to be printed, thus avoiding wastage.

1930s Green Bus Timetable

Of no practical use whatsoever to us in the 21st Century, but an interesting glimpse into the routes and services provided by those lovely old green buses from Hants and Dorset.
Looks as if the timetable is every bit as difficult to understand as they are today! This comes from a 1930s Pavilion programme.

Hants and Dorset Motor Services Limited
IN ASSOCIATION WITH THE SOUTHERN RAILWAY COMPANY

BOURNEMOUTH, CHRISTCHURCH, HIGHCLIFFE, MILTON, MILFORD-ON-SEA, LYMINGTON.
Depart Bournemouth.—8.45, 9.45, 10.45, 11.45 N.S., 12.0 S.O., 12.45 N.S., 1.45, 2.45, 3.45, 4.45, 5.45, 6.45, 7.45, 8.15, 9.45
Depart Lymington.—8 30 N.S., 9.15, 10.15, 11.15, 12.15, 1.15, 2.15, 3.15, 4.15, 5.15, 6.15, 7.15, 8.15, 9.15.

BOURNEMOUTH, CHRISTCHURCH HIGHCLIFFE.
Depart Bournemouth.—8.45, 9.45, 10.20 N.S., 10.45, 11.20 N.S., 11.45 N.S., 12.0 S.O., 12.20 N.S., 12.45 N.S., 1.20, 1.45, 2.20 2.45, 3.20, 3.45, 4.20, 4.45, 5.20, 5.45, 6.20, 6.45, 7.20, 7.45, 8.20, 9.45.
Depart Highcliffe.—8.0 N.S., 9.14 N.S., 10.2, 11.2, 11.33 N.S., 12.2, 12.30 N.S., 1.2, 1.30 N.S., 2.2, 2.33, 3.2, 3.35, 4.2, 4.15, 5.2, 5.35, 6.2, 6.35, 7.2, 7.45, 8.2, 8.35, 9.2, 10.2.

BOURNEMOUTH, CHRISTCHURCH, BRANSGORE, BURLEY.
Depart Bournemouth.—8.25 N.S., 10.30 N.S., 11 B 30 N.S., 12.45, 2.30, 4.45 B, 6.0, 8 B 20 N.S., 9 B 30 S.O., 8.15 T.S.
B Bransgore only.
Depart Burley.—9.10 N.S., 12.40 N.S., 2.10, 5.15 N.S., 5.55 S O., 7.35 N.S., 8.15 S.O., 9.15 T.S.
Depart Bransgore. — 8.50 N.S., 9.45 N.S., 12.50 N.S., 1.50, 2.20, 5.25 N.S., 6.5, 6.40 N.S., 7.45 N.S., 8.25 S.O., 9.27 T.S.

BOURNEMOUTH, CHRISTCHURCH, RINGWOOD, FORDINGBRIDGE AND SALISBURY.
Depart Bournemouth.—8.5 N.S., 9.5 N.S., 10.5, 11.0 N.S., 12.0, 1.5 N.S., 2.5, 3.0 N.S., 4.0, 5.5 N.S., 6.5, 7.0 N.S., 8.0, 9.5.
Depart Salisbury.—8.0 N.S., 9.0 N.S., 10.0, 11.0 N.S., 12.0, 1.0 N.S., 2.0, 3.0 N.S., 4.0, 5.0 N.S., 6.0, 7.0 N.S., 8.0, 9.0.

BOURNEMOUTH, FERNDOWN, ST. IVES, VERWOOD, RINGWOOD.
Dep. Bournemouth.—8.0 N.S., 8.45 N.S., 9.45 S., 10.45 N.S., 11.45 N.S., 12.45 N.S., 1.45, 2.15 V., 2.45, 3.45, 4.45 N.S., 5.45, 6 V 45 N.S., 7 V 30 S.O., 7.45, 8.45, 11.0.
From Ringwood.—8.50 N.S., 9.15 N.S., 9 V 45 N.S., 10.15 N.S., 11.15, 11 V 45 N.S., 12.15 N.S., 1 V 30 N.S., 2.15, 2 V 45 N.S., 3.15, 3.45 N.S., 4.15, 5.15, 6 V 20, 7.15, 9.0, 10.15.
v Includes Verwood.
s West Moors on Sundays only

BOURNEMOUTH, CHRISTCHURCH, MUDEFORD.
Depart Bournemouth.—8.35 N.S., 9.30, 10.55, 12.30, 1.30, 2.30, 3.30, 4.30, 5.30, 6.0, 7.30, 9.20.
From Mudeford.—9.30 N.S., 10.15, 12.10, 1.45, 2.25, 3.10, 4.10, 5.10, 6.10, 6.40, 8.10, 10.25.

BOURNEMOUTH AND POOLE.
The Route will be to and from the Omnibus Station, The Square, Bournemouth, round the Square, and then via Poole Road to County Gates, Lindsay Road, Archway Road, Bournemouth Road, Parkstone, Park Gates East, Parkstone Road to the Library, High Street, Poole.
Week Days, leaving Bournemouth at 5.50, 6.0, 6.20, 6.40, 6.50, 7.0 a.m., and then every 10 minutes up to and including 11.30 p.m.
Sundays, leaving Bournemouth at 8.30, 9.0, 9.30, 9.40 a m., and then every 10 minutes up to and including 11.30 p.m
Week Days, leaving Poole at 5.50, 6.0, 6.10, 6.20, 6.40 a.m., and then every 10 mins. up to and including 11.20 p.m.
Sundays, leaving Poole at 8.0, 8.30, 9.0, 9.30, 9.40 a.m., and then every 10 minutes up to and including 11.20 p.m
This Service is duplicated during Busy Periods : 8 a.m. to 9 a.m., and 2 p.m. to 6 p.m.

BOURNEMOUTH—POOLE
SPECIAL NOTICE
From 5.50 a.m. to 9.40 a.m., Omnibuses leaving Poole at 10, 30, 50 minutes past the hour, proceed via Longfleet, also on the return journey leaving Bournemouth at the hour, 20 and 40 minutes past the hour—then, from 9.45 a.m. to 10.15 p.m., Omnibuses leaving both Bournemouth and Poole at the hour, quarter-past, half past, and a quarter to, will proceed via Penn Hill Avenue and Parkstone Road. At all other times, Omnibuses will proceed via Longfleet and Bournemouth Road. After 10.15 p.m. all Omnibuses will proceed via Bournemouth Road and Longfleet.

CONDITIONS OF SERVICE
Passengers are most particularly requested to note that the conditions relating to this service are :—That no persons can be carried on the above time-table Omnibus who wish to **Commence and Finish** their journey in the Borough of Bournemouth ; passengers can be picked up en route for points Outside the Borough, but the first stop on the outward journey from Bournemouth at which passengers will be allowed to **Alight** will be at the Omnibus Stand, County Gates, in the Borough of Poole ; passengers coming into Bournemouth from outside the Borough can alight at any of the official stopping places.

STOPPING PLACES
In the Borough of Bournemouth are : The Omnibus Station, The Square ; St. Michael's Church ; West Station Entrance (viz., on the Bournemouth side of the Hospital on the outward journey, and opposite the Hospital on the inward journey) ; and from there direct to the County Gates Stand. In the Borough of Poole the stopping places are: County Gates; Corner of Lindsay and Leicester Roads ; Corner of Archway Road and Penn Hill Avenue ; Archway Road ; and from there to Poole the stops recently used by the Trams.

BOURNEMOUTH, POOLE, LYTCHETT, WAREHAM.
Depart Bournemouth.—10.5, 12.5 N.S., 1.45, 3.5, 4.30, 7.30, 8.45, 10.45 T.S.
From Wareham.—8.45 N.S., 11.0, 1.45, 3.0, 4.30, 5.30, 8.30.
See Company's Time Table for particulars of special through fares and connections for Corfe Castle, Swanage, Weymouth, etc.

OMNIBUSES RUNNING THROUGH CHRISTCHURCH.
To Christchurch.
Depart Bournemouth.—7.45 N.S., 8.5 N.S., 8.25 N.S., 8.35 N.S., 8.45, 9.5 N.S., 9.30, 9.45, 10.5, 10.20 N.S., 10.30, 10.45, 11.5 N.S., 11.20 N.S., 11.30 N.S., 11.45 N.S., 12.5, 12.20 N S., 12.30, 12.45, 1.5 N.S., 1.20, 1.30, 1.45, 2.5, 2.20, 2.30, 2.45, 3.5 N.S., 3.20, 3.30, 3.45, 4.5, 4.20, 4.30, 4.45, 5.5 N.S., 5.20, 5.30, 5.45, 6.0, 6.5, 6.20, 6.45, 7.5 N.S., 7.20, 7.30, 7.45, 8.5, 8.20, 9.5, 9.30 S.O., 9.45, 10.45 W.S.

From Christchurch.
Dep. Town Hall.—8.15 N.S. 9.10 N.S., 9.25 N.S., 9.35 N.S., 9.40 N.S. 10.10 N S., 10.15, 10.25, 10.35 N.S., 11.15, 11.25, 11.35, 11.45 N.S., 12.15, 12.35 N.S., 12.40 N.S., 1.15, 1.35, 1.40, 1.55, 2.10, 2.15, 2.35, 2.40, 3.15, 3.20, 3.35, 3.45, 4.15, 4.20, 4.25, 4.35 N.S., 5.15, 5.20, 5.35, 5.45, 6.15, 6.20, 6.30 N.S., 6.45, 6.50, 7.0 N.S., 7.15, 7.35, 8 5 N.S., 8.15, 8.20, 8.35 N S., 8.45, 9.15, 9.35, 10.15, 10.35.

BOURNEMOUTH, KINSON, WIMBORNE, BLANDFORD, SHAFTESBURY.
Depart Bournemouth.—8.45, 10.0 N.S., 12.0, 2.0, 3.0, 5.0, 7.0, 9.15 W.S.O.
Depart Shaftesbury. — 8.55, 10.25 N.S., 11.25 N.S., 12.25, 2.25, 4.25, 5.25 N.S., 7.25, 9.40 W.S.O.
To Blandford only. — 7.45 N.S., 10 F 0 p.m.
From Blandford only.—8.55 N.S., 2.15 S.O.
F Via Ferndown
THERE IS A FREQUENT SERVICE BETWEEN BOURNEMOUTH AND FERNDOWN GOLF COURSE See Company's Official Time Table for Particulars.

BOURNEMOUTH, SANDBANKS, STUDLAND AND SWANAGE.
To Swanage.—*8.10, 9.45, 10.45, 11.45 N.S., 12.15 S.O., 12.45 N.S., 2.10, 3.15, 4.15, 5.15, 6.30, 10.45 T.S.
From Swanage.—*7.55, 9.45, 10.45, 11.45 N.S., 12 15 S.O., 12.45 N.S., 2.10, 3.15, 4.15, 5.15, 6.30, 7.30 T S
* Mondays only

BOURNEMOUTH, COUNTY GATES, CANFORD CLIFFS, SANDBANKS.
From 9.0 N.S., 9.25 N.S., 10.0 N.S., a.m. to 8.0 p.m. ½-hour service (no 'bus at 1.30) is run from Bournemouth to Sandbanks, then 8.5 S O., 8.30, 9.0, 9.25, 10.0. 11.0 T.S., and from Sandbanks to Bournemouth 8.30 N.S., 9.30 N S., 10.0 N.S., after which ½-hour service (no 'bus at 1.30), till 9.0, then 9.30, 10 0, 10.30, 11.25 T.S.
N.S.—9, 10.15, 11.15, 11.45, 12.45, 1.15, N S.—10.30, 10.45, 11.15, 11.45, 12.15, 12.45, 1.15 and 1.45.

THERE IS A FREQUENT SERVICE BETWEEN BOURNEMOUTH AND FERNDOWN GOLF COURSE
SEE COMPANY'S OFFICIAL TIME TABLE FOR PARTICULARS

N.S.—Not Sun.   S.O.—Sun. only.   T.S.—Thurs. and Sat. only.   S.S.O.—Sat. and Sun. only.   W.T.S.—Wed., Thurs. and Sat only
N.W.S.—Not Wed. or Sat.   N.W.S.S.—Not Wed., Sat. or Sun.   W.S.—Wed. and Sat. only.

ALL 'BUSES LEAVE THE OMNIBUS STATION IN THE SQUARE.

Issued subject to the Conditions, etc., as Printed in the Company's Official Time Table, which can be obtained, at the charge of 1d., from any of the Company's Offices, or from the Conductors.

By Order, W. W. GRAHAM, General Manager, Royal Mews, Norwich Avenue, Bournemouth. Telephone 2264.

The Fall of the Popular Restaurant

A SAD DECLINE

The **Popular Restaurant**, also known as **The British Restaurant**, **The Ocean Rooms** and **Oasis** has had a chequered life. It's popularity as a restaurant was not echoed when its purpose changed. When **Eldrige Pope**, the Brewers from Dorchester, took over the facilities, they had hopeful plans to build it into a strong commercial venture and a leading part of the eating and drinking life of the town. Sadly, it was not very successful from a trading point of view. The area was taken over by the **Beach Services** for a while, but now lies

In all its original glory

dormant, empty and neglected - a large building in a prime position but of no current use to the holiday trade and certainly not a good advertisement for one of the leading seaside towns in the country.

As it is in 2005 - dying and sad - with no-one to feed and no-one to entertain

The entrance to OASIS in 2005. Similar to a P.O.W. Camp? And right next to Pier Approach.

FAMILY TERRACE AND BAR

Oasis

All too often today, a visit to the theatre does not include the buying of a programme - because it will be too expensive. That's not always been the case. A theatre visit of today, anywhere in England will offer patrons programmes which resemble a glitzy magazine, containing vast amounts of reading on the show - its stars, producers, writers (if a play) or composer (if an opera or musical).

All information will be accompanied by superb photography, drawings and sometimes puzzles. This applies across the entire spectrum from grand opera to Ken Dodd or Joe Pasquale. What it will no longer do however, is give you a unique flavour of the venue in which you see the show, apart from the theatre's name and a few details of officials. Even the latter may not be present in some programmes.

Bournemouth's theatres of yesteryear always offered programmes which somehow encapsulated the atmosphere of the building. So, the **Boscombe Hippodrome** (now Opera House) gave programmes with a line of drawn chorus girls in perspective tapering to infinity or a drawing of **Boscombe's Chine Hotel**. The **New Royal**, a chorus girl swinging on a large sash suspended from a crescent moon. The **Palace Court theatre** had a neat sober programme with a small motif of the building's façade. Bournemouth **Pavilion** was no exception. All its various programme formats across the years managed to convey the flavour and ambience of the building. Its earlier programmes, apart from the war years and immediate post-war years, displayed the borough coat of arms, proclaiming its civic background.

Earlier programme covers were in full colour with views, sometimes photographs, in the pre-war years, of the Pavilion and its beautiful surroundings of gardens, pine trees, fountains, sky and sea. All gave a sense of opulence.

My collection of programmes dates from 1933, August 6th, 1933 being the first. The page measured 8 5/8 ins. x 10.5 ins. On the front cover was a drawn and painted view of the Pavilion taken from the rock garden at the side and was typical of the twenties/thirties art in that it was romanticised. The colouring was unrealistic and chocolate boxy in appearance. A deep white border surrounded the picture. The actual programme was crammed with advertisements both local and national. **Beales**, **Brights** (now Dingles), **Prices Music Store** were juxtaposed with **Schweppes** and

**BOURNEMOUTH
PAVILION**  PROGRAMME

London Hotels. The Municipal Orchestra under Sir Dan Godfrey shared the programme with theatrical presentations under the heading **"Concert Hall"**.

The size of 1930s programmes remained constant but front covers changed to actual photographs of the Pavilion, some oblique views from Westover Road; some of the rock garden and stream looking seawards. Colour must have been by hand in those days. The title **"Concert Hall"** seemed to disappear about 1938 to be replaced simply by **"Pavilion"**. Looking at these pre-war pictures gives the feeling of balmy, care-free days - people strolling in the gardens under summer blue skies with fleecy clouds. No-one looking at them would guess the sinister storm clouds gathering in Europe or the horror that was to be unleashed within such a short span of time.

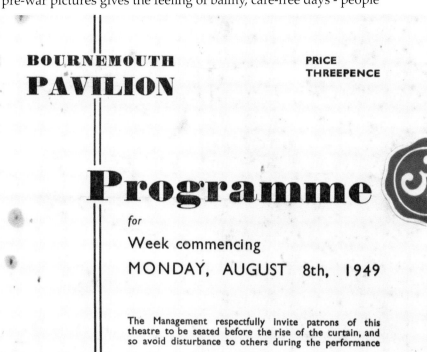

BOURNEMOUTH
PAVILION

PRICE
THREEPENCE

Programme

for

Week commencing
MONDAY, AUGUST 8th, 1949

The Management respectfully invite patrons of this theatre to be seated before the rise of the curtain, and so avoid disturbance to others during the performance

My first memories of the Pavilion date from the later war years as a very small child. Programmes by then had been reduced drastically in size to 5 by 4 inches, a wartime economy which lasted up to the end of 1950. I, of course, knew nothing of such economy measures and just accepted them as typical Pavilion programmes with their plain chocolate coloured seals with **3d** in white - same price as their pre-war

BOURNEMOUTH PAVILION

EMILE LITTLER'S
ALL STAR PANTOMIME
MOTHER GOOSE

CHRISTMAS 1949 NEW YEAR 1950

counterparts! They contrasted with the advertisement-bedaubed Boscombe Hippodrome programmes, one sheet folded usually in blue print on semi-glazed paper. Yet somehow these programmes still typified the Pavilion. How, one might say? Difficult to put into words. Maybe the black printing on parchment coloured rough unglazed paper, gave a message that the Pavilion was to be taken more seriously than its Boscombe rival. Whatever, they were marvels of clever compression in wording. Printed weekly, they gave the two municipal orchestra concerts Sunday, 2.45 p.m. and 7 p.m., the theatre shows and coming attractions, together with details of corporation transport services. One lovely touch to the front cover was a request: **"Patrons are respectfully requested to refrain from smoking pipes during the performances"**. Surely an insight into the sociology of the era more macho than today, would you say?

The transfer of the orchestra to the Winter Gardens in December 1947 gave greater room for theatre information and, at Christmas 1948, programmes for **Emile Littler**'s first Bournemouth pantomime **"Little Miss Muffet"** were actually printed in green with a green and red holly motif on the borders of the front cover, although they were the same size. The printers were the **Richmond Hill Printing Works**, Yelverton Road, but somewhere in the late forties the tender moved to **Suttons** of Boscombe.

Christmas 1949/50 saw Emile Littler's second Bournemouth pantomime with a programme measuring 6.5 x 9.5 inches. **"Mother Goose"** had a bright orange border with midnight blue background and white wording and design. A copy is on display in the Pavilions's memorabilia displays in the corridor nearest Bath Road. The programme was glazed and with wording and photos of the stars, plus scenes from the show in blue. But for the rest of 1950 there was a return to economy size.

It was in 1951 that the programme covers again returned to full colour with an oblique view of the Pavilion taken from left of building showing pines, rhododendrons, flower beds, blue sea and hazy sky. The scene occupied the whole of the cover with a half-inch border at the top and 1¾ inch at the bottom in yellow ochre (appropriate to sands) with '**Bournemouth Pavilion**' written in aquamarine. The Borough coat of arms was in the bottom right-hand corner, and the price was 6d. They were beautiful, perhaps the best. Inside advertisements appeared once more for **Harvey Nichols**, **Citax**, **South Western Table Waters**, **Strong's of Romsey**, **Bournemouth Wine Co.** and the famous **Creemier Ice Creams** made in Palmerston Road. *(See Page 180)*

For some reason, these lasted two years only. Why, I shall never find out, but they were replaced by another coloured cover. Again, there was the same olique view with coat of arms to top centre position against a blue and white sky. '**Bournemouth Pavilion**' appeared in white and ochre wording on a maroon oval shaped backing - the same colour as the proscenium house tabs (curtains). The rear cover had a black and white photo inset of the Ballroom and Popular Restaurant with a stylish couple dancing. This was to be the format for the remainder of the fifties and indeed until about 1962. Towards the end of the 1950s glazed paper replaced the matt.

(The cover and some pages from the Opening Ceremony Programme appear from Page 13)

PATRONS ARE RESPECTFULLY REQUESTED TO
REFRAIN FROM SMOKING PIPES IN THE AUDITORIUM

LUCULLUS RESTAURANT · BALLROOM · POPULAR RESTAURANT
AVAILABLE FOR PRIVATE PARTIES AND BANQUETS
LOUNGE BAR – SALOON BAR – PUBLIC BAR

Bournemouth
PAVILION
PROGRAMME

After 1962, the colour cover disappeared to be replaced by a plain red or blue cover with Pavilion Theatre written at a slant across the front. The contract had by now been moved to **Brown & Son**, Ringwood, Hants. Advertising had steadily increased throughout the 1950s and into the 1960s.

By the mid 1960s, programmes had again changed. A 1966 programme in pink measured 6 ¾ ins. x 9 ¼ ins. and had 'Pavilion' in white lettering with the borough coat of arms in black at bottom right hand corner; the price by now - one shilling, printed by **Stilwell Darby & Co. Ltd., S.W.1**, who continued to print into and through the 1970s. An established format became the norm after a period of changing designs. The wording 'Pavilion Theatre' appeared perpendicularly in white on the front cover, near the staples. Background colours changed weekly; blues, scarlets, oranges, purples and greens being used in rotation. Insets now began to appear written by Eric Shorter on a multiplicity of theatrical topics, not always apposite to the show being seen. These were printed on coloured paper different from the white glazed paper

of the actual programme information. Exceptions to these were the pantomimes which carried their own special covers in colour.

Occasionally, shows brought their own programme, such as the Prospect Theatre Company's 1977 tour of Bernard Shaw's St. Joan, venues being listed on the inside cover. And this was to become the increasing norm into the 1980s and 90s. Larger and more elaborate programmes seemed to become the order of the day with a vast increase in the price to accompany the trend, no doubt to support the research and writing of the information on stars, composers, authors and producers.

I still tend to buy a programme, but what has been lost? Yes, there is that something - that indelible mark of the theatre itself. The awareness that the programme being handled was very much of the Bournemouth Pavilion, not depersonalised by being part of a large tour. There was something exciting about handling the programme with mainly local advertisements, especially the coloured ones. They even, when new, had a sort of smell about them that was part of the unique Pavilion atmosphere. Recently, a man I met through a local choir said, "The Pavilion is different from anywhere. It's got its own feeling." Much more exciting than, dare one say, Southampton or Poole. Somehow picking up those old programmes, reading and handling them, brings back the excitement - nostalgia, of course - but why not?

Year after Year it returns - Year after Year it fills the theatre
'That'll Be the Day' - one of the most successful shows of all time

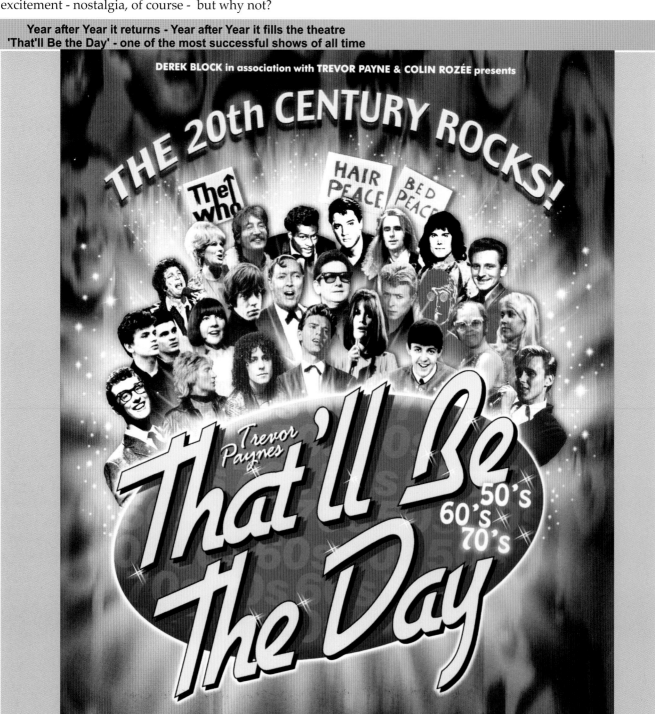

The Chairman of the **Bournemouth and Boscombe Light Opera Company**, **Brenda Baker** says that many marriages have been created through friendships begun with the company. None have been as dramatic as an incident at the end of the final performance of 'My Fair Lady' in 2004. The leading lady was **Becky Weeks** *(Page 58)* who had been friendly with **Simon Bagnell** *(Page 143)*, the theatre's Stage Manager. They'd been together for a year and Becky says that she had forgotten Simon's birthday and felt very guilty. Brenda takes up the story: "We had always had long speeches after the last performance so we decided that we'd stop them and just let the curtain come down. But Simon came to me and begged me to have some speech so that he could be invited on stage. The story was that he

wanted to thank the company for fifty years of shows, and mention that the theatre had just celebrated its seventy-fifth birthday. He told me why he desperately wanted to do this, but had to let me into the secret, so I had to be very careful about what I said." Becky continues the story: "I had no idea what was going on, but Simon came on stage and made his speech, but then he didn't walk off, but he turned to me, called me forward, got down on his knee and asked me in full view of the audience to marry him. The entire cast and the audience just roared with approval. It was a moment that no one will ever forget." And we wish Becky and Simon all the very best for their marriage.

Simon wins his fair lady

THERE was an unexpected ending to Bournemouth Boscombe Light Opera Company's recent production of My Fair Lady that had most of the cast and audience reaching for their handkerchiefs, and for the very best of reasons.

As the final performance ended, company chairman Brenda Baker made her closing speech, during which she thanked Pavilion stage manager Simon Bagnall for his hard work during the week.

But no one, save those very few who were in the know, could have imagined the theatrical coup that came next.

Simon, who began working at the Pavilion part-time when he was a 14-year-old schoolboy, becoming stage manager last year, duly appeared to take his bow.

Then, in front of the entire audience and company, he called his girlfriend, Becky Weeks, who had been part of the chorus, to the front of the stage, went down on one knee and proposed to her. And yes, she did say "Yes".

Becky, 24, who also works at the Pavilion, first appeared with BBLOC when she was 12,

Courtesy of Bournemouth Daily Echo

PROPOSING: Simon Bagnall drops down to one knee

playing one of the children in Fiddler on the Roof.

Since then she has been in many of their shows, and has also played leading roles for both Poole and Parkstone and Theatre 2000.

Also, at 14 she spent a season with the National Youth Music

Theatre, appearing with them in Toronto and New York in a production of The Ragged Child, and has appeared in a number of TV programmes.

But My Fair Lady is undoubtedly the show that both Becky and Simon will remember for the rest of their lives.

Another high-profile wedding was organised at the Bournemouth Pavilion in 1958. **Bob Monkhouse** was starring with the **Beverley Sisters** in '**The Big Show of 1958**', and at that time **Joy Beverley**, the oldest of the three sisters had been courting England Football Captain, **Billy Wright**. They got married at Poole Registry Office during the summer season in front of a row of photographers from every national newspaper. What tremendous publicity for the Pavilion's summer show!

1960

March - New **heating system** was installed at the cost of £31,000.

April - 'Don't Shoot, We're English' was a whacky entertainment starring **Michael Bentine**.

June - The Bournemouth **Pier Theatre** opened, designed by the Borough Architect. The first long-running season was what was described as a 'sophisticated' revue, had amongst its cast **Ted Rogers** of 'Three, Two, One' television fame.

June - General Manager, **Arthur Clegg**, was suspended after an audit of accounts. He was subsequently dismissed and the Fraud Squad was called in.

September - The theatre was unexpectedly and suddenly closed **because of structural wear to the stage fly-tower.** The show, 'Salad Days', was cancelled. The repairs would take six months, leading to the cancellation of Emile Littler's 13th Pantomime, which would have been 'Aladdin' starring **Frankie Howerd**.

December - Peter Wass was appointed as General Manager.

1961

January - Report published on how to **make the Pavilion pay**.

March - **Fraud Squad** reported back to the Council.

April - Repairs and renovations were completed at the cost of **£150,000**.

April - **Sybil Thorndike** and **Lewis Casson** appeared in '**Waiting in the Wings**'.

May - **Nicholas Parsons** in '**Doctor at Sea**'.

July - Former General Manager, **Arthur Clegg**, was jailed for fraud for four years.

September - **Popular restaurant** closed for the winter months.

September - Bournemouth and District Citizens Alliance hold a **Festival of Dancing** in the Ballroom.

November - the first-ever visit of stage version of the BBCtv series '**The Black and White Minstrel Show**' starring **Leslie Crowther**, **George Chisholm**, **Tony Mercer**, **John Boulter** and **Dai Francis**. All the singing was **pre-recorded and mimed** to a 'live' pit orchestra. This show came back many times with several successful summer seasons. In recent years, the BBC has denounced the show, regretting that the corporation ever put it on because of its political incorrectness.

Alliance
Festival of Dancing
at the
PAVILION
BOURNEMOUTH

Channel Counties Championships

FRIDAY
SEPTEMBER 29
1961

PROGRAMME

1/-

November - **Margaret Lockwood** and **Derek Farr** played the leads in the terrifying play, '**Signpost to Murder**', which brought gasps a-plenty from the audiences.

The year was a real treat for fans of Dorothy **Reynolds and Julian Slade**, the duo who wrote the ever-popular musical '**Salad Days**'. This show itself played in November, just a month or two after the theatre had hosted the musical's sequel. Called '**Wildest dreams**', it never really came up to the same standard, although there was one very funny scene where a group of young people go to a very serious chamber music recital and get a fit of the giggles. It was guaranteed to get everyone laughing.

December - Pantomime was '**Goody Two Shoes**' with **Richard Hearne** (Mr. Pastry) and **Kenneth MacKeller**.

(n.b. the shows for the year 1961 are featured in a full article on Page 182)

1962

October - **Peter Wass** resigns as General Manager.

December - **Adam Faith** starred in 'Aladdin'.

(n.b. the shows during this year are featured in a full article on Page 182)

1963

Arnold Wesker's 'Chips with Everything'

Summer Season - **Millicent Martin, Tommy Cooper** and the **Kaye Sisters**.

December - **Danny La Rue** was in 'Cinderella'.

1964

September - **Jack Dangerfield** became General Manager.

Summer Season - **Bruce Forsyth** and **Edmund Hockridge**.

December - The pantomime was '**Puss in Boots**'.

1965

May - The Pavilion was found to be too small for the Conference of the **National Association of Round Tablers**. A large marquee was erected on the forecourt.

Summer Season - **Arthur Haynes, Yana** and **The Seekers**. During the run, **Judith Durham**, the lead singer of the Australian Group, 'The Seekers', collapsed on stage during a performance. When Harold Fielding had booked the group, they were virtually unknown, but during the months preceding the show, 'The Seekers' had become number one chart toppers, with their song '**I'll never find another you**'.

The usual money problems occurred, and the Pavilion, at the end of the year, was **in debt by £191,000**. Many people asked if it should be razed to the ground.

December - '**Mother Goose**'.

1966

March - Manager **Jack Dangerfield** resigns, and only 26 people apply for the post after a national advertisement.

June - New manager **Douglas Dawson** was appointed on a salary of £2,400 per year.

November - Three month **car-parking permits** increased in price from £3.0s.0d to £6.5s.0d. more than double!

December - **Diana Dors** in '**Jack and the Beanstalk**'.

1967

May - Permission was given to build a **footbridge** from the Car Park into the Lucullus Room, thus allowing access without walking through the main building.

July - The idea of a **sunken beer garden** alongside the West Terrace was floated.

Summer Season - **Des O'Connor, Margot Henderson, Kenneth McKeller**.

November - Plans were drawn up to speed the **traffic flow** around the forecourt.

December - '**Robinson Crusoe**'

1968

January - Decided that the original **fountain in the Pavilion forecourt**, which was forty years old, should be demolished. It cost £12 a week to run, and when in full flow, caused patrons to get wet. (Aaahhhh!)

August - A **new fountain** was proposed which would cost £4,000 to build. The cost of water would drop from £111 to about £20, and it was claimed that the new device would allow a much better view of the Pavilion. It was claimed that the original fountain was beyond repair.

September - **Big Night Out With the Stars**, organised by the Bournemouth Round Table, The Canford Heath Church and the Christchurch Round Table. And how's this for a star line-up? **Pearl Carr and Teddy Johnson, Eric Delaney** and his Band, **Ivor Emmanuel, The New Faces, Dickie Henderson, Frank Ifield, Hugh Lloyd and Terry Scott, Ken Platt** and **Semprini**.

December - **Harry H. Corbett** starred in 'Aladdin'.

1969

March - Work on the Pavilion forecourt meant that guests to a special function had to wade through 'rivers' of water.

May - **New fountain** opened.

June - Permission was given to play **Bingo in the Ballroom**.

December - '**Cinderella**'.

The Truth

28 FACTS ABOUT THE BOURNEMOUTH PAVILION when it was built

1. One national newspaper has described the building as the "**New Wonder Pavilion**", so called because of the magnitude of its conception, the nobility of its design, the artistry displayed in its adornment, and the skill and craftmanship that have gone into the equipment.

2. The contract for the **foundations** alone amounted **to £47,000**. Carried out by Jones and Seward, Ltd a local firm.

3. The Pavilion is much **larger than some of England's cathedrals**. It is larger than Exeter, Wells and Rochester Cathedrals.

4. The tunnels (ducting) by which fresh air (water-cooled or steam-heated) is pumped into the building **are big enough to drive a vehicle** through.

5. While the Pavilion was being built, the number of men working on the site varied weekly, and at some stages there were **as many as 250 men** at work.

6. **20,500 cubic yards of earth and sand** had to be excavated, and the foundations included 5,000 cubic yards of concrete, 1,200 cubic yards of reinforced concrete, 1,050,000 bricks, 98 tons of steel joists, 70 tons of reinforcing rods and 8,630 cubic feet of Portland stone.

7. The superstructure contract was for **£136, 585** - also carried out by Jones and Seward, Ltd.

8. Over **320 tons of steel** were used in the superstructure.

9. The reinforced concrete used **Bridport gravel from the Chesil Beach**. The small, round pebbles were ideal as they fitted around the steel rods so closely.

10. About **570 tons of gravel** was used.

11. Over **25,000 cubic feet of Empire cast stone** was used in the superstructure.

12. The roof was covered in **Dawson's patent italic tiles**.

13. A **cinema projector** is at the rear of the screen.

14. **Portland stone** was used in the foundations - up to plinth level.

15. **1,500 ash-trays** were installed in the concert hall, on the backs of seats.

16. The number of people working at the Pavilion was about 170, sixty of them being waitresses, for whom a special uniform had been devised - a **plain black frock with a white apron**, and a cap "the like of which has never before seen in Bournemouth".

17. The building process was hampered by the **unusual site** with an awkward slope, and also by the fact that the Belle Vue Hotel - on the site already - could not be demolished at the outset.

18. The electric power installation consists of **32 electric motors**, varying in size from 35 horse-power for electric fans, down to one quarter of one horse-power for labour-saving devices in the kitchens.

19. In addition to other lifts, the **floor of the orchestra pit can be raised** to the level of the stage. Other lifts to left and right of the orchestra bring the organ console into view. *(The mention of lifts 'either side' is confusing - there is only one lift for the organ, and as far as is known, there has only ever been one.)*

20. It was the **only structure building of its kind** on the south coast, and was a cause of pride for Bournemouth residents.

21. Built in well-designed gardens, the Pavilion had an interior combining **elegance and comfort**, and planned to meet completely the many-sided appetite of a public clamouring for entertainment and amusement.

22. The new **remarkable building** was an effort to keep the town, one of the south's leading resorts, abreast of the times.

23. The building was recognition of the vastly changed tastes of the people, and a bold attempt to satisfy their altered needs, and to keep Bournemouth where she had been for years - in the very **forefront among the English coast resorts**.

24. The concert hall is a **luxurious chamber** with warm colouring in shades of pink and terra-cotta, and gilt ornamentation. Theatrical, variety and cinematograph performances can be given there.

25. The organ is a mark of **the building's modernity** and completeness. The console rises to stage level and sinks out of sight as the occasion demands.

26. Comfort is the keynote, with its thickly carpeted floors and its tip-up chairs.

27. The **promenade** around the balcony will be a boon to those who find a long-sitting irksome; it is roomy and looks full onto the stage.

28. The **rubber-tiled floor** of the promenade will render footfalls noiseless, and the audiences in other parts of the hall will suffer no disturbance.

View into Pleasure Gardens from
West Corridor

Centralised Vacuum Cleaning

At various points around the Pavilion are small circular vents. The one of the left is on the floor in the front of the auditorium, near the orchestra pit, and the one on the right is at the bottom of the east main staircase. There are many more in various situations. These are vacuum points for cleaning. In the boiler-room, beneath the ballroom and stage, is a central vacuum pump. The system has been out of action for many years. *The manufacturer's name is STURTEVANT)*

Was the Pavilion Worth the Money?

SIGN OF A NEW ERA

The people of Bournemouth paid £250,000 for their new Pavilion. Was the cost and the effort really worth it? The Bournemouth Daily Echo *was very proud of the complex.*

𝕭𝖔𝖚𝖗𝖓𝖊𝖒𝖔𝖚𝖙𝖍 𝕯𝖆𝖎𝖑𝖞 𝕰𝖈𝖍𝖔

"The Pavilion was the only structure of its kind on the South coast, and Bournemouth could be well proud of it. There was cause for pride in its impressive exterior, commanding a position which dominated the surroundings and yet complemented them gently. It wasn't intrusive or garish, but bold and distinguished, set in the most glorious of natural surroundings. The interior combined elegance and comfort, and perfectly provided all the needs of a Bournemouth public who demanded quality entertainment. And the great quality about the magnificent and remarkable building was that it was a grand effort to keep one of the leading coast resorts abreast of the times. In an age where many folk had cars, where dancing was carried out between meals from midday to midnight, and where crowds were no longer thrilled by the slower delights of a bygone age, they yearned for something which reflected more vividly the times in which they lived.

"This Pavilion was the symbol of a new era. It was recognition of the vastly changing tastes of the people, and a bold attempt to satisfy their altered needs. Critics of the day suggested that the visitors could not fail to feel a sense of magnificence and luxury. There was nothing second-rate in the place, but there was much originality and artistry. The electric light fittings were much acclaimed - in the vestibule, there were 'flaming' torches, both creative and original, pendant lamps, painted red and shaped like street lamps illuminated the stairways, and in the Concert Hall, the light holders, dropping from the ceiling, had the appearance of wonderful exotic flowers. The golden glass petals around the lights widened out from the sharp point in the figure of a spreading shuttlecock. Fanning out from the top of the lowest ring of petals came another and another. In the large central light, there were four such rows. The effect was alluring, great barbed arrow-heads of golden light."

These chandeliers were taken down during the Second World War because it was felt they were dangerous should the building be struck by a bomb. They were replaced by metal cups, and these still hang in the Concert Hall to this day. Their origin is unknown - some argue that they were purchased from a Town Hall in the north of England, possibly Leeds or Rotherham. Rotherham Council confirms that there were changes made to their lighting in their Assembly Rooms at this time, but have no record of any sale to Bournemouth. Ex-Chief Engineer of the Pavilion complex, Peter Knight, says that he thinks they were made especially for the building by G.E.C. Current Stage Manager, Simon Bagnall reckons they are German in origin. This is one mystery which the Pavilion will probably hold in its own memory for ever.

The Circle in 2005. Note the 'cup-like' chandeliers, and the Pavilion's own lighting and sound control points just to left of centre

Remember that this is 1929, and yet the system of heating and ventilation boasted that the air was constantly purified. The claim stated that the Pavilion will be found to be one of the best ventilated buildings in the country, because the methods used for maintaining proper atmosphere at all seasons and for keeping pure air in circulation, are of the latest and most approved kind.

Mumford, Bailey and Preston, a large company which had Bournemouth works, were the engineers who carried out the engineering installation for the warming and ventilation of the entire complex. The following is difficult to grasp, but this is how it all works.

Steam Heated Batteries

The ventilation of the building is maintained by a balanced mechanical system. Fresh air is allowed into the building through a main air shaft connected by an underground duct to the chamber in the basement. The entering air is first dry-filtered and then heated by passing over steam-heated batteries. From the batteries, the air is delivered to the various rooms by means of two motor-driven centrifugal inlet fans through a system of underground ducts which are connected to the various inlets in the rooms. These inlets are incorporated in the architectural decorations, and in this respect, a great deal of careful planning had been necessary to produce the results obtained. The inlet fans are capable of handling **55,000 cubic feet of air** per minute.

Sea Water is Cooled

For summer use, there is an arrangement for pumping brine through the batteries for cooling the incoming air instead of warming it. The extracting section of the ventilation plant is operated by means of two main extracting fans located in the chamber in the basement. Generally, the vitiated air *(that which has been made impure)*, is extracted from the various rooms through extract gratings which also form part of the architectural decorations. This air is eventually discharged into the atmosphere through two main exhaust shafts.

The heating of the administrative sections and the corridors is by another separate system, called **"atmospheric direct vapour heating apparatus"**, which is economic and easy to control. A central operating point allows engineers to control the heating of the entire complex and instruments show the steam pressures and water temperatures maintained on the boilers and plant throughout the day.

Lifts and Sea Water Washing

The same company also provided the lifts for the orchestra pit and for the organ console, and also supplied a complete pumping plant for providing river water to supply the fountains in the Pleasure Gardens, and for general watering purposes. Other tanks store sea-water supplies for street watering and for giving sea water to various houses and hydros in the town. These pumps are capable of delivering **14,500 gallons per hour**.

Still Too Hot! Or Too Cold!

So now we all know. This was an amazingly forward-looking system, although history showed that it was never very successful. The complexity of it all has made it very difficult to improve the system for modern needs, and consequently, patrons often complain that the building is too cold or too hot. Many of the ducts have, over the years, been blocked, either deliberately for health and safety reasons, or by accident by contractors who didn't understand the system.

Hidden Mystery

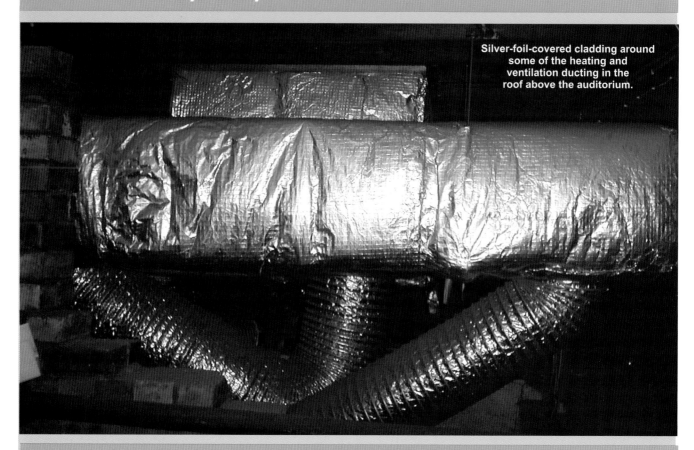

Silver-foil-covered cladding around some of the heating and ventilation ducting in the roof above the auditorium.

Audience Awaiting Organ Concert

Steep learning curves!

GRAHAM SHEARING

*While a student at Queen Elizabeth School in Wimborne, **Graham Shearing** was awarded an AVCE Double Award in Performing Arts after two years in the Sixth Form. At 21, he's now a member of the Bournemouth Pavilion Stage Crew.*

"I always felt destined to work in the theatre, having spent a lot of time at school in the drama studio, and I was made responsible for the sound system in the main hall, where there was quite a lot of work to be done in improving the facilities. I also worked with some local amateur groups, including *The Swan Theatre* in Wimborne, where I was their technical adviser. When a Trainee Technician job became available at the Pavilion, I was appointed along with **Ryan Oliver** *(Page 138)*, and we both attended a course in Lighting and Sound at the Northcott Theatre in Exeter, gaining a B. Tech.

A lot to be learned

"As far as I'm concerned, all is going well for me here. We have to do everything connected with stage craft and, although my heart is set on designing theatre lighting, I've now been able to learn some of the skills involved with the fly-rail, and I spend quite a lot of time up on the grid when shows are being fitted up. As far as lighting is concerned, I'm lucky to have **Sean Tomkins** *(Page 140)* as my mentor, and he's teaching me a great deal about lighting techniques. I particularly enjoyed a chance in 2005 to step in for Sean to light the weekly organ concerts when he was on holiday.

"We've all been working recently on the up-grading of the sound system in the Ballroom. We replaced all the wiring and all the main speakers, with a new amplifier and mixer. This was a steep learning curve, and Ryan and I learned a good number of practicalities in cable laying and so on. The project also gave me a great insight into the Ballroom itself, and I realised that there's a lot more to it than just a dance floor with a small stage. The Pavilion is planning some new ventures for the Ballroom in the future, and I'm glad to have got to know my way around it a bit better.

The Fly Rail

The fifty-line counter-balanced stage flying system

Tickets by Post

JENNY PEART

Now....

....and then!

and before then!

Jenny Peart has worked in the Ticketing Office of Bournemouth Entertainments for many years. Now the **Administration Co-Ordinator**, *she's had such happy times.*

"I started at eighteen, initially at the Pier Theatre for the Sooty Show, and it while I was there that I met my husband, who was fishing on the pier. Although I trained as a graphic designer, I went full-time in the Box Office; there's no doubt that theatre is in the blood, and if you start working there and like it, you're hooked for life. I work nowadays on the postal side of the operation. All letters for bookings come to me, and it's my job to deal with all the customers' needs. We call them patrons, and make sure they get the best seats possible. Some of the letters are totally indecipherable; this can be a problem if you can't read the address, because you can't call them to check what they want.

"One person, who writes quite regularly, puts all her requests on the little square sticky post-its, and the writing is so small I can hardly read it. We always keep a record of everyone who writes because makes it easier to process when they contact us again. Some people book so many tickets that they have their own file. These are the real fans of theatre-going. We don't get as many letters as we used to, because many people book by credit card.

Only on the Gangway, Please!

"It's quite common for us to receive requests for seats before we have confirmation of a show, and they often send us a cheque in advance. They get to know where certain artistes are appearing through their fan clubs, who give them advance notice. **Daniel O'Donnell** is particularly popular and so is **Cliff Richard**. We have a list of patrons who will always want to see certain artistes, and we tell them when that artiste is coming back - it's a sort of advance warning system. Every single letter which comes to us is processed by me. Sometimes we get special requests or demands! Some people will only buy gangway seats, some will only buy right or left gangway seats and nothing else will do. Some people have a deaf ear and so need to be on a certain side of the auditorium. Each patron has a customer number which tells us of any special requirements, and the computer programme warns us when we click into that patron's file.

"In some ways the job has changed a lot, but in others, it's still the same. In the late 1960s, we had to clock in every day on time with a special machine which clipped a little notch in the bottom of your card, but nowadays, our computer clocks us in when we sign on first thing. I've made a lot of 'phone friends' over the years, people who call me by first name and it's as if I've known them for years.

Not just the Pavilion

"My job is absolutely enormous, because we book the seats for all the Bournemouth Theatres - the Windsor Hall, the Tregonwell Hall, the Pavilion and, until this year, the Pier Theatre. This means that if we're booking seats for several weeks in advance, we can be selling and distributing thousands and thousands of tickets. But it doesn't stop there, because we also book for the AFC Bournemouth Stadium, all the Bournemouth Symphony Orchestra external concerts across the region, and many of the music festivals as well. Many of these have to be sent out by recorded delivery. All the time we have to be aware of security; I can remember once we found a bag left, and had to have a full security check just in case.

"As a child, I appeared with the **Anglo-Saxon Ballet Company** who produced a great big show every year for the Waifs and Strays, and I also appeared in one or two of the Bournemouth and Boscombe Light Opera Company productions. My grand-daughter has taken up the theatre mantle and she's just started working at the Pier Theatre as a lighting technician - so the link continues.

"I really love my job, and the people we work with in the Ticketing Office are lovely. I enjoy every minute of it."

View from hatch-way above the front stalls.

For more details, see Sean Tomkins' article on pages 140-142.

Programme Advert 1980

Kristen Greenep

STAGE CREW - HEAD FLYMAN

*The **fly-tower** is the large square building above the stage, where backcloths and curtains can be 'flown' out of sight above the stage. This is managed by a series of counter-balanced bars and operated by the Head Flyman. At the Bournemouth Pavilion, this is **Kristen Greenep**.*

"I went to school at Queen Elizabeth in Wimborne Minster and, quite honestly, I had no idea what I wanted to do for a living. I was interested only in one thing and that was football, which I played as much as I could. When I left, I went to the Bournemouth and Poole College of Art and Design at Wallisdown and worked on a three-year course in Audio-Visual Production. The College is doing very well, and has had several of its films shown on Channel Four. In my time, we made a film highlighting the dangers of drug abuse which was hailed by the Police. I was never too keen to go out on the shoots but always wanted to be a technical man behind the scenes. I worked at **The Lighthouse/Arts Centre** in Poole for a while and when a full-time job at the Pavilion became available in 1999, I applied, was appointed and was straightaway thrown in at the deep end. I found I had to focus far more than I ever had done before, but thoroughly enjoyed the experience.

Well Balanced and Counter Balanced

"One of the great things about working at the Pavilion is that **everyone pulls together**, and we make a **good and effective team**. Most of the shows have quite a lot of equipment to hang, and the first thing I have to do is to estimate the approximate weight of each item. Each backcloth or each set of drapes (curtains) or each lighting bar has to be **counterbalanced** by adding a series of weights into the cradles at the side of the stage. We have **fifty bars** and it's very common for them all to be used in one show. Each weight, which is shaped like a flat gold bar, weighs 28 lbs, and each cradle will take up to 22 of these. In the grid, there are some **500 weights** to be spread as required. It's a tradition that a new flyman starts at the top - at the top of the grid that is, so it's up the two vertical ladders to the very top part of the fly-tower and then to place the weights in the cradles as directed from below. The busiest day I had was when I loaded **5,100 pounds of weights** in one day - that's well over 230 weights to move and lift into place! I've recorded the event in chalk on the iron girders at the grid level. The heaviest show I've ever worked was '**Annie**'.

Amateur Shows are Good

"Working the shows can be very busy indeed, and we often have to have two or even three more staff to operate the lines. My job is not only to co-ordinate the work, but to take the lion's share of the physical action. I find it very worthehile working in the flies, and it's extra rewarding when there are lots of cues and when everything goes exactly to plan. The musical '**Chicago**' had lots and lots of nitty-gritty cues requiring a very strong concentration. I loved it. I enjoy working with the amateur groups, too - **BBLOC** (Bournemouth and Boscombe Light Opera Company) are brilliant, as are **Big Little Theatre School** - these shows give the staff a real chance to work together with the directors and make the show perfect. With the touring shows, we have to do what we're told by the company managers, and this can take away our own creativity.

"I do lots of other things as well as the work on the fly-rail - when we had the show '**Singing in the Rain**', I was working on filling up a **500 litre tank** with water. We did it with a hosepipe, and while the tank was filling we went off to get some food; yes, you guessed it - we misjudged the time it would take to fill, and, when we got back, the **tank had overflowed** - there was quite a mess. Ice shows are fun, too - the ice is about three to four inches deep and arrives as a frozen mush in lorries! We unload it in wheelbarrows, and tip it into the troughs on the stage. It smells a bit fishy. Then, at the end of the week, we all behave a bit like kids when we have to smash the ice with large mallets to break it up, and then dispose of it. While it's good fun, it's very demanding and back-breaking work and the enjoyment doesn't last too long. We're always glad when we've finished.

One of the Best Theatres in the Country

"The Pavilion really is a **great place to work**; the job can be extremely stressful and we spend most of our lives in the building, but the job makes everything worthwhile and we all work together like **a big happy family**. We're so privileged to have such a lovely theatre with original and mostly unchanged decor; I reckon it's **one of the best theatres in the country.** All right, the floor in the auditorium creaks a little in places, but the atmosphere is cosy and warm. Many of the people who live in Bournemouth have little idea of what there is on offer at the building and so they don't use it properly, and so there's so much wasted resource. Wouldn't it be good if we could use the excellent bakery by the ballroom to make our own bread and cakes and sell them in a cafe with those wonderful

Up into the gloomy heights of the fly-flbor and grid

views across the Bay. There's also room for another ballroom which could cater for a younger audience. What's on offer and **all the potential here needs to be made known;** so many folk think that there's just a theatre and that's it. When it opened back in the 1920s, it was designed as a town meeting place - what a shame that it still doesn't serve that function. "I love it here and I can't think of any better place to work."

SID KERLEY - Head Flyman 1950s and 1960s

In the 1950s and 1960s, the **Head Flyman** was **Sid Kerley**. He was a lovely character who, instead of swearing when everything was collapsing around him, used to say the word **"Quack!"**. When things got really difficult, he would shout the word! Sid had worked at the **New Royal Theatre** in Albert Road until it closed in 1957, and he moved to work with John Laurie, the Pavilion Stage Manager. When he left he spent the rest of his working life as Caretaker at the old **Portchester School** in Portchester Road, Bournemouth, where he was popular with staff and pupils, not only because he was an excellent caretaker, but because he was most supportive of the sporting activities. For many years, he ran the **Portcastrians** Old Boys Rugby Club. All his life, Sid had been a staunch supporter of 'Boscombe' - as he would have called **AFC Bournemouth**, and he was a well-known and well-liked personality in the Boscombe area until his death in 2003.

Bournemouth Pavilion - 76 Years of Shows

Marketing and Promotions
ABI SINGLETON and TRACEY RAWLINS

Until the middle of 2005, in the offices above the coffee bar in the foyer of the Bournemouth Pavilion, right at the top, there was a door labelled 'Marketing and Promotions' - another of the busy departments in the running of the theatre. Now that the B.I.C. renovations are complete, the department has moved into new offices. The two Marketing and Promotions Officers are Abi Singleton and Tracey Rawlins. Abi is a local girl who was educated at Avonbourne School and St. Peter's School, and who gained her degree at the Arts Institute in Bournemouth. Tracey comes from Cardiff, and has been at the Pavilion for eight years, following similar jobs in theatres in Cardiff and Southampton.

"There are four of us in the department, because we work with **Lucy** and **Esme** as well. We have a splendid job which is very demanding and exceptionally rewarding; probably the most obvious part of the work is the **Mailing List** to patrons who have decided that the best way to keep in touch is to pay a small fee to be kept informed. We have several hundred people on the list who receive regular updates of what's on in all the **Bournemouth Entertainments**. Also, when someone books a show here, we ask them if they'd like to be told about similar events in the future. If they agree, we place them on our enormous data-base and keep them up to date with all the shows we think they'll like. This data-base has in excess of **50,000 people**; they're not all from Bournemouth and the immediate area, but come from far and wide. We have to remove names from the data-base after two years and the information is destroyed. This data-base also provides us with information of which shows were the most popular and those which had a limited interest.

"We are responsible for compiling the **regular brochures** and this is a complicated job, because new shows and events are being organised all the time. Just as we think we're done, another show is arranged and so we have to slot that one in too. Most popular are our season brochures which used to be published monthly, but now they're quarterly, and because we like to keep moving with the times, we've launched a **new-look brochure** in 2005 which has a lot more information, and is much better organised according the venues with more space for the larger shows. The new B.I.C. will be very busy and our new-style brochure reflects that. This is very exciting. For the production of the brochure, we send all the information to a professional firm of type-set-designers who shower us with proofs before we accept the final version. With the designers we decide on printers, and another of our jobs is to phone around and get lots of quotations.

"Most people remark on the **banners** we place around the town on lamp posts - in 2005, we had a big campaign for '**High Society**'. No one in town could claim that they hadn't heard about the show! As soon as the Entertainments Department, who are based at the B.I.C., have confirmed a show, we get on with the advertising. Some of the one-night shows have their own handbills and fliers which we over-print with our details. We are not responsible for the paid adverts in the papers and so on, but it's our job to write the **press releases** and get them to the correct places. Writing a press release is not as easy as most people think; we have to ensure that we get all the facts in early to interest the journalists who might use them. We often go on courses to keep us up to speed. The advertising in newspapers is nowadays looked after by an agency, and these ads are paid for by monies from the theatre and from the promoters. Obviously, the Entertainments Department and our Promotions Offices are very closely intertwined.

"Sometimes we organise **special press nights** when we invite all newspapers - local, regional and national - **local radio stations**, **local television** and **magazines**. These evenings are only for those invited and we use them a lot for long-run shows such as pantomimes.

We also are responsible for **Press Calls**, when a special time is arranged to meet artistes, and we put together a rota for the individual reporters and so on to visit. These are in some ways similar to **Photo Calls**, when local press photographers, etc., are invited for a '**photo opportunity**'. We're always on the look-out for innovative and exciting ways to do these and they often won't be at the theatre. We have to throw ourselves right into these, and when **Noddy** played the Pavilion, I (Tracey) had to get dressed up as the puppet!

"**Competitions** with local media are a very successful method of promoting shows; we often work with the *Daily Echo*; we might have just a simple reduced ticket-price offer or a two-for-one, but sometimes we get quite inspired with originality! For the pantomime at Christmas 2004, we arranged a '**Beanstalk Challenge**' for schools, and the winning school got to see the pantomime, '**Jack and the Beanstalk**'. We worked with the star and author of the show, **Chris Jarvis** *(Page 225)*, who now lives in Bournemouth, and he was brilliant. He is most supportive of our work here - he loves the Pavilion and gives so much time to help us promote it. What we like about competitions is that they generate **editorial** - it's what we call the '**trust factor**'; many people don't trust advertisements, but they do trust editorial. **Local Radio Stations** are also given tickets for their programmes to hold their own competitions, and sometimes it's appropriate to send tickets to national radio.

"And that leads us on to another area of our work in **organising interviews** on radio programmes. We've learned which programmes are most suitable for each show and we try to persuade presenters to talk to the stars of the show. For BBC stations, we use the satellite studio in the B.I.C.

"**Discount vouchers** are another method of generating interest - we can use them with letters, adverts, and fliers, and from them, we can research into the most successful ways of promoting a show. The results can help us see how the audiences got to know about the various shows and which is most satisfactory? Brochures? Posters? Direct Mail? This research, of course, costs money, but the results make

it very worthwhile.

"One good method of advertising is **buses**! We can pay for a complete back panel, or for a complete side, and we find this very successful. **Yellow buses** drive constantly around the town, and if they're carrying a message about the Pavilion, then that can't be bad. We also use **large outdoor banners** across the front of the theatre.

"We love talking about the job we do, because we love the job! It's never the same two days running, it's busy and exciting, and there's no part of the job we don't like - occasionally some of the

promoters can give us some distress and pressure, but they just want the best for their shows. We've made our own department motto which says '**BRING IT ON!**'"

'The King and I' was one of a series of well-known and well-loved musicals throughout the Summer of 2005. Others included 'High Society', 'Annie', and 'Joseph and His Amazing Technicolor Dreamcoat'

Sounds O.K.
RYAN OLIVER

*Ryan Oliver is a member of the stage crew, a small, dedicated and close-knit team who ensure the technical best for the Bournemouth Pavilion. Some of his work is concerned with **sound reproduction and operation**.*

"I'm not employed particularly as a sound-man, although usually if there's work to be done in this area, it comes my way. There's a **24-way operation desk** in the back of the circle, and from there I can control all the microphones, correct their levels and open or shut them as required, as well as introduce any other sound sources there might be, such as CD-players, mini-discs, cassettes, and so on. But my job is to get involved with all aspects of stage work, as a member of the team, so it's hands on everything - scenery, lights, props, you name it, I'll do it.

It's Computers for me

"I love the **creative side of the work** best and my real love is computers and finding out how they can be used to enhance performances; computers are now used in stage design, theatre design, lighting design and sound design - in fact, all aspects of theatre. I recently rigged up my own lap-top computer so that it could link by radio to the theatre's main lighting control. This meant that I, or Sean, the chief electrician, could operate every lighting circuit in the theatre from wherever we were - in the orchestra pit, on the stage, in the stalls - anywhere. This could be a great help when we're doing fit-ups for shows, because we can see exactly what we're doing from anywhere in the auditorium, so we can set and adjust the direction of lights and then check they're all right without actually having to bother anyone else - so, in a way, it would help with sensible and economical use of staff resources. But, it's an expensive computer program, and it would be difficult to afford it.

"I'm very lucky in the way that I came into the job; I was a student at **Oakmead School** in Bournemouth, and was always involved in the **Expressive Arts Department**, working on the technical side of things for school concerts and dramatic productions. Most schools nowadays use the students in this department to help with school assemblies and meetings, and so they get hands-on experience as they're learning. At the same time, I managed to get a little unofficial work experience with a local firm that specialised in setting up and operating lighting for schools, colleges and small amateur drama groups, and it was here that I gained more interest and more practical knowledge. When it came round to the time for school work experience, the careers teacher managed to fit me up with a job here at the Pavilion. I was literally thrown in at the deep end in the middle of summer season, and so I had to learn quickly! It gave me a chance to get to know all the staff here. Following on from that, the school allowed me to work at the Pavilion one day a week, so every Monday, here I was - it was great, and so it became obvious that I would seek a job in this area of work.

Work Experience - AT SCHOOL!!!

"And the chance came much closer to home than I would have thought possible. The Expressive Arts Department at Oakmead School decided that they would appoint a **Technician** to work permanently within the department, to provide support and knowledge to the students. Yes, you guessed right - I got the job, and worked for about a year with the **GCSE groups and the drama groups**, assisting and advising on their assessment pieces, and working on school assemblies which needed technical support. It was a good year.

"Then a job as **Trainee Technician** came up at the Pavilion and I was once again lucky to be appointed; some of the training is done as you actually do the job, some just comes naturally when you find you have to do it, but there's also a commitment by the theatre to send you on training courses, and I spent several weeks on a course at **Exeter University's Nuffield Theatre**, where we were taught all about stage art and craft. It was a thoroughly enjoyable time, and very worthwhile. What happened to me in getting the job here is an excellent example of schools and work-places collaborating to get the students employed.

Acoustics are improved

"Some people who come to shows at the Pavilion have always complained about the poor acoustics, particularly for speech in plays. This has now largely been overcome. I'm told that the centre of the stalls around row J was always notoriously bad, and apparently, people booking seats would refer to it as 'the dip', and ask not to be given seats there! Not so long ago, probably five or six years, the speaker set-up was repositioned; there are now two banks of three 'cluster' speakers above the canopy, and underneath the balcony, there are a series of small speakers which are, in fact, in slight delay. It's only a fraction of a second, and is all computer controlled and designed. The idea is that members of the audience who sit under the balcony will hear the sound at the same time as it's taken to travel from the main speakers in front of the auditorium. It's all very clever.

The Perils of
Radio Microphones!

"There are many **different types of microphone**s, and it's important that the correct one is used for each individual situation, so I have to have some knowledge of their qualities and their weaknesses. **Radio mics** are very good though not without problems! Each person using one has a little box, about the size of a cigarette packet. This is the battery power and also the transmitter of the sound; sometimes, those using them forget to switch on the power, and if that happens, I can't control the sound at the desk! Another potential hazard with radio mics is that people, having done their scene, go off stage and forget to switch the mic off. So, as desk-controller, I have to make sure that all mics are closed down as a person leaves the stage, otherwise the audience might hear sounds it shouldn't! If there are a lot of radio mics on stage at the same time, it can sometimes be frustrating to find the correct one, especially if an actor or singer is in the wrong place on the stage, or, worse still, if an actor has picked up the wrong mic!. But it's all wonderful work.

"My job is not just for the Theatre, but we all work everywhere in the building if we're needed, and sometimes we go the **B.I.C.** as well. We've just been doing lots of work in upgrading the **Pavilion Ballroom** facilities, and we have some portable sound systems which might be required in the **Lucullus Room**, or even in the foyer. So sometimes, I might find myself operating one of these. There's always a technical person on duty whether there's a show or a function taking place or not, so we work different shifts which fit around all the hours that the complex is open.

"It's a great crew here - we all work hard but we have fun, we pull each other's legs, we have jokes, but the team spirit is next to none because everyone is totally committed to the job. Amidst the fun we know the need to be professional and safe. We have an enormous variety of work, each day bringing new challenges and new problems, and that's what's so great about it. The **building too is magnificent** - amazing in fact. There's so much here which takes you back in history and somehow oozes a sense of security. The only sad part is that when we have excellent and big shows here, sometimes we don't have as big an audience as they deserve."

THE WEST ARCHIVE

Part of the archive of old posters and programmes. This is in the West Corridor towards the Ballroom. See if you can find Jeremy Beadle, David Essex, Chris Ellison, Terence Donovan, Chris Jarvis, Ruth Madoc, Wayne Sleep, Max Bygraves, and a few more! The Archive is well worth a browse on both sides of the Stalls.
(See Page 43)

Nowhere better.......
SEAN TOMKINS HAS THE 'BEST JOB IN THE WORLD'

As Deputy Chief Electrician at the Pavilion Theatre (there isn't a Chief!), **Sean Tomkins** *is obviously totally dedicated to his work, and he exudes pure enthusiasm for the theatre in general and for the Pavilion.*

"I can think of **no better job** in the world, and I know of **no better place** than the Pavilion to do it. I have great respect for the Pavilion and it's like working with a respected member of my family. I like all the work, but while enjoying the challenges created by the touring shows, I'm particularly happy when I've got the chance to design the lighting myself. I regularly provide the lighting for the weekly Compton Organ Concerts and these are a great **chance to experiment** with lamp positions and colour mixes, and it's gratifying when people actually mention that they liked what you've done. I'm told that some theatres have similar organ concerts and let the organist play in the houselights or, in one case, in general working light. I like to be as imaginative as possible and give the audience something to look at, thus enhancing the music. For a show to sound good, it also has to look good. We all like it when an organist or the **Bournemouth Municipal Orchestra** make comments to us, sometimes publicly, about how they've appreciated what we've done on stage.

Pavilion still has a lot to offer

"We've had some wonderful touring shows here in my time, and I especially remember 'Chicago'. It was an enormous production of one of the greatest **and most successful shows** ever on the stage. They had a marvellous and extremely professional crew. The amusing thing for me was that I had only one lighting cue to do right at the beginning of the performance. All the rest of the lighting was controlled by the company's staff, but that doesn't mean that I had nothing to do. We all work together on the stage and there's always something to be done with props or scenery or on the fly-rail. I loved the extended run of **'The King and I'** in the summer of 2005, and it's good to know that after 76 years of taking in shows, that the Pavilion still attracts some big and top productions with well-known and first-rate artistes. There's no question that the **theatre still has a lot to offer** in the way of entertainment to those who live here and to the thousands of visitors.

The Orchestra Back at Home

"We welcomed back the Bournemouth Symphony Orchestra in 2002 on a more regular basis. Although people come to hear the music, it's good to be able to design some lighting for the concerts, thus highlighting the musical settings with some adventurous lighting ideas. And this is the kind of work I particularly enjoy. What you do have to watch is that you don't go too far - **stage lighting is only an aid** to a show - not an end in itself, and too much alteration and movement can detract from the real purpose of the show.

Nothing like a good GOBO! Not to mention a Fresnel and a Profile!

"Many of the shows nowadays do most of the lighting operation themselves. They can plug up their pre-programmed switchboards into our system and they just have to press the right buttons at the right time. All the creativity in the lighting has been prepared elsewhere and is just replicated in all the theatres the show visits. We have to be alive to new systems, new ideas and new techniques; I love the **new 'moving' lights**, which can be set from the switchboard and moved about the stage to point in different directions. Some have special technology inside them which allows the colour of the beam to change through two moving colour-wheels which can, when mixed, provide an almost infinitesimal number of colours; the operator can control the discs and mix the colours as he wishes. There's also a special disc in some lamps. It's called a **'gobo'** and on the disc can be various shapes and patterns cut to let the light through. These can spin and give wonderful effects of movement on stage settings. They were used very effectively in the show **'High Society'** in 2005, when a white garden set was made almost real with these lights which gave the effect of the sun shining through tree branches. There are two different types of stage-light - a **fresnel** spot and a **profile** spot; the fresnel lamp gives an area of light with a soft edge, whereas the profile spot gives an area of light with a hard edge. And these new lamps can be either, and are superb spots revolutionising stage lighting and operation, but which are extremely expensive!

Safety Conscious

"We often have to go up into the dome above the auditorium to check on safety cables on the chandeliers and we're always conscious of our own safety and the safety of the audiences and artistes. The girders up there are enormous - far bigger than would actually be needed to support the real weight, but this 1920s iron-work was well-designed and well-constructed, and would be suitable for any extra weight which future builders might place on it.

"If you sit down right in the middle of the first few rows of the stalls, and look up, you'll see the vent above you is usually partly open. It's about six-feet in diameter and is still used sometimes for some front-of-house spotlights; it was put there for a spot on the organ and also for a stand-up comic who wouldn't move much. It would have been an horrendous place to work with no safety barrier or harness, and with today's health and safety requirements, would not have been allowed; the heat up there is unbelievable and would have been a lot worse when you were standing next to a hot 1000 watt lamp! Mind you, the view from the hatch is dramatic and magnificent, with people appearing like little ants below. *(See photograph on Page 133)*

Theatre is in the blood

"The 'theatre' is definitely **in the blood** of my family - my dad's a professional comedian and my older brother runs a stage school. When I was at Henry Harbin School in Poole, I was able to do my **work-experience at the Mowlem Theatre** in Swanage, but I knew even before that, that I wanted to work in the theatre. At the Poole and Bournemouth College, I studied computers and then, because the **theatre yearning** was so strong, I took a B. Tech. National Diploma on the technical side of the theatre. There were only six of us, and it was a

great course.

Spotting in a Truss!

"At that time, the electrician at the Pavilion was **Barry Beresford** - he eventually became stage manager, and he had a small company called "**Crew Call**", which gave those interested a chance to learn about theatre in a practical way in the Bournemouth Theatres. This gave me - and many others - a great opportunity to learn about big rock shows and these were massive, and on a couple of occasions, at the Windsor Hall in the B.I.C., I found myself '**truss-spotting**' - that's where you're literally strapped at the top of a pole with a spotlight. Very frightening! So, through Barry, I was able eventually to get a part-time job at the Pavilion. I was 19 then and have been here six years, although my post actually requires me to work at all the venues in Bournemouth's

Entertainments. I didn't actually target the Pavilion for a job, but it's where I always hoped I'd finish up. I've never had any formal training in stage lighting techniques, so the job is a good opportunity to experiment - I can learn what's possible and the audiences soon tell me if they don't like it!

"Sometimes, we finish up in the 'lime-box' at the back of the theatre - you have to go outside to get into it, but it's a large area. We call it a 'lime-box' - some would call a projection box, because in days gone by, the light for the follow-spots was generated by pointing two carbon-arcs towards each other, thus creating a very, very bright white light. The arcs also gave off a tremendously acrid smell, and the operators were actually given a **milk allowance** in their salaries to help dampen the effects of inhaling it! The box also had little chimneys to get rid of the smoke. Nowadays, the light is created in other ways, which are much more environmentally friendly.

Stage Crew in Scanty towels!

"I like every show we have at the Pavilion - each one brings a **new challenge** or a new idea and from that we all learn a little more about stage work. One of the best stars we ever had was **Jeremy Beadle;** he's known for giving other people a hard time in a humorous way, but he also doesn't mind taking it as well! On the last night of his pantomime, he told us all we could do whatever we wanted; that's unusual nowadays, because most shows insist on sticking with the usual pattern right to the end. Everyone on stage was involved, and at one point in the show, the girls came out from a supposed shower scene - and the stage crew all followed wearing just towels. The audience, and Jeremy Beadle thought it was a great ruse.

Broken Train

"I remember once - in fact we still go cold when we think about it - in an amateur show, there was a **concertina-train.** Obviously, because the stage isn't as wide as a train, it all bunched up in the wings. We, on the stage crew, stood behind the front part, and pulled it across the stage. Unfortunately, half way across, **it broke in half,** and we were pulling only a small piece of the train! I was with the stage manager, and he shouted, **"Oh, my gosh** (it was really a bit stronger than that!), it's snapped in two!" There was nothing we could do, and just had to cover as best we could. Mercifully no one was hurt. Sometimes things can go wrong and you have no choice but to laugh it away. On another occasion, in the pantomime **"Snow White and the Seven Dwarfs"** starring **Marti Webb**, a cloth being flown-out caught the corner of a little scenery cottage and it totally collapsed. The most important thing was that no one was hurt, but it really was very funny - not that we thought so at the time!

"It would be good if the Pavilion could revert to its original plan, and become a **central meeting point** where people come for a drink, and a coffee and then have a sit-down to enjoy some of the lovely views from the back of the building. That would be the dream, and we'd see the building in full use and providing everything residents and visitors need for entertainment. I love the building - **long may it continue to thrive."**

Programme advertisement in the 1960s.
The Nanking Chinese Restaurant was almost next-door to the New Royal Theatre. It is long closed.

Simon Bagnall
PAVILION STAGE MANAGER

Simon Bagnall is the Stage Manager of the Bournemouth Pavilion and his connections with the building are long established. He is particularly interested in the building as it would have been in 1929 at the official opening.

"Although the publicity at the time claimed that the stage was big enough and well-enough equipped to take **big London shows**, this wasn't really the case. The stage was very small, there was no grid and **virtually no wing-space**, and there were matching staircases on either side of the stage which led to the sides of the circle, probably the basis of the steps which now lead down to the exits from the toilets on either side. As far as is known, the orchestra pit lift and the organ lift were in situ, but the stage was greatly enlarged when what is now the **Phoebe Bar** was added - this spans from west to east, whereas the original plan had two smaller bars (lounges), one either side, spanning north to south.

Mysteries Galore!

"There are **lots of mysteries** about the building and its fittings, such as the current **chandeliers** which hang in the auditorium. I'd always been led to believe that the original glass chandeliers had been damaged during the dreadful bombing raids in 1943, but we now know that the concerts by the Bournemouth Municipal Orchestra on that day actually took place as advertised, so any damage caused must have been minor. The large chandeliers which now hang in the theatre are a similar mystery; folk-lore suggests that they were bought from a town hall somewhere in the north of England, but, in fact, they appear to be of German origin, with German colour-coded wiring and it would seem likely that they were custom-built for the Pavilion. One suggestion was that they came from Rotherham - and the libraries' archive there can confirm that changes were made to the lighting in their Assembly Rooms during the war. While this by no means conclusive, it is possible evidence that that's where they came from. It's these kinds of mysteries which make the Pavilion such a **fascinating place** to work.

"We know that the footlights and the **five lighting battens** were almost original - although not often used nowadays, they still worked until very recently when they were taken down, but the **footlights** remain and these are particularly useful for such shows as pantomimes. Changes in the style of theatre lighting had made the battens totally redundant. On-going massive changes in theatre

The large auditorium chandelier and some of the marvellous art-deco work of the ceiling

lighting mean that spotlights are much more versatile and can pinpoint stage areas much more accurately than the battens which give a rather cold general spread of light. And nowadays there's not so much worry if lamps can be seen by the audience. It's interesting, too, that the Pavilion, in the lime/projection box, was the first theatre in the country to have **four carbon-arc lights** upgraded to **Xenon lights**.

From Safety Curtain to Revolving Stage

"Another mystery is the enormous **Safety Curtain**, the "iron" as it's called; history has the story that it was in position at the opening in 1929, but it would seem unlikely that it could actually have been flown out. The plans of the stage at that time would seem to suggest that there just wouldn't have been enough room. We do know for sure that the revolving stage was added in the early enlargement of the stage in 1934, and this revolve was still working - albeit a little erratically! - until 1994, when it was covered over. Some of the mechanisms remain, and it's likely that it would still work if we uncovered it and plugged up the control, which is now stored under the stage *(See photos on Page 204)*. During the years, some shows managed to use it to good effect, but most of the touring shows ignored it because other theatres didn't have a revolve and so the scenery wasn't built to accommodate one. If shows need a revolve nowadays, they bring their own portable mechanisms which can fit onto any stage.

Advanced Building Techniques

"When the building was finished, it had the biggest **unsupported Circle** in the country, constructed on a cantilever system which was bolted to upright RSJs (rigid steel joists). Most of the building was with **RSJs clad in concrete**, and built on sandstone. I went under the auditorium when we were making some repairs in the theatre, and underneath there is just sand - all very eerie! The land site was sloping and was used very sensibly by the architects and the builders, who used it to their advantage. There was little earth-movement needed but the foundations go very deep. Provision was made for extreme weight on them, and the ballroom foundations are strong enough to have another floor built on top. The heating initially was by steam and then oil-fired boilers, and the building was the first in the town to have three-phase electricity; this was all **locally produced at Branksome** and provided the theatre with 400 amps.

"I came to the Pavilion first of all in 1984 when I was on **work-experience** at St. Peter's School in Southbourne, and it wasn't long before the fascination took over and I started casual stage work when I left school. I went for several years on tour but always finished up working here on and off. **I love theatre** in general, and this is my local theatre. In my younger days, I used to build my own model theatres using coloured sweet wrappings for the lights. In fact, my childhood ambition was to control the lights, and when I came here for work experience, this urge was made even more intense - the lamps were so big and so stylish, with real character, and I longed to operate the lighting system for shows.

Danny La Rue and Postman Pat with his Black and White Cat!

"The first show I worked as a casual was **Danny La Rue**, and during the performance, the chorus girls used to rush off to make quick changes! I used to bunk off school, to do my job which was to **collect the microphones** from on stage. Of course, I was found out; my teacher phoned the stage manager and I was sent back to the classroom. Not deterred, I was back for **The Grumbleweeds** and I can remember that my first cue was to see dancers come safely on stage through a giant oversized piano. But it was still the lights I really yearned for - so desperate in fact that I paid for a course in theatre lighting which taught me how to operate a **Gemini Switchboard** such as the Pavilion was using at that time. This, of course, meant that I had a head-start. I can still recall that board which was frequently going wrong and not doing what it was supposed to, but there was a back-up system. Then came my break through the unlikely characters of **Postman Pat and his Black and White Cat**; as the man who was switchboard operator at that time didn't report for duty for this show, I was asked if I could cope. Cope? Of course I could, and so my childhood dream was realised.

"I had such happy times here and remember the worst get-outs we did were after ice-shows, when all the hard ice has to be chipped up - a dreadful back-breaking and extremely hard job. We were extremely busy, with wet pipes and pool lines.

So Much Grief

"The Pavilion has **suffered so much grief** over the years that I sometimes wonder if it's jinxed. Many local people don't particularly care about it, it's **not much loved** and they dislike it because of prejudices about the heating and the sound, and the local newspapers have always tended to give it **negative publicity**. The Winter Gardens, which has a very good acoustic for the Symphony Orchestra, is very limited in comparison; an old indoor-bowling-green which has extreme limitations as a theatre, whereas the Pavilion is a complete entertainments centre and complex. Both have their place in the town, and it seems a great pity that one is balanced against the other. Under-investment has made the Pavilion start to crumble; instead of **extensive renovation**, there has been a succession of 'bitty-bodges'. This is a shame, because the Pavilion is a **beautiful building** and deserves much more respect from the residents and from the council. It's on public land, and should definitely remain as a municipal venue.

Poor Sound is Not Always our Fault

"The **acoustics** have always been criticised, and in fairness, they are very much dependent on the man who is controlling the sound; he has a difficult task in that whether the theatre is full or nearly empty, he has to satisfy every member of the audience. Often the problems are not of our making; if a show comes in on tour, their own sound engineers can set up microphones and speakers which are unsuitable - the Pavilion was designed in an era when there was no such technology as recorded sound, and so it's hardly surprising that some electronically-generated sounds are difficult to get right.

Grand Old Theatre

"I love the building, I love the Theatre, and **I love my job**. I'm proud to be working in such a grand old theatre and sharing its memories of virtually every top actor, singer, musician, performer who ever toured the country. It's grand.

Wartime Concert

This programme was loaned by Gwen Chapman of Poole (See Page 102), and shows a star-studded 'cast'. Sir Henry Wood and Malcom Arnold* - now an internationally-known composer - would have made a formidable team. Note, too, the unusual starting-time, presumably because of war-time restrictions.

*Now Sir Malcolm Arnold, CBE. He was born in 1921, and is a prolific composer, including Nine Symphonies - and he aslo wrote the score for the film 'The Bridge on the River Quai'. Star names have always appeared at the Pavilion!

n.b.
Presumably, the actor George Baker, who played Inspector Wexford in the Ruth Rendell Mysteries on ITV is not the same person as the narrator here. He would have been only 12 years old at this time!

THE PAVILION - BOURNEMOUTH

Thursday, March 4th, 1943, at 6.15 p.m.

MUSICAL CULTURE LIMITED

presents

THE LONDON PHILHARMONIC ORCHESTRA
(Leader - JEAN POUGNET)

Conductor :
SIR HENRY J. WOOD

Narrator :
GEORGE BAKER

Solo Trumpet - MALCOLM ARNOLD
Solo Organ - PERCY WHITLOCK

Programme and Notes price 6d.

Timely Device
NEVER STANDS STILL AND IS CONSTANT

The Pavilion has co-ordinated time!

The master clock on the left is in the Catering Office, and it controls many important clocks throughout the Pavilion.
From Top to Bottom: Reception Clock, Manager, Bob Bentley's Office Clock,
Forecourt Clock and Technical Co-Ordinator, Chris Knighton's Clock

1970

February - £1,120 was spent on the fountain with new jets to mask the bowls and pillars. A management spokesman said, "We wanted to improve the fountain, but not spend too much money."

June - **Douglas Dawson**, General Manager, investigated by police.

December - Dawson found guilty of theft.

December - 'Dick Whittington' starred **The Barron Knights**.

1971

January - **Douglas Dawson**, General Manager, resigns.

February - **Luis Candal** becomes General Manager.

March - The Pavilion was the **victim of a hoax**. 225 seats were booked by a Southampton School for a matinee of the **Royal Ballet**. No one turned up for the seats, and the school claimed it had no knowledge of any such booking.

March - The 1,500 seats in the auditorium are put on the market as plans start for their replacement.

May - A Councillor queried the need of spending £5,000 on doors at the Pavilion.

May - Alderman Derek Scott said, "I don't think the Pavilion will be knocked down for ten or fifteen years."

July- **Traffic jams** were a problem in Westover Road between the two performances. Police blamed **selfish, thoughtless and arrogant drivers** who queue jumped to take car-parking spaces as they became empty. *(Some things never change!)*

August - Mike of the comedy duo, **Mike and Bernie Winters**, was taken ill during a performance during the twice-nightly summer season.

October - Letter in the Echo complains that late-comers in the audience were allowed entry at all times, thus disturbing the enjoyment of the show for others.

November - **Theatre closed** for redecoration and alterations. There had been many criticisms of the dark and dingy decor from the 1960s, so **lighter, pastel shades were used** - two pinks, reds, blacks and blues. New theatre seats were installed in red, and the seating plan took on a new layout. The **stage was re-laid** with a cork underlay, but the existing revolve stayed in situ. The cost of all the refurbishment was £111,500.

December - 'Puss in Boots'.

1972

February - Chamber of Trade described the conditions at the Pavilion as '**not good enough**', and some members wanted it pulled down and rebuilt.

February - The **South Terrace cafe** opened.

September - Refunds were given to some members of the audience at a show called '**Stars from the Black and White Minstrel Show**'. The show was described as '**atrocious and pathetic**'.

October - The Delfont Organisation lost the contract to present summer shows after a six year run.

November - Students at the Bournemouth College design a large mural for the **Viking Bar**.

December - Plans were presented to provide a new entertainments and conference centre on the present site. This would, supposedly, be built within four years.

December - The '**new**' fountain, built just three and half years ago, was **knocked down** following public criticism. Some had likened it to a collection of kettle drums and an oil refinery.

December - 'Robinson Crusoe'.

1973

February - It was agreed that the Pavilion should start a **mailing list** advertising future productions.

February - Because of abysmal attendances at plays at the Pavilion, there was to be an experiment that **two people could enter for the price of one**.

March - **Pavilion Ballroom** comes under stick for not opening on Saturday evenings. Many thought that a need was being neglected.

March - **Coloured toilets** were discussed for the Ladies. It was felt that white was rather clinical.

Easter - The Pavilion saw its first-ever **seven-night-a-week show**, starring **Larry Grayson**.

September - **Sam Bell**, Manager, said that plays were too expensive to bring to the Pavilion. He also denied that summer shows at the Pavilion and in the Winter Gardens were **excessively noisy**.

December - 'Aladdin'.

76 Years of the Bournemouth Pavilion

Phil Silvers, following his enormous success in television's 'Bilko', played in **'A Funny Thing Happened on the Way to the Forum'**, a stage farce which had originally starred Frankie Howerd.

Among other shows were **'Fiddler on the Roof'** and a group of television stars in **'Not Now Darling'**.

January - The Council spent some time in discussing the major issue as to who should appear at the theatre on Good Friday - **Des O'Connor or Rupert the Bear!**

March - A rather **unfortunate decision** was made to dispose of nearly 1,500 **music scores** worth hundreds of pounds. They had been the life-blood of the pit orchestra before its demise.

May - Plans for a new **conference centre** suggested that the Pavilion would need a change of use.

September - The summer show **'Those Good Old Days'** - was extended by another week.

October - A gloomy report was published that inflation had 'eaten up all the profits'.

November - New West Terrace extension was started to be built. Cost would be £100,000.

December - The pantomime, **'Cinderella'**, starring **Dickie Henderson** and **Arthur Askey** ran for **nine weeks**, and was watched by **95,000** theatre-goers.

June - The dreadful **West Terrace extension** was opened with bar and cafe. The main aim was for it to be used as an extension area for exhibitions. It cost **£100,000** which was to be paid for by the profits from the Catering and Entertainments Committee. Although some attempt was made to make the building look similar to the original, the overall effect

is one of inferiority, and it altered the whole face of the West Terrace until the present day, taking away the original idea for a pleasant promenade with a sea view. The construction in 2005 is idle and in decay.

The roof of the extension building in 2005, as seen from the Top West Terrace.

October - **Luis Candal**, the General Manager, spent £2,700 to replace the cutlery and crockery. In true British style, it was purchased from Sheffield and Stoke-on-Trent. Luis commented, "A lot is taken by holiday-makers, particularly knives, which they 'borrow' to cut up their beach snacks."

November - **Good news**, at last. The show, **'Boeing-Boeing'** was reported to have been seen by **10,000 people** in the theatre's summer season. This was an **all-time record**.

December - **'Jack and the Beanstalk'**.

February - An idea for offering **bargain tickets** was dismissed by the council.

April - Sound system was to be upgraded and updated. Also, a **new lighting switchboard** was installed at the side of the Circle. It was an MMS (Modular Memory System), and was the first fully computerised lighting operation.

April - The Pavilion was reported to be **in the red** to the tune of £38,000 0ver the past twelve months. There was discussion as to whether the theatre could afford to continue offering subsidies for local amateur shows.

December - Robin Hood

1977

March - Popular singer **John Hanson** gives his final performance as '**The Student Prince**'.

April - Council Committees fight it out over whether the Pavilion forecourt should have **cars or roses**!

May - A touring theatre company reports appalling audiences for a production of Shaw's '**St. Joan**', saying that box office receipts were less than half what they had been in any other town of the nine-week tour. *(This is an excellent example of how Bournemouth folk seem to shun any kind of culture, although they complain that there is none!)*

June - Bournemouth Council report that the Pavilion is '**the heaviest loss unit**' in Entertainment Services.

June - **Big Bands** came back to the Ballroom.

July - Eric and Ernie **Morecambe and Wise** played several Sunday shows.

July - It was suggested that the **forecourt fountain** should be demolished to make more room for car parking.

August - new concrete steps were built from the south-east end of the ballroom into the car-park.

September - The **rose versus car** saga continues. There were to be 43 new car-parking spaces and a new water-feature. One councillor thought the fountain should be covered with tarmac.

October - The Pavilion's **main boiler** had to be repaired, during which operation a cloud of black smoke poured from the cellar, falling on cars in the car-park. There were several insurance claims for damage. It was announced that **John Inman** would star in next year's summer season.

December - Councillors say that women are afraid to go out at night because there is so much violence in the town. *(27 years on and still no change!)*

December -'Aladdin' with **Lenny Henry** and **Don McLean**.

1978

January - Pantomime, '**Aladdin**', hit a problem when **Scruffy**, the canine star fell sick. A new dog was sought and the post awarded to local Jack Russell '**Skip**'.

February - Entertainer and broadcaster, **Don McLean** hits out strongly at **local apathy** over the pantomime. He said, "Locals don't deserve a pantomime."

March - **Jack Jones**, the general secretary of the Transport and General Workers Union, was honoured on the Pavilion stage at his retirement.

March - Pavilion site considered as the place for Bournemouth's new Conference Centre.

March - **Sadlers Wells Ballet**

April - **Poole Arts Centre** opened with a 1,500-seater Concert Hall, a 600-seat theatre and a small cinema, as well as other rooms. Many of the shows which had up until now played the Pavilion preferred to go to Poole. Also, the **Bournemouth Symphony Orchestra** transferred to the **Wessex Hall**. These events certainly changed the entertainment scene in Bournemouth for ever.

April - A new forecourt fountain was proposed, featuring dolphins. This displeased some people, especially those in Poole, because the dolphin is the sign of the Borough of Poole!

May - Actress **Googie Withers** made a return to the British stage at the Pavilion.

July - A suggestion was made that local hotels should be offered **special rates for tickets** at Pavilion shows. This idea is now (in 2005) being successfully employed at the Pier Theatre by a private theatre company!

September - The **London Contemporary Dance Theatre** put on two world premieres.

October - £8,000 **losses** reported.

November - **Dulcie Gray** plays Agatha Christie's Miss Marple in '**A Murder is Announced**'.

December - Pantomime was '**Dick Whittington**' with BBCtv's **Crackerjack** team, including **Ed Stewart**.

Other stars at the Pavilion this year included **Arthur Askey**, **John Hanson** in 'Lilac Time', **Danny La Rue** and **John Inman**. **Basil Brush** also graced the stage!

1979

February - The **black clouds of death** certainly hung over the Pavilion and it looked as if the final curtain was to fall. More losses were announced, and the Council admitted that Bournemouth was falling far behind Poole in entertainment.

March - **Fiftieth Anniversary celebrations**. In spite of the gloom, a special charity ball was held for the Pavilion's fiftieth birthday. A celebratory message said: *We can all thank the foresight and intelligence of those people who created this well-loved building whose 50 year record has amply proven its value to the town.* *(What a shame that the town hadn't shown a similar proof to the Pavilion!)* The Echo described the Pavilion as **"the focal point of the social and entertainment life of the town."**

April - An unusual local story developed which accused the **Pavilion Ballroom Dance Band** of denying talented local musicians the chance to play.

April - The **Safety Curtain** cable brake snaps. The show had to be stopped and the audience sent home. The cable is five-eighths of an inch thick.

Claims on a web-site that the curtain was raised by using the orchestra pit lift are not only make-believe and fantasy but totally impossible. The show playing the theatre was 'Play it Again, Sam'!

April - In spite of the continuing doom about the Pavilion, the Council claims that there was much needed improvement, as the building had had nothing but a lick of paint in fifty years.

May - Political decisions are known to change, and alarming winter losses are likely to mean the closure of the theatre in winter months. It was also announced that the summer show bookings for Paul Daniels were booming. There was a

Festival of Dance Week in the Ballroom.

October - There were audience walk-outs at the show 'Fings ain't what they used to be'.

October - A week was lost and the theatre became dark following the cancellation of the Vienna Ballet. There was no problem with ticket sales, but the company had suffered a disastrous fire which destroyed most of their costumes.

December - The Pantomime programme picture was painted and designed by a Dorchester girl. The pantomime was 'Babes in the Wood' with Matthew Kelly and Elizabeth Estensen (now Diana in the Woolpack of Emmerdale).

Picture well illustrating the dominance of the motor-car
over the Pavilion Forecourt

What Needs to be Done?

PAVILION REDEVELOPMENT

from "Bournemouth Online" dated 1st December, 2004
www.bournemouth.gov.uk/News/major_town_developments/Pavilion/default.asp

(Since the opening of the Bournemouth Pavilion) "......numerous alterations have been undertaken, including the addition of two storeys to either side of the main entrance in the early 1950s, and the replacement of the large fountain in the forecourt by a smaller one in 1968. In 1998, the building was listed Grade II and its future has therefore been protected.

The Pavilion now falls short of present-day standards in a number of respects:

The **auditorium** requires modernisation to improve comfort and acoustics, the **stage** and access arrangements need to cater for modern touring productions and the performers' **accommodation** needs to be upgraded.

The once grand and dominant building is now **masked behind overgrown trees**, a car park and an elevated road.

Front of House space is inadequate with difficult access for people with disabilities.

The building **lacks the resources** to encourage and develop new audiences and to undertake education and community projects."

The Past in the Present

Pavilion Theatre, Bournemouth
Sunday 9th October 2005
At 7.30pm - Doors Open 7pm
Director – Stephen Godsall, Entertainments Manager - Chris Jenkins
with Christian Knighton and the Pavilion Organ Fund
proudly present

Picture Palace
Memories

Recreating a halcyon evening at a Super Cinema,
with the Mighty Compton Organ & Steinway Piano.
Nostalgic Film excerpts - Archive Newsreel - Cartoon
and a special Cine-Variety Show with

Rosemary Squires - nightingale of song
Peter John - the very best of comedy
Donald MacKenzie at the organ
Michael Brent - Piano

Stalls seats £7 - Seniors & Students £6
Circle seats £8 - Seniors & Students £7

Box Office 0870 111 3000
www.bic.co.uk & www.pavilionorganfund.org.uk

Bring back the old times! An evening of cine-variety was held at the Pavilion in October 2005 - bringing memories of the 1930s and 1940s.

Malmesbury Park School

BENJAMIN JAMES KILCOYNE and
KIRK BUTCHER

One summer's afternoon, just before the school holidays, I came across a small group of pupils from Malmesbury Park School who were on a Town Centre fact-finding visit, and who had come into the Pavilion Foyer. I showed them around the auditorium and we took a look at the stage where the crew were getting ready for a show later that day. Two of the pupils went home and wrote poems about their unexpected visit to the Theatre. The poems are superb, and I reproduce them exactly as they were sent to me.

THE PAVILION

ITS SO LARGE AND OLD,
IT'S A JOY TO ALL,
ALL THE TICKETS ARE SOLD,
BUT THERES ONLY THE ONE RULE,
JUST TO HAVE FUN THERE!
UNDER THE HUMUNGUS CHANDERLEIR,
ALL THE STAFF JUST CARE.
GO FOR A NICE BEER,
ALL THE BARS ARE OPEN,
1560 RED SEATS IN ROWS,
THE BIG STAGE IS OPEN,
WITH ALL THE BEST SHOWS,
LUSH BLUE WATER FOUTAIN OUT SIDE,
THE HUMUNGUS STAGE IS GREAT,
THE BUILDING IS SO WIDE,
COME DOWN WITH YOUR MATE.
IT'S A GREAT ADVENTURE
AND A GOOD DAY OUT

Pavilion

Seats that scatter across the room.
Red rose seat like the fire of doom.
Chandeliers that peer like a once silk web left for ever more.
Waiting for a spider to come through the door.
The stage like a wall, width by tall.
The ceiling makes you feel as if you're in a ball.
Not strait, not normal at all.

BY BENJAMIN JAMES KILCOYNE

© PAVILION ORGAN FUND

I love Kirk's idea of the auditorium being like the inside of a ball. Wish I'd thought of it!

I really liked going into the pavilion it was the best trip I ever had and it was the first time I went into the pavilion thanks and good by
Kids today never had it so good.
By Kirk butcher

Goons with Neddy Seagoon?

JOHN CRESSWELL on Goons and Ballet

*John Cresswell is a local author and social historian who has written a complete history of the Streatham Hill Theatre in London. He had already started some research into the Bournemouth Pavilion, and he very generously handed over all his notes and thoughts to me. I sincerely thank him for his magnanimity; the **News Diary** section for the 1930s and 1940s is considerably fuller for his help. (H.A.)*

"I can recall going to see what was billed as '**Stars of the Goon Show**' in 1955, with **Joseph Locke** on top of the variety bill. Although '**The Goon Show**' was highly successful on the radio, it definitely needed **Harry Secombe** - but he wasn't on the bill, although **Peter Sellars** and **Spike Milligan** both did individual stand-up routines. I can remember my school friends and I were rather disappointed. *(See Page 194)*

In 1957, I made my first venture to the ballet to see the **London Festival Ballet** in '**The Nutcracker**'. I may have gone earlier in the week and I recall that the audience was not large (although I had remembered seeing that earlier references to the Festival Ballet indicated full houses. Once hooked on ballet, I used to go regularly to the Pavilion whenever a company visited, buying the tickets on the day booking opened, because they were always popular and often sold out. The three main companies were the **Festival Ballet**, the **Royal Ballet** (touring company) and **Ballet Rambert**. It was pretty much the same diet and I became fed up that all we got from '**Swan Lake**' was Act II - never the complete ballet. It was this starvation diet that made me go to London to see ballets in full - especially modern ballets."

Classic Show

PAVILION THEATRE

BOURNEMOUTH   Box Office Tel. 25861

Entertainments Manager DENNIS L. J. HALL

Week commencing Monday 12th May, 1980

Nightly at 8.00 p.m.   Matinee: Saturday at 2.30 p.m.

PATRICK FYFFE and GEORGE LOGAN

present

★   ★

DR. EVADNE   **DAME HILDA**

HINGE AND BRACKET

in

STACKTON TRESSEL FAVOURITES

Stalls, Circle: £3.25 £2.75 £2.25   OAP's and Children: £1.25 to matinee

Parties: 1 free seat in 10 ex. on reduced prices

Box Office open each weekday 10 a.m. to 8 p.m.

G. & M. Organ Ltd., Theatrical Printers, Wrington, Bristol.

The hilarious Hinge and Bracket, round about the time of the amazingly successful BBCtv series "Hinge and Bracket at the Buxton Opera House"

MEMORY
John Matthews
AUTOGRAPHIC RECORD

John Matthews has been a regular patron of the Bournemouth Pavilion for more years than he cares to remember, and has an enormous collection of autographs, making a wonderful record of the stars who have played the Pavilion.

"My interest was not only to see and hear the artistes perform but also to get their autographs. My intention was to provide some kind of record of the stars who appeared in Bournemouth. I have several books of autographs going back to the 1940s, when I remember the Stage Door man was very straight-laced. The trouble nowadays is that you can see a signed name in the book and realise that most people are too young to know who they are! Also, like most people of my age, my memory isn't what it used to be, and I sometimes can't remember whether I saw the artiste at the Pavilion, or the Winter Gardens, or the New Royal Theatre. It's a fascinating hobby and I've made many friends while waiting at the Stage Door after shows. **Maurice Denham**, **Harold Berens**, **Jack Warner**, **Basil Radford**, **Gladys Ripley**, **Richard Attenbrough** - I could go on for ever, and each name brings back a personal memory. One of my favourites is the actress **Evelyn Laye**.

I saw her in 1948 at the Pavilion, and she was lovely. I like the jazz bands, too, such as **George Melly** and **Chris Barber**. And back in the 1950s, I saw a show with **Peter Sellers** and **Spike Milligan** with the harmonica player from the Goon Show, **Max Geldray**. But none of these was the star of the show

- the star was the singer **Josef Locke**. It was a great show. *(For full programme details, see Page 194)*

But my most treasured autograph has to be Richard Attenbrough when he played the Pavilion in 1950.

(John also has a very rare copy of the Programme for the visit of The Prince of Wales to the building site of the Pavilion in 1926. There is a picture of what appears to be a very well-developed concert hall. This can be seen in the News Diary on Page 6)

The Things You Find!

KARL BLANCH reflects on Cleaning Duties

*If you think that a cleaner in a theatre just picks up sweet papers and vacuums the carpet, then talk to **Karl Blanch**. Karl was a seasonal cleaner for **Bournemouth Services** in the mid-1990s, and worked frequently at the Pavilion. He explains the system:*

"We were working in teams of eight people and started work at six in the morning, working for three hours. In that time, we had to clean everything - and I mean everything! The foyer, the brass, the theatre, the wrought iron railings, the stairs, the toilets - you name it, we cleaned it. And it was a job that you couldn't skive at, because you knew you were being watched all the time by CCTV cameras. When the morning shift was done, we were off until four in the afternoon when we did another two hours. I remember that not everybody pulled their weight, and sometimes you found yourself doing more than a fair share of work.

"In the theatre, we had all the litter to pick up under the seats and between the fold in the tip-up - here we'd find all sorts of lost property including umbrellas, coats, hats and small handbags - it's amazing what can hide itself between that narrow fold. We'd often find the odd coin or two on the floor but my most amazing find was a wad of bank notes for £600! We found that they had been dropped by an elderly lady who presumably didn't trust her bank. It's amazing just what people bring to the theatre with them.

"The most annoying elements of the theatre cleaning were the sticky sweets and chewing gum left on the backs of the seats, and on the carpet, often trodden in. Toffee was dreadful and could take an age to scrape off, then wash, then vacuum. And, of

course, there were the cardboard ice-cream containers and plastic spoons. Very few people thought to take them out with them! Once we'd got all the litter up, it was time to vacuum, but this didn't take too long, although we were only using ordinary domestic cleaners. Remember there are about 1500 seats in the theatre, so it was quite a task.

"In the toilets, we often found rolls thrown down the pans, and so they were often completely blocked, but it was the foyer where much hard grafting had to be done. Take a look around at the amount of brass there is - around the display cabinets and all over; it all had to be cleaned properly every day and left looking shiny. The wrought-iron work was awful to clean but had to be properly wiped,

dusted and then polished, and the terrazzo floors were first swept, then mopped and finally buffed every day.

"The box office had to be dusted and vacuumed and the conference room on the east landing of the foyer steps had to be checked. Also, we were responsible for the steps outside the entrance to the foyer - these had to be cleaned and swept, and the forecourt checked for litter. And, of course, all the bins had to be emptied - so you can see that there wasn't any time for dithering because the shifts were quite short for the amount of work to be done. And, I forgot to mention the brass around the circle barrier - lots of it, and the soft floors in the promenade behind the seats - they had to be washed and polished.

"Occasionally, something unusual happened - one day when we all had to do the cleaning very quietly because **Joe Pasquale** was doing a sound-check. This sort of thing - although very rare - made us feel part of the whole show. Sometimes, I was put on the dressing room cleaning, and this was fascinating because the artistes used to put their own mark on them. They made the rooms their own and we had to respect their privacy. We seldom saw them but the rooms had a very special atmosphere.

"The ballroom was an absolute nightmare to clean - if there had been a lively party the night before, the floor was covered deep with party-poppers, broken glasses, spilt beer and all sorts of litter. But we always managed to get it all spick and span. I really enjoyed my time at the Pavilion - there's something about the atmosphere of the building which makes it a good place to work."

The Original Bournemouth Pavilion Lighting SWITCHBOARD

The first (1929) lighting switchboard and batten.

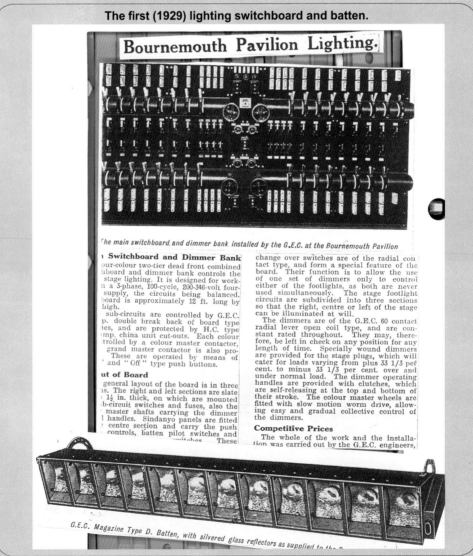

Bournemouth Pavilion Lighting.

The main switchboard and dimmer bank installed by the G.E.C. at the Bournemouth Pavilion

Switchboard and Dimmer Bank
our-colour two-tier dead front combined board and dimmer bank controls the stage lighting. It is designed for work- n a 3-phase, 100-cycle, 200-346-volt four- supply, the circuits being balanced. board is approximately 12 ft. long by high.

sub-circuits are controlled by G.E.C. p. double break back of board type es, and are protected by H.C. type mp. china unit cut-outs. Each colour trolled by a colour master contactor, grand master contactor is also pro- These are operated by means of and " Off " type push buttons.

ut of Board
general layout of the board is in three s. The right and left sections are slate 1½ in. thick, on which are mounted b-circuit switches and fuses, also the master shafts carrying the dimmer l handles. Sindanyo panels are fitted centre section and carry the push controls, batten pilot switches and itches These

change over switches are of the radial con tact type, and form a special feature of the board. Their function is to allow the use of one set of dimmers only to control either of the footlights, as both are never used simultaneously. The stage footlight circuits are subdivided into three sections so that the right, centre or left of the stage can be illuminated at will.

The dimmers are of the G.E.C. 60 contact radial lever open coil type, and are con- stant rated throughout. They may, there- fore, be left in check on any position for any length of time. Specially wound dimmers are provided for the stage plugs, which will cater for loads varying from plus 33 1/3 per cent. to minus 33 1/3 per cent. over and under normal load. The dimmer operating handles are provided with clutches, which are self-releasing at the top and bottom of their stroke. The colour master wheels are fitted with slow motion worm drive, allow- ing easy and gradual collective control of the dimmers.

Competitive Prices
The whole of the work and the installa- tion was carried out by the G.E.C. engineers,

G.E.C. Magazine Type D. Batten, with silvered glass reflectors as supplied to the P

Behave Yourselves!!

KEN BATT recalls a
MAX WALL MOMENT

Revd. Ken Batt, Vicar of Holy Epiphany Church in Bournemouth, was born and brought up in Christchurch and was a member of the Priory Choir; he has a couple memories of the Bournemouth Pavilion.

"In 2005, we went to see **Aled Jones**, this wonderful personality, and it's amazing how the Pavilion, which is always thought of as a theatre and concert hall, is also a good place to hear religious songs. Aled sings many such songs, and they fit in every bit as comfortably as the songs from the shows and the big rock groups. The lady who I found amazing was his supporting act, a young lady called **Keedy**. She had a very unusual voice and as she sang so beautifully, she physically punctuated her voice with wide sweeps of the arms and hands, and gentle and precise curling of the fingers. The movement was every bit as important as her singing. I suppose she was rather like a classical **Shirley Bassey**.

Thoughts of Max Wall

"While I was sitting there in the interval, as my wife went off to buy an ice-cream, my mind went back to the mid-1950's when I was a paper-boy in Christchurch, and all the paper shops were encouraged to buy tickets for one particular performance, to go and see **Max Wall** in the pantomime, **'Mother Goose'**, at the Pavilion. The idea was that the newsagents could show their appreciation of what all the delivery boys and girls were doing - a kind of thank you. So it was, that what seemed like hundreds of children - me included - found ourselves in the theatre to see this oddest of comedians.

A Bit too Ridiculous?

"Now, I really don't remember us being badly behaved, but I was aware that some of the audience were not too amused by his antics of pretending to try and play the piano when the lid was down. Apparently, this was part of his charm - a sense of the ridiculous. But it seemed as if the youngsters thought it was all **too** ridiculous and so the

auditorium got rather noisy! Then, to our astonishment and, I suppose, embarrassment for those who were misbehaving, the curtain came down, all the house lights came on and an announcement was made, asking - or was it telling? - us to be better behaved and allow Max Wall to get on with his act. I remember nothing more about the show, but I do recall vividly this situation."

Well, the audience at that performance might not have been too impressed, but the Bournemouth Daily Echo *critic thought that Max Wall was brilliant, and wrote several paragraphs extolling his performance and his originality. But, then again, he wasn't a teenage newspaper deliverer!*

HIS COSTUMES

At the head is Max Wall, as Mother Goose, not in the grand style of pantomime dames, perhaps, but a dame who is going to be a great favourite. His approach to the part is conversationally subtle, and in his scenes with Billy Goose, the Squire, Gretchen and the village policemen his brilliant timing and grand sense of the ridiculous reveal him as a droll without equal in this type of humour.

Petite Fois and Ice-Cream Bombs
MARGARET CAVE relives happy days in the Pavilion Kitchens

"The Bournemouth Pavilion, since its opening in 1929, has always been an important venue for corporate Dinners and Dances. These require a large staff and large kitchens. **Margaret Cave** *worked in the kitchens for the Lucullus Room, the Popular Restaurant and for the Ballroom in the 1950s and 1960s.*

"I was the **patisserie assistant**, making the cake for the Popular Restaurant and for the Tea Dances in the Ballroom. My job was to make the small fancy cakes, and so I worked carefully with the baker. Great big sheets of **sponge cake** would be passed through the hatch, and I cut these up into the cakes, and then decorated them. I also helped with the sweets and desserts. The fruit salads were made in large bowls, into which I put the cut apples, pears and oranges and mixed them together. Everything was fresh in those days, and nothing came out of a tin.

"Our work rotas were posted in the kitchen, and we mostly worked Mondays to Fridays, but sometimes we would be taken off the rota on a day during the week so that we could work at the weekend for the really big functions, when everyone would work. We worked split-shifts, usually in the mornings and then the evenings, but sometimes when we were very busy, we would work all day and evening as well. For the big functions, we made the sweets and had to make them attractive to present to the customers, so I was able to use my own imagination and I much enjoyed the creative side of the work. There were fewer choices of dessert in those days, and what I really enjoyed making were the **ice-cream bombs** - tutti-frutti bombs! They were placed onto oval stainless steel dishes, and when they were brought in to us, we had to cut them into portions, and then pipe the cream up into each section, before decorating with brandy snaps. Other sweet courses were **Dutch Apple**, and Sultanas in Stewed Apple, but I don't remember what they were called. While working on these, we were also making the fruit salads for use in the two restaurants.

"One very popular and very lovely sweet I recall was **Meringue Glace** - that was meringues, with ice cream and real cream, and that often appeared on the menu. The Head Chef was called **Mario Leto**, though we all called him Jack, and there was Dennis working with me on the sweets - he was the Sweets' Chef.

"I can still see those enormous kitchens - they were so long, and we had a special room just off the main kitchen and designed for the sweets. Ralph was the baker and we also made lots of sausage rolls and presented them on silver platters. Each one of them was made by Ralph himself, long before the days of pre-prepared frozen foods in plastic sachets. He also made the most delicious **chocolate eclairs**. We always enjoyed the days when pancakes were on the menu, because they were fun. The pancakes themselves were really very small, made in what was like an omelette pan, and three of them would make up a single portion for serving in the restaurants.

"The butcher had his own room where all the meats were hung up on separate hangers. Sometimes, the kitchen porters were drafted in to help with the preparation of the vegetables. We all had to make sure we were spotlessly clean and that all the worktops and utensils were kept washed, but there wasn't quite the same obsessive attention to cleanliness as there is nowadays. But we did have a very happy working environment and we all got on well together, and we certainly worked hard - but we didn't mind because we all enjoyed the job so much.

"I doubt if I could find the kitchens today; I can't even visualise how we got to them, but they seemed a long way from anywhere else in the building. During breaks, we used to sit outside and just talk, but there wasn't very much spare time! I can remember **Peter Ward** who was excellent at cake decoration. One highlight was when **Manchester United** came to play in Bournemouth; we cooked breakfast for them and all the fans were able to come in have a breakfast too.

"There were no such things as after-dinner mints at the Pavilion during my time there, but we used to make **petite fois** instead; **peppermint creams dipped in chocolate**, **marzipan pieces** and the rest, all attractively positioned on oval steel plates and a plate for each and every table. They were happy days, and I have some lovely memories."

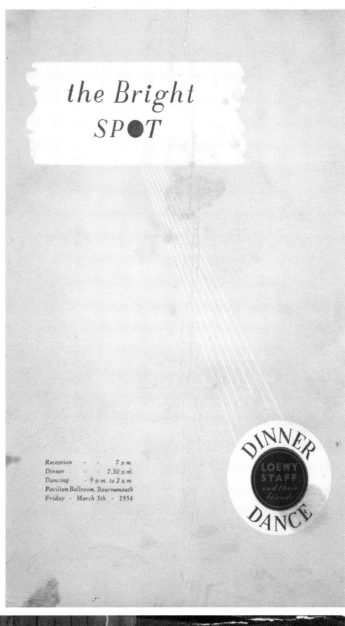

the Bright
SP●T

Reception - - 7 p.m.
Dinner - - 7.30 p.m.
Dancing - 9 p.m. to 2 a.m.
Pavilion Ballroom, Bournemouth
Friday - March 5th - 1954

DINNER
LOEWY STAFF
and their friends
DANCE

Top Right:
A typical 1960s Menu
Bottom Right:
Tasting Session with Mario Leto

Copyright:
Haviland Picture Sales

Michael Lunn

VIVID MEMORIES OF THE ORIGINAL DECOR

*The Bournemouth Pavilion can have no greater fan than **Michael Lunn**, a retired schoolmaster who has, it would seem, more knowledge and memories of the Pavilion than anyone. He is an enthusiast extraordinaire! He tells wondrous stories of transformation scenes in pantomimes throughout the years, recalling scenery movement, colours and costumes in vivid detail, and he has a collection of programmes and handbills spanning the entire seventy six years of performances, as well as a superb collection of memorabilia about the theatre's history. Ask him what pantomime was at the theatre in 1954, or 1942, or any year, and he'll know straightaway the name of the show, and probably the principal stars and the impresario too. And if that's not enough to convince, then he has a large model of the theatre in one of his bedrooms, a model which replicates the decor as it was in 1929, and which has a full working stage and lighting set-up, with scenery, backcloths and miniature performers. Even the tiny seats tip up! It's a fascinating labour of love.*

"My first visit at the age of four was to the 1943 pantomime '**Jack and the Beanstalk**', presented by impresario **Harry Benet**, who put on shows every Christmas for many years, right back to 1934. I was

so small that my feet didn't touch the floor in the circle, where I sat in a gangway seat; I remember the lovely sherry-coloured seats, and I still smile when I remember that my spring tip-up seat shot me upwards when I craned forward to see the stage. To this day, I am still a little wary of the seats! The house tabs (the main stage curtain) made a particular impression on me as a lad**; old gold with yellow and rusty-red flames** spiralling from the stage level, and the **Bournemouth Borough Coat of Arms** clearly visible on the top of the proscenium border (pelmet). The ceiling was pale blue, embellished with rows of stars with a gold centrepiece, and an architrave and frieze in a biscuity colour; the pilasters (pillars) were cream and the organ chambers on each side of the proscenium arch were green. Somehow, I have this feeling for

The Proscenium Arch of Michael's Model of the Bournemouth Pavilion. Michael built the model with Margaret Barnes

colour, and I can still see all this quite clearly in my imagination.

"The original seats in the theatre were called **St. George's Theatre Chairs** (I've never been able to find out what particular qualities these chairs had), but they were replaced in 1938 with plush seats and tubular ashtrays. In 1971, the seats were again changed but these were inferior in quality, cerise in colour, and lacking any real personality.

"Back to my first visit - I actually remember some of the people there, and also the scenery sets in the pantomime, particularly a backcloth which depicted a castle with turrets, and with the giant's henchmen being dressed in green. Although I was mesmerised by the show itself, I was also totally fascinated by the ventilators around the ceiling. And, in March 1945, I watched **Celia Lipton** as **Peter Pan**.

overlarge; and the whole scene was surrounded by a blue-green sea and was for me rather too "chocolate boxy". The Purbecks had three peaks, which looked rather like small volcanoes. The words **SAFETY CURTAIN** were written in sepia just below the horizon. And in brown letters in the middle of the curtain were the splendid words *"By orderly conduct from the audience, this hall can be emptied in three minutes"*.

"The Pavilion complex itself is a building typical of 'between First and Second World War design' - a so-called **restrained nineteenth-century** scheme, which lacks any real flamboyancy, with the Concert Hall (now Theatre) very much influenced by the needs of the **Bournemouth Municipal Orchestra**. I think that the vaulted ceiling is rather suspect for good acoustics. But, set in its right context, in a town

Michael's Model
Pavilion with the
Safety Curtain

"The **Safety Curtain** originally had a fanciful painted scene of **Poole Bay**, spanning from the Purbecks to the chines, with the horizon about two-thirds of the way down. I've replicated it on the curtain of my model of the theatre, and at one time, we were trying to arrange for the present curtain to be painted up in the same way, but this proved too difficult. **Corfe Castle** and **Studland** featured, both

where no major entertainments centre existed, it was just right.

"I read somewhere a folk-lore story that the architects and planners had forgotten the need to have the sprung floor in the ballroom - and hence the rather low ceiling!"

(See Michael's comments about the Bournemouth Pavilion Programmes on Page 118)

Above: Michael Lunn's Model Theatre. *Below:* The Real Theatre in 2005

Patricia Spooner

WORKED WITH FOUR MANAGERS

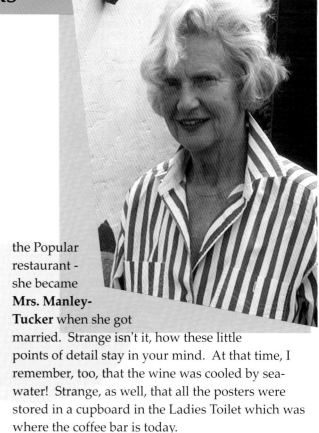

COUNTY BOROUGH OF BOURNEMOUTH

Patricia Spooner

PARTY BOOKINGS ORGANISER

Pavilion Theatre 25861

Winter Gardens 26446

Pier Theatre   20250

Patricia's Calling Card in the 1970s

*There can be few people who worked with four Pavilion managers, but **Patricia Spooner** did, and she recounts her happy times at the Pavilion.*

"I've lived in the area for well over fifty years, and my work took me to the Pavilion on two quite lengthy occasions. In the 1950s, I worked in the general office as an assistant in the catering and other departments. In those days, the offices were where the Circle Bar is now and they were all in a row. The switchboard was on the left of the foyer as you enter. I can remember there was one whole family who ran the kiosks and were also commissionaires - their name was Coole. **Stuart Bacon** was the Entertainments Manager at that time. My job was to organise the eternal and dreadful memos which flew about the offices like paper darts, and they kept the staff informed of what was going on and told them what to do. I also prepared and typed - no computers in those days! - programmes for the dancing and dealt with all the letters from **Arthur Clegg**, the manager; although he eventually left the job ignominiously *(see Page 124)*, he was absolutely charming. For the shows, he wore full evening dress with tails and he always stood under the foyer clock welcoming people as they came in. When you went to the theatre, you really were made to feel that you were somewhere special, and Mr. Clegg was a lovely man to work for.

"I've always tried to remember the names of the people I worked with; in the 1970s, I recall a commissionaire called **Frank Burton**, who used to wear white gloves, with that distinctive maroon uniform and gold-braided hat. He had taken part in the Normandy Landings. In the 1950s, a **Mr. Rowsell** was in charge of the stores and he, I believe, had been in a Japanese P.O.W. Camp; and there was **Miss Randall** who ran a very tight ship as the manager of the Ballroom, and **Miss Calcott** who ran

the Popular restaurant - she became **Mrs. Manley-Tucker** when she got married. Strange isn't it, how these little points of detail stay in your mind. At that time, I remember, too, that the wine was cooled by sea-water! Strange, as well, that all the posters were stored in a cupboard in the Ladies Toilet which was where the coffee bar is today.

"I also dealt with all the complaints, and the mailing list, as well as ensuring that all the flowers for special functions were booked well in advance - this included the banquets and dinners in the Lucullus Room. The Pavilion was a lovely place to work and very prestigious because the complex was the centre of everything. Life was easy in those days; I had no car but could catch the Number 25 trolley-bus from the Queen's Park Hotel, and glide to the Pavilion. The Ballroom was at the height of its success, and the band leader was **Hayden Powell** and I can remember the lovely gold chairs they had. People who visited Westover Road used to wear hats and gloves, as it was a very special road, rather like London's West End. The shows we had in the theatre were all movement and colour. We had little to do with the staff who worked on the other side of the curtain - front-of-house and back-stage just didn't mix - it wasn't the done thing.

"I moved elsewhere until 1972 when I applied for job of publicity co-ordinator for the **Black and White Minstrels** which were presented by the impresario, **Robert Luff**. The job had been advertised in the Echo under the 'Situations Vacant Male' section. How things have changed! I was surprised to get an interview, but I did, with the manager **Leslie Beresford**. And I was offered the job, probably because I was cheaper than the men! I started on £4 0s 0d per week, but this rose to £4 12s 6d. The Entertainments Manager was **Sam Bell** and he was a little remote, but he always noticed you when he needed you, and **Leslie Beresford** was extremely fair and very smooth. They liked what I had done with the Black and White Minstrels and so they gave me more work on Pantomimes and for the Pier Theatre. During my time there, **Dennis Hall** (*See Page 94*) became the Entertainments Manager and he is lovely, a splendid man to work for.

"So my job was publicity, working on mailing lists of party bookings and keeping in regular contact with the local Tourist Information Offices. I spent much time with regional coach companies like **Colessium** and **Angela Coaches** in Southampton - if they had good bookings, so did we! Groups came in from far and wide; such places as Swindon, Exeter, Camberley, Portsmouth and an

even wider area than that; **Rimes of Swindon** was a particularly big coach company. Many local firms had annual outings and I used to encourage them to come to the Pavilion every year. I did this for eight years, and they were good times. I smile when I recall once booking the entire theatre to a company called **Lancing Bagnell**, a fork-lift truck company in Basingstoke. The show was a pantomime sometime in the 1970s. They caught the train into Bournemouth Central Station and then came down to the theatre in coaches. Dennis Hall also used to book the brass and wind bands for the **Pine Walk Bandstand**, and I used to distribute leaflets for those as well - and the **Fisherman's Walk Bandstand**.

"In 1980, I decided to move on, and I formed a promotions company of my own, but it was the Pavilion which had sent me into a successful career. I loved my time there, and we all got on well together, and I still keep in touch with my friends to this day."

Bill and Betty Longman

MEMORIES OF 'PARLOUR MAIDS' AT TEA DANCES

"We attended Tea Dances with **Sim Grossman's Orchestra and Singers** in the 1940s and 1950s. The cost was 1s 6d (about 8p), which included a pot of tea and a cream cake, being served in the interval by **'Nippys'**. These were waitresses dressed in the style of Lyons Tea Shops - a little like the parlour-maids of earlier years. They wore **long-sleeved black dresses** with white **collars and cuffs**, with a pleated pinafore edged with lace; they had headbands which I think were lace interwoven with black velvet. I'm not sure that the Pavilion waitresses always wore headbands. Evening dances were 2s 6d (about 13p) which included refreshments of a sandwich, sausage roll or vol-a-vent, and coffees were also served.

"There was a special Coronation Ball in 1953, arranged by the **De Haviland Aviation Company**. We can't remember how much it cost, but we remember that supper was served as well. On occasions, we had two-course meals in the Lucullus Restaurant for 5s or 7s 6d.

Happy days!! And incidentally, we may be 85 years young, but we're still dancing."

Pavilion Ballroom TEA DANCES 4 to 6 EVERY AFTERNOON (Except Sundays) Admission : 1/- (*including Afternoon Tea*)

1934

Many Secrets
PETER KNIGHT

*As the **Engineer** at the Bournemouth Pavilion between **1970 and 1985**, Peter Knight has many fascinating facts and memories.*

"My involvement with the Pavilion begun when I was three years old. The **Waifs and Strays Society** - now called the **Church of England Children's Society** - used to put on a show each December, presented by a London producer called **Robert Hope**. My parents knew him, and as a consequence, they were often in the shows, and I was called in once or twice. My main involvement with them was to be the caller, making sure all the cast were on stage at the right time.

"I had so many happy years at the Pavilion and saw many changes. In the early 1908s I suddenly found myself saddled with the **Liberal Party Conference**. In those days, such events were organised by the Information Bureau; although that seems a little odd today, in fact it was very sensible, because they were able to flag up all the hotels for the delegates to use. My job not only covered the staging and management of the event, but also the control and use of the media, and all the vehicle parking too.

Steam Heating and Glass-Faced waterfall

"My predecessor was **Les Darke**, whose official title was **Chief Electrician**, but he did much more than that and was a well-known character who was responsible for all the general maintenance of the Pavilion. In his day, there was a **resident plumber** on the staff and a **resident stoker** who was responsible for the control of the coke boilers. When the oil boilers were installed, he stayed on. The whole building was originally **heated by steam**, and the change over to more conventional systems was very difficult. Beneath the West Terrace is a cavernous room which was a pump-room, through which was pumped sea water which came in from large pipes in Poole Bay. This was used for washing the streets in Bournemouth, and the flanges which covered the entrance to the pipes are still there. The pumps themselves weren't removed until in new extension was built on the West Terrace in the 1970s. Also, at that time, there was a **glass-faced waterfall** on the side of the Terrace and the water from this came from the fountain in the forecourt.

"The steam heating fed the kitchen ovens and there were lots of steam outlets around the kitchens which were used for cleaning the floors. I'm told that there was an early attempt to cool some of the water as a **primitive air-conditioning device**, but I've not found any evidence of any such machinery. The only cooling plant I know of was the wine cooler which used a gas called **Methyl Chloride**, a gas which is lethal!

A warm draught

"Air was sucked in from the yard below the Stage Door and passed through heating coils which was then passed up through concrete chambers to the two decorative shells in front of the theatre auditorium, just above the organ chambers. The air came out through the grid, filtered through the theatre and was sucked back through grills underneath the circle and at the back of the roof above the circle, and then it passed back through specially constructed ducts above the two side corridors to the theatre and above the Promenade in the Circle. These ducts are still in existence, but fire safety regulations closed some of the ducts many years ago. Consequently, only a small volume of air can now pass through the system.

Lighting changes

"When I started, the stage lighting switchboard was a **Thyratron Board**, where each dimmer was operated by a series of three large electronic valves. *(See picture on next page)* Although, at the time, it was very progressive and very effective, there were lots of problems associated with the valves, which often meant that the lights wouldn't go out properly. The valve racks were placed on bricks underneath the stage by the West Terrace - quite a distance from the stage. That wasn't helpful when the show required a blackout! As I remember, there were only three of them in existence, one in Manchester, one in Covent Garden and the one at the Pavilion. On the advice of **Bert Sandy**, an ex-ATV staff man who was working with us at the time, I took out the old board and replaced it with an old ATV board which had wire-wound dimmers - in some ways a backward step, but it did have **180 separate dimmers**, and also was the first board at the Pavilion to have a memory bank - albeit, somewhat limited. Ironically, this memory system was from **Compton Theatre Organs**, so it must have felt quite at home, being placed close to the Pavilion organ console! The next switchboard was an **MMX board**, the first fully computerised lighting operation. Oddly enough, all three of the boards I've mentioned were made by **Strand Electric**.

Two Pictures of the Thyratron Board. This board is not the board at the Pavilion, but a replica. The photograph on the right is of the valve racks. *Photos by permission of Jon Primrose from Strand Archive*

"Much of the stage operation today goes back to 1934, when a major refit took place, making the stage wider and deeper. It was a massive rebuild which included **under-stage dressing rooms**, a full **counter-balanced fly rail**, a **scenery lift** to bring scenery up from the entrance at Stage Door level, a **revolve**, a full **lime/projection box** with four **carbon-arc lights** (these were a bit of a nuisance because they had to be cleaned after each time they were used), three for follow-spotting and one for a slide projector, and strangely, the orchestra pit was made smaller. At one time, it stretched out underneath the stalls slightly. There is evidence under the orchestra pit lift of the old arrangement where there's a skirting board. The revolve was supported on **sixteen vertical wheels** all connected by an **endless steel rope**. In order to reduce noise as the revolve went round, the wheels had rubber tyres and I recall, on one occasion, the rubber had worn away, so my colleague **Len Pope**, tried lining the wheels with **Ferodo Brake** Lining. But the first time the revolve was used, the lining all fell apart. So the revolve could only be used when the orchestra was at full volume to drown the sound made by the unlined wheels on the stage. As was so often the case, there was no money available to make the necessary repairs, so I went to **Revo** at Christchurch; they couldn't help, but recommended a company in the midlands who were able to re-tyre the wheels in **polyurethane**. We had to send the wheels away and support the stage in other ways. *(See Page 206)*

From Carbon to Xenon

"Going back to the carbon arc lamps in the projection box, these were replaced with **Xenon Lights**, which I would describe as **'evil'**! They are much better and much brighter than the old carbon arcs, much more efficient and much easier to work.

One of the Xenon Lamps in the lime box at the Pavilion

Their **light output is phenomenal**, made by using the rare gas Xenon.

"The chandeliers in the auditorium were put up as replacements to the original glass chandeliers during the war, and as far as I know they were made specially for the theatre by G.E.C. There are stories that they were bought from a hall in the north, but I'm not so sure.

"Yes, I have **many happy memories** of the Pavilion it was a fascinating building to be part of, and it holds lots of secrets."

Plastered Principal Boy!

ROGER BENNETT

Roger Bennett (pictured left with Grandad), one of the regular members of the audience to the Bournemouth Pavilion weekly Compton Organ concerts, has a memory of the theatre over sixty years ago.

"Although I was born and lived in Southampton, my elder brothers and I were frequently visiting Westbourne where our paternal grandparents lived in retirement in Alum Chine Road. It was there that we spent all our summer holidays; in fact, we were there in September 1939 on holiday when the **Second World War** was declared.

Plastered Principal Boy

"My first visit to the Pavilion Theatre was at Christmas time in 1942, when, as a young school boy I had a thrilling experience. My mother had obtained, booked by my grandparents, tickets for the pantomime '**Mother Goose**', starring that wonderful Music Hall entertainer, **Nellie Wallace** in the leading role. Two things were memorable about that occasion. Firstly, it was announced before the start of the show that Nellie Wallace had had

a fall, and had broken her leg, but that she insisted on appearing as usual and she did, with her leg clearly visible and set in plaster. *(Some news sources claim that she broke her wrist! We believe Roger)*

"Secondly, it was a rare motor journey, because **petrol rationing** had severely curtailed motoring. But sufficient coupons were made available to make the trip. My mother, Aunt Gladys and cousin Sheila and I, mother at the wheel, drove from Southampton through the New Forest in the family **1935 Austin 10**, to Bournemouth. I recall today, the car was navy blue with black mudguards! It was a memorable outing which was enjoyed by us all. The return journey, too, was exciting, for I remember the headlights in those days were none too bright or powerful as we made our way home via Lyndhurst.

Entrance to Lucullus Room below East Corridor

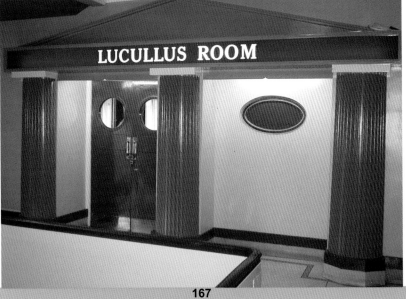

*Tony Bond was the Stage Manager at the Bournemouth Pavilion from 1970 - 1977. He took over from the legendary John **Laurie**, who had been in residence for well over twenty years, and who was, says Tony, an absolutely brilliant stage manager. So how had Tony come to succeed him?*

"I had worked in repertory in Leicester and then gone on to the **Royal Academy of Dramatic Art** (RADA) where I taught stagecraft. I first came to the Pavilion in 1952 when I applied for a job with a company called **Ballet Joux** - and that was the beginning! I immediately fell in love with this theatre with its enormous stage, the best I'd ever seen. In fact, for ever after this visit, I used the Pavilion as an example of good stages in most of my lectures and workshops - all my colleagues knew exactly the way I felt. When John Laurie announced that he was going, an advert was placed in *The Stage* for someone to act as his deputy for a while and then take on the job permanently. Many people think that a stage manager has an easy job with little to do, but in reality, the job is extremely demanding and requires many skills. I hadn't seen the advert, and when I walked into the staff common room at RADA, someone said, "So, you're leaving then?" I had no idea what he meant so he showed me the advert. I applied, got the job and spent a very happy seven years or so in the position. I think the job and the theatre were both fantastic - this was the Pavilion's hey-days with so many big shows, week after week. We had the **Royal Opera House**, the **Welsh National Opera**, the **Royal Ballet**, the **D'Oyly Carte Opera**, and so on, non-stop exciting and demanding work - the only days we weren't open were Good Friday and Christmas Day - until the early 1970s when concerts were started on Good Friday. And for the privilege of doing this job, I took an enormous salary drop from my work at RADA, and welcomed the prospect of an **85 hours working week**!

"In those days, the pantomimes didn't open until Christmas Eve - it was a sort of sophisticated dress rehearsal when any unforeseen problems could be ironed out - and that made the Boxing Day matinee something quite special. I always think that the moment when you fade down the houselights for that Boxing Day show is the best moment of the year; all the five-year olds stop chattering and a definitive hush spreads through the auditorium. I remember one year, just as the curtain went up, a little voice shouted, "**It's in colour!**" - what better start to a season could you have than that? These were the days of big orchestras - 30 or even 40 musicians, and 12 dancers as well as the local dancing school juniors - I remember particularly the **Maureen Headford School**. The amateur shows were wonderful, too, but they were sometimes quite difficult and certainly hard work.

"The weekend would be like this; immediately the previous show finished on Saturday night, say at about ten o'clock, we'd have to get all the scenery and lights out and this would take possibly up until about four on the Sunday morning; then we'd all be back at nine for a full day's work to prepare for a dress rehearsal on the Sunday evening. Shows at this time were beginning to travel by road, but some still arrived by rail, in which case we had to load up the lorries at the station - at that time, the dock was near where B&Q is now and then unload them again at the stage door.

Brilliant Casuals

"I was lucky to work with the entertainments' manager, **Leslie Beresford** - not only was he a superb manager, but also a great man who always made sure that if we

Tony in 2005 looking across the stage

needed something, we would get it. Some of the big shows, like the Opera Companies, would have more than one show in the week - sometimes a different show each performance, so we had get-outs and get-ins every day. And we always opened on Mondays, and spent most Sundays working right through. I was supported by the best team possible; there was **Malcolm** and **Roger** on the full-time staff - always consistently brilliant and efficient, and then there were the casual staff - we call them that, but they often worked as many hours as the full-timers! They weren't just folk who came in for evening performances and changed scenery to earn a bit of pin money, but they were real professionals who knew the trade right through. I recall **Pat Phethean**, **Bob Willis**, **John Price**, **Graham Filbey** the wingman, **Denis Philpott** and **Alan Day** - these were the men who made the shows what they were, who made the staging so professional. **Dickie Henderson** said that his opening night was the finest he'd ever had anywhere in the world.

"The hey-day wasn't to last for ever. In the 1970s, the Corporation stopped giving touring shows any guarantees against losses and the result was tragic - all the **Arts Council Sponsored Companies** stopped coming here, and this made for a much altered pattern of shows. **The Palace Court Theatre**, opposite, was doing well with touring shows and pre-London runs, and they took some of the smaller shows while we took the larger ones. It was a tremendous shame that there wasn't more liaison between the two theatres.

Goodbye to the Big Shows

"This new pattern meant that the really big companies came no more, so after a long-run pantomime - perhaps up until mid-February - we'd have a succession of one-week plays; at that time, we never had anything for less than a week's run, and many of them were pre-West-End try-outs. We'd have a couple of twice-nightly Easter concerts, and then, after a big summer season, we'd have some more plays up to the pantomime. The summer shows at this time were wonderful - **Black and White Minstrel Show**, **Mike Yarwood**, **Des O'Connor**, **Mike and Bernie Winters**, **Shirley Bassey**, **Morecambe and Wise**. The most successful of them all was **Mike Yarwood** who succeeded in selling every seat in the house, twice-nightly for the entire season!

So Many Memories

"Looking back, I've got so many memories - there was a great television rivalry between **Des**

O'Connor and **Morecambe and Wise**; during Des O'Connor's performance one night, the **Johnnie Wiltshire Band**, who accompanied the comedian as he told his jokes, started to play "**Give me Sunshine**", the signature tune of Eric and Ernie! And Des didn't even notice! Sunday evenings were excellent, too. Sometimes, **ATV** used the Pavilion as a rehearsal for the following week's "**Sunday Night at the London Palladium**" - the audience didn't know this, but it meant that we got big stars like **Tom O'Connor** and **Sascha Distell** playing for our Sunday audiences. And this was a real compliment to the staff at the Pavilion and it showed that it was known that they could cope with the very best.

"**Ken Dodd** shows were always unpredictable and were always without any real plan. Ken's known for his long over-running act and it was quite often that the second house at 8.40 would not start until well after nine! One night, Ken Dodd went out into the Foyer where hundreds of people were waiting to get in for the second house and he shouted, "Do you care?" And they all shouted, "No!" The Sunday shows often had no real plan to them and usually no real information, so we had to make it up as we went along, choosing the lighting colours according to the tone of the songs. Wonderful days.

One year, we had the stage version of the BBC hit sit-com "**Dad's Army**", with all the regular cast. They brought with them a new lighting switchboard, which had all the lighting cues programmed into it. On the first night, there was supposed to be ten-second fade of stage lighting to black-out, followed by a spotlight on **Arthur Lowe** - Captain Mainwaring. But he was left standing in the dark, and it took some time to work out that the switchboard could cope only with one lighting cue at a time - as the ten-second fade hadn't finished, the light couldn't come up on Lowe. He was not best pleased! During "**A Funny Thing Happened on the Way to the Forum**", starring **Phil Silvers** - and this is the first time this story has been told! - I noticed some smoke coming through the scenery flats. Racing round to investigate, I found that a stage light had set fire to one of the curtains. I quickly extinguished it and the show went on totally oblivious!

In another show, **Kenneth McKeller** starred with the Television Toppers dance troupe. During a routine, a large and high scenery flat began to topple over onto the stage where the dancers were

performing. I just watched dumbfounded, but in actual fact, when a scenery flat falls - and it's rare - it falls very slowly, because the canvas construction acts like a sail and slows down the rate of descent. The stage manager controlling the show, one **Perry Brown**, acted quickly by signalling the dancers downstage and getting the flyman to drop in a cloth, in front of the falling flat. He succeeded just in time, and the audience probably didn't even notice, and afterwards Perry complimented me in being so calm about the situation. He said that many stage-managers would have panicked! I didn't have the heart to tell him that I was so amazed and impressed at the way he dealt with the situation that I was rooted to the spot!

"I used to love running the actual shows myself. This wasn't all that common, because most of the big shows had their own stage managers and it was their responsibility to oversee the smooth running of each performance. I remember when the **Tokyo Ballet** came, the stage manager and the electrician were so frightened of the headphones system of cueing, that they made me do it. Both were giving me cues - one by tapping me on the right shoulder, and the other by tapping me on the left shoulder. I had to remember which tap was which, and give the appropriate cues to my staff!

"**Ballet International** were a regular visiting company, and when they wanted a theatre to do a complete refit of their shows, they chose the Bournemouth Pavilion for a week. One transformation scene needed fifteen staff members! We showed the director how it worked, but he wanted to see it again - and then again! I couldn't understand why he wanted to see it repeated, so I gave the staff a good talking to and told them to tidy up their work. Eventually, the director accepted it, and I asked him what had been wrong. He said, "Nothing was wrong. I've just never seen it done properly before, and I wanted convincing."

"What shall I do?"

"One show I shall never forget was the pantomime, "**Aladdin**", starring **Roy Castle** in 1973. He was a lovely man to work with - such a vibrant personality. One scene required him to chase around the stage with the lamp, while he shouted, "What shall I do? What shall I do?" One night, from the audience came a child's voice which shouted, "**Rub the bloody lamp!**" When the laughter and cheering had died down, Roy Castle said, "It's all right for you, you've obviously read the story." At the end of the season, the cast and staff made a collection for him and bought him a silver plate to remember the show. When **Margot Henderson** - another lovely person - first came, she was intrigued by her trailing microphone cable which always seemed to be the same distance from her wherever she walked on the stage. She couldn't believe that a man used to let out the cable from the side of the stage as she walked away, and then pulled it back in when she walked back. This was, of course, the way we were able to stop singers tripping up. So the next night she deliberately walked back and forth and watched the cable following her!

"Another regular show was the fast-moving variety show called "**The Fol-de-Rols**", often starring **Jack Tripp** and **Denny Willis**. Once, on the Monday, the show's stage manager lost his nerve and refused to give the stage and lighting cues - the big theatre had frightened him, so he gave up and went home! So, I had to follow the script from the prompt copy and keep the show running - I've still got that script as a treasured memory. "**The Black and White Minstrel Show**" always went through without cues, as much of the music was pre-recorded. **Max Bygraves**, too, used some kind of recorded backing music which had been known to go wrong on some occasions!

Yarwood or Bygraves?

When **Max Bygraves** was appearing once at the **Winter Gardens**, we had **Mike Yarwood** at the Pavilion. Now Mike used to do a very good impression of Max, and unbeknown to the impersonator, Max was backstage! When he imitated Max's voice and movements, Max walked on to the corner of the stage and pointed at him. Mike Yarwood just couldn't understand why there had been such a tremendous roar of laughter from the audience!

"The organ was always a good and controversial talking-point. Should it go or should it stay? It was in a very poor state of repair, and sometimes the console was in the way of musicians in the pit. At one stage it was suggested that it should be taken out to make more room. Then I appointed a stage electrician called **Richard Smithers**. I didn't know at the time, but he was a superb theatre organist, regularly playing at the **Southampton Guildhall**, and who had played professionally for years under the name of **Tony Fenton**. One day, I heard him playing the Pavilion Compton Organ, and I was amazed at how good it sounded. The potential was there and I argued that we should keep it. So it was that a small team of folk grew up, especially **Len Bailey** and a young casual stage-hand called **Christian Knighton**, who gradually over a period of years have restored the instrument to its former glory. Of course, Christian is now the Technical Director for the entertainments under Bournemouth Council. *(See Pages 65 and 219)*

Where have all the bells gone?

"I don't know much about the operation of organs, but I knew that there was supposed to be a line of sleigh bells in the one of the organ chambers - but that they'd all disappeared. Eventually, I had an idea as to where they'd gone, and I was right! They'd dropped inside some of the organ pipes, and I spent hours in the chamber with a fishing line, pulling out the lost bells.

"Anyone who's ever been to a show at the Pavilion knows that the orchestra is housed on a large flat lift which can be at stage level or can be about 7 feet below. One night, I was in the prompt corner just before the show started, and one of the musicians appeared from the auditorium through the curtains on to the stage, claiming that he'd left his trombone in the dressing room and had come to get it. He'd been unable to get out of the door at the bottom of the pit, so he'd climbed out in full view of the audience to get on stage!

My Essential Panic Box

"As stage manager, I always used to keep what I called a **"panic box"** - in it were a few essentials, like a pair of scissors, some needles and thread, sellotape, you know the sort of stuff. It came in very useful when **Olivia Newton-John** appeared here one Sunday evening. She was wearing a very tight pair of black trousers and, unknown to her, the zip had broken. When she went on stage, a lady in the front row pointed it out to her, so she rushed off in a very embarrassed state, and we were able to put my panic box to good use! **Norman Wisdom** insisted on learning all the names of the staff, and when he came on stage each evening, he spoke to them personally. His act was very much a set piece, and one night he noticed that a spotlight had gone out in the auditorium. He stopped his act, came over to the prompt corner and told me about it. Then he went back, but he'd forgotten where he was, so he started the whole act all over again. **Freddie Starr** was another interesting comedian, and totally

unpredictable; he was a total controller of the audience, but the length of his act varied tremendously. In one show, the dancers decided to play a joke on him - part of his act was a very good impression of **Tommy Cooper**, complete with red fez. This was kept upside down on a table on stage. The dancers put a large amount of talcum powder inside it, and then waited at the side of the stage to see him put it on! But Freddie knew what they had done and kept teasing them by pretending he was going to put the fez on, and then putting it back down again. Eventually, he walked to front of the stage and handed the fez to the **musical director** in the pit asking him to put it on. And, of course, he did!

Boiling Waters!

"During my seven or eight years as stage manager, we had quite a few of **Jimmy Curry's** water effects - they're an excellent attraction and very effective, but they always have the potential for disaster! I recall once when we had the **Waltzing Waters,** which had scores of individual jets, someone thought it funny to fill the water tank with washing powder. The poor engineer in charge had to clean out every single jet. And, on another occasion, we had the tropical cascades as a spectacular finale to the first half. Gallons and gallons of water were poured through scenery made to look like a mountain stream. It was worked by having a forty-feet wide tank, one foot deep at the back top of the stage. This was almost the entire width of the proscenium opening. It was pivoted with a wheel to turn it, so that all the water could be tipped into the scenery channels. Some of the cast complained that the water was too cold, so we put some heaters in. Oh dear! One night, just before the act was to start, I found that the water had boiled. There was no way we could stop it, so I warned everyone on stage to be aware, and when we tipped the trough, all the steaming water gushed down, making the effect even more wonderful.

Screaming woman in négligée!

"One show we had was called **"Pyjama Tops"** and starred **Fiona Fullerton**. Part of the stage set was a large glass-fronted swimming pool which was about twelve feet deep. Lots of semi-nude girls used to swim about in front of the audience. During the show, Fiona Fullerton had to sit on the side of the pool and then jump down backstage, being helped by someone on stage level. Our properties man was **John Price**, so we invited him to help the lady off her perch. One thing we didn't tell him was that she would only be wearing a see-through négligée! And also, we failed to mention that when she jumped off she was to let out a loud scream. On the first night, she jumped, she screamed - and John was so surprised that he dropped her! And that's not the only tale of that show, either. After the final performance, the fire brigade kindly helped us to empty the pool by pumping out the water. Half way through, the drain appeared to block, so they found another one and sucked out the water into that. Next morning, the boiler-man from down below came to see me in some panic, saying that water was seeping through the walls into the boiler room. On investigation, I found that the water from our swimming pool had been pumped into the old coal-hole!

"And one final story I must mention. In those days when the **Playhouse** was also taking touring shows, we had a very large get-in with twelve enormous lorries - I think it was the **Welsh National Opera**. Before we had finished unloading them, another two arrived - that was all we wanted, and we thought we'd never finish unloading let alone get the show onto the stage. I had a call from the Playhouse, saying that they had 'lost' two lorries for their show that week. I jokingly remarked that they were quite welcome to a couple of ours. But the joke was on me - the two new lorries which had arrived at our stage door were, in fact, the show for the Playhouse. The drivers, being new to the town, had seen all the other lorries in our car-park and thought they must be for us.

"They were fantastic days, my days at the Pavilion, an exciting job which I loved and which I had wanted ever since my first visit in 1952.

"Wonderful theatre, wonderful staff, wonderful shows, wonderful work."

The Stage and Auditorium in 2005

The Proscenium Arch in the Bournemouth Pavilion is 45 feet wide. The actual height is 40 feet, but this looks much lower because of the rounded lighting gantry which hangs across the top. This gantry was added in the 1950s. *(See Page 86)*

Two Chances to get a girl friend!

TREVOR AND ANN WITTS

Trevor Witts spent seven years in the Royal Navy, then worked in cinema management before moving to Bowmaker Limited. Although he hasn't always lived in Bournemouth, he has a great affection for the town and was able to return to work in the Bowmaker Head Office in Christchurch Road before retiring.

"My early memories of the Pavilion take me back to before and during the **Second World War**, when my parents took me to the theatre to see Christmas Pantomimes and other stage shows. My mum was as a fan of **Richard Tauber** and the **Mantovani Orchestra**. One evening, we went to see a big band show but we had to leave early to catch the last bus home to Christchurch.

Sid Fay - Drummer more exciting than dancing

"It was during the war that I first encountered the **Pavilion Ballroom**. My mother would take my older sister to evening dances there, and I would be taken along rather than be left at home. As an early teenager, I was not too interested in ballroom dancing, but the 'live' music was an attraction and I used to go up onto the bandstand and **sit alongside the drummer**, Sid Fay. This was much more fun than sitting at the table!

My First Drum Kit

"I seem to remember that Sid was a fireman in Winton and I bought my first drum kit from him. It cost me £5, but my mum flogged it many years later whilst I was abroad in the Navy. I can remember too, Sid's son, Don, who played the clarinet very well. Soon after the Second World War,

whilst I was in the Navy in the Portsmouth area, I used to come to the Saturday afternoon Tea Dances in the Ballroom with what could be best described as a 'gang' of youngsters from the Christchurch/Highcliffe area. We always booked the same tables - they were B4 and B3, so we all knew where to find each other, at the east end of the dance floor between the entrance door and the far corner. Some of the girls at the dances would wear gloves, and some even wore hats as well! On Bank Holidays, there was an added bonus to the day out - morning Coffee Dances as well. So, if you had no girl friend, you had a double chance of finding one! It was jolly good fun. The journey from Portsmouth was no problem, either coming by train or hitch-hiking, which in those days was easy, particularly if you were in uniform.

Meet me under the clock in the Foyer

"The whole Pavilion building was **attractive and impressive**, but the ballroom was especially good, with a warm and pleasant atmosphere. There was a common arrangement made by the young people all over town and beyond **'meet me under the clock in the foyer at the Pavilion.'** This was a regular meeting place, where you knew you would meet your friends and everyone knew exactly where it was. Many years later, in the mid-nineteen-seventies, I was working as training officer for Bowmaker Limited near the Lansdowne. The Company always held the **Directors' Dinner and Dance** each year for all the staff in the Pavilion Ballroom. This was a big occasion, with dinner jackets and long dresses, a real perk for the staff. I certainly missed them when I was posted to Sheffield for a couple of years, but I was fortunate enough to be moved back to Head Office in time for the last such function which was in January 1984. It reminded me of earlier visits, sitting with Sid Fay around forty years earlier and subsequently attending those Coffee Morning and Tea Dances."

(Ann's memory is on next page)

DAVID PUGH LIMITED Presents

THE 'HIT' TELEVISION COMEDY
BREAD
ON STAGE FOR THE VERY FIRST TIME
Featuring Brand New Adventures of the Boswell Family
By CARLA LANE

PAVILION THEATRE
BOURNEMOUTH

*Trevor's wife, **Ann**, has an amusing story concerning the Pavilion Theatre, back in the 1980s, when actor **Kenneth Waller** was in the role of **'Grandad'** in the stage version of the BBCtv sit-com, **'Bread'.***

"We were friends of the actor because he and Trevor had been in the same class at school. After the performance, we went backstage into his dressing room. And this was where the trouble started. We spoke for a while as he wound down from the show, and then he took us over to the Palace Court Hotel for a drink and a chat. When we eventually got home, I realised with horror that I had lost an opal brooch which was of really great sentimental value. I hardly slept a wink and, at first light, I went back to the Pavilion forecourt and had a good search. There were 'No Entry' signs outside the foyer, but I ignored them and went in. By this time, the cleaners were in and the staff were very helpful and searched all around the seats in the area where we had been sitting (I still had the ticket stubs), but to no avail. I mentioned that we had been to Ken Waller's dressing room and they kindly took me to see if the brooch was there. And it was - on the carpet! I actually cried when I found it. But the staff had been wonderful."

Memories of 76 Years
of the Bournemouth Pavilion

The Foyer in 2005

Bitten by the Theatre Bug

HUGH ASHLEY reminisces

Not only schooldays ......

Enormous, intimidating and fascinating - those words would describe my feelings when first I visited the Pavilion to see a pantomime with my parents, sometime about 1950. I remember not what the show was or who was in it, or indeed anything about it at all, but I knew that here was something special, and the atmospheric warmth of this gargantuan building has attracted me ever since. At about the same time, when at St. Michael's School on the West Cliff, I took part in some kind of children's show, I think for Good Friday, when hundreds of us from all over town stood on the stage for a performance of music. This may well have been one of those instrumental shows featuring school children musicians, but I was part of a small accompanying choir, and remember quite well having to climb an extremely steep set of wooden steps behind the scenes to gain a seat on the raised platform. Strangely, I recall one of the pieces we sang; how I remember is just one of those quirks of the mind which stores unimportant information while discarding the real facts we need, but it was by Tchaikovsky - *The Legend (Crown of Roses)*, and whenever I hear it now, I think on that surreal visit to the Bournemouth Pavilion fifty-five years ago. And that, I suppose, was when I became hooked on the theatre, as an compulsive sensation, a yearning, a vocation which grasped me forever.

New Royal Theatre

Anyone who has ever worked in the theatre will tell you that the experience is like an injection of a powerful drug, which takes control of your life. My second and most powerful injection came in the summer of 1957, when **Jimmy Edwards** and **Norman Evans** starred at the Pavilion in "**The Big Show of 1957**". I wasn't there, but I was very conscious of the power of that great variety show, because I was working, as a 15 year old Bournemouth School boy studying for G.C.E. in nine subjects, at the nearby **New Royal Theatre** in Albert Road, for a season of twice-nightly variety starring **Edmund Hockridge**, **Daisy May and Saveen**, and comedian **Joe Black**. My dad knew the Theatre Manager, **Geoffrey Unsworth** and he had got me a job as props boy on the show. I was hooked, and when the theatre closed just four weeks after that season, because the owner **Will Hammer** had fallen off his bicycle and died, I literally wept at what seemed like the death of an old friend.

Yes, the theatre bug had well and truly bitten. So it was, that a year later, I found myself at the Bournemouth Pavilion, backstage, again as a properties assistant, working on "**The Big Show of 1958**" starring **Bob Monkhouse**, **Denis Goodwin** and the **Beverley Sisters**. Here was a theatre vastly different from the cosiness of the New Royal - the stage was enormous, the stage crew varied, large and unknown, the atmosphere at first daunting. I was working under one of the legendary Stage Managers, the Scot, **John Laurie**, who inspired hard work through fear, yet was loved by all for his efficiency. With him was **John Ralls**, the Property Master, who "lived" in a small room in the back wall of the stage amongst an unbelievable amount of unlikely gear, all of which would be, or had been, used for shows or plays, including a kettle and a pint bottle of milk - yes, the tea was made here.

Aircraft Hangar

The stage itself seemed like an aircraft hangar - the New Royal had been cramped and warm, but this was spacious and awesome. All around were tall curtained wings to mask the backstage area from the audience, and scenery flats three times my height, reaching towards the grid, which seemed as high as Salisbury Cathedral. Across the stage was just as far, stretching across the well-worn boards with its famous revolving stage. I couldn't believe that I was here, working in this well-loved and much respected theatre. Could I survive this new work-place? Oh yes - I could, and I did - survive and thrive.

This was a land of make-believe, of laughter, of drama which would use and absorb me for years to come. John Ralls, my immediate boss (line-manager, I suppose he'd be called today) was delightfully cheerful, a breath of fresh air, always on the ball, fast walking and intensely humorous. During the interval he would sing-along with **Harold Coombs** at the organ, making up new and silly lyrics - such as "Don't throw mince pies at me", and we all used to join in with him. He was a joy - a privilege to work for. He was no mean sign-writer, either - he made posters both large and small, and painted the words **NO SMOKING** onto the back wall of the stage - they're still there to this day.

There were others I remember; **Cecil** who worked at Wellworthy's in Lymington, a small man with great strength both physically and spiritually, a man who taught me how to "walk" a scenery flat on my own, a man who just smiled his way through life. There was a milkman whose name has gone, but I think it might have been **Jack** - who spent the entire performance changing over colour frames in the big, now old-fashioned floodlights which filled each entrance to the stage area. There were two younger men, **Alan** and **Steve**, who knew how to get the job

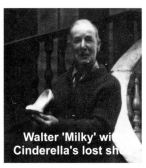

Walter 'Milky' wi Cinderella's lost sh

done quickly and had a pretty strong line in dubious jokes. And there was another milkman, **Walter**, but we all called him **Milky**; he had a lovely Dorset/Hampshire accent and he plodded on getting the job done slowly but effectively, totally ignoring the light-hearted jibes about his age. When there was a breathing space, we all sat just outside the stage at the top of the steps to the stage door and dressing rooms, and smoked and complained about the management and the way of the world. This was the O.P. side - Opposite Prompt, the Prompt corner being on the left side as we faced the audience.

Prompt Side

On the Prompt side were yet more staff, including **Dennis** (guess what we called him!) who pulled the ropes for the "runners", the curtains that closed across the stage for scene changes; then there was the switchboard operator, **John Wyatt**, who operated the electronic lighting switchboard (more of which later), and **Sid Kerley**, the Head Flyman who skilfully controlled the fly-rail, dropping in drapes and cloths and lights and so on. Sid later went on to be Caretaker at the old Portchester School, where he worked tirelessly with the Old Boys Rugby Club. In the distance, at the back of the auditorium, which always felt as if it must be on the other side of Westover Road, three more staff, led by **Tony Joy**, worked in the dreadful atmosphere of the lime-box, where bright spotlights, generated by pungent burning carbon arcs, highlighted the stars as they cavorted across the stage below. Here was a wonder

world of team work presenting laughter and music to hundreds of people twice nightly, at 6.15 and 8.40.

The atmosphere of this stage enveloped those who worked and played there, and united them in a common togetherness of purpose - if your heart didn't sense that, you didn't work there for long. Why would you want to work such unsocial hours cut off from natural light? I felt I was the luckiest schoolboy in the world to have such a job. Even now, nearly fifty years on, the stage is almost unchanged and there's still that unity of resolve, where the current team of **Christian**, **Simon**, **Kristen**, **Sean**, **Ryan** and **Graham** work cheerfully together for aims that are timeless and unchanging. In the 1950s, my values had not been fully realised, but I knew that this wasn't just a theatre, it was the Bournemouth Pavilion, part of the fabric of the town's entertainment, and it was to be part of me, too, for ever. This wasn't, perhaps, a real world, yet it was a grand world to live in.

Bob Monkhouse

Then there was the show itself; dancers opening a vast kaleidoscope of colour, wonder, humour and music - a show filled with big star names such as **Bob Monkhouse**; he was young, he was fun, he was generous with praise and thanks - each and every week of the ten-week (or so) season, he sent a crate of **Double Diamond** beers for the stage crew. His finale act has stayed with me too; an impeccably accurate impersonation of the American pianist, **Liberace**, seated at a white grand piano covered with glittering candelabras. That white piano still lurks on the Pavilion stage, or just underneath it, currently being converted to be operated from the organ console, and Bob Monkhouse finished the act by standing up and singing "I'll be seeing you in all the old familiar places", with the last line altered to 'I'll see you under Boscombe Pier' - and suddenly his black jacket lit up in hundreds of white Christmas tree lights and the audience, twice nightly, collapsed with delight. He was to become one of the greatest stand-up

comedians and scriptwriters of all time, who had the biggest joke book, and the quickest delivery of humour ever known. And where did he have one of his first summer seasons? Of course - at the Bournemouth Pavilion.

Joy and Billy Wed

And the **Beverley Sisters** - well-established and extremely popular, delighting the audience with

close harmony and gentle sisterly banter. During the season, Joy, the oldest, got herself married at the Poole Registry Office to the England footballer **Billy Wright**. When I hear a recording of them singing their signature tune, "Sisters", I remember all the added publicity the show and the theatre received the next morning in the national press.

The rest of the show has largely disappeared from memory, although I remember that **Denis Norden** was a rather nervous man, who wasn't too keen on public appearances, and I recall, too, a so-called spectacular scene called "**The Burning Oil Wells**". Not surprising that this should have notched itself permanently in my mind, because I was directly involved with its workings. The idea was that the audience were shown the scene of an oil-well, and the pit orchestra played dramatic music as the chorus and dancers, in a strict choreographed routine, pretended to be workers there. Suddenly there was a loud stage "bomb" and the stage erupted into a burning inferno! I was positioned underneath the revolving stage with a broom handle - I still feel apprehension at this! - and, when the bomb went off, I had to thrust the broom upwards to dislodge part of an oil-well cap - it was made of wire-enforced paper-mache. A large fan underneath the stage with me started to blow cold air across some roughly cut orange strips of silk and they billowed upwards like flickering flames. And I just kept my head down until the curtain fell

for the interval, as the orchestra blasted forth in agonising chords of destruction, and **Harold Coombs** lightened the atmosphere with a selection of songs from the shows on the organ. I never saw that scene from the audience point-of-view, but I'm told it was very effective. Not a great technological stage production, but a very clever illusion. This was again all part of my learning process, a realisation that people could be entertained without sophistication; over the years, I have heard so many people reminisce about the burning oil-wells - simple yet convincing. And as soon as it finished, it was off to set the second-half opening, which I think was a cowboy scene involving a revolving fence. Happy days! Oh, and one final memory - the smell underneath the revolve; it was dusty and musty and somewhere in the atmosphere was a spice which I never identified.

John Ralls, the Bournemouth Pavilion Property Master in the 1950s and 1960s. Always smiling and always cheerful, nothing was too much trouble. He was slightly eccentric, always smartly dressed, and was actually almost completely bald. In this picture, his 'hair' is in fact a peacock feather he's wearing as a wig. I have no idea why. Note the 1950s scooter and motor-car in the background at the stage door.

During the interval, after setting up the opening of the second half, the stage crew dispersed for ten minutes, some to the bar for a quick pint, and others to the west corridor which links the foyer to the ballroom, where we stood at the windows and watched the holiday-makers milling across the Pleasure Gardens below. Amidst the background of hustle and bustle inside, we could hear the Pavilion Ballroom dance-band, at that time with a drummer who also sang - one Tony Blackburn, before his disc-jockeying days and before his winning stay in the Australian jungle.

Difficult Get-In

Once the season had started, the routine became easy and relaxed, a joy to work, and even better to get paid for the privilege. The last night was again sad, when all the chorus girls cried buckets because they wouldn't see the stage crew again, and when all the now familiar scenery flats and curtains would be taken away. This was my first-ever pull-down and get-out, and fascinating it was, even though it went on well into the daylight of the next morning. The Pavilion has what is termed as a 'difficult' get-in and get-out, in that the stage is well above the level of the stage door exit, through which all scenery, props and costumes go. Because of its difficulty, a small extra fee was paid; I don't remember exactly, but I think my rate of pay for the work was something like £5, which to me, still at school, was more than acceptable.

The problem of the differing levels is overcome by a lift in the east front corner of the stage, a lift designed to take several people and much heavy gear. So the way it was done was as follows: take down all drapes and borders, fold and carry onto lift. Then the props needed packing away into large wicker baskets and taken to the lift. Then all the scenery flats had to be moved onto the lift, and then the additional lighting equipment. The lift took only a small amount at a time, and so it was up and down many, many times to clear the stage. The main difficulty was the high flats - sometimes 18 feet, even 20 feet, and up to six feet wide. These had to inched round the difficult corners by the stage door, off the lift and out through the double doors. The lorries used were large Pickford's Removals vans, and each full one was termed as 'a load'. There would probably be only three vans, but they could be filled up to three times each, because in the 1950s and 1960s, the scenery was travelled by British Rail. So - once the lorry was full, it was driven with some of the staff to Central Station and then unloaded into a railway truck. When that was complete, it was back to the stage door for the next load. If the one carriage was insufficient, we had to wait while another carriage was shunted it, and in the middle of the night, this often wasn't the fastest of procedures! Kristen (today's Head Flyman) tells me that nowadays, some of the really big shows have dozens of road trucks of equipment - and still the same small lift which has been feeding the stage with lights and scenery ever since the theatre opened. *(See Page 46)*

The use of trains for transport slowly died out in the 1960s and 1970s and most shows now travel using experienced firms who specialise in theatre equipment movement So, let's recap the procedure - equipment on to the lift, off the lift into the van, off the van into the railway carriage. It was a long and slow process, but deep down, we loved it. I remember one summer season, when **Des O'Connor** was the star; it wasn't the biggest show we'd ever seen but it arrived by rail on Sunday morning, unusually at Bournemouth West Station, now destroyed by the town's inner-by-pass. We waited at eight in the morning for the first load. And we waited. And we waited. By about half past nine, the Stage Manager, John Laurie was decidedly angry - as he often was! - and it was ascertained that British Rail had sent the carriage to Weymouth by mistake. We were told it would be back by about eleven. So by the time the scenery actually arrived, we had been paid - not, let it be said, by the Corporation, but by the impresario - for three hours doing absolutely nothing. There was, too, a knock-on effect that the stage wasn't ready for a rehearsal later in the day.

Dickie Valentine, who deputised for David Whitfield in 'The Big Show of 1959'. Destined to be an international star singer, he was tragically killed in a motor accident.

There were many shows before the next summer season, including **Tommy Cooper** in the Pantomime '**Puss in Boots**', but Summer 1959 saw **Arthur Haynes** and **David Whitfield** in '**The Big Show of 1959**'. My main memory of this one was the several guest appearances of **Dickie Valentine**, who used to replace **David Whitfield** when he was unwell. Dickie Valentine was an amazing singer and impersonator who finished his act with a sad song called 'The Clown that Cried', thus ensuring a standing ovation. I remember, too, David Whitfield wore a white jacket with a red carnation and started his act with 'Throw Open Wide your Window, Dear'. What a strange thing to remember!

![A never-before-seen picture of David Whitfield and Arthur Haynes doing a promotion for Ind Coope Breweries]

A never-before-seen picture of David Whitfield and Arthur Haynes doing a promotion for Ind Coope Breweries. Notice comedian Freddie Frinton in back seat (left). Remember his wonderful drunken butler sketch with actress May Warden?

Buttons - the Magician!

Pantomime that year starred **David Nixon** as a magician Buttons in '**Cinderella**' with **Erica Yorke** as the 'handsome' Prince.. The Ugly Sisters were played by **Dawkes and Webb**, and there were the usual flour-throwing scenes and - if I remember correctly - a small team of ponies who pulled the pumpkin-shaped carriage. Also, there was an amusing scene with a trick car which eventually appeared to blow up; quite how it fitted into the story, I have no idea! It was all good fun and very popular.

That's Life!

My third summer season was another Harold Fielding extravaganza, with comedian **Al Read**, Comedienne **Dora Bryan** and - amazingly - **Marty Wilde and the Wildcats** for the music. The idea was that the

show would appeal to all age groups. During the season, the Property Master, John Ralls, went on holiday for a couple of weeks, leaving me in charge of the props - a not-too-demanding role! I remember one thing especially - in a Dora Bryan sketch set in a travel agents, she insisted on having a piece of Dundee cake as a prop. Each night, I faithfully cut the slab for her. Marty Wilde wooed not only the younger members of the audience but the more mature as well with a well selected programme that finished with the old semi-religious song 'My Prayer'. Never fails and never failed for Marty either. Marty Wilde's drummer was Brian Bennett, who was later to join the Shadows; as a young man he wanted to be an orchestral conductor, and spent lots of time in the dressing room doing imaginary conducting of symphonic music. Al Read, of course, was a gem, a comedian who saw the funny side of people and made us all laugh through ourselves. Apart from his stand-up second-half routine and his famous signature song, 'That's Life', his main sketch was of a drunk who came across a sign which said 'Police Notice No Parking'. The drunk saw it upside down and the audience collapsed with laughter as he tried to read it. Clean and harmless fun - an absolute gem of humour. These Big Shows were in the beginnings of the glory days - if there ever were any - for the Bournemouth Pavilion, twice-nightly large houses and the theatre ringing with good music and belly-laughs. What else is entertainment all about?

Hugh at the switchboard in 1961. It was customary, at that time, for full-time stage crew to wear ties!

With that show sent back to the store, it was time to look forward to the pantomime - 'Aladdin' starring **Frankie Howerd**, but fate decreed that it was never to be. During a two-week run of the musical 'Salad Days', the theatre was found to be unsafe and closed for several months.

How Tickled I Am!

By the summer of 1961, the theatre was back in operation with yet another Big Show - this time with a very young **Ken Dodd** with **Alma Cogan**, the lady who claimed not to wear the same dress twice, as the principal singer. For me, this was the finest-ever show at the theatre and was to be the point of no return for me. Ken Dodd is such a funny man that you laugh before he speaks - that's true of 44 years ago, and it's true today as proved when he appeared at the Pavilion in 2005. He's noted for long story-telling sessions which often resulted in the first house at 6.15 over-running well beyond the supposed start time of the 8.40 performance. Add to that the problem that Bournemouth Corporation Buses all finished soon after half past ten and you'll see that quite a lot of people had to taxi or walk home! I'm not too sure of the length of season but I think it was about fifteen weeks.

Who Needs A-Levels?

Half way through this season in mid-August, I received the news I had been expecting that I had failed my A-levels and so I needed a job. Coincidence would have it that the Electrics Dayman, John Wyatt, who operated the lighting switchboard, had resigned and quite quickly I found myself in a full-time job in a building where I felt so much at home. As the show was well-established, the lighting cues were well documented and I quickly fell into the twice-daily pattern of the show. I used to work mornings with my direct boss, Chief Electrician **Alex Holland**, and another dayman, **Tony Joy**, whose job was to run the lime/projection-box upstairs and make sure that all the follow-spots were working and maintained. Mornings saw general maintenance and cleaning, and most afternoons, between 1 p.m. and 5.30 were free. This altered if the weather was bad, because the bands that regularly played in the Pine Walk Bandstand during the summer months would come into the theatre and give their concerts there, to a handful of damp and somewhat depressed holiday-makers who couldn't afford to go the cinema! If this happened, I would gain a couple of extra hours work, keeping the stage appropriately lit for the music.

At 5.30 p.m., I was back on duty, my first job being to switch on the electronic lighting switchboard. The main control was in the Prompt Corner on the stage, but the real workings of it were downstairs, underneath the promenade which led to the gardens. It was a large room, with large-sized wardrobe-like banks with hundreds of large valves, like the old radio sets, but each one was about six inches high. Each lighting dimmer had three valves which used to glow when they were working, and if one of the valves stopped functioning, the light would be a third below its maximum. These were a real problem, because we were forever switching them about from channel to channel to keep the lights working as best we could. There never seemed to be enough money to buy any new ones. Another problem was that they took about twenty minutes to warm up before they'd work! On two occasions, through misunderstandings, the board wasn't switched on in time for them to warm up and we had to delay the start of first house for a few minutes. Sometimes, a valve would blow during a performance and we had to make a dash from the prompt corner, across the stage, down the 25 steps, round the four corners past the canteen to change the faulty valve. *(See Page 166 for Pictures of Board)*

The switchboard itself was floor-standing with two large panels, both with identical controls. About 120 dimmers were on each side and the idea was that one cue would be on the left, and the next lighting cue set up ready on the right. When the lights needed to change, a central control was turned to change from one board to the other. A log of each cue looked something like this:

Board A *(Cue 17)* (3 secs)

```
* * * 0 0 0 * 0 0 0 * * 3        4 4 0 * * * 0 0 * 6 6 0

0 0 * * 7 9 0 * * 8 * 0         0 0 0 0 0 * * 8 8 8 8 0

* * * * * * * * * *            * * * * 0 0 0 7 7 7 8 0

* * 8 8 9 9 9 * * 0 0 *
```

Cue 18 - Fade out all FOH (10 secs)

Board B *(Cue 18)* (3 secs)

```
0 0 0 0 * * 7 7 * * 0 0        6 6 7 5 5 5 5 5 5 * * *

* * * * * 0 0 0 0 0 9 9        0 0 0 0 0 * * 8 8 8 0

* * * * * * * * * *            0 0 0 * * * * 9 9 9 5 5

* * 9 8 9 0 0 0 9 * * *
```

Cue 19 - Go to FU all (5 secs)

This all looks very complicated, but it was all very straightforward - a system developed by Alex Holland, and very simple and effective.
Each "*", "0", and "number" represents a dimmer. The "*" represents the dimmer at full, the "0" represents the dimmer at off, and the numbers represent the intensity of light as printed on the plastic sliding dimmers. Each dimmer worked one - and one only - light.

The "cues" were numbered as in the Prompt book which the stage manager used - he would merely say, "**Go 17**" and you'd set the lights for that cue, in the time indicated, e.g. a five-second fade. "**FOH**" is stage jargon for "**Front of House**", and referred to all spotlights on the auditorium side of the main curtain. "**Go to FU all**" is not as rude as it

sounds, but merely tells the operator to bring up all stage lights to full intensity. This is only a basic representation of the operation of the board, but any more would only become too complicated.

Just Like an Elephant!

It's a strange fact of life that, as you get older, some things you never forget - I struggle to remember the number of my wife's car or what I had for breakfast this morning, but I could sit at that switchboard today, over 45 years on, and remember exactly how to operate it. It was easy, and most enjoyable. The only disadvantage was that you had no idea what your lighting looked like, because you were backstage. How I envy Sean and his crew nowadays who can sit at the back of the circle and see exactly what they're lighting.

Very little went wrong during these early weeks, because life at the switchboard was very repetitive, but I recall one night making a very grave error; in the middle of Ken Dodd's first half stint, he had - as ever! - long overrun, and the stage manager was waving him off. For reasons I never understood, while setting up the board for the next cue, I totally blacked out the stage, leaving Ken Dodd in a follow-spot only. I soon realised what I'd done and brought the lights back up. I imagined being given my cards, because Ken quickly concluded his act and came off. I never heard a mention of the error, and believe that he had thought the blackout was a stage-manager's warning to get off stage. It was my first error, and I was mortified - but more would follow in my year to follow as electrics dayman.

So come with me now on a year's work as stage electrician at the Bournemouth Pavilion from June 1961 until October 1962.

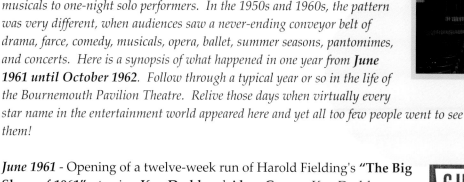
In 2005, the stage presents a tremendous amount of variety from big musicals to one-night solo performers. In the 1950s and 1960s, the pattern was very different, when audiences saw a never-ending conveyor belt of drama, farce, comedy, musicals, opera, ballet, summer seasons, pantomimes, and concerts. Here is a synopsis of what happened in one year from June 1961 until October 1962. Follow through a typical year or so in the life of the Bournemouth Pavilion Theatre. Relive those days when virtually every star name in the entertainment world appeared here and yet all too few people went to see them!

June 1961 - Opening of a twelve-week run of Harold Fielding's **"The Big Show of 1961"**, starring **Ken Dodd** and **Alma Cogan**. Ken Dodd was a young man who had already charmed radio audiences and when he came to Bournemouth, he charmed up to 1500 people twice-nightly. He was extremely funny - in fact, quite 'tattifilarious', and a lovely chap as well. Alma Cogan, who is sadly no longer with us, was full of cheer and joy and her happy voice and songs matched her bright and colourful dresses. **Rawicz and Landauer** were a duo of pianists, who sat both facing the same way. Although they couldn't see each other, their playing and style was impeccable. I most remember them for the closing item which was the theme from the film 'Exodus'; the whole pit orchestra (and pit orchestras were big in the 1960s) joined with **Harold Coombs** at the Compton Organ, and as the final crescendo built, the organ was dominating over all the other musicians, and Rawicz and Landauer's dizzy fingers were playing hard but could not be heard. It was spine-tingling and the audience reception was rapturous. Happy

days, and a happy show, forever indelibly marked into my memory.

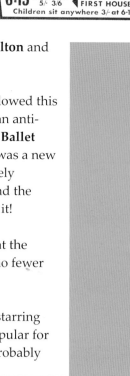

Sundays had different shows which featured such stars as **Joan Regan**, **John Hanson** and **Edmund Hockridge**. **Ronnie Hilton** and **Semprini** also played.

Week 25ᵗʰ September - Whatever show had followed this 15-week bonanza of fun would have seemed an anti-climax. But, all was well, because, **The Royal Ballet** were presenting three different shows. Here was a new experience for me - hours spent setting minutely positioned lamps, a set of very important and very accurate lighting cues, and the prospect of working through at least two nights to fit up each show. I loved it!

2 Weeks 2ⁿᵈ October - And if that wasn't initiation enough into my new job at the Pavilion, what should follow but **The D'Oyly Carte Opera Company** with no fewer than seven different shows. More hard work, but more fun.

Week 6ᵗʰ October brought the first play of the winter season - '**The Gazebo**' starring **Alan Melville**. Alan was a well-known raconteur on television and very popular for his astute and sharp wit. I remember nothing at all about this play, which probably says more about me that it does the play!

Week 23rd October - Whitehall farce followed; **John Slater** and **Andrew Sachs** in 'Simple Spymen' - exactly what you'd expect. John was a very popular and much-worked actor in films and on television, and Andrew Sachs was to become Manuel, the waiter, in the 1970s television sit-com 'Faulty Towers'. I remember being told to 'Shush' by Mr. Sachs when I walked behind the set during a performance!

Week 30th October - From farce to light-hearted bumbling comedy with **Cicely Courtneidge** and her husband **Jack Hulbert**. The play was called '**The Bride Comes Back**'. **Robertson Hare** also starred, and I think he may have appeared at the Pavilion on more occasions than any other actor. Cicely and Jack were very pleasant but, as might be expected, a little aloof from stage staff.

Week 6th November saw the first-ever performances at the Pavilion of '**The Black and White Minstrel Show**' featuring the BBCtv stars **Tony Mercer**, **Dai Francis** and **John Boulte**r, with **Leslie Crowther** as the comedian. This really was delightful week, but many of the audience were disappointed when they realised that the singing was all pre-recorded. From my point of view on switchboard, it was the busiest time I had ever spent in the job.

All good wishes
Robertson Hare

Week 13th November - Back to farce with **Cyril Smith** and **Joan Emney** in '**Watch it, Sailor**'. Lots of laughs, but not much to do for stage crew, because there was just one 'box' set, and the lighting was full-up all the time!

Week 20th November - The farewell tour of '**Salad Days**', possibly one of the most delightful musicals ever to play the Pavilion - or even the British stage. Lovely music, amusing and entertaining lyrics, and some of the worst (or best!) puns you'll ever hear. This is a show which just won't go away from my life I was working at the Pavilion when it had to close down because the fly-tower was unsafe, I was working it again now, and when I moved to the Palace Court Theatre later, I worked the musical for a fortnight over the coldest winter for years in 1963. And in 2005, I revived all the happy memories the show has when I saw it at the Buxton Opera House in the summer. No sex, no violence, no swearing, no filth - just entertainment pure and simple. More, please!

Week 27th November - A pre-West End production of a terrifying play called '**Signpost to Murder**', with three of the really big acting names of the era - **Margaret Lockwood** (always elegant and glamorous), **Derek Farr**, and **Ian Hunter**. The set was a 'split-set' - several rooms across the stage - and there were a couple of rather gruesome images of blood-covered bodies in the bath, I recall.

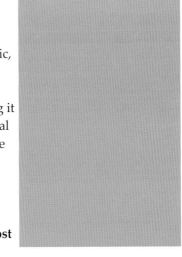

Week 4th December - Two separate plays from **The Old Vic Company**, about which I remember nothing.

11th - 23rd December - Theatre closed for pantomime rehearsals. As stage crew, we had much cleaning and maintenance to do. These were strange days, rather quiet and empty, and we learned that the theatre was only real when it was open and doing its job of entertaining.

23rd December, 1961 - 3rd February, 1962 - The 14th Emile Littler Pantomime, and a good example of how you build a show around a cast. This is what he did; he took **Richard Hearne (Mr. Pastry)**, dancing the Velita, **John Gower** singing beautiful songs, **Billy Burden**, the Dorset comedian

from Wimborne, the **Dagenham Girl Pipers** (yes - the Dagenham Girl Pipers!) and **Jimmy Curry's** amazing wonder highland waterfalls, and he mixed them all into '**Goody Two Shoes**'. It was superb! What better than to hear the Dagenham Girl Pipers playing 'Auld Lang Syne' in the middle of a pantomime? I recall having a bit of a thing about one of the

EMILE LITTLER'S 14th Bournemouth Laughter Pantomime

GOODY TWO-SHOES

Late and Early, *Town Councillors*	...	THE COX TWINS
Muddles, *the Mayor's Son*		BILLY BURDEN
Twiggie, *the Old Woman's Maid*	...	JUEL MORRELL
Bluebell, *the Old Woman who lived in a Shoe*		CLIFFORD HENRY
Penelope, *a Troublesome Horse*		THE MILES TWINS
Fairy Goodhope	...	JANE BOLTON
Goody, *one of the Old Woman's daughters*		CHRISTINE YATES
Mr. Pastry, *the Mayor of Merry-Go-Round*		RICHARD HEARNE
Robin Adair, *a village carpenter*	...	JOHN GOWER
The Yellow Dwarf		BRYN BARTLETT

CURRIE'S WONDER WATERFALLS

THE DAGENHAM GIRL PIPERS

THE ZENA MARTELL CHILDREN

EMILE LITTLER'S YOUNG LADIES

THE NORMANDY SINGERS

The Pantomime Produced under the direction of Emile Littler
by George Barnes

Scene 1	... ...	THE VILLAGE OF MERRY-GO-ROUND
Scene 2	... ...	THE FARMYARD
Scene 3	... ...	INSIDE THE SHOE
Scene 4	... ...	A LANE NEARBY
Scene 5	... ...	THE MAYOR'S NEST
Scene 6	... ...	THE BALLET OF THE SEASONS
	INTERVAL	
Scene 7	... ...	DOWN IN THE LOWLANDS
Scene 8	... ...	UP IN THE HIGHLANDS
Scene 9	... ...	PUDDING ROW
Scene 10	... ...	A WEIRD WOOD
Scene 11	... ...	COURTYARD OF SHOE PALACE
Scene 12	... ...	VAUXHALL GARDENS

The Pantomime written by Emile Littler
Music and Lyrics by Hastings Mann
Scenery and Costumes designed by Physhe
Dances arranged by David Gardiner

Harold Coombs at the Organ
Pavilion Theatre Orchestra under the direction of Charles Tovey

The entire production made in the Emile Littler Workshops at Pantomime House, Birmingham. Costumes made under the supervision of C. L. Trobridge. Hats by Sheeta. Shoes and Nylon Stockings by Gamba. The Dagenham Girl Pipers' uniforms are all supplied by Courtaulds Fibres. Gloves by Milore. Wardrobe care by Lux. Orchestrations by Charles Tovey.

girl pipers and I often wonder what happened to her as she got older.

Week 5ᵗʰ February - After the noise and fun of the pantomime, a one-set play with nothing but dialogue was just what we needed. '**My Place**' was another pre-West End production and starred **Diane Cilento** and **Barry Foster** (later to be ITV's Van der Valk Dutch detective). The only part of the play I recall was the beginning, when Diane Cilento was draped across a bed centre stage!

Week 12ᵗʰ February - Yet another pre-London play starring **Joan Miller**. The play was called '**A Loss of Roses**'. Set in Kansas, it was described as a bitter-sweet romance which scandalised Broadway in 1959. I don't recall any scandal here, nor many people in the audience.

Week 19ᵗʰ February - Once again, appalling audiences greeted a rather heavy philosophical drama by Jean-Paul Sartre putting forward the view that 'hell is other people'. Those who did come and see it largely hated it, and few understood it. **Constance Cummings** and **Jill Bennett** starred in '**In Camera**'. For me, the entire week had a touch of unreality, and the atmosphere of the theatre was subdued and confused. This was a worthy play, but we were unworthy to receive it. Later in life, whilst at college, I had to study Sartre, and I still don't understand him!

Week 26th February - So what we needed was some light relief and we certainly were given that. Ted Willis' play **'Doctor in the House'**, was performed by the members of the cast of ITV's early soap opera, 'Emergency Ward 10'. Just look at the names in the cast **Jill Browne**, **John Barron** (who was to become Reggie Perrins' desk-bound boss in 'The Fall and Rise of Reginald Perrins' - you remember the one who used to say 'I didn't get where I am today.....' - and notably **Charles Tingwell**, who returned to his native Australia and still, even at the age of 82, makes occasional guest appearances in the Grundy Television soap 'Neighbours', and **Desmond Carrington** who to this day (he was 79 in 2005) delights BBC Radio 2 audiences with his nostalgia programmes broadcast 'live' from his home in Perthshire.

Week 5th March - Then came the annual offering from the **Bournemouth and Boscombe Light Opera Company**, Sigmund Romberg's **'New Moon'**. Never be in any doubt that this company's shows are top quality, and my memory is one of a group of male singers calling, 'When I'm calling you-ooh-ooh-ooh-ooh-ooh-ooh,' from the wings.

Week 12th March Sadlers Wells Opera, a company that brought with them top names, and enormous stage sets.

This week, they performed no fewer than seven shows in seven days, so there was quite a lot of overtime. Interesting to note, too, that the top ticket price was 12/6d - five half-crowns! That's just over 62p.

Week 9th March - Poorly planned scheduling by today's standards, but the Opera was immediately followed by the Ballet in the form of the **London Festival Ballet**, another heavy work week, and another week of culture.

Week 26th March - And the heavy and big shows continued with a two-week run of a major musical straight out of the Adelphi Theatre in London's West End, where it had been seen by over half a million people. Meredith Willson's **'The Music Man'** tells of a travelling musician who cons parents into buying expensive instruments for their children to form a band. There were brilliant performances, notably of the full cast and the song '76 Trombones', but for me the gentler 'Lida Rose', sung as an unaccompanied male quartet by **The Square Pegs**. This was a show-stopper every night. Memory bends the truth, but I seem to recall that this show didn't open until the Tuesday evening, because the fit up needed two days - Sunday and Monday. This show was the

provincial premiere of the tour, and it was prestigious for the town and for the Pavilion that Harold Fielding, the impresario, should have selected Bournemouth for this important occasion.

Week 9th April - **Mary Preston** starred in another post-West End Music, '**Irma La Douce**', where an ex-cop in Paris falls in love with a prostitute. This was a well-loved musical and a very good booking for the Pavilion, and back on the list of popularity in 2004 with the new film starring Ewan McGregor.

Week 16th April - Incredible, but the musicals kept on coming, and this week saw the return of one of the most popular singers of the era, **John Hanson**, a singing heart-throb of the 1950s and 1960s, giving all his tenor power to the Mario Lanza role of '**The Student Prince**'. There weren't many empty seats for this, which was a very straightforward and uncomplicated production, one that proves that good theatre doesn't necessarily need millions of pounds thrown into it.

Week 23rd April - At last, a week with something a little quieter - a post-West End play, '**The Amorous Prawn**' starring the great, wonderful and popular **Evelyn Laye** and a heart-throb from Ivor Novello's days, **Barry Sinclair**. The plot revolved around General and Lady Fitzadam who lived at a remote army outpost in Scotland, and who were carrying out their last assignment before the General retires......

Week 30th April - Another play, this time on a pre-London tour, had four enormous acting stars, **Geraldine McEwan**, **Charles Gray** (a Bournemouth actor, born in 1927, who made his name as the villain in the James Bond film, 'You Only Live Twice', and who died in 2000), **Derek Chinnery** and **Geoffrey Chater**. The play was '**Everything in the Garden**' by Giles Cooper, and was a surreal attack on suburban complacency. This was one of the supposedly 'forward-looking' dramas which used risque words to make the audience shrink in disbelief. Not really my scene, but there weren't many lighting cues!

Week 7th May - Then followed a play of real controversy, '**Billy Liar**', with **Trevor Bannister** and **Lynn Redgrave**. Billy was a typical late teenager who told lies all the time. The controversy was because his father kept shouting the word 'bloody' over and over again. Probably wouldn't make much difference nowadays, but the Bournemouth audiences hated it, and walked out in high numbers. This was a post-London tour and I seem to remember that Albert Finney had played in the title role in the West End. Some years later, Trevor Bannister was to criticise the Bournemouth Pavilion, saying it should have been pulled down years ago. He later appeared as Mr. Lucas in the television comedy show, 'Are You Being Served?'

Week 14th May - **Sadlers Wells** returned with a splendid bright and colourful version of '**Orpheus in the Underworld**', complete with can-can. At the end, the cast disappears into hell by way of an underground train. Wonderful stuff!

Week 21st May - A musical by Lionel Bart should, surely, be a theatre filler. But not necessarily this one, '**Fings ain't what they used to be**', with gangsters, tarts and gamblers, and with only the title song worth remembering. This came straight out of the Garrick Theatre in the West End.

Week 28th May - In the 1960s, when summer shows were still being very successful, it wasn't uncommon for them to tour around the country before moving into their summer home. '**Make it Tonight**' was destined for many weeks at the Lido Theatre in Cliftonville, but came to the Pavilion for a week. It starred **Jimmy 'That's Yer Lot!' Wheeler**, the slick cockney comedian with the little moustache and the black hat, **Tony Hughes** and **John Gower**. The opening scene was a small production number where all the cast pretended to board a plane for their holidays. This dog-eared photograph shows the setting, with me pretending wave goodbye but I didn't get any further than the switchboard!

This was super show and great fun to work. Let's hope the people of Cliftonville enjoyed it too!

2 Weeks 4th June - With summer threatening fast, '**The Fol-de-Rols**' arrived, that delightful revue show of music and sketches with **Denny Willis** and the famous Huntsman dance-song, **Joan Mann** and **Norman Caley** whose arms got longer as he sang, and who always made me laugh when he came on stage and pretended to saw the end off a piece of wood. When he'd finished, the opposite end to the one he'd been sawing fell to the stage; silly but funny!

Sundays in June, July and August - a variety of stars including **The Temperance 7**, **Paul Jones** (who has Bournemouth and Portsmouth connections) from Manfred Mann, **Rawicz and Landaeur**, **Winifred Atwell,** who was lovely, lively and exuberant, and **Shirley Bassey**, who gave the musical director a hard time, but sang with all the power and magnificence that she was noted for. Truly wonderful - and for me, a memorable moment when she personally thanked me for the 'beautiful lighting I'd done for her songs'.

July/August/September - What was described as the greatest stage spectacle ever seen in Bournemouth! '**The Big Show of 1962**'. Just look at this - and all for a top price of 10/6d. And there's so much to say about this one; **David Nixon** was a real gentleman and a joy to work for with his slick wit and his magic. One night he wasn't at all pleased with the electrics staff on the stage. One of his tricks was to suspend a lady in mid-air about twelve feet above the stage, with suitably sinister and subdued lighting in reds and purples. We had spent the day washing the lenses and bulbs in the lights which shine from the canopy at the top of the proscenium arch. So, when they came on, being so much cleaner, they were considerably brighter, and they completely gave away David's suspension illusion. He was not happy, but we reduced the power for the second house. **Joan Regan** was - and is - also lovely, a gentle personality who charmed the audience with her delightful and distinctive voice and with her chat about her family. **Terry Hall**, the ventriloquist, and **Lenny the Lion** were extremely clever and when he came back-stage, he would chat cheerfully with the stage crew and you suddenly realised that you weren't talking to Terry, but to the camp Lion. He was brilliant. *Speed Maniacs* was an illusion created by putting David Nixon in a wooden car in the centre of the stage and projecting a film of a road moving fast into the distance; it was simple yet quite effective. The *2-Ton Tilting Mirror* was exactly that, and gave a breath-taking reflection across the stage and audience. **Jimmie Currie's** *Tropical Cascades* were, as all his water effects, superb and were operated on the same principle as a garden water effect - the water poured down the scenery, flowed into big tanks in the dressing rooms, and was pumped back up for a return performance. And, finally, the *60 Foot Model Liner*; this was actually a bit of a con (and that's what good stage illusions usually are - and does it matter?), but very,

very effective. The liner was painted on a very wide curtain which was 'wiped' across the stage on curtain rails, bunching up at each side of the stage. The painting of the liner on the curtain was luminous, and so the ship looked as if was passing across the theatre in a blue haze of ultra-violet moonlight. All well and good but......! One night, the motor which pulled the curtain across the stage, stopped when the liner had reached about half way. So there was a static liner in front of a tittering audience who were beginning to enjoy what was obviously a problem. But things got worse, because the only way we could get the liner out of the way was to fly it - and the audience nearly collapsed when this supposed great ocean liner was seen to disappear up to the theatre roof. This show was directed by **Dick Hurran**, one of the really great show directors. It was such a happy show, that it's firmly entrenched in my memory bank of good and worthwhile times. The Stage Director for the season was **Bryan Penders**, whose name appeared in the 1980s and 1990s as a director of many light-entertainment programmes on BBC1.

2 Weeks 24th September - Following on the fun of the summer season was always difficult, and this year saw a much-heralded brand new play, pre-West End and, in fact, a world premiere. 'Kill Two Birds' was written by one of the great television and stage writers of the decade, **Philip Levene**, who wrote dozens of episodes of 'The Avengers' and much more besides. This play starred **Roger Livesey**, **Renee Asherson** and **Tony Britton**. The first night had a well-papered house (i.e. one where a large number of complimentary seats had been given out) and most of the national press theatre critics were there. The opening scene was a dark stage which should have been lit up when a character walks on and 'switches' a wall switch on the set. I, on switchboard, on cue, would bring up a bank of spotlights to represent the table and standard lights on the set. When I did the cue, the whole stage went to total blackout, and to this day, I can hear the stage director screaming at me in a hoarse whisper 'Bring the lights up, bring the lights up!' There were a few teeth-clicks and gentle intakes of breath from the critics, and when the lights came up a gentle ripple of light sarcastic applause, like raindrops on silver paper, spread through the auditorium. Oh dear - not a good start. The director of this play was **Robin Midgeley**, who has since done a great deal of direction in television drama.

Week 24th September - **Renee Houston**, **Cyril Smith** and **Patricia Hayes** starred in a farce entitled **'Rock-a-bye Sailor'**. Full lighting throughout and, once again, just what you'd expect. Not a very exciting ending to my full-time job at the Pavilion.

And that ended my stay as Electrics Dayman at the Bournemouth Pavilion; I had been tempted away by the Palace Court Theatre over the road as their electrician. The Pavilion had showed me virtually everything the British theatre could offer over the past fourteen months, and I had had a whale of a time. There was sadness but, as life worked out, I was to be back as a casual for several more years to come. The Pavilion is part of my heritage, my learning platform in stage-craft and entertainment. I shall never forget it. Being back on the Pavilion stage for the compiling of this book, working with Christian, Simon, Kris, Sean, Ryan and Graham has brought back all the happy times, all the busy fit-ups, all the problems for solving; life in the theatre is always exciting and varied, and although technology has moved on apace since my day, the lure of the stage still beckons with an enticing finger - once you're entrapped by it, you're caught for ever. If only I were forty years younger.......

Week Commencing 8th October, 1962
Nightly at 7.45 p.m.   MATINEES Wednesday and Saturday 2.30 p.m.
STALLS 9/6 7/6 6/- 4/-   CIRCLE 9/6 7/6 6/-

TOBY ROWLAND LIMITED
IN ASSOCIATION WITH PERTPIC LIMITED
presents

RENÉE **CYRIL**
HOUSTON **SMITH**
IN
THE HILARIOUS NEW "SAILOR" COMEDY

**ROCK-A-BYE,
SAILOR!**
BY
PHILIP KING and **FALKLAND CARY**
WITH
JOHN WARNER
IAN CURRY   **IAN MacNAUGHTAN**
WANDA VENTHAM   **JANET BUTLIN**
MARGARET ST. BARBE WEST
AND
PATRICIA HAYES
Directed by **DENNIS MAIN WILSON**
Setting by **KEN CALDER**

Bournemouth
PAVILION
PROGRAMME

1980

In this year, **Dulcie Gray** appeared in 'Lloyd George Knew My Father'.

January - The Council agreed that the Pavilion Theatre, in future, should **close during November, February and March**.

March - There was a successful run of 'Fiddler on the Roof', starring **Alfred Marks**.

March - Secret report was discussed by Council members over the viability of the Pavilion. Should it **become a shopping arcade** or indoor market?

April - New **kitchen equipment** for the **Lucullus** and the **Ballroom** cost £3,685.

May - The suggestion was again put forward that the Pavilion site should be considered for the new Bournemouth Centre.

June - Councillors demanded that the conference centre be abandoned in favour of a **revamp of the Pavilion**.

October - Luis Candal announced that the Pavilion was **not to close**.

November - An Echo critic slammed the population of Bournemouth for their **'pitiful response'** to the top quality West End show, 'Ipi Tombi'.

December - **Diane Lee** (half of the singing duo, Peters and Lee) starred in the pantomime, 'Sleeping Beauty'. This was the first year the panto played on Sundays.

December - High drama on the **Compton Organ** front! Speculation arose that there were plans to **sell the instrument** as a preliminary to rebuilding the Pavilion as a Conference Centre.

1981

June - October A long-running season to celebrate the 21st Anniversary of **'The Black and White Minstrel Show'**.

October - A row blew up with the entertainments department in Poole; a play, **'The Dresser'** had been booked to play the Pavilion and advertised. Then the promoters pulled out and took the play to the **Towngate Theatre** in Poole. It's known that Poole gave some guarantees, but that Bournemouth didn't.

November - **Dennis Hall**, the Entertainments Manager, succeeded in booking the musical 'Annie' for the 1982 summer season. Booking opened immediately. This was the first of many **prestigious bookings** managed by Dennis

Hall. *(See Page 94)*

December - The traditional pantomime 'Aladdin' starred **Clive Dunn** and **Roy Hudd**. Clive Dunn had appeared in Ice Shows at the **Westover Ice Rink**, and he was probably best known for his portrayal of **Corporal Jones**, the butcher, in the BBCtv sit-com, 'Dad's Army'. He also topped the charts with his song called **'Grandad'!** Roy Hudd is an authority of **Music Hall**, and played a very successful role in ITV's 'Coronation Street' as Alfie Shuttleworth, the undertaker.

1982

January - The Council reiterated that the **Pavilion would not close**.

February - A **secret report** on the Pavilion Complex was debated by the Town Council.

March - Yet another suggestion was made for the future of the Pavilion - that the building could become a **'fun-palace'** for children. But, once again, the council said that the Pavilion would **survive for at least another four years**.

May - Megastar, **Dame Edna Everage** (Barry Humphries) had a successful few days in the theatre. The show was not without controversy, and caused a furore over billing between conference organisers and theatre management. *(See Pages 95 and 96)*

Summer Season - the long-awaited musical 'Annie' was a wonderful show, but lost £12,000. Debate and argument centred around local cinemas who had shown the film version at the same time, in spite of pleas by Pavilion management to hold back the film.

July - An announcement made it clear that there would be **no more big band names** in the Ballroom.

November - A suggestion came that the Pavilion should be leased to a **private operator**.

December - Next year's summer season was confirmed as the stage version of the BBCtv sitcom 'Hi Di Hi'.

December - A petition to **'Save the Pavilion'** was launched as the traditional pantomime, 'Aladdin', opened with **Tommy Trinder** and **Joyce Blair**.

January - The petition put together to '**Save the Pavilion**', gained momentum after the pantomime had to close a week early through lack of support. The comedian, **Tommy Trinder**, stood on the forecourt steps and took signatures. He was supported by Wimborne comedian, **Billy Burden**, who described the Pavilion as 'the best'. The council suggested that the theatre should remain closed except for summer seasons, and that the next pantomime should be held at the Winter Gardens (which, incidentally, had no facilities to put on such a show!).

January - Echo headline read **"DOORS CLOSE FOR FINAL ACT"**. Everyone was convinced that the theatre would close, but......

February - A week of **Sadlers Wells Ballet** was a virtual sell-out. It was as if the Bournemouth people knew that they had to show some support in order to save their theatre. What a shame this support was so short-lived!

April - Lansdowne Baptist Church booked the theatre for a week later in the year for an ambitious evangelical project.

April - **Spandau Ballet** (a ballet of a different type to Sadlers Wells!) filled the seats for two nights.

May - The euphoria following the two successes was quelled by Stage Manager, Malcolm Lane. He caused much discontent by telling the press that there was not enough staff provided by the management to man the prestigious '**Hi Di Hi**' show with the television series cast. The management responded by announcing that the show would go ahead and summoned Malcolm Lane to a disciplinary hearing.

June/July/August - Summer season A stage version of the BBCtv hit-comedy series '**Hi Di Hi!**' All the television names were there, and one or two besides **Simon Cadell**, **Paul Shane**, **Ruth Madoc**, **Jeffrey Holland**, **Felix Bowness**, **Barry Howard**, **Ben Warriss**, **Su Pollard**, **The Webb Twins** - what a cast and what a show! Brilliantly funny entertainment. *(I can remember meeting one or two of the cast for interviews on BBC Radio Solent; Simon Cadell was every bit the gentleman he was in the show, gentle, thoughtful and kind; Ruth Madoc was lovely, and Felix Bowness was Felix Bowness, always humorous and always cheerful. He was, for years the warm up comedian for BBC Television shows and, known particularly at Sandown on the Isle of Wight, where he delighted audiences with his style for many years. He played a series of Sunday shows at the Pavilion during the 1960s and he had the knack of reducing an audience to its knees with laughter. H.A.)*
Incidentally, **Ben Warriss** was one half of the famous comedy duo, **Jewell and Warriss**, Jimmy and Ben, who had great success on radio and on stage in 1940s and 1950s.

June/July/August - Sunday shows were handled by **Little and Large**, **Max Bygraves**, **Jim Davidson** and **Val Doonican** - but not all at the same time!

July - Losses of £187,000 were announced across the whole operation of Bournemouth Entertainments.

August - An earlier decision to cancel the pantomime was queried by the local Hoteliers who demanded a rethink.

October - **Lansdowne Baptist Church** hail their evangelical rally as a tremendous success. Once again, the Pavilion proved its versatility to house farce, comedy, drama, variety, ballet, opera **and** be suitable for religious worship.

October - The summer season at the Winter Gardens, starring **Mike Yarwood**, was reported as being 'a disaster'.

December - A touring company presenting '**The Wind in the Willows**' found that the Pavilion stage get-in lift was not big enough to get their car on stage!

December - There was **no pantomime**. The theatre remained 'dark'. The bad decision to axe the annual pantomime had actually been carried out, and many Bournemouth people could not believe the stupidity - particularly hotel proprietors.

1984

This was the year which saw the opening of the **Bournemouth International Centre**.

February - **Renovation and redecoration** of the Pavilion plan was agreed. The public was invited to name some of the public rooms.

June - new carpets were laid in the auditorium.

June - A plan was put forward to provide **under-16 discos** in the Ballroom on wet days.

October - Elvis Costello and **Clannad** both gave concerts.

November - John Nettleton, played a week in '**When the Wind Blows**', and **Hans Christian Anderson Fairy Tales** were told by the Western Association of Ballet Schools.

December - A local company criticised Pavilion management for buying upholstery for the refurbishment from a London supplier.

December - **Ted Rogers** was the star of the pantomime, '**Goldilocks and the Three Bears**', with **Lynsey de Paul** in the title role.

**News Diary
1980 - 1989**

1985

February - £200,000 was provided to spruce up the theatre.

April - The Restaurant was renamed as **WEDGEWOOD ROOM** and opened. The former names had been **Lucullus** Restaurant and **The Captain's Table**.

Summer (June/July/August/September) - The summer show starred **Keith Harris and Orville**, but audience support was very poor. Keith Harris, who lived locally, was said that 'Bournemouth people didn't support' him. *(Nothing new there, then!)*

September - **Ronnie Corbett** does a one-night stand.

November - (and this is funny!) The newly named **WEDGEWOOD ROOM** was found to be copyright and could no longer be used. One councillor suggested they call it the **Lucullus Room**. The name seems vaguely familiar!

December - 'Cinderella'.

1986

January - £200,000 needed over a period of six years **to keep the rain out** of the theatre.

February - £60,000 was spent on tidying up the Bourne Stream where it passes the West Terrace.

March - **Ballroom re-opens** after extensive refurbishment.

March - Discussions took place over the possibility of **ticket and show sharing with Poole**.

April - Council **asked for ideas** from companies about possibilities for the redevelopment of the Pavilion.

April - The restored Ballroom and Phoebe Bar (between theatre and ballroom) were hailed as a **success and a great new asset** to the town. The Ballroom was fitted with **air-conditioning**, with six units, all roof mounted *(See Picture Page 199)*. The £500,000 spent had restored the Ballroom to its original style and character.

April - **Ticket sales** at the Pavilion Theatre were described as **catastrophic**.

June - The idea of a **Fun Palace for Children** to replace the Pavilion was rejected, and there was to be no amusement arcade.

June - In spite of news of poor ticket receipts, the Pavilion management reported that the complex **'did much better in the last financial year'**.

July - Thursday nights become **Wrestling Nights** in the Ballroom.

September - The **Bournemouth Operatic Society** cancel a two-week production run because of extremely poor advance ticket sales.

November - **Eldridge Pope**, the Dorchester Brewery, put in a bid to run the lower floor of the Pavilion.

November - Plans were unveiled for a new-look town centre with a **department store in place of the Pavilion**.

December - Eldridge Pope are given the contract for the lower floor. Not yet approved by Council.

December - Pavilion **budget slashed** by the Council.

December - **Anita Dobson** stars in 'Aladdin'.

1987

January - Pavilion **stage crew** put on a spoof version of the pantomime, raising £76 for the Macmillan Unit.

February - Plans for redevelopment of Pier Approach/Pavilion.

April - Councillors pushed forward an idea that the lower floor of the Pavilion (formerly Popular Restaurant) should be 'privatised' and leased to Eldridge Pope, the Dorchester Brewers, to make a Family Pub. Other councillors were in strong opposition.

Summer season - The West End musical 'Evita' starring **Rebecca Storm**.

September - Eldridge Pope announced plans for an **extension single-storey** building on the West Terrace.

October - Poor attendances once again for the musical 'Evita'. Low box office receipts were blamed on a **negative press**.

December - Pavilion **slash draft budget** at the request of the Council Finance Committee.

December - **Lorraine Chase** (now Stephanie in ITV's **Emmerdale**) and **Matthew Kelly** star in pantomime 'Jack and the Beanstalk'.

1988

April - The **axe was poised** over the proposed redevelopment plans.

May - Two groups still wanted the Pavilion and seafront development to go ahead.

May - There was a public display of the proposed development plans. The Pavilion was to have a multi-purpose hall and a **Covent Garden-style shopping mall** on the South Terrace. Some residents called the scheme **'vandalisation'**.

June - 81% of the public agreed with the proposed development plans.

June - It was confirmed that **Ladbrokes** were the chosen developers.

August - National postal strike, but **Postman Pat** still played at the Pavilion - with his cat!

December - Councillors approve the plan.

December - **Paul Shane** in 'Dick Whittington'.

January - Letters in the Echo deplored the **possible closure of the Ballroom** just two-and-a-half years after the £500,000 refurbishment. The Council agreed to keep it open.

January - The developers Ladbroke said they might well pull out of the Golden Acres. Development plan, which was to build new seafront facilities.

October - Ladbrokes pull out of the multi-million pound development scheme.

December - **Marti Caine** in **'Snow White'**.

The West Terrace as it was intended to be - in 1934

21st Century Forecourt

FACT

From All Sides!

Many Faces! One Pavilion!

JOSEF LOCKE

PETER SELLERS

SPIKE MILLIGAN

MAX GELDRAY

and

ALL STAR VARIETY SHOW

1. OVERTURE ... "Amporita Roca" ... ... *Texidor*

2. THE THREE KELROYS ... ... On the Bounce

3. MAX GELDRAY ... ... With his Harmonica

4. MEDLOCK and MARLOWE ... ... Celebrity Night

5. SPIKE MILLIGAN ... Late of the Human Race

6. DUNCAN'S COLLIES ... ... Canine Actors

7. INTERMISSION

   Selection of Melodies from "Love from Judy" ... *Hugh Martin*
   "White Horse Inn" on Ice ... ... *Benatzky and Stolz*

   HAROLD COOMBS at the PAVILION ORGAN

8. MEDLOCK and MARLOWE ... ... To Entertain Again

9. JOAN and ERNEST ... ... Reflection in Rhythm

10. PETER SELLERS ... From Radio's "Goon Show"

11. **JOSEF LOCKE**

    At the Piano :
    Will Fyffe, Junr.

    Pavilion Theatre Orchestra
    under the direction of
    BYRON BROOKE

Above: This programme comes John Matthews' collection and is from July 1955. It shows a typical variety show, with all the individual acts totally self-contained and self-sufficient. Max Geldray appeared as an harmonica player with the Goon Show in the radio series. Note especially Act 6 - 'Canine Actors'! Note, too, that the Borough Organist, Harold Coombs, is billed as part of the entire show, and not as a separate interval act. Some audience members were disappointed that Peter Sellers and Spike Milligan did not interact at all.

An Early View

Right: An early picture, where the Pavilion appears to be all but finished. Notice the two lounges behind the fly-tower - these were lost when the fly-tower was extended in 1934, and the bar we now call 'Phoebe' replaced them. At the top of the picture is the old Westover Ballroom, which provided much early opposition to the Pavilion. Notice that the Belle Vue Hotel is still there right in front of the ballroom.

1990

January - Plans to spend £90,000 on forecourt fountain.

January - Big losses were reported from last year's summer shows.

February - Cloakroom staff were violently pushed aside as revellers stole armfuls of coats.

March - **Jim Davidson's** idea to put on a wartime musical show fell through.

April - A suggestion was that **National Lottery money** might help to revive the theatre's fortunes.

May - Veteran Band, **The Chieftains**, described the Pavilion as "beating the Royal Albert Hall".

May - Annual Council Meeting held at Pavilion, when the Mayor switched on the **re-furbished fountain**.

July - **Prince Edward** attended a very successful **Royal Variety Youth Showcase**.

July - Councillor attacks the Pavilion management for 'appalling marketing strategy'.

August - The **Holiday Revival Bar** was used for an **open-air disco**. There were no order offences but two complaints were received.

September - A show was cancelled through strike action by the stage crew. Union bosses said that they could no longer subsidise the Pavilion through their low wages.

September - **£1,500,000 needed** to refurbish the Pavilion in order to turn it into a major concert venue.

September - Record-breaking advance bookings for Pantomime.

October -Announced that the Pavilion had lost £43,000 during the summer season.

December - The new **canopy and illuminated signs** across the entrance to the Pavilion was opened, giving the complex a festive feel.

December - 'Aladdin' with **Matthew Kelly** and **Su Pollard** - and an unlikely star, **Gordon Honeycombe**, the ITN Newscaster, who was living in Bournemouth.

1991

January - **Westover Ice Rink** closed for ever. This saw the end of not only session skating, but also bright and colourful summer shows and pantomimes.

June - The canopy lights above the Pavilion main entrance fail. They were still under guarantee and had cost £28,000 when installed twelve months ago.

July - Popular BBC Organist, **Dudley Savage**, for years the presenter of '**As Prescribed**' from the Compton Organ of the ABC Cinema in Plymouth on the BBC West region and then Radio Two, gave an organ recital at the Pavilion.

July - 'Buddy' plays the Pavilion but local shops refuse to sell the Buddy Holly disc. **Luis Candal**, Entertainments Director, severely criticises them.

September - The **Assemblies of God** with 100,000 believers world-wide, held a conference at the Pavilion and the B.I.C. The event was relayed by satellite across the whole world.

December - 'Jack and the Beanstalk' starred **Max Boyce**.

1992

February - Memories were revived by two one nighters, the **Bay City Rollers** and **Billie Jo Spears**.

March - **Alan Price** and the **Band of the United States Air Force** each played their own brand of music, and the **Chippendales** took off their clothes.

April - **Ken Dodd** made his annual pilgrimage from Notty Ash, and the **Bolshoi Ballet Stars** delighted fans - but not in the same show!

April - There were doubts for the Pavilion's future as a plan for an indoor theme park was discussed. It was later denied that there had ever been any suggestion that the building should be demolished. The Echo described the Pavilion as '**one of Bournemouth's most cherished buildings**'.

June - **Danny La Rue** played a week's variety, and **Russ Conway** gave a one-off performance.

July - **The Troggs** and **The Merseybeats** played in '**Sounds of the 60s**', while '**Thunderbirds FAB**' delighted children both young old.

July/August/September - Summer season was '**Elvis The Musical**'. As is traditional at the Bournemouth Pavilion, audiences were appalling.

August - The BIC, Pavilion and Pier Theatre **slashed seat prices** as a recession struck the town's entertainment industry. The Director, **Luis Candal**, said, "Excellent shows, but fewer bums on seats."

October - The **William Temple Association** held a meeting in the Lucullus Room to 'promote a better understanding of religious matters.

1993

April - Bumper business reported in an **Easter Bonanza**, where shows played to capacity houses.

July - The Best of British Jazz starring **Kenny Baker**, **Don Lusher** and **Jack Parnell**.

July/August - Summer saw **Christopher Cazenove** in a glittering production of the all-time favourite musical '**The Sound of Music**'. (But not an all-time favourite with Bournemouth audiences, because they stayed away in their hundreds.) On Sundays, **Bobby Davro** appeared with his special brand of humour.

September - Management express disappointment at small audiences for '**The Sound of Music**'.

September - an unusual production called '**Return to the Forbidden Planet**'.

October - **Jimmy James** and **Paul McKenna** both played one nighters, and the auditorium was filled with 'oooohhhs' and 'gosh' when the **Chippendales** stripped off all their coverings. Entertainment of different nature came from **George Best** and **Rodney Marsh**, who did not take off their clothes.

The Ballroom had a busy summer with **Old Time and Modern Sequence Dancing** on Mondays, **All-Star Wrestling** on Tuesdays and **Summer Dances** on Wednesdays. Thursdays and Friday saw **Summer Discos** and general **Dancing** completed the week on Saturdays.

December - A busy month for the Ballroom with **The Mel Douglas Dance Affair** on the 15th and 22nd, and Tea Dances with **The Pete Papworth Duo** on the 16th, 23rd and 30th.

December - **Roy Hudd** and **Geoffrey Hughes** appeared in the pantomime, '**Babes in the Wood**'.

1994

January - Pavilion Press Officer, **Tony Hardman**, opened a memorabilia gallery in the two side corridors of the Pavilion. *(See Page 43)*

February- **Paul McKenna** amazed the audience with his psychic powers, and **Chas and Dave** joined forces with **Warren Mitchell** as Alf from the BBCtv sit-com '**For Better For Worse**'.

March - A recommendation went before the Council that **Pay and Display machines** should be installed for use in the Pavilion Car Park. Also, the 50p concession for theatre patrons was to be abolished.

March - Ice Ballet performed. It was '**Sleeping Beauty**' by the **Russian All Stars.**

March - For five nights, the stage version of Roald Dahl's popular children's story, '**Big Friendly Giant**'.

April - Ballroom **Wrestling** is under threat through poor support.

July/August - The summer season was carried by two comedians in repertory, **Billy Pearce** and **Joe Pasquale**.

October - Management blamed excellent weather for poor attendance at summer shows.

December - Boxer **Nigel Benn** became a disc-jockey for the night in the Ballroom.

December - Pantomime starred **The Krankies** and **Lorraine Chase**, with **Buster Merryfield**, all in '**Robinson Crusoe**'.

December - The Ballroom hosted an **Antiques and Collectors' Fair**, as well as a **New Year's Eve Dance**.

1995

Throughout the year, the now normal pattern of short runs performances came from the likes of **Richard Digance**, **Joe Longthorne**, **Ken Dodd** and **The Bachelors**. The **Bert Kaempfert Orchestra** gave a concert, and also the **Cliff Adams Singers** made a rare stage appearance.

March - A report was produced of a strategy to halt the decline in ticket sales.

April - **Tommy Steele** brought joy and happiness to large audiences - '**What a Show!**'.

May - **Richard Todd**, the film actor and war veteran who was brought up in Wimborne, stars in '**Brideshead Revisited**'. Appalling audiences, with one show playing to only 30 people.

June - **Barbara Dickson**. Sunday nights throughout the summer starred **Danny La Rue** in '**The Goode Olde Dayes**'.

Summer season - a mixture of '**Buddy**', '**Hot Shoe Shuffle**', and '**Three Steps to Heaven**'. The Ballroom held the **Red Hot Salsa Grand Summer Ball**.

September - Strike by Theatre staff led to show cancellation.

October - the mega-star singer **Howard Keel** (star of American Musicals, and also of soap '**Dallas**') was followed the next day by **Squeeze**. '**Robin, Prince of Sherwood**' had a ten-day run.

November brought a feast of ballet with both the **Ballet Rambert Company** and the **Western Association of Ballet Schools**. Also '**Scrooge The Musical**' had **Anthony Newley** in the title role.

December - **Marti Webb** appeared in a production of '**Evita**'.

December - **Les Dennis** and **Kathy Staff** gave their all in the most popular of all pantomimes, '**Cinderella**'.

1996

The idea of an **£8 million Ice Rink** on a site nearby was scrapped, because it would have meant demolishing part of the Pavilion Ballroom.

February - 'Hot Ice Show'.

April - The Pavilion became the centre of the **Jewish Community** and was converted for a conference into 'a little corner of Jerusalem'. This was for the **3000th anniversary of King David** declaring Jerusalem the Jewish capital.

May - 'My Cousin Rachel'.

June/July - Two big shows 'Calamity Jane' and 'Barnum', the West End circus musical.

Summer season saw **Joe Pasquale** playing Mondays, Tuesday and Wednesdays, with **Max Bygraves** on Thursday, Fridays and Saturdays.

November - **Jools Holland**.

December - **Ian Botham** and **Allan Lamb** brought their particular brand of entertainment and humour to the stage.

December - The pantomime was 'Dick Whittington' with **Paul Daniels**.

1997

January - The Wessex Branch of the anti-smoking organisation, ASH, called for a **no smoking ban** in the Pavilion.

January - one of many performances over the years at the Pavilion of 'Fame - The Musical'.

February - After 42 years of use, the stage had to be resurfaced. The work cost £16,000 and took nearly two weeks. **Ballet Rambert** were the first company to tread the new boards, and the revolve was covered over, although the workings were left intact.

March - Stars of the **Romanian National Opera**. This was reported to be an absolutely first-class evening but, as usual, poor attendance. Where do all the Bournemouth culture lovers go when there's some culture on stage?

May - The Smurfs - were we talking about culture?

June - Theatre was evacuated during the performance of 'Carmen on Ice' because of an electrical fault.

July - Comedian, **Jim Davidson**, walked out of the theatre leaving a 900-strong audience just before the curtain went up. He complained about the theatre management and said that no one had even offered him a glass of water.

July/August/September - Summer season with **Bradley Walsh** (now two-timing Danny in 'Coronation Street') on Mondays, **Jethro** on Wednesdays and **Jim Davidson** on Thursday, Fridays and Saturdays.

September - The audience walked out on a play called '**The Surprise Party**', starring **Ruth Madoc**, **Peter Duncan**, **Frank Windsor** and **Matthew Kelly**. The play was described as "bad taste". The Echo reported that no one from the theatre was available for comment.

December - In place of the traditional pantomime, 'Peter Pan' flew the stage.

1998

The Pavilion became a listed building. English Heritage stated: **"The Pavilion is an excellent example in good condition of a purpose-built multi-entertainment venue, and remains remarkably homogenous given the variety of stylistic idioms it portrays." (***Think that's probably a compliment!) (See Page 212 for details of Listing)***

February - Enid Blyton's '**Noddy Goes to Mars**', and **Rowan Atkinson** played two nights of revue.

August - The **Ken Mackintosh Band** played the Ballroom.

September - Five schemes before council on future development of the Pavilion.

September - **Lily Savage**, aka Paul O'Grady, played for four nights, and the **Ted Heath Band** gave a concert.

Shows throughout the year included '**The Magic of Sinatra**', '**Pirates of Penzance**' starring **Paul Nicholas**, **Lee Hurst**, **Paul Merton** and **Postman Pat**.

December - The pantomime starred ice-skating champion, **Robin Cousins** in 'Beauty and the Beast'. Local actor, **Buster Merryfield** also starred.

1999

June - **Lionel Blair** and **Trevor Bannister** said that "the Bournemouth Pavilion is one of the least favourite venues in the entire acting world." Bannister went on to call the building "a monstrosity which should have been pulled down years ago." *For the record, Trevor Bannister is an actor who made his name while he appeared in the BBCtv sit-com, 'Are You Being Served?', where he played second-fiddle to John Inman as Mr. Lucas. Lionel Blair is Joyce Blair's brother.*

Among stars to appear at the Pavilion this year were **Gene Pitney**, **Roy 'Chubby' Brown**, **Dominic Kirwan** and **Leo Sayer**. The Theatre hosted the **Disney Channel Kids Awards**, and **Opera and Ballet International** presented 'Nabucco'. **Patrick Moore** gave a lecture on the stars at night, and the summer season had different artistes each evening of the week, **with Joe Pasquale**, Freddie Starr tribute, **Gerry and the Pacemakers**, **Jethro** and the 'That'll Be the Day' team. There was a **Dolls' House and Miniature Fayre** in the Ballroom, and the **Glen Miller Orchestra** gave a concert performance.

November - The Ballroom hosted the **Classic Gold 828 Millenium Party**.

November - **Ruth Madoc** starred in the musical '**42ⁿᵈ Street**', and '**Peter Pan**' appeared - paradoxically on ice!

December - A return for the colourful and foot-tapping musical, '**Joseph and His Amazing Technicolor Dreamcoat**'. The **Russian National Ballet** also played, as did the **State Opera of Wroclaw** who performed '**Aida**'.

December - **David Essex** was '**Robinson Crusoe**'.

MEMORY — Own Costumes - and a Bun!
EDNA SIMS

*A local girl from Parkstone, and then Boscombe, **Edna Sims** joined the **Bournemouth and Boscombe Light Opera Company** when it started in the 1950s. They have played at the Pavilion ever since on an annual basis, and Edna was in the chorus for many years. (See Pages 41-42 for more details on BBLOC)*

"They were always happy days and I loved them. My first show was the first-ever for the Company, '**Katinka**', which we performed at the **Boscombe Hippodrome**, and it was then that I learned you can let yourself go when you're on stage and really enjoy yourself. I can never remember being at all nervous. One of my favourites was '**Hello Dolly**' - it was a happy and lively show - and for that production, I made my own hat; it was common in those days for all the cast to make extra costumes and props themselves. '**Fiddler on the Roof**' was a little different, and we played it all with no make-up, but I remember we all had buns in our hair, but everything was very plain, in fact a rather dreary production, but absolutely wonderful.

"'**Blue Danube**' was another success for me, with extremely colourful costumes, as was '**Show Boat**'. When you're on stage, you feel as though you are a different person - in another world. I recall once that one of our dancers came off stage and tripped over some cables, nearly bringing the scenery down, and there we were - hanging on to the scenery making sure it stayed put! I'm 86 now, but still have some beautiful memories of my time with BBLOC."

Another of Beales' Faithful Adverts - this one was in 1980

Places you might not see
A PICTURE TOUR OF THE LESS ACCESSIBLE AREAS

?

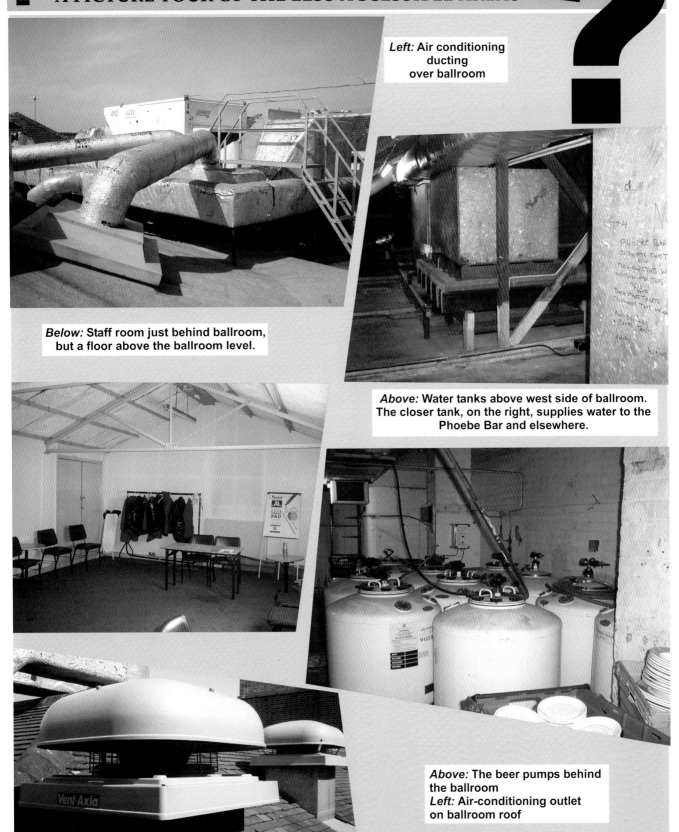

Left: Air conditioning ducting over ballroom

Below: Staff room just behind ballroom, but a floor above the ballroom level.

Above: Water tanks above west side of ballroom. The closer tank, on the right, supplies water to the Phoebe Bar and elsewhere.

Above: The beer pumps behind the ballroom
Left: Air-conditioning outlet on ballroom roof

Underneath the stage and the several floors of kitchens and storage, is a vast catacomb of open space, some of it below sea-level - THE CELLAR. This houses some important machinery and the heating system for the entire complex. In the days when Blake, Avon and Vila fought the Federation in the cult BBCtv Series 'Blakes 7', this cellar could easily have been used as a setting for several episodes. The atmosphere is sinister and dramatic, the warmth is clammy, and you walk with an eye across your shoulder in case you catch some old spirit from the past floating casually by. When I left this space one sunny spring morning, I felt a different person - and I still experience a sense of awe and surprise at this vast space under this enormous building, spending most its life in lonely and peaceful solitude.

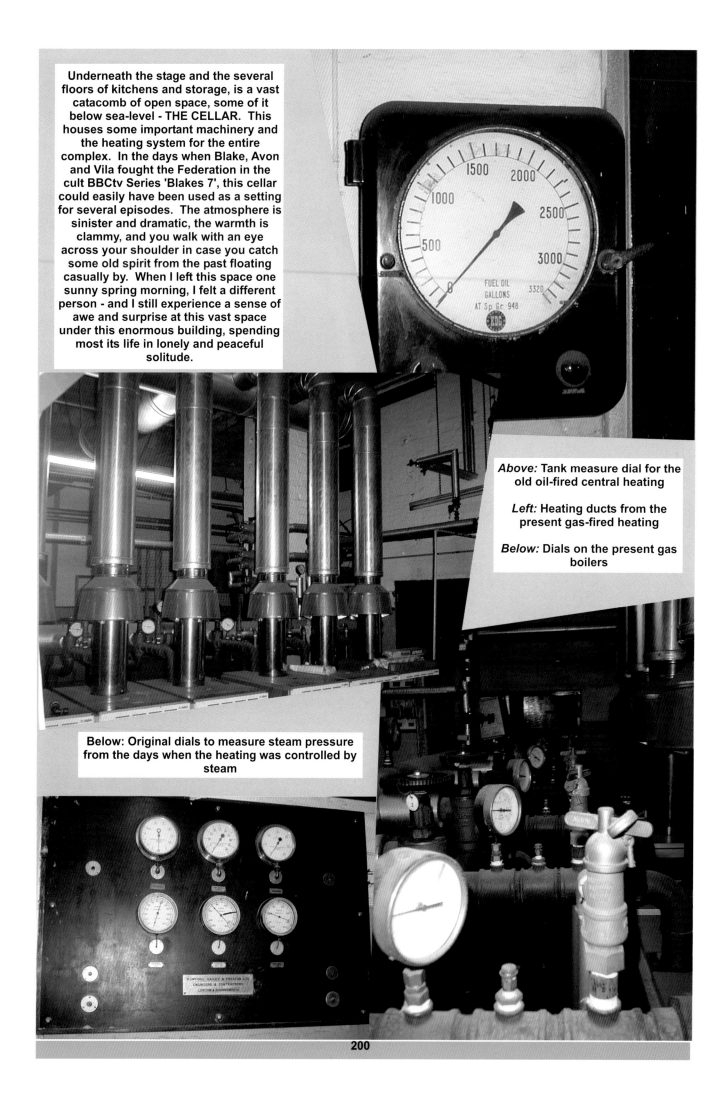

Above: Tank measure dial for the old oil-fired central heating

Left: Heating ducts from the present gas-fired heating

Below: Dials on the present gas boilers

Below: Original dials to measure steam pressure from the days when the heating was controlled by steam

Above: **Nest of Crockery in Ballroom Stores**

Above: **Extractor Fan/Pump for removing heat from auditorium**

Right Centre: **This picture gives no real impression of an enormous space underneath the west corner of the Pavilion Theatre, near the West Terrace. It is the old Pump Room, where sea-water was extracted from the Bay and used for making steam for heating and cleaning. The flanges where the pipes go out to the sea are still in position. This area could be converted into a large art gallery or drama studio/theatre. With removal of the partition walls, it would become an immense area with great potential.**

Bottom Right: **The gas central heating system from behind the line of boilers.**

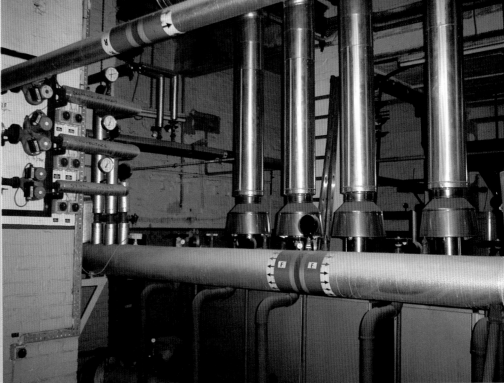

A View from the Top......

The climb to the roof is not easy - lots of rungs and steps and plenty of heavy breathing! But it's worth the effort for the magnificent views from the top. Most of these photos were taken during a very cold spell in the winter of 2004-2005 and the icy wind was chilling.

Left: A view from the top of the fly-tower towards Old Harry Rocks.
Centre: From the fly-tower across to the B.I.C. and Punshon Memorial Methodist Church in Exeter Road.
Bottom: Looking westwards up the Bourne Valley. The gasometer at Branksome can be seen on the horizon just to the right of the tower of St. Andrew's URC in the Square.

Metro Palace Court Hotel - to the north

**Odeon, Ice Rink, Beales,
St. Peter's Spire, Portman
Building - to north-west.**

Below the West Terrace

The Number Boards

PROSCENIUM ARCH ORIGINALS

LEFT

Thought to be entirely original, the two number boards on the proscenium arches are controlled from a switch-box in the Prompt Corner. The amusing fact about them is that the highest number they can display is 19! This means that 20 minute intervals cannot be displayed! On either side of these boards, can be seen two more 'remains' of boards which we think were used during the Second World War to display information about the state of air-raids.

RIGHT

The Stage During a Show Fit-up

'THE KING AND I' 2005

FACT

Stage Miscellany
DIPS and LIFTS and LAMPS and ROPES and REVOLVES and ....

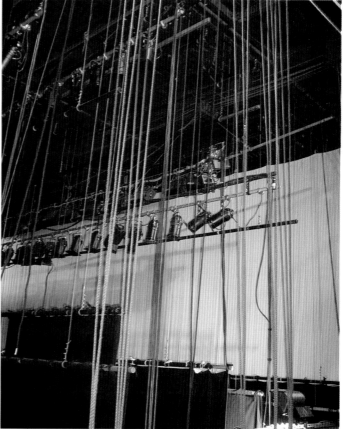

Top Left: A view from the top of the fly-tower on the grid. The stage is some forty feet below.

Top Right: A line of contemporary lamps across the vast expanse of stage.

Bottom Left: Looking across the grid from east to west.

Centre Right: From the Prompt Side Fly Floor looking towards the back wall.

Bottom Right: A stage dip where floor-standing spot and flood lights can be plugged in These are set into the stage, and the numbered lid closed down to stage level. The stage has many such dips.

The Revolve

MUCH LOVED and MUCH MISSED

This strange and old-fashioned piece of technology is the control which operated the Pavilion's famous revolving stage. The revolve was installed in 1933 when the stage was enlarged, and it was a successful part of many pantomimes and summer shows. Now, it's covered over, although the machinery is still in situ. Both Christian and Simon are pretty confident that, if it were uncovered, it could be persuaded to work again. But, that's hardly likely to happen, because revolving stages in today's theatre need to be much more flexible and sophisticated. This control used to stand in the wings about half way back, and could be unplugged and taken away when not needed. It now 'lives' underneath the right organ chamber, put out to grass to live in quiet and peace. In the 1950s and 1960s, members of the stage crew were always pleased to be asked to operate it. I remember when John Laurie asked me to work it, I was over the moon. All you had to do was to turn the lever left or right, and the revolve would turn clockwise or anti-clockwise. Wonderful memories!

This is what it is like underneath the stage - very cramped

R.I.P
We revered you when you spun, We miss you now your work is done.

1933 - 1971

ALWAYS CALLED "THE IRON"

These are the original controls for the eight-ton Safety Curtain, with levers and safety cage, to ensure that they couldn't be touched by accident.. As the iron drops, when it falls to about four feet above the stage, it hits a compression brake which lowers it gently onto stage level.

In one show in the 1960s, the brake showed signs of wear, and let the curtain slip and the iron very slowly crept down. We had to press the 'raise' button two or three times during a performance, which was very noisy and very distracting to actors and to the audience.

The Pavilion Safety Curtain has a small screen painted on the middle of the audience side, and advertisement slides can be shown from the lime/projection box.

The Law states that the Safety Curtain must be lowered at some point during each and every performance, so that the members of the audience can see that it is functioning properly.

The purpose of a theatre safety curtain is, in the event of fire, to prevent the air-flow from backstage to front-of-house, and to contain smoke and flames on either side.

FACT

The Stage Lift

Because the Stage Door is 20 feet below the level of the Stage itself, a special lift has been built to bring the scenery, props and lights up from the loading bay. We believe this lift to be original. The control on the left is clearly marked with 'up' and 'down' and with 'slow' and 'fast'. By today's fast-moving standards, the markings should be 'slow' and 'even slower'! The lift is still used every time a show comes in or goes out. The control is very similar to those in department stores' lifts of days of yore. For a big show, the lift will be in use possibly all day - or longer - because its capacity is quite small. Easing the large scenery flats around the difficult corners from the Stage Door has become quite an art, but is still very difficult and requires much patience. (See Page 46)

The plate below, which is affixed to the back wire-wall of the lift, is self-explanatory.

MAXIMUM SAFE DISTRIBUTED LOAD 1 TON 10 CWTS

KNIGHT & Cº (ENGINEERS) LTD
WINCHMORE WORKS LONDON N14

One of the
smaller
dressing-rooms

Fire Hydrant
at
Stage Door

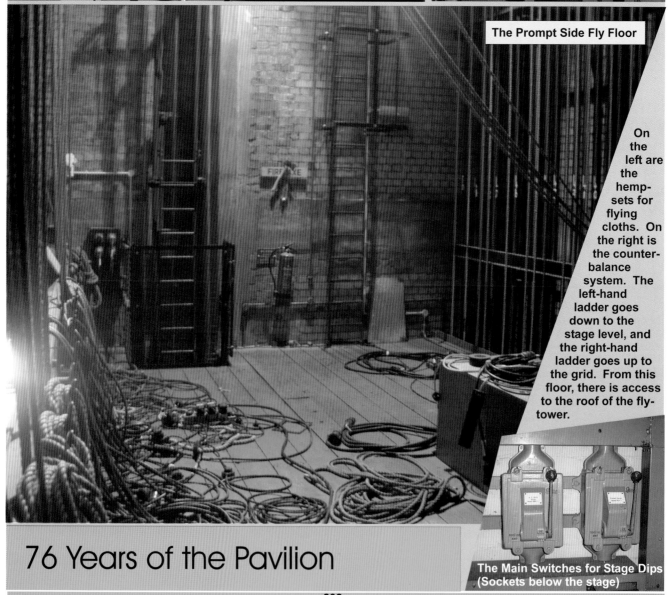

The Prompt Side Fly Floor

On the left are the hemp-sets for flying cloths. On the right is the counter-balance system. The left-hand ladder goes down to the stage level, and the right-hand ladder goes up to the grid. From this floor, there is access to the roof of the fly-tower.

The Main Switches for Stage Dips (Sockets below the stage)

76 Years of the Pavilion

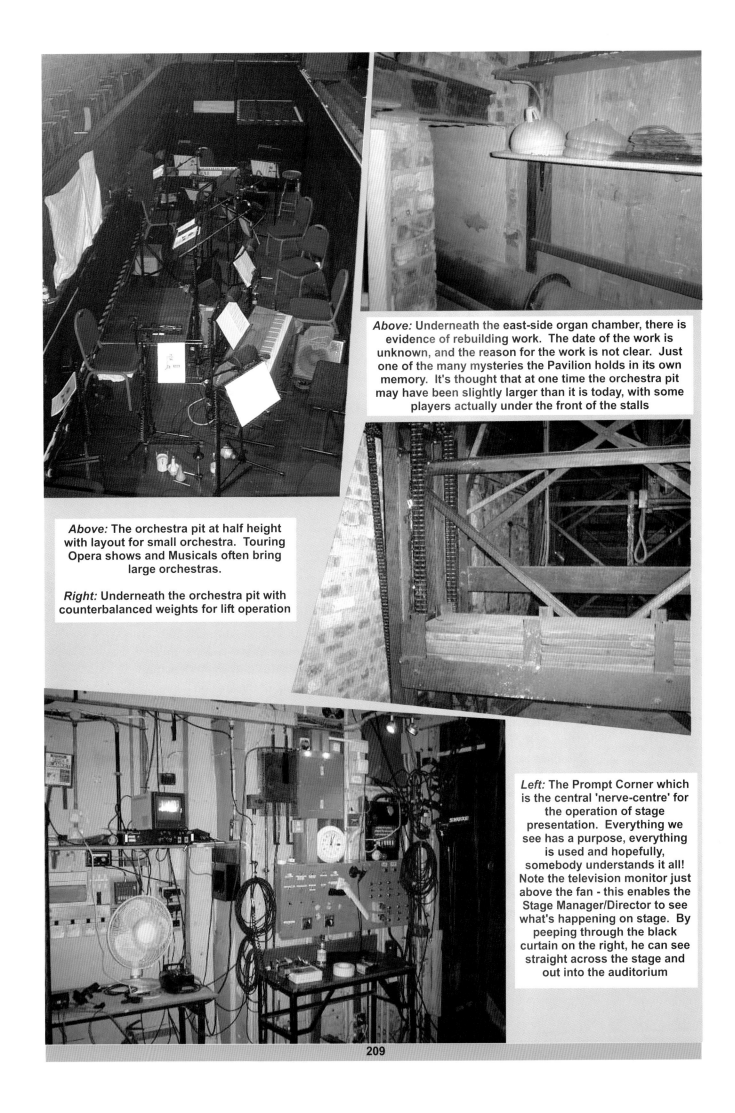

Above: Underneath the east-side organ chamber, there is evidence of rebuilding work. The date of the work is unknown, and the reason for the work is not clear. Just one of the many mysteries the Pavilion holds in its own memory. It's thought that at one time the orchestra pit may have been slightly larger than it is today, with some players actually under the front of the stalls

Above: The orchestra pit at half height with layout for small orchestra. Touring Opera shows and Musicals often bring large orchestras.

Right: Underneath the orchestra pit with counterbalanced weights for lift operation

Left: The Prompt Corner which is the central 'nerve-centre' for the operation of stage presentation. Everything we see has a purpose, everything is used and hopefully, somebody understands it all! Note the television monitor just above the fan - this enables the Stage Manager/Director to see what's happening on stage. By peeping through the black curtain on the right, he can see straight across the stage and out into the auditorium

OSCAR THE CAT

During the 1960s, a black and white cat used to live both inside and outside the Stage Door. He was popular with staff and artistes alike and was thought to keep any mice that might consider a home near the staff canteen well away. He was called Oscar, and of course he never went hungry, because everyone used to feed him. Although no one really owned him, he was probably the most overfed and contented cat in Bournemouth. What eventually happened to him is unknown, but Oscar was a favourite friend to many famous stars during his reign at the Stage Door.

UNSEEN WORK PLACE

Between the Ballroom and the back of the stage are four extensive floors of storage for food and equipment, kitchens, bakery, preparation areas, serving area, cellars and staff rooms. For a member of staff to walk down from the staff room on the roof of the Ballroom to the cellar below, he needs to use 78 steps. This is an unseen part of the Pavilion and is absolutely enormous, providing the essential requirements for functions.

FIRST STAFF

On the photograph of the staff on the opening day, there are 197 people, all lined up on the forecourt of the Pavilion. This does not include any who were off-shift or who were ill or on holiday. The picture can be seen in the West Corridor on the left.

I have a lasting and tangible memory of my early days at the Bournemouth Pavilion. During a Pantomime season in the early 1960s, I got my toes caught under a twenty foot scenery flat. The nail was damaged, and eventually came off - underneath it was a perfectly formed new nail. This procedure has continued about every three years ever since when I discover a perfect new nail! I'll never forget that scenery flat!

CEILING Versus MIRRORS

In the 1960s, a hanging ceiling was put into the Ocean Rooms - formerly the Popular Restaurant - a polystyrene monstrosity which more or less covered up all the wonderful features of the old decor, such as the enormous mirrors. When the Dorchester Brewers, Eldridge Pope, took over the running of the area on a long-term lease, they took out the ceiling to bring back some of the original features. They also took over the 'SHED' - that's a colloquial name (i.e. the truth!) for the 'extension' to the Ocean Rooms on the West Terrace. This had been built to house exhibitions for the town, but when the BIC was opened, it lost any real need. There were plans to make it into a small theatre, but these never materialised.

Early press notes about the Pavilion suggest that there were two identical lifts either side of the orchestra pit - one for the Compton Organ. What the second lift could have been for is not mentioned. There is certainly evidence under the orchestra pit that some previous construction was in place (*See Page 209*) on the left hand side. It is unlikely that the truth will ever be known. Just another of those fascinating mysteries which the building holds!

Outside and In.....

OUR PAVILION

Classic picture showing the 'wedding-cake' effect of the building. Mid to late 1950s. New Offices are in place with their uncharacteristic flat roofs, there is no ostentatious canopy and there's the old fountain!

BACK-STAGE VIEW

Backstage photograph during the 2002 Pantomime "Cinderella" starring Ruth Madoc and Chris Jarvis

SCHEDULE

The following building shall be added to the list:

SZ 0890   BOURNEMOUTH   WESTOVER ROAD

768/12/10047   The Pavilion Theatre and
                                      surrounding raised terrace and steps

GV   II

Entertainment complex of theatre with ballroom and supper rooms, one of latter now used as public house. 1928-9 by G Wyville Home and Shirley Knight, winners of a competition in 1923 assessed by Sir Edwin Cooper; remodelled in 1934 and in the 1950s in the original style. Sir E Owen Williams was the consultant engineer. A beaux arts composition in stripped classical style. Red brick with Empire stone dressings; pantiled roofs. The plan is of two halves on a steeply sloping site, with the theatre on two levels at the front, and the ballroom to the rear with the supper room and public house below reached by corridors and stairs to either side of the theatre. Entrance to theatre and ballroom has three-bay front, with round-arched openings to front and renewed first-floor windows set between broad classical pilasters under deep stone cornice and parapet. Pavilions to either side raised in the 1950s in similar style. Roof surmounted by iron crestings. Behind it a flytower was raised in 1934 and rebuilt in the 1950s with bands of stonework. Side elevations retain some original windows with metal margin lights and fan-shaped tops, again set in three- bay composition between pilasters. Rear elevations with renewed windows under deep eaves cornice, the ground-floor public house with original metal fenestration under late C20 awnings. The interiors survive very completely in a variety of styles reflecting the importance of Grecian and Egyptian influences in the late 1920s. Entrance hall reached via vestibule with original pendant lights and with plaque commemorating the opening by the Duke of Gloucester on 19 March 1929. The three-bay entrance hall has decorated terrazzo floor, dentilled cornice and paired Doric columns, and inner arcade with rounded moulded archways, now partly blocked by reception desk and office. Similar fluted mouldings to corridors at either side, which curved round and down to serve the theatre stalls and the bar and ballroom beyond. At either side of the entrance hall are open-well staircases which rise to the first-floor bar and circle; they have upswept timber handrails and metal balustrading, and are top-lit by Regency style circular skylights. First floor bar over entrance hall of three bays with circular ceiling mouldings. The 1518-seat theatre is roughly square in plan and has a full-size stage and a circle, re-raked in 1934 to provide better sight-lines for plays. It is entered from 'silence corridors' on both levels, with Egyptian- style mouldings to the cornices of the doors. The theatre itself is in a restrained early C19 style, with square columns to the rear and sides of the circle and a shallow groin vault with festoon decoration. The balcony front has a shallow roll moulding with fluted decoration, and the motif of the doors is repeated over the rounded and ribbed ante- proscenium, which conceals the pipes for the original Compton organ, which sits to the side of the stage and is reached via the organist's personal green room. Ballroom with richly moulded ceilings and pendant lights (renewed to original design in modern materials). Beneath it is the Lucullus Room, a restaurant, reached via staircases with iron arch-moulded balustrading. The Lucullus Room is entered via double doors between fluted Doric columns, and retains original wall decoration with shallow fluting and mirrors in an elegant moderne style which is advanced for its date. The ceiling with shallow recess defined by concave plaster moulding.

Beyond it the larger restaurant is now a public house, with deep, double-height space surrounded by original mirrors with fan-shaped decoration set between broad piers with fluted tops. The ceiling similarly banded and with similar mouldings. Around the Pavilion is a terrace with steps leading down to the Pleasure Gardens, which are on English Heritage's Gardens Register, and with which it forms an important entertainment ensemble. The Pavilion is an excellent example in good condition of a purpose-built multi-entertainment venue built to serve a major seaside resort. Other resorts do not have such a complete and complex example of this style and period. It was sympathetically extended and improved in the 1930s and 1950s, and remains remarkably homogenous given the variety of stylistic idioms it portrays.

Source: 'The Builder', 22 March 1929

Signed by authority of the
Secretary of State

TA Ellingford

Dated: *19 January 1998*

T A ELLINGFORD
Department for Culture, Media and Sport

PROGRAMME OF COMING ATTRACTIONS - SPRING 1939

THE PAVILION PROGRAMME

The Pavilion attractions are continued throughout the year

THE CONCERT HALL

This Hall has a fine revolving stage, which makes it practicable to present the most spectacular productions. Performances nightly, and matinees as announced. At the time of going to press bookings are as follows :—

Week commencing :—

April 24th	-	Fay Compton in "Drawing Room."
May 1st	-	Closed for Alterations.
May 8th	-	"Weep for the Spring"
May 15th	-	Yvonne Arnaud in " Plan for a Hostess."
May 22nd	-	Engagement Pending.
May 29th	-	Variety Company.
June 5th	-	Engagement Pending.
June 12th	-	Variety Company.
June 19th	-	Vic-Wells Ballet Company.
June 26th	-	Engagement Pending.
July 3rd	-	"Band Waggon"
July 10th	-	Variety Company including Jack Hilton and his Band.
July 17th	-	"Me and My Girl."
July 24th	-	"Wild Oats."
July 31st to August 21st	-	Variety Companies.
August 28th	-	D'Oyly Carte Opera Company.
Sept. 4th	-	Variety Company.
Sept. 11th	-	"White Horse Inn"

ORCHESTRAL CONCERTS

The Bournemouth Municipal Orchestra (60 performers) is the largest permanent Municipal Orchestra in the world. It provides a comprehensive programme of concerts every week throughout the year, except for a fortnight's vacation during the Spring. The Orchestra is directed by Richard Austin and the leader is Harold Fairhurst.

Well-known Soloists appear in conjunction with many of the Concerts, the following engagements have been made :-

23rd March	Marie Korchinska (Harp)		6th July	Ellen Ballon (Pianoforte).
30th March	Harriet Cohen (Pianoforte)		13th July	Muriel Taylor (Violoncello).
6th April	Lamond (Pianoforte)		20th July	Irene Kohler (Pianoforte).
13th April	Eda Kersey (Violin).		27th July	Austin Dewdney (Pianoforte).
20th April	Norman Tucker (Pianoforte).		3rd August	Charles Lynch (Pianoforte).
27th April	Phyllis Sellick (Pianoforte).		10th August	Mark Hambourg (Pianoforte)
4th May	Zacharewitsch (Violin).		17th August	Lance Dossor (Pianoforte).
11th May	Estelle Wine (Pianoforte).		24th August	Alfredo Campoli (Violin).
18th May	Antonia Butler (Violoncello).		31st August	Susan Slivko (Pianoforte).
25th May	Dorothy Manley (Pianoforte).		7th September	Gordon Bryan (Pianoforte).
1st June	Melsa (Violin)		14th September	Frederick Grinke (Violin).
8th & 15th June	Orchestra Vacation		21st September	Leslie England (Pianoforte).
22nd June	Meyer Rosenstein (Pianoforte).		28th September	Florence Hooton (Violoncello).
29th June	John Sterling (Pianoforte).			

THE MUNICIPAL CHOIR AND ORCHESTRA

Sunday, April 23rd - "JUDAS MACCABÆUS"

Soloists: Janet Hamilton-Smith, Vera Healy, Edward Reach, Tom Williams

"BUBBLES" CONCERT PARTY.

Will Seymour's Brilliant Company of Artistes. On Boscombe Pier, commencing Whit-Saturday, May 27th at 8.15 p.m.

During May and June :
Performances at 8.15 p.m. daily (except Sundays) also Matinees at 3 p.m. on Mondays, Wednesdays and Fridays.

During July, August and until September 16th :
Performances daily (except Sundays) at 3 p.m. and 8.15 p.m. with special children's Matinees on Tuesdays and Thursdays.

2000

July/August/September - A mixture for the summer season - Mondays had show songs in 'Beyond the Barricade', Tuesdays had 'The Summer 60s', while Wednesday the theatre played host to 'Jethro Bull*cks to Europe' Show. **Shane Richie**, before he took up residence in Albert Square as Alfie Moon, played his one-man show on Thursdays, and the 'That'll Be the Day' team covered both Friday and Saturday, leaving **Canon and Ball** for Sunday night comedy.

September - 'Phantom of the Opera', played for a week, and **Abba Gold** and the **Magic of the Minstrels** played one nighters.

September - A disastrous summer season was reported, and a proposal that the Pavilion should become a casino was announced.

September - **The Ted Heath Band** gave a concert and from the opera world came 'Figaro' and 'Aida', with **Opera and Ballet International**.

November - £200,000 was needed urgently for essential repairs.

November - A stage version of the television comedy series 'The League of Gentlemen' started off the month, and 'The Circus of Horrors' played five nights at the end.

November - A show entitled 'Supergirly' was described as "naughty but nice", and **Darren Day** played the lead role in a production of 'Carousel'.

December - **Barbara Dickson** performed an evening of songs.

December - 'Aladdin' was the pantomime and starred **Jeremy Beadle**.

2001

January - 'La Boheme' from **Opera and Ballet International**.

March - The annual **Bournemouth and Boscombe Light Opera Company** production was 'Oliver'.

April - The Ballroom hosted a **Woman's World Exhibition**.

October/November - **West Side Story**.

November - **Errol Brown** and **Paul McKenna** both performed one man shows, and 'Carmen' and 'Turandot' came from the **Chisiman National Opera**. There was also an evening of 'An Explosion of Percussion'.

December - **Jack Dee** filled the theatre for a one-night show, and there was a **Royal Marines** Christmas Spectacular. And a real must to be missed - an evening 'Stars of Stars in Their Eyes'. Balancing common sense was the **St. Petersburg Ballet Company**.

December - **Sid Owen** and **Wayne Sleep** told the tale of 'Dick Whittington' in the annual pantomime.

2002

The year started well with **Gene Pitney**, a **Glen Miller Tribute Concert**, a **Salute to Sinatra**, and the very real **Ken Dodd**.

July - A £10 million plan was unveiled to turn the Pavilion into a major **Performing Arts Centre**.

July/August/September - the enormous production of 'Chicago' with **John Altman** (Nick Cotton in 'Eastenders'), was followed by 'Singin' In the Rain'. Two slightly smaller shows were **Postman Pat** with his cat, **Jess**, and an **Audience with Tony Benn**. Both **Nana Mouskouri** and **Mary Black** gave concerts and Opera International performed 'Aida'. Also among those appearing were **Martha Reeves**, **Edwin Starr**, **Roy Chubby Brown** and the **Band and Bugles of the Light Division**.

August - In the Ballroom, **Ken Mackintosh Big Band** played for the **2002 Gala Ball**.

September - Council held a meeting about the Arts Centre plan - behind closed doors.

October - The Bournemouth International Centre and the Pavilion were reported to be in line for a **grant of nearly £10 million** from the Government's Private Finance Initiative.

November - The **Adult Education Service** backed a suggestion that they could be housed in the Pavilion.

December - The Council was told that it would cost **£30 million to revamp** the Pavilion.

December - **Ruth Madoc** starred with **Chris Jarvis** in the pantomime, 'Cinderella'. (See Page 211)

2003

Throughout the year, there were discussions about the future of the Pavilion, including plans by the **Trevor Osborne Group**, who had thoughts of a casino and an enlarged car-par, with a show-bar. One suggestion included the Odeon Cinema opposite which would have been included in the new complex, possibly as the theatre. Much opposition was received to the casino.

February/March - '42nd Street', a musical set in Broadway, had a cast of 90 and a 'live' orchestra.

May - There was a change of administration at the Council. **Liberal Democrats** took control from the **Conservatives**. **Council Officers** were asked to **explore all options** for the Pavilion development and report back to the council at a later date.

Summer - Summer Shows included a touring version of the 1960s television hit-programme, **'Fame'**.

December - 'Snow White' with **Marti Webb** was the pantomime.

2004

January - **Bill Wyman**'s Rhythm Kings.

February - A Johann Strauss Gala with the **Bournemouth Symphony Orchestra**. Full house, and mostly enjoyed by everyone except the die-hard whingers who say the acoustics are bad.

February - The much-loved children's character gave a tinkle or two in **'All New Adventures of Noddy'**, and **Elkie Brooks** brought back memories in a one-night show.

March - **The Drifters** 50th Anniversary Tour reached the Pavilion, as did 'Solid Silver 60s' with **Peter Noone** and **Wayne Fontana**. The BSO gave its **'Last Night of the Pavilion Proms'** to another full house.

April - As ever - **Ken Dodd** with his diddy laughter show. Also there was an evening with **Sir Henry Cooper**.

April - **Council Cabinet** selected the **Trevor Osborne Group** to run the Pavilion, subject to further clarification. Following a meeting that heard representations from both Trevor Osborne and from **Future 3000**, Councillors decided that the Trevor Osborne Group provided the most attractive proposal that could be progressed to meet the Council's requirements.

Details of the proposals included:
1. **Retaining the Theatre** and Ballroom.
2. Adding a new **Studio Theatre**.
3. Introducing a **'Discovery Centre'** - an interactive, educational facility
4. Recreating the **Pavilion Forecourt** into an open square.

A **Council Statement** confirmed: *Getting the Pavilion refurbished is a high priority for the Council. The Trevor Osborne Group's proposals would be widely attractive throughout the year and in all weathers.*

May - Bournemouth Symphony Orchestra once again with '**A Night at the Opera**'.

September - an unusual stage show straight from the West End - '**Round the Horne**', a stage version of the very popular radio series which had starred Kenneth Horne and Kenneth Williams. Top-class impersonators took the audience through two complete programmes, using a stage set designed to look like a radio studio.

December - A welcome return visit of **Chris Jarvis** (Entertainer, impressionist, author, CBBC presenter, director - who now lives in Bournemouth) with 'The Bill's' **Chris Ellison** (Burnside) for the excellent traditional pantomime, '**Jack and the Beanstalk**'. This was one of the most successful pantos in the history of the Pavilion, noted for its freshness, its brightness, its fun and its cleanliness. This is what the finale looked like.

This year, following complaints from many people that the Pavilion doesn't host enough cultural events, **Christian Knighton** and the **Pavilion Theatre Organ Fund** started a series of Sunday afternoon recitals on the Pavilion's **Concert Grand Steinway**.

Discussions had continued with the **Trevor Osborne Group**, and their future plans.

2005

Spring and Summer - a season of first-rate musicals, staring with '**High Society**', followed later by '**The King and I**', '**Annie**', and '**Joseph and His Amazing Techicolor Dreamcoat**'. '**That'll be the Day**' filled in several weeks with their immensely popular and successful music show featuring music from the last four decades. Another week was provided for with the West End Production of '**The**

Rat Pack', a superb show with top-rate impersonations of **Frank Sinatra**, **Sammy Davies Jnr.**, and **Dean Martin**.

August - A special event for **VJ Day** invited veterans of the Second World War to a cream tea in the Pavilion Ballroom. The Council underestimated the demand and received 730 requests for tickets when there were only 596 seats.

August - *'The Daily Echo'* published a feature entitled *Theatre of Dreams - Pavilion set for major transformation.* Plans were unveiled to return the Pavilion to its **former glory**, offering a state-of-the-art theatre and cabaret facilities, a casino and restaurants with swish new decor, landscaped grounds and vastly improved car-parking facilities. If the Council's development partnership with the **Trevor Osborne Property Group** stays on course, the next five years could see an estimated **£28 million** spent restoring the battered and faded venue ('Echo's' words not mine!) to a cutting edge 21ˢᵗ century entertainment complex. **Jonathan Ogden**, the Group's leisure and entertainment consultant said, *"The Pavilion was built in the very best location. Its relationship with the town and the beach are superb."* The first phase which is scheduled for the first half of next year, will be crucial to an on-going bid to re-establish **Bournemouth as a world class resort**. Jonathan added, "We want something that's high quality and elegant." Refurbishment plans for the Ballroom will restore decorations and art deco light fittings and open up the long obscured

panoramic views across the Bay. The Theatre will enjoy a new stage, seating and technical facilities, while there will be a garden restaurant and 600 car parking spaces operating on a pay-as-you-leave basis. The Casino, he concluded would not be big and brash, but very stylish.

October - Following its success last year, **'Round the Horne Revisited'** returned, with a new show.

November - Performance by **Alexander O'Neal** had to be cancelled because of power failure. A fire at a scrap yard in Parkstone had caused massive power cuts across Bournemouth and Poole.

December - Concert by the **Royal Marines Band** was interrupted for half an hour when dust was seen falling from the grid above the stage. Freak winds had caused damage to the windows at the top of the fly tower. At no time was anyone in danger.

December - 'Aladdin', written, produced by and starring Bournemouth's **Chris Jarvis**. Co-star is **Ray Meagher**, who plays Alf Stewart in the Australian soap, **'Home and Away'**.

In the year, one nighters included, **Ballet International** with **'Swan Lake'**, **Katherine Jenkins**, **Les Dennis** in a stage version of ITV's Quiz success, **'Who Wants to be a Millionaire?'**, an evening of **'Bellydance'**, Classical Boy Band - **G4**, **Jack Dee**, **Michael Ball** (filling the theatre twice), **Max Bygraves** and **Jimmy Tarbuck**. Who says the Bournemouth Pavilion is a spent force?

Sean Tomkins' lighting for the Mayor-Making Ceremony in 2005, highlighting the art-deco features

Mayor Making Ceremony 2005

Organ Concert 2005

More examples of the colourful lighting by Sean Tomkins assisted by Ryan Oliver and Graham Shearing

The Ups and Downs of the Bournemouth Pavilion

The Bournemouth Pavilion was built on a sloping site - hence, wherever you go, you'll have to experience the steps! For the record, here are some of the steps which artistes and patrons will have to count while they get their breath back!

Stage Level to Dressing Room - both sides	24 steps
Ballroom West Side to Toilets and Lucullus Room	21 steps
Ballroom East Side to Toilets and Lucullus Room	21 steps
Ballroom West Side to gardens level	42 steps
Ballroom East Side to below car park level	43 steps
Circle Centre Aisles (x3) from Promenade to railing	13 steps
Circle Side Aisles (x2) from Promenade to railing	11 steps
Foyer West Side to Circle Bar and Circle	32 steps
Foyer East Side to Circle Bar and Circle	32 steps
Forecourt into Foyer	4 steps
Circle East (Ladies) *to Car Park Exit*	36 steps
Circle West (Gents) *to Outside Terrace*	37 steps
Stalls East out to Car Park	9 steps
Foyer to Toilets	2 Circular steps
Foyer to Coffee Bar	2 Circular steps
Dressing Rooms to Bottom of Orchestra Pit	12 steps in two tunnels
Stalls to Stage level via Proscenium Arch	5 steps each side
Ballroom Staff Room to Lower Cellar	78 steps
Foyer to Conference/Committee Room	18 steps
Foyer into Box Offices	34 steps
Foyer into Lime/Projection Box	27 steps, + 12 rungs of ladder, + 2 steps up, + 1 step down, + 4 steps up
Foyer to Office Doors on West Side	18 steps
Offices to top floor on West side	16 steps
Coffee Bar to West Top Terrace	5 steps
West Corridor to Top Terrace	4 steps
Top terrace to West Terrace	47 steps
West Terrace to Gardens (Over river)	19 steps

In 1929, when the building was opened, little thought was given to those who might find steps difficult for health and physical reasons. The design of the complex is such that it is very difficult to build lifts, although there is a lift from the West Ballroom Door to the West Terrace

Technical Co-Ordinator

CHRISTIAN KNIGHTON

A theatre complex as large as the Bournemouth Pavilion has many technical resources and technical staff. These are co-ordinated by Christian Knighton, who has made his mark on theatres in Bournemouth since the mid-1970s. His untiring work and leadership with the Compton Theatre Organ has restored the instrument to its former glory, with regular concerts bringing hundreds of people to the theatre each week.

"I went to St. Michael's Junior School in West Hill Road, still with its gas lighting, before going on to Portchester School and then to Bicknell School. When I left, I was tempted by an apprenticeship at my father's workplace, which was the Radio and Television Department in Beales. I eventually took a course in electronics at the Bournemouth and Poole College at the Lansdowne. This career choice seemed to be wrong for me and a teacher suggested that I might like an electrician's job in the theatre. I had, at that time, no experience whatsoever in that field, but was encouraged to go and see the Stage Manager at the Pavilion, Tony Bond. When I arrived at the Stage Door for an interview, I can remember a rather belligerent stage door keeper, who had no idea who I was or why I was there; he sent me "round to the left, up the stairs and turn left, and you'll find him in the room on the left". I had no idea of the layout of the theatre and really was not helped by his attitude, but I followed the directions and eventually, after wandering round the stage on my own, met Tony coming out of his office at the back of the stage. The 'interview', which was really just a chat, seemed to go all right, and Tony offered me casual work, and promised to contact me when any was available. Just two days later, he called me and offered

me some work. He was a wonderful stage manager and painstaking in his training; he taught me how to run a flat without it falling over, he taught me how to sweep a stage properly - that is everything into the middle - and he taught me how to tie knots, such as those needed to tie flats together. In those early years of training, I was immediately hooked on the theatre and on stage work - like so many others, I got the bug. My first show was the 1975/6 pantomime, 'Jack and the Beanstalk', and I went on with 'The Royal Ballet' and 'The D'Oyly Carte Opera Company'. These were all big shows, and the experience I gained was invaluable. This was a superb opportunity; although I was only a trainee casual, here I was working with the biggest touring shows in the country. I knew what I wanted to do with my life!

From Rupert Bear to Jon Pertwee

"Then another challenge, when I was offered a twenty-three week season as Assistant Stage Manager at the Pier Theatre. I left my college course in favour of working up to four shows a day, starting with "Rupert Bear and Windlings" at 11am & 3pm, then twice nightly performances of "Birds of Paradise" an evening show which caused quite a stir

in the town because it featured topless girls. And that wasn't just for Monday-Saturday because there were Sunday shows too. I remember the singer John Heddle Nash appearing there throughout the season, along with Jan Fyffe, who was the sister of Patrick Fyffe, who played Dame Hilda Brackett of the popular comedy duo, Hinge and Brackett. I was doing general stage work which meant building and striking sets every day for each different performance. I was working from about ten in the morning, often until midnight.

"Sadly, I wasn't too happy with some aspects of the job, so I asked to leave after about 17 weeks of the season, but another door opened when I was appointed as electrician at the Playhouse Theatre in Hinton Road. This had previously been the Palace Court Theatre when it was owned by the Bournemouth Little Theatre Club, but they had moved on, and the theatre was in the hands of the Louis Michaels' Theatre Group - a professional management company who managed a small string of theatres including, the Theatre Royal, Bath, Richmond Theatre, Devonshire Park Theatre, Eastbourne, Theatre Royal Haymarket, London and the Strand Theatre, London. Their production company, Triumph Productions, brought many star-names in pre-West End provincial tours, often straight from the Theatre Royal in Bath. This was a full-time job where I was responsible for all aspects of theatre electrics - setting, lighting control, follow-spotting and maintenance, and it was most rewarding. I loved it, watching such stars as Dulcie Gray, Brian Rix, Jon Pertwee, Melvyn Hayes, Eric Sykes, Hattie Jaques, Irene Handl, David Jason, Dora Bryan, Douglas Byng, Patrick Cargill, Jimmy Logan, Gerald Harper, Hannah Gordon and many more. I stayed there for nine years between 1977 and 1986.

"During my later time at the Playhouse Theatre, I had also been working for a local lighting company, AJS Theatre Lighting. I was able to gain more technical experience in setting up lighting and sound rigs, and designing lighting for shows all over the area. This job worked in tandem with the theatre, because more and more films were being shown and so there was less stage lighting work to be done. Then in 1986, after the death of Louis Michaels, the Playhouse was sold to settle death duties, and I went full-time with AJS.

From the National Theatre.....

"To be honest, I gradually became a little fed up with the work I was doing, and needed a new challenge. Since my time at the Pavilion, Tony Bond, the stage manager, had moved to the National Theatre in London where he was Technical Advisor responsible for Technical Services. He ran his own company called *Theatre Techniques* and I worked with him for three years based at the National Theatre and elsewhere on the 'administration of maintenance', which meant categorising equipment - in short, I had to find all the items on the inventory, and then log them down, marking each one with the appropriate security tagging. I had to find every spotlight, every microphone and every prop, including all the swords, daggers, guns, rifles and staves and torches! It was a great time, and taught me a good deal more about theatre administration. I was also lucky enough to see a succession of fantastic shows at the National Theatre and learn more just by seeing the best technical effects from the greatest designers of the day.

.....to the Pier Theatre!

"In 1989, the Bournemouth Pier Theatre required some help with a production, so I went back to work with four plays which were in repertory over eight weeks, and which, unusually, changed on a nightly basis. The company liked my work and so I was invited to become the Stage Manager. This lasted for three years until the B.I.C. took over control of the Pier Theatre, and I was offered further work by the Council but in the same job! This was, obviously, only seasonal, so I went back to AJS Lighting as a Service Engineer, thus giving me two strings to my bow.

Technical Co-Ordinator

"All was well - my life in the theatre had taken me to many interesting places and given me excellent experience in many fields of administration and practices. When AJS was sold in 2000, there were, co-incidentally, big changes at the Bournemouth Pavilion. The Stage Manager at that time, Roger Stares, retired, Barry Beresford took the role as caretaker Stage Manager and in May of that year, an advert appeared in 'The Stage' inviting applications for the permanent post. I applied, but in all honesty, had little hope of getting the job. There were six candidates called for interview, including some who already had senior stage management jobs in other theatres around the country. We were put through an extremely gruelling day with group exercises and psychometric tests!

"No one was more surprised than I was when, the following day, Chris Warren, the Technical & Engineering Manager, offered me the job. I still wasn't sure and took two days before accepting and joined on the understanding that I was allowed the chance to restructure the department and my role. I re-wrote my job description and created the post of Technical Co-ordinator.

"I was able to appoint Barry Beresford as Stage Manager, and Simon Bagnall as the Chief Electrician, and when Barry died, Simon stepped up into the role of Stage Manager. Natural staff losses since then have enabled us to build up a first-rate and wonderful stage crew. My job is to oversee all the equipment and its usage, and to ensure that the staff is being deployed sensibly and effectively; my accrued knowledge at AJS has allowed me to redevelop practices in the most economic manner. I suppose that my business background has helped to save the Council some money!

Not Just the Pavilion

"My job, which covers not only the Pavilion, but also the B.I.C., cuts across three areas, namely entertainment, exhibitions and conferences - the really big money-spinners for the Bournemouth Council. So amidst the daily routine of mundane tasks, my mind is filled with conferences which might not be here for two or three years. I have frequent meetings with possible clients where we negotiate what technical expertise and equipment they might need and so on. The Exhibition sector of work is ongoing, and some organisations are repeat business working continuously from year to year. With conferences, I have to know how many presentation screens might be needed, where they'll be required, how much audio-visual equipment will be used and so on. I need to ensure that all the necessary equipment is available and that there are appropriate and qualified staff to operate them. In the entertainments field, we can have four or five different shows on at any one time in the two venues. I have to know exactly what lighting, sound and staging is needed for each of them, and arrange additional casual staff to maintain all our required services. The majority of the stage-related expertise is at the Pavilion, and most of the very large shows which come to the B.I.C. bring all their own gear and crew. The visiting company will tell me how many staff they will need to fit-up and get-out, and I arrange what they need. The B.I.C. has some really big shows on the way, such as 'Little Britain' and Status Quo, and an enormous band, Prodigy. The newly refurbished Windsor Hall will be the biggest on the South Coast, having room for up to 7,000 in the audience.

Facilitator

"So my job is to act as a facilitator; I must have the contacts and the knowledge, and the three areas are intermingled all the time. It's like being a juggler with countless balls in the air at any one time, and not one of them can be dropped. I believe that the internal infra-structure in the venues must work well; all the staff must be aware of what's happening, what is required of him/her and where he/she fits into the overall success of each and every project. My job is to rota the staff in the places where they can use their own particular knowledge and show their own special expertise. They must be used sensibly, fairly and effectively in a way which brings them job satisfaction as well as providing the very best for the various clients. There are eight full-time staff on the technical crew, but these are heavily augmented by casuals, all who have to be booked and monitored.

"I totally trust the stage crew and don't interfere with their work at all unless they ask me for advice or help. Simon has overall control of the stage operation, and I wouldn't want it any other way.

All Knowledge Must Be Passed On

"One of my great mentors was Tony Bond, the Stage Manager *(See Page 168)* who gave me my first chance, and his philosophy was that all his knowledge should be passed on to his trainees. I carry on that philosophy so that all knowledge can be maintained and improved. We have very little changeover of staff, but we do have a great amount of flexibility; when staff are expected to work, often at very short notice, right into the early hours and perhaps over night, we expect total dedication, so we must allow some understanding if they want to pop out during the day for a personal matter. This is a two-way process; they work hard when they need to, and we all give and take.

The Magnificent Compton Organ

"Although I have been at the Pavilion on a full-time basis only since May 2002, I have, in reality, never been away from the building, because of my association with the Compton Theatre Organ. I have no ability to play the instrument and there is no musical background to my life, and strangely enough it wasn't the music which attracted me to the instrument and which caused me to dedicate my free-time to its maintenance. When I started as a casual, the organ hadn't been used for some years; Harold Coombs had died in 1964 and Reggie White had stopped playing, so no one in the theatre realised its true potential. Until, that is, Richard Smithers was appointed as the Chief Electrician. He was a professional theatre organist who had worked under his stage name Tony Fenton. When he was only 16, he was billed as ABC's youngest ever organist! After leaving the Pavilion he moved to the newly opened Poole Arts Centre and then onto the Southampton Guildhall, where he played the Compton Organ from which he had broadcast a series of programmes on BBC Radio Solent and recorded a video and cassettes. Whilst he was at the Pavilion, he showed us just what the instrument might do, if it were brought back up to scratch. This is where I came in, because I was fascinated by the electrics which operated the instrument - wiring and relays and electro-magnets - they amazed me in what they could do. Theatre organs use a system where one rank of pipes can be used to produce several notes at the same time - it's called an 'extension organ'; this is an amazing piece of early electrical technology which totally captivated me. With guidance from Richard and from Len Bailey, himself an organist who had been doing a

over eighteen hundred metal pipes arranged in twenty-two ranks, and split between the two rounded chambers on either side of the proscenium arch. These are literally hollow concrete towers and all the sound is 'released' through the top by a system of wooden shutters, rather like venetian blinds. The shutters are controlled by the organist, and the sound bounces off the dome falling back into the auditorium. There aren't just pipes in the two chambers - there are drums, cymbals, sleighbells, xylophones and so on, and a series of special effects such as an aircraft drone. These would have been designed to be used in the days of silent films when an organist provided all the background music and

little playing for some shows at the theatre, I worked on the repair of the instrument, and I have been with the project now for twenty-six years. But we have never done anything to take away from the original design of John Compton. We have improved, we have enhanced and we have renovated, but we have never detracted from the original plan. Tonally, the organ is exactly the same as it was when it was installed in 1929, and it is now one of only a handful of theatre organs which operate successfully within their original environment. The only change was made by Compton themselves when they added, at the request of Percy Whitlock (Borough Organist) in 1932, a Clarinet stop and a Concert Flute. There are

effects. The construction of the instrument in such cramped conditions is nothing less than a technological miracle, and the electrics which operate it all are just magnificent. The best place to hear the full stereo effect is to the sit in the stalls, in the centre just in front of the circle.

"The Wobbles"

"In the early days of my involvement, we had dreadful trouble with the organ going flat whenever the tremulants were used - tremulants do just as you'd expect - they waver the notes, by exhausting amounts of wind and thus make the true theatre organ sound. One of our faithful organists, Phil Burbeck who's played dozens of concerts here, calls it 'the wobbles'. We found that the air from the regulators was being fed into the rank of pipes only at the one end and this was just not enough to cope when the tremulants were on, because the ranks of pipes were so long that all the air had been used up before it reached the top register. So we overcame the problem, by sending air in from both ends of the ranks of pipes. And so it goes on, cleaning, replacing, rewiring - a never-ending task, but well worth the effort because today we have an organ which probably sounds better than it did seventy-six years ago and which is praised and loved by all the top-line professional organists who come week by week to give concerts. Most of them consider it a privilege to be asked to play such a grand instrument. Derry Thompson, from Maiden Newton, was the first tuner and builder to work on the project and he, Len Bailey and I formed BKT Productions (the initials of our surnames!), who put on regular concerts at lunchtime. In those days, we were pleased if one hundred people turned up, whereas nowadays we expect upwards of four-hundred for our weekly concerts. Our current builder is Tim Trenchard who comes from Shillingstone in Dorset, and his work and effort is untiring, hours of careful and dedicated work to keep the instrument up to standard. We have no official funding from the council, but we maintain funds by collecting change - and notes! - in old organ pipes at the end of each concert. The council is very supportive of our work in other ways, such as allowing use of the theatre on a very regular basis. My aim has always been to encourage awareness of the instrument by local people and by visitors; it's a glorious piece of social history which deserves our efforts and must be preserved.

"One possible future development would be to have a new console which is on a movable platform, as they do in many churches nowadays. This would enable us to place the console wherever we wanted it, but, of course, the lift which enables the audience to see the player slowly rising into view is a very important part of the whole concept of theatre organs. If we did decide on this way forward, we would emphasise that the sound of the actual instrument would remain unchanged.

Exciting Project

"Another rather exciting project is not far away. We have a Boudoir Steinway Piano which was slightly damaged on the woodwork, but which was perfectly intact in its workings. Tim Trenchard has 'electrified' the instrument with a digital interface which will enable it to be played by the organist from the organ console. Although other theatre

Christian introducing a weekly organ concert

organs, such as the Wurlitzer in the Blackpool Tower, have pianos built into them, our project would probably be unique, and would not only be a topic of amazement, but would further enhance the lovely sounds of the organ.

Mike Yarwood on his Back!

"My years at the Pavilion, albeit often only as a part-timer, have been wonderful. As a member of the stage crew, I remember an amusing incident at one of the Mike Yarwood Shows. For the walk-down at the end, we were using the stage revolve, rather like the finale to ITV's 'Sunday Night at the London Palladium', and it was always a little reluctant to start, juddering a bit as we worked the control. Artistes standing on it would be seen to sway a little as it got itself up to speed. One night, Mike Yarwood actually fell right over, and as the revolve passed the audience, there he was lying flat on his back with his legs waving in the air. You can imagine the audience just loved it.

"The 'Black and White Minstrel Show' played at the Pavilion on many occasions, and what many people in the audience didn't know was that all the choral singing was pre-recorded while the orchestra played 'live' in the pit. There were two tape machines so that if one wouldn't work properly, the other could be used instead.

"One night, both machines failed! So all the principals and lead singers had to gather round the riser-mic (that's the microphone in stage centre which can be raised and lowered as required) and sing into that. One or two of them had rather rough throats, and the result wasn't quite as good as the recording!

"Currie's water falls are always a source of potential disaster. In one show, a hole had to be cut through the stage through to Dressing Room 7, under the stage, where there was a large water-tank. The water from the waterfall poured through this hole into the tank to be pumped back up to stage to go through the waterfall again. At the rehearsal, the hole was found to be too small to take the volume of water, and so there was a large flood - like a mini tidal wave gushing across the stage down into the orchestra pit. Happy days!

The Skeleton

Early 1927 - the building begins

Stage Manager John Laurie 1935 - 1972

All photographs courtesy Bournemouth Daily Echo

The Pavilion Pit Orchestra

At the Stage Door in c. 1970. Byron Brooke holds the baton. Photograph courtesy Daily Echo

Chris Jarvis
PRAISE FOR THE PAVILION

Chris Jarvis is a man of many skills and talents - actor, comedian, impressionist, playwright and director, who is known to countless millions of children, parents and grandparents who see him on the CBeebies Television Channel. His pantomime in 2004, 'Jack and the Beanstalk', was one of the most successful ever at the Pavilion. And he likes the Pavilion Theatre.

"I have so many fantastic memories of working at the Bournemouth Pavilion. I directed **'Cinderella'** here 3 years ago, **'Jack'** last year and in 2005 I'm back with **'Aladdin'**. Pantomime is the highlight of my year and those seasons spent in Bournemouth have been extra special - so much so, I moved here!

"I'm passionate about panto and spend most of the year preparing for it. With so much hard work, the venue has got to be perfect and the **Pavilion really hits the spot** when it comes to staging these traditional family shows. There

are obvious reasons why it's so good but there is **something magical** about it which is harder to explain and has more to do with its reputation and the **ghosts of so many great artists**. The theatre's glorious past in producing top pantomimes is well documented - just walk down the outer corridors and look at the posters!

"The Pavilion building itself is also **rather fabulous** with its art deco exterior and fountain. It would be wonderful to restore more of the building's past glory inside, especially in the auditorium, and further improve the acoustics. However, great work goes on - often unrewarded - in preserving the theatre's jewels like the organ.

"It's always good to see so many different people using the Pavilion. I imagine the place was rather exclusive in the '20s judging by the rather downstairs-looking assortment of staff lined up in the old photographs. But now the Pavilion is a lot more accessible and really does belong to everyone in the Bournemouth community: line-dancers, tea-dancers and panto-goers alike.

"On a personal note, I think a lot of what makes the Pavilion so special is to do with the **people who work here**. When the **Tsunami** hit on Boxing Day 2004, we produced a one-off fund raising show that made over **£20,000 for the relief fund**. This was made possible by the speedy response of the theatre staff and management, notably **Simon** and **Christian** who staged it with just a few days preparation. The show was remarkably professional and technically slick yet totally unrehearsed - a real testament to everyone in every department.

"The Pavilion helps to make Bournemouth one of **Britain's finest seaside towns**. What it provides for the community in terms of entertainment is clear but it's also a stunning landmark unlike the Imax Cinema - the butt of many a panto joke.

Chris Jarvis

There have been Pantomimes at the Bournemouth Pavilion since 1934. There were two years without one, first in 1960-61, when the Theatre fly-floor was being rebuilt, and secondly in 1983-84, when the Council decided to abolish Pantomime at the Theatre. Many local hoteliers were very unimpressed with the idea!

Duncan Honeybourne
DORSET PIANO RECITALIST

"The Bournemouth Pavilion is a **beautiful concert hall**, a veritable "**period piece**"! Acoustically it possesses a warmth and fidelity which makes it a perfect and very special venue for solo piano recitals and chamber music. Furthermore, a building with such a distinguished history absorbs into its character the resonances of the artistic triumphs which have taken place within its walls, and the spirits of the great artists of musical history who have appeared there since it was opened in 1929.

"It has been an immense privilege for me to give the two inaugural **piano recitals** on the gloriously sonorous and subtle new **Steinway** in the Pavilion, and I hope that these concerts will herald a new dawn for chamber recitals in Bournemouth. This gem of a concert hall cries out to be used and loved by new generations, and it deserves to be cherished by a town whose noble place in **British musical history** is unique and huge - in fact out of all proportion to Bournemouth's relatively small size. Used to the full, the Bournemouth Pavilion should take its place alongside the Bournemouth Symphony Orchestra as another permanent memorial to the vision and endeavours of the formidable and ever-enterprising **Sir Dan Godfrey**.

"As Bournemouth's musical history moves forward through the twenty-first century, many new and exciting ventures and venues take their place alongside the old, yet this welcoming hall represents a flame from the past which can continue to keep a rich heritage aglow whilst nurturing and celebrating the new and progressive. For me as a **Dorset-born artist** it has been an intense privilege to be associated with the hall, and to establish this new tradition here."

The Auditorium in chaos......
REFURBISHMENT OF THEATRE in NOVEMBER 1971

A seatless auditorium

Photograph courtesy of Bournemouth Daily Echo

The "Oh No!" Fountain

The 1960s fountain that everybody seemed to hate.

Critics thought it looked like a collection of oil drums.
Photo courtesy Bournemouth Daily Echo

The old Seating Plan

WHERE YOU WOULD HAVE BEEN SEATED PRE-1971

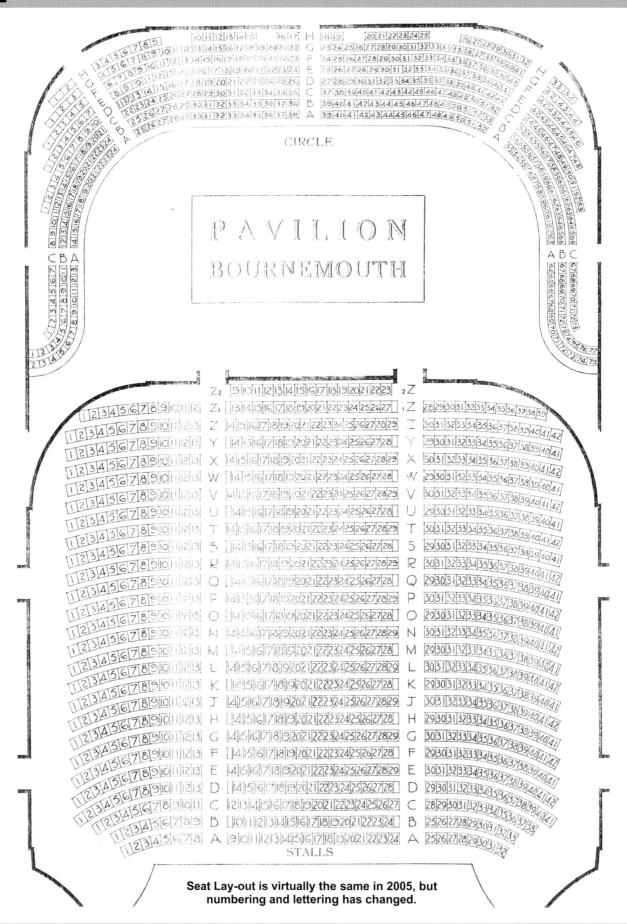

CIRCLE

PAVILION
BOURNEMOUTH

STALLS

Seat Lay-out is virtually the same in 2005, but numbering and lettering has changed.

MEMORY BANK

Thanks for the Memory!
A MISCELLANY OF NOSTALGIA

COLIN ROBINSON

*In July 1982, the **Pavilion Ballroom** once again proved its versatility by hosting a **Real Ale Festival** organised by CAMRA. **Colin Robinson** was a volunteer as a barman.*

"It sounds a bit strange holding a beer festival in a ballroom, but the occasion was most successful, taking place on Friday and Saturday evenings. All the barrels were placed around the dance floor, and all the beer came straight off the barrels - no gases needed to help them along! It was open to the general public, and several hundred people arrived on each evening. I can remember one beer was called **GBH** - but this was not what it seemed; the contents of the barrel had nothing to do with fighting, but the letters stood for '**Godson's Black Horse**', and it was made by a London Brewery.

There were lots of other beers including some from **Eldridge Pope**'s in Dorchester, and we drank them out of half pint glasses, being allowed as many as we wanted! The Pavilion also had their own bar up and running as that was part of the arrangement, but the event was massively expensive, and so it was only held once at the Pavilion. Similar events still take place, but CAMRA has to hire a more modest venue."

VERA BROCKHURST

"I can remember well that my father, **Cecil Macklin**, was employed as a carpenter by Jones and Seward, in the construction of the revolving stage at the Pavilion. He used to remark on how proud he was to be involved in the work on such a prestigious building."

ANONYMOUS

Another memory recounted to the author second-hand was of a father and son who lived at Three Legged Cross, between Ferndown and Verwood. As the work force on the Pavilion building site was hired on a daily basis, they would walk in from Three Cross to see if there was any work, and if not, they had to walk all the way back. That was in the days long before the fast-moving A338 spur road from Ringwood into Bournemouth.

PAT WITHERIDGE (nee Howard)

"In the 1960s, I used to work at the **Royal Victoria Hospital** in Shelley Road in Boscombe, before I moved over to the **Ear, Nose and Throat Hospital** on Poole Road near the old Bournemouth West Railway Station. I well remember the annual **Matron's Ball** in the Pavilion Ballroom. This was a real chance for all of us to really dress up. Also, we used to go to Saturday evening dances on a regular basis. It was a really great meeting place, and although I met my husband there, I stopped going when we got married!"

PAM WILLIAMS

"When I was in my teens in the **early 1950s**, there really weren't all that many places to go in Bournemouth. But my friends and I, and most of our generation would use the **two corridors** either side of the Theatre to meet up and see what was going on. It was just right for us, in the centre of town, and close to the seafront. We loved it there, and I feel that the Pavilion is **part of my early life** and of my up-bringing. I think we all take it for granted nowadays, but I think most people would be very sad to see it pulled down."

ALICE CHAPMAN

*(I am indebted to **Darren Wall** who recounts some memories recalled by his grandmother, **Alice Chapman** who was actually present at the opening of the Pavilion, working as a waitress. She continued to work there for some time afterwards. H.A.)*

"The **head waiter** at the opening of the Pavilion was a German by the name of **Mr. Meyer**, who was later succeeded by **Mr. Stinton**. **Mr. Hutchinson** was the General Manager, who interviewed prospective employees at the Town Hall. **Mr. Donergani** was the catering manager, who later unfortunately perished in the war. The shows were opened by a band called **Paderiski**, and were supported by the four-piece **Houston Sisters**. Among those appearing in the first shows included **Georgie Wood, Flotsam and Jetsam, Gracie Fields** and **Sir Dan Godfrey**. The **Star Waltz** competition was held in the ballroom. One could join the tea dances for 1/6, a price which included sandwiches and cakes. Professional dancers, 'hosts' and 'hostesses', were available at a charge of **1/- per dance**. On a visit to Bournemouth, **Amy Johnson** had dinner in the **Lucullus Room**. The army requisitioned the Pavilion during the war, and the **King** paid a brief visit." *(This visit was in October 1941 - see Page 48)*

SHEILA NELSON

*Living in Bournemouth since the early-1950s, **Sheila Nelson** recalls a keep fit occasion in the **Pavilion Ballroom**.*

"The really big icon in the Keep fit world was **Eileen Fowler**, and in the 1980s, she came to the Pavilion for an event organised by all the local keep-fit clubs. Eileen was getting on a bit at that time, but she was marvellously fit and she encouraged us to work-out together. It's an example of how the Pavilion can become the centre for **virtually any activity**.

"In the early-1950s, I can **remember seeing a production of 'La Boheme'** with the Sadlers Wells Opera Company. What I recall most was the most enormous lady singer! And the Pavilion is also part of the annual **Taxi Run**, where local taxi drivers club together to take out under-privileged children - they have teas, picnics and go off for a drive, often to Swanage. This all starts on the forecourt of the Pavilion.

'Queen' Eileen is a sell-out

IN Keep Fit circles I suppose "queen" Eileen Fowler is already a legendary figure and even though she is now in her seventies, her following is as great as ever.

Evidence of this will be seen in Bournemouth tomorrow afternoon at the Pavilion when Eileen will be demonstrating her considerable talents. All tickets went weeks ago.

Her last visit in 1977 was a sell-out. She's now cutting down on her travelling commitments so this could be the farewell appearance in this part of the world for the woman who held her first class back in 1934. Her visit is being organised by the East Dorset Keep Fit Association. Several demonstrations by local classes will entertain the audience in the interval.

SHEILA REID

***Sheila Reid** was born in Moordown and has lived in Bournemouth all her life. For many years she worked in the dairy in Muscliff Lane. Sheila remembers the **Pavilion being built**.*

"I had just left school and we used to go into town to watch the builders. This was an exciting time for Bournemouth people and something very different. We used to check regularly by walking down Westover Road; in those days, late mid-to-late 1920s, **Westover Road was like London's West End**, very up-market and the Londoners who came here for their holidays used to love shopping there. The Pavilion was going to be **very special** - something which belonged to us and would be among the best entertainment centres in the country.

"Later, I particularly recall the **lovely fountain** in the forecourt with its beautiful colours, and on the Square side of the building there was lovely **waterfall** which was also lit in bright colours. My particular vivid memories concern the Tea Dances with the band leader **Sim Grosman**. He was wonderful and used to ask the dancers what they wanted to have next - he would even come down off the stage and ask individual dancers in a very polite and friendly way. The waitresses were, by today's standards, very old-fashioned and wore black and white dresses as they brought you a pot of tea and a fancy cake. All the plates and cups and saucers were proper china, not the horrible plastic things you get today. But I was more interested in the dancing than the food - the rumba, the foxtrot, the tango - they were all marvellous. After my marriage, I used to go with a girl friend because my husband was at work, and there was one old man who always used to ask me for a dance. The whole afternoon was **very classy and friendly**, there was no rudeness and **no anti-social behaviour**. We knew how to behave properly in public. This was **our ballroom** and we looked forward to going there and made sure we enjoyed ourselves in this distinctive 'palace'.

"The ballroom was often hired out for special functions, and the **Convent of the Cross** always went there every year, and I know that the **Samaritans** have a regular function there nowadays. During the Second World War there were lots of **Canadians**, **New Zealanders** and **Americans** in Bournemouth based at **Sopley Camp** and at **R.A.F. Hurn** (now the International Airport), and we used to enjoy their company at the dances.

"The **theatre was good** too and we always used to go the pantomimes; I loved the ballet scenes and remember especially a production of 'Cinderella'. I saw **Gracie Fields** there and was taken to meet her in her dressing room; she was a lovely lady and gave me a signed photograph. I recall, too, a musical show called '**Flora Dora**', which had lovely costumes, gay and light, and some pretty music. This was sometime in the 1930s. I've been going to the theatre there ever since and recently went to a Strauss evening with the Bournemouth Symphony Orchestra.

"There's one very sad story from the war times. One day I went to a wedding at the **Church of Sacred Heart** on Richmond Hill; the groom was an airman who had been given a special 24 hour leave to get married, and then he had to go straight back to the war. After the ceremony we went to the **Pavilion for the reception**. At that time, it was impossible to buy proper cake ingredients such as fruit and eggs,

so the **wartime wedding cakes** were very small, but made to look big by building a cardboard pretend-cake around it - it looked good but the real cake was very small. I can remember walking down the corridor from the foyer to the ballroom; well, we weren't walking at all - we were running, jumping and skipping all holding hands as we went, and we ran into the ballroom all singing happily. We were all dressed up, but you needed coupons at that time and good clothes became very expensive. And we all drank orange juice for the reception. We had a wonderful time, but tragically, two of the men from the wedding party were killed very soon after in the war.

"I vividly remember **V.E. Day** at the Pavilion; hundreds of troops lined up in the forecourt and there was a march-past down Westover Road. Everyone was dancing in the streets and holding hands - the Pavilion grounds, the gardens, the Square were all absolutely packed with people rejoicing, and all the lights came on, the first time for years because of the blackout laws. I remember sharing a taxi home with five American men, and they insisted on paying the fare!

"Yes, the Pavilion has great memories for me even though it's **not quite as old as I am!**"

MAUREEN PHILLIPS

"My memories of the Pavilion start in **the late 1940s** when I recall going to pantomimes and other shows. It was the ceiling of the theatre which has stayed foremost in my memories - it was pale pink at the edge merging into a blue which was **dotted with stars**. You can imagine that my young imagination was filled with wonder, because it was, during the war, forbidden to peek out through the curtains at home to view the stars. I don't think the present decoration of the ceiling has anything like the same charm. As well as pantomimes, I can recall going to the **Ballet** with my sister, and we always found our visits to be very exciting. There's something about the Pavilion which has **a compelling charm**. I used to love the fountain as well in the forecourt, but this was closed during the war, and I can remember being so pleased when it reopened with such lovely colours. I worked for a while for a firm of accountants called **Hibberd, Bull, Gow and Ford**. Every so often, the management arranged for us to have a night out by giving us some money. One year we decided to go to the **Lucullus Room** where we had a marvellous meal before going upstairs to the theatre. **The Pavilion is lovely**, and has so much to offer."

The PAVILION   Bournemouth

Telephone 2654   Box Office 5861

General Manager : ARTHUR CLEGG

WEEK COMMENCING MONDAY, 9th MARCH, 1959.   NIGHTLY at 7.45

Matinees : Wednesday and Saturday at 2.30

PLAYERS VENTURES LTD.

present

The Boy Friend

A New Musical Comedy of the 1920's

Book, Music and Lyrics by Sandy Wilson

The Management respectfully invite patrons of this theatre to be seated before the rise of the curtain, and so avoid disturbance to others during the performance. The right is reserved to refuse admission, and to make any changes in the cast necessitated by illness or other unavoidable causes.
The taking of photographs in this theatre is strictly prohibited.

There is more to choose from at Bournemouth's Finest and Most Modern Store . . .

Beales

the centre of interest for shoppers with its Restaurant high above the town and selling floors of gifts through which the shopper can wander at will

PHONE: BOURNEMOUTH ONE

A show memory from 1959

SHEILA and DOREEN BRUSHETT

*Although **Sheila** has now left Bournemouth, **Doreen** has lived here all her life. As sisters, they often visited the Pavilion during the **Second World War**.*

"The **British restaurant** *(at different times known as the Popular restaurant, The Ocean Room and Oasis)* was probably the only place in town during the war where you could buy cooked meals. **Rationing restrictions** limited other restaurants, and even the Pavilion had to take coupons from the customers - so we didn't go very often, but I remember visiting the restaurant when I was about twelve or thirteen. Our parents couldn't afford to go, so we really felt privileged when we were taken out. Wartime regulations ensured the **food was very basic**, but we didn't mind because it was great to be there.

"Then later, I recall going to Saturday evening dances when **Joe Loss and his Band** and other bands would play, sometimes, with vocalists who later became very famous like **Lita Rosa** and **Denis Lotis**. I used to love the music, but much preferred it when there was no singing. On **Boxing Days**, the ballroom always had a coffee dance, and we used to go to those when we could.

"I still smile at a visit we made to the theatre in 1946; one of the major Ballet Companies was putting on '**Swan Lake**', and soon after the performance started **all the lights went out** because there was a power cut. We had to wait about half an hour, but we stayed in our seats and thought the whole thing was wonderful. This was our first visit to a ballet and the production was nothing less than beautiful with excellent dancers. As it was our first time, we've never forgotten a lovely brand new experience made even better because the lights went out!

"On Sheila's **twenty-first birthday** - it must have been **1958**, we made another visit, this time to the summer show to see one of Harold Fielding's spectaculars starring **Bob Monkhouse**, **Denis Goodwin** and the **Beverley Sisters**. *(Sheila is sure that it was Des O'Connor, but he didn't appear at the Pavilion that year)* My parents had informed the company of the special birthday, and it was mentioned on stage and all the lights dimmed. Sheila was most embarrassed.

"The Pavilion is a lovely place, a very **special and unique building**. My late husband used to tell me of what happened there on **V.E. Day**. There was a big party in the forecourt when lots of troops came and lined up while others marched down Westover Road. He said that the party spread right through the gardens into the Square and lasted well into the next morning."

Reminder of a 'lost' Coach Company - A Programme Advertisement in 1980

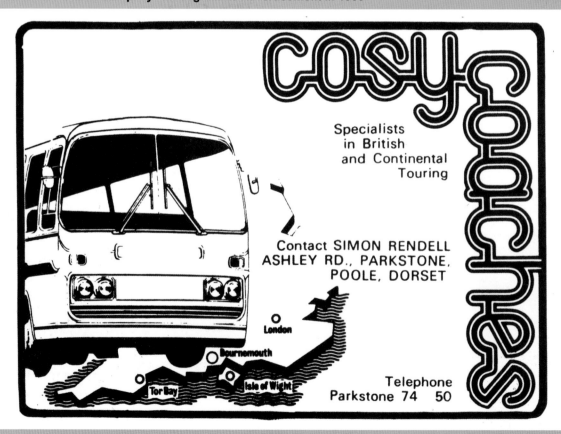

cosy coaches

Specialists in British and Continental Touring

Contact SIMON RENDELL ASHLEY RD., PARKSTONE, POOLE, DORSET

London
Bournemouth
Tor Bay
Isle of Wight

Telephone Parkstone 74 50

In All its Glory
PUBLICITY POSTER - EARLY 1950s

The Affluence of the Past
SILVER-PLATED TEAPOT BY MAPPIN AND WEBB

As used in the Opening Years of the Bournemouth Pavilion. This one has lost its lid! Found in an old cupboard behind the Ballroom, the pot needed much careful and dedicated cleaning! The Bournemouth Coat of Arms between handle and spout is very worn but just visible. This is just one example of the silver service operated by the Restaurants in the 1930s.